CW00688316

Anglican
Baptismal Liturgies

Edited By
Phillip Tovey

CANTERBURY
PRESS
Norwich

© Phillip Tovey, 2017

First published in 2017 by the Canterbury Press Norwich
Editorial office
3rd Floor, Invicta House
108–114 Golden Lane
London EC1Y 0TG, UK

Canterbury Press is an imprint of Hymns Ancient & Modern Ltd
(a registered charity)

Hymns Ancient & Modern® is a registered trademark of
Hymns Ancient & Modern Ltd
13A Hellesdon Park Road, Norwich,
Norfolk NR6 5DR, UK

www.canterburypress.co.uk

All rights reserved. No part of this publication may be reproduced,
stored in a retrieval system, or transmitted,
in any form or by any means, electronic, mechanical,
photocopying or otherwise, without the prior permission of
the publisher, Canterbury Press.

The Author has asserted his right under the Copyright,
Designs and Patents Act 1988
to be identified as the Author of this Work

British Library Cataloguing in Publication data

A catalogue record for this book is available
from the British Library

ISBN 978 1 78622 020 2

Printed and bound in Great Britain by
CPI Group (UK) Ltd

Contents

Acknowledgements and copyright sources

Copyright

Every effort has been made to apply for the relevant copyright permissions. Should there be errors in this then please contact the author through the publisher and efforts will be made to rectify the situation. In some cases, Provinces have made the decision not to copyright their texts, examples of this being, the Episcopal Church in United States of America, the Episcopal Church in the Philippines, the Church of Ceylon (Sri Lanka), the Diocese of the Seychelles. In the case of translations, the copyright rests with the Province in the original language and with the translator in the English translation.

Permissions Granted

Holy Baptism 2006 (including Affirmation of Holy Baptism for Confirmation and Renewal) © The General Synod of the Scottish Episcopal Church.

The Book of Common Prayer Vol. II: Y Llyfer Gweddi Gyffredin Cyrfrol © The Church in Wales 1984.

Services for Christian Initiation: Gwasannethau Bedydd a Chonffyrmasiwn © The Church in Wales 2007.

Church of Ireland: Material from *The Book of Common Prayer* copyright © RCB 2004.

*Liturgia da Igreja Lusitana,*1991 [in Portuguese] © Lusitanian Church; translation © Joseph Fernandes.

Order of Baptism for celebration in any season [in Spanish] © Reformed Episcopal Church in Spain; translation © Andii Bowsher.

Book of Alternative Services, © 1985, The General Synod of the Anglican Church of Canada.

Livro do Oração Comum 2015 [in Portuguese] © Episcopal Anglican Church of Brazil; translation © Joseph Fernandes.

Libro de Oracion Comun y Manual de la Iglesia Anglicana 1973 [in Spanish] © Diocese of Chile; translation © Andii Bowsher.

Igitabo Cy'Amasengesho 1973 [in Kinyrawanda] © The Province of the Anglican Church of Rwanda; translation © Stephen Nshimye.

Igitabo C'Amasengesho 2012 [in Kirundi] © The Anglican Church of Burundi; translation © John Niyondiko.

Kitabu Cha Sala Kanisa La Jimbo La Tanzania 1995 [in Swahili] © Anglican Church Tanzania; translation © Bridget Lane and Ian Tarrant.

Liturgie pour L'initiation Chrétienne 2012 [in French] © Diocese Mauritius; translation © Damian Scragg and Phillip Tovey.

Buku Re Munamato Wevese 1972 [in Shona] © The Church of the Province of Central Africa; translation © Rainah Madzorera.

Baptism and Confirmation from *An Anglican Prayer Book, 1989* © Provincial Trustees of the Anglican Church of Southern Africa.

Kitabu cha sala kwa watu wote 1998 [in Swahili] © The Province of the Anglican Church of Congo; translation © Bridget Lane and Ian Tarrant.

Common Prayer: Church of Pakistan [in Urdu] (1985, 2005) © Church of Pakistan; translation © Evelyn Bhajan and Augusten Masih.

Prayer Book of the Church of Bangladesh [in Bangladeshi] 1997 © Church of Bangladesh; translation © John Webber.

Service Book 1999 © The Church of the Province of South East Asia.

Initiation Rite: Holy Baptism and Confirmation/Reception within a celebration of Holy Communion 2016 [in Chinese] © Hong Kong Kung Hui Sheng; translation © Chunwai Lam.

Anglican Prayer Book (2004) [in Korean] © Anglican Church Korea; translation © Br Christopher John and Nak-Hyon Joseph Joo.

Book of Common Prayer 1990 [in Japanese] © Nippon Sei Ko Kai; translation © Lydia Morey and Shintaro Ichihara.

A Prayer Book for Australia 1995, author the Liturgy Commission of the General Synod of the Anglican Church of Australia © the Anglican Church of Australia Trust Corporation.

Anglican Prayer Book 1991, © Anglican Church Papua New Guinea.

A New Zealand Prayer Book He Karakia Mihinare o Aotearoa 1989 © The Anglican Church in Aotearoa, New Zealand and Polynesia, used with permission.

Revised Order of Holy Baptism 2001 © Anglican Church of Melanesia.

Confirmation and Re-affirmation of Baptismal Faith © Joint Liturgical Group 1992.

Order of Services 1988, © Mar Thoma Syrian Church.

Permission applied for

Common Worship: Christian Initiation 2006 © Archbishop's Council Church of England.

The Book of Common Prayer 1995 © The Church of the Province of the West Indies.

Our Modern Services 2002 © The Anglican Church of Kenya.

Book of Common Worship 2013 © The Church of Uganda.

The Book of Worship 1995 © The Church of North India.

Book of Common Worship 2006 © The Church of South India.

Other acknowledgements

I wish to give thanks for the help to the following people who have provided me with different information. The help was theirs, the misunderstandings mine.

The Most Revs: Clyde Igara, Paul S Sarker, Joseph Mar Thoma.

The Rt Revs: Bismark Avokaya, Terry Brown, George Conner, Dibo Elango, Henry Scriven, Oliver Simon.

The Venerable Ricky Rountree.

The Rev Canons Dr: Alison Barnett-Cowan, John Gibaut, Christopher Irvine.

The Rev Drs: Michael Hunter, Shintaro Ichihara, Chun Wai Lam, Ruth Meyers, Juan Quevedo-Bosch, Tomas Madella, Kevin McGinnell, George Matthew, Eileen Scully, Elizabeth Smith, Nicholas Taylor.

The Rev Canons: Cynthia Botha, William Challis, Brian Griffiths, Ian Tarrant.

The Revs: Evelyn Bhajan, Andii Bowsher, Richard Christopher, Joseph Fernandes, Michael Hughes, John Kafwanka, David Lounge, Shemil Mathew, Josie Midwinter, John Niyondiko, Stephen Nshimye, Mathew Phipps, Dushantha Rodrigo, Anderson Saefoa, Adel Shokralla, Jane Shaw, Manasseh Tuyizere, John Webber, Charles Wohlers.

Br: Christopher John SSF.

Dr: Judi Berinai, John Chesworth, Narmmasena Wickremesinghe.

Karen Brayshaw, Talia Carr, Anne Hywood, Bridget Lane, Rainah Madzorera, Augusten Masih, Abir Mitra, Lydia Morey, Ken Osborne, Damian Scragg, John Stuart.

Abbreviations

ASB   Church of England, *Alternative Service Book*, (London: SPCK, 1980).

BCP 79   The Episcopal Church, *Book of Common Prayer*, (New York: Church Hymnal Corporation, 1979).

BEM   World Council of Churches, *Baptism, Eucharist and Ministry*, Faith and Order Paper No.111, (Geneva, World Council of Churches, 1982).

G   David N. Griffiths, *The Bibliography of the Book of Common Prayer 1549–1999*, (London: The British Library, 2002).

J   Peter Jagger, *Christian Initiation 1552–1969* (London: SPCK, 1970).

IALC   Inter Anglican Liturgical Consultation.

Preface

The collection of baptismal texts in this book brings together most of the current texts used in the Anglican Communion. This volume is the fourth in an unplanned series of books of baptismal texts written by a succession of different authors, and it stands as a companion to Colin Buchanan's *Anglican Eucharistic Liturgies 1985 to 2010*. Unlike the series of books on eucharistic texts, the previous volumes have not covered every aspect of baptism and Christian initiation, and the previous volume finished in 1969. A complete set of Anglican liturgies of baptism, confirmation and associated rites would require a very large volume indeed to cover the period 1969 to 2016. Thus for simple practical reasons the concept of this book is to provide a comprehensive snapshot of the Anglican Communion and its baptismal liturgies frozen at the date of 2016.

The previous volumes in the series are: E.C. Whittaker, *Documents of the Baptismal Liturgy*, 3rd edition edited by Maxwell E. Johnson, (London: SPCK 1960 and 2003); J.D.C. Fischer, *Christian Initiation: The Reformation Period*, (London: SPCK, 1970); and Peter J. Jagger, *Christian Initiation: 1552–1969*, (London: SPCK, 1970). The latter volume concentrated on infant baptism and confirmation, thus being only a partial collection of texts. Alongside these volumes should be mentioned Thomas F. Best (editor), *Baptism Today: Understanding, Practice, Ecumenical Implications*, Faith and Order Paper No. 207, (Collegeville: Liturgical Press, 2008), which includes in it a helpful ecumenical collection of liturgical texts.

This volume approximately follows the order and some of the conventions of *Anglican Eucharistic Liturgies*. It thus includes an introductory paragraph to each of the Provinces. There has been a standardization of the format of texts so that in this book they have a commonality. Rubrics, notes and directions are included in *italics*. **Bold** type is used for corporate responses. ***Bold italics*** is used for the responses of candidates and or godparents. Headings are in a variety of forms depending on the level and are standardized as much as possible across the texts. This is not the way that many of the texts are laid out, indeed there is a variety of approach throughout the Communion, but for the purpose of comparison standardization is useful. Each text is numbered but this does not necessarily correspond to original numbering and is an editorial approach. Some original texts have numbered paragraphs and others do not. Not every text is produced in full. Editorial comment on the text is included in double brackets. Many of the texts are set within a Eucharist, and where that happens the eucharistic material is omitted, as it can be found in companion volumes. Sometimes there is provision of propers or alternative materials; these are included in the degree to which they are baptismal in nature, e.g. a set of intercessions as an option may be included in the baptismal Eucharist text, but if they are more general intercessions not specifically related to baptism they will not be included here.

Various footnotes are included that cross reference to two important works. G refers to David N. Griffiths, *The Bibliography of the Book of Common Prayer 1549–1999*, (London: The British Library, 2002). This is a significant contribution to the study of Anglican liturgy listing the various editions of the Book of Common Prayer in English and in other languages. If the book referred to is in English, then Griffiths' convention is to give the date followed by the number of his listing e.g. 1672/6, which means it was published in the year 1672 and Griffiths lists it as number 6 in his book in 1672. If the book is in a different language, then the languages are listed by number followed by the number of his listing e.g. 36:2 which means that it is the second book listed in French. The other cross reference that will be used will be to Jagger *Christian Initiation: 1552–1969*, thus referring you back to the previous work where relevant, and the footnote will simply say, J 51–59, which indicates the page numbers. For further information on The Episcopal Church I would refer you to Paul V Marshall, *Prayer Book Parallels*, (New York The Church Hymnal Corporation, 1989).

Even concentrating on the currently used texts there is still a vast amount of material e.g. *Common Worship: Christian Initiation* of the Church of England is 377 pages long. It includes pre-baptismal material (catechumenate), thanksgiving for the birth of a child, Holy Baptism, Baptism and Confirmation, much alternative material, affirmation of faith, reception into the Church of England, rites of reconciliation and a service of healing. My book will focus particularly on baptism and confirmation, for adults and children, and will mention in the introduction other material that exists. Increasingly services are online and thus readers will be able to follow up further interests.

The introductions to each chapter will try to bridge the gap between 1969 and 2013 indicating if there were any other baptismal texts in that period, although they will not be included. There is a complication in that in some Provinces traditional rites exist alongside contemporary rites. This is further complicated by periods of experimentation when temporary booklets may have been important, but are very easy to be missed.

It is a complex task to try to collect Anglican liturgies together into one volume. There is no one library that has a complete collection of these liturgies, not even Lambeth Palace Library. Some Provinces have had very difficult circumstances and while a particular prayer book may be the provincially stated book, on the ground something different may be used. Likewise, some Provinces have a rich collection of alternative texts but in reality only a small selection is actually used in parishes. This book does not try to solve such problems and simply gathers the texts as they exist. There is a further complication that some Provinces have to deal with a multiplicity of languages. As they are translated, it may be that there is some textual revision e.g. the 1662 baptism and confirmation rites in Northern Uganda, when I worked there, had been 'enriched' by parts of the 1928 Prayer Book when translated into Acholi. Such complications are beyond the scope of this book, which will concentrate on official Provincial rites. It may well be that some texts have been left out of the collection and I would be glad of readers sending further information for correction and addition.

Peter Jagger developed some abbreviations for the rites and Colin Buchanan has a complex series of abbreviations for the eucharistic rites. It is not possible to completely follow Colin Buchanan's approach; as baptismal texts do not necessarily come out at the same time as eucharistic texts. In general, the identification of rites will be by the

Province and date that they were produced. Where abbreviations are used they will be identified in the abbreviation section in the introductory material.

This book is the result of much goodwill and friendship across the Anglican Communion. Of particular importance to me has been the Inter Anglican Liturgical Consultations which have formed bonds of friendship between Provinces both in terms of liturgical thinking and genuine friendships. I have attended most of them from 1989 onwards. This has enabled me to visit Provinces I probably would not have gone to otherwise. Many friends from the IALC, a network that shows 'the bonds of affection' as real, have helped in this book and for that I wish to give thanks.

Phillip Tovey

A. Introduction: The Worldwide Scene

1. Baptismal liturgy and theology in the Anglican Communion 1948–2016

Anglicans have been having a long debate about baptism, confirmation and Holy Communion, as part of entry into the church, the sacramental theology of these elements and their liturgical expression. There have been significant reports at both international levels and in local churches. Sometimes reports from particular Provinces have been influential in other parts of the Communion. Certainly liturgically in this period there has been considerable borrowing of rites between Provinces. There has also been ongoing ecumenical debate, both in a bilateral and multilateral mode. This chapter aims therefore to look at these interprovincial, ecumenical and provincial reports that have contributed to the ongoing debate within the Communion. What will become clear from this is Anglicans are still not completely of one mind and settled on the core issues, and there is still considerable diversity between Provinces in their baptismal approaches.

The Lambeth Conference 1948

Immediately after the Second World War baptism and confirmation was addressed in a report at Lambeth 48. The report began recommending *The Theology of Christian Initiation* by the archbishops of Canterbury and York and commended its study.[1] Having said that it admitted that there was still much work to be done on the subject and that this was urgent. It centred on the recommendation that a fuller conception of Christian initiation is required and that this should start with a combined service of adult baptism and confirmation. Infant baptism should then follow as an adaptation of that rite.

The report, however, was fairly conservative. While considering the possibility of confirmation being at an early age, with renewal of vows later, it supports the traditional pattern of baptism followed by confirmation. Thus it hints at some of the discussion that had already begun, and will continue in spite of this report. It tries to tackle the question of the relationship of the Holy Spirit in baptism and in confirmation. It rather

---

1 Archbishops' Theological Commission. *The Theology of Christian Initiation: Being the Report of a Theological Commission Appointed by the Archbishops of Canterbury and York to Advise on the Relations between Baptism, Confirmation and Holy Communion*. London: S.P.C.K., 1948.

ducks the question by putting the issue in a wider context, but rejects the idea that somehow the Spirit is operative in one act but not in the other. In so doing it rejects the more extreme views of Gregory Dix[2] and holds to a more traditional approach.

It then tries to tackle the issue of indiscriminate baptism. It is aware that there is considerable unease and thinks churchmen (sic) need greater teaching in the area encouraging frequent instruction through sermons on baptism. In dealing with the issue of those who bring their children baptism without seeming to grow in the fellowship of the church, it recommends the possibility of a catechumenate for the parents of such children.

Concerning confirmation, the report notes that many still fall away after being confirmed. The report believes that people should only be confirmed after a personal response to the gospel. As for baptism, it suggests further preparation both long-term in children's work and short-term in preparation for the confirmation event. It suggests that all getting confirmed should have a basic rule of life comprising daily prayer and Bible reading, regular worship, and self-discipline (almsgiving and service). It again notes that in some parts of the Communion a catechumenate is used for a more extensive preparation. It sees a need for continual training in the Christian faith in a post-confirmation context, recommending refresher courses.

The report finishes with a note on the use of chrism in confirmation. It would appear by 1948 three Provinces were already using chrismation at confirmation. The report allows the use of chrism providing the sign of laying on of hands is maintained.

The resolutions of the conference 100–112 hold to the traditional sequence of baptism, confirmation and admission to Holy Communion. The conference wants to support infant baptism and recognizes that the parents have a major share in bringing the child up in the faith. It wants to see baptism as administered in the main service of the church and bring the local congregation into the responsibility of helping candidates into full fellowship. No unbaptized person should act as a godparent. It recommends keeping a baptismal roll. It also opens up the possibility of those who have been confirmed having a later opportunity for reaffirmation of vows.

Thus the 1948 report tries to maintain a traditional pattern and suggests the need is for more pastoral preparation of candidates for both baptism and confirmation. While this is a continual recommendation within Anglicanism, the report also shows various cracks appearing and the suggestion of more radical approaches. These are to become more apparent in future conferences.

The Lambeth Conference 1958

While holding to the myth that the 1662 Book of Common Prayer is the bond of unity in doctrine and worship for the whole Communion, the 1958 Conference had to admit that Provincial independence means that each particular Church has the right to develop its own prayer book. Thus this conference brought together some rules and suggestions as to how various services might be revised. In the discussion of features two aspects concerning initiation were regarded as essential. One was that holy baptism

---

2 Dix, G. *The Theology of Confirmation in Relation to Baptism*. London: Dacre Press, 1946.

be with water and the threefold name, the other was that confirmation be by the bishop with prayer and the laying on of hands.

With regard to Christian initiation the conference commended the study of three reports, *Baptism and Confirmation Today* from the Church of England,[3] *Prayer Book Studies 1* from the Episcopal Church[4] and the Church in Wales *Revised Services for Experimental Use: Holy Baptism and Confirmation*.[5] The conference encouraged the revision of the service of adult baptism on a primitive pattern culminating in first Communion. It suggested the revision of services to create this combined service as urgent.

The report even suggested elements of the baptismal service which need to be included, which are:

1. The ministry of the Word.
2. The renunciation.
3. A profession of faith.
4. The promises:
   a. to hold fast to the Christian faith;
   b. to obey God's commandments;
   c. to bear witness to Christ.
5. The blessing of the water.
6. Baptism in the threefold name.
7. Signing with the cross.
8. Reception into fellowship of the church.
9. Thanksgiving for having been sealed by the Holy Spirit.
10. Prayer for growth in the Christian life.
11. An exhortation to the congregation.
12. An exhortation to the candidate to live in the power of the Holy Spirit.

While these elements are incorporated into many services, this did not form a rigid framework to be followed by the Provinces.

The resolutions of the conference on the prayer book, 73–75, commend ecumenical study of liturgy, the report itself and urge that revision should be the recovery of the worship of the primitive Church.

The 1958 Conference tried to build on the 1948 resolutions, but realized that the trend would be for further liturgical revision with the growing impact of the liturgical movement. It tried to set some parameters for this with regard to baptism and confirmation, but the more Anglicans investigated the theology of the practice the more diversity developed.

---

3 Joint Committees on Baptism Confirmation Holy Communion. *Baptism and Confirmation Today.* London: S.P.C.K., 1955.

4 The Episcopal Church. *Prayer Book Studies: I. Baptism and Confirmation.* New York: Church Pension Fund, 1950.

5 Church in Wales. *Revised Services for Experimental Use: Holy Baptism and Confirmation: Bedydd Santaidd a Chonffirmasiwn.* Swansea: Llan and Welsh Church Press, 1969.

The Lambeth Conference 1968

This conference did not directly touch on questions of initiation; nevertheless, it further opened up the situation. In a section on the ministry, resolution 25 asks each Province to explore the theology of baptism and confirmation, particularly in regard to the commissioning of the laity. This may reflect the discussion in some circles of confirmation as a commissioning to ministry within the church.

The report, the renewal in ministry, is concerned about the lack of commissioning for the laity analogous to ordination. This is a somewhat strange concern as it seems to have the cart before the horse. However, it suggested two alternatives:

1. Infant baptism, followed by admission to Holy Communion after instruction, followed by confirmation in young adult life for responsible ministry.
2. Infant baptism and confirmation administered together, followed by admission to Communion after instruction, followed by episcopal commissioning later in life.

This is rather remarkable as these experimental lines are recommended alongside the traditional pattern of baptism, confirmation and Holy Communion. Diversity is increasing within the Communion, and one archbishop admits that he returned to his Province to rethink the position completely.

The conference also tackled confirmation from an ecumenical perspective. One reading of the 1662 confirmation rubric might suggest that Anglican confirmation was essential to receive Communion. However, in line with ecumenical concerns the conference suggested that Provinces adapt their constitutions so that baptized members of other churches may be welcome at the Lord's Table. Thus the absolute necessity of confirmation was being eroded within Anglicanism, on the one hand through its own internal discussion of the theology of baptism and confirmation, and on the other hand in relation to the ecumenical movement.

1968–1988

The 1978 Lambeth Conference did not address questions of baptism and confirmation, but there was considerable discussion in light of a major period of liturgical reform. In this period the Church of England produced the *Alternative Service Book 1980*, and the Episcopal Church produced the *Book of Common Prayer 1979*. These were to be highly influential around the Communion. There was also detailed discussion of questions of initiation. *Prayer Book Studies 18 Holy Baptism with the Laying-on-of-hands* was the basis for the 1979 book.[6] In it the Episcopal Church embraced a baptismal ecclesiology, with baptism being full initiation and confirmation being a pastoral rite. The Church of England, however, dithered. The Ely report of 1971 had recommended that baptism is recognized as 'the full and complete rite of Christian initiation'.[7] In light of that it suggested that clergy be allowed to admit persons to Communion, and that confirmation be a service of commitment and commissioning. After a muddled discussion in diocesan

---

6 Standing Liturgical Commission. *On Baptism and Confirmation*. Prayer Book Studies 18. New York: Church Pension Fund, 1970.

7 Commission on Christian Initiation. *Christian Initiation: Birth and Growth in the Christian Society*. GS 30. London: Church Information Office, 1971.

synods and again in General Synod, insufficient majorities were achieved to take this new direction, which left the church trying to revise its liturgy without a clear theology. Indeed, what happened was that parishes were allowed to take the proposed alternative route with the permission of their bishop, thus bringing a variety of approaches within the one church. This muddle continues till today.

Another input to the discussion was the influential *Baptism, Eucharist and Ministry* 1982 from the World Council of Churches.[8] This multilateral document was discussed in all Provinces of the Anglican Communion as well as in partner churches around the world. The report criticized an apparent indiscriminate approach to baptism in Europe and North America, something that Anglicans had already been discussing and so it reinforced the issue. It questioned the need for any separate rite to be interposed between baptism and the Eucharist, thus undermining the traditional Anglican requirement of confirmation. It affirmed the renewal of baptismal vows as a regular celebration. It said that baptism should always be celebrated in the setting of the Christian community. It looked for vivid signs of the gift of the Spirit. In all of these areas Anglican practice was considered and questioned.

In the celebration of baptism BEM suggested the minimum of the following elements:

1. the proclamation of Scripture;
2. invocation of the Holy Spirit;
3. a renunciation of evil;
4. a profession of faith in Christ and the holy Trinity;
5. the use of water;
6. a declaration that the candidate is a child of God, member of the church, and witness to the gospel.
(7. The sealing of the baptized with the gift of the Holy Spirit,
8. participation in Holy Communion.)

The last two elements are seen as essential in some churches but not in others. In the context of liturgical reform this provided a background for the reconsideration of traditional Anglican practice, and the encouragement in certain directions, not least baptism as full initiation.

A further body, developed in this period, was to have a significant input into baptismal questions, the International Anglican Liturgical Consultations. In light of liturgical development, the Anglican Consultative Council of 1987 proposed an Anglican Communion Liturgical Commission. This in fact never came into being, instead liturgists proposed the IALC, a network of liturgists who gathered together every two years to discuss issues of mutual interest. IALC 1 in Boston 1985 addressed the issues of baptism and Communion, 'since baptism is sacramental sign of full incorporation into the church, all baptised persons be admitted to Communion'. It asked that Provincial baptism rites be revised such that there was no distinction made between adult and infant baptism. It suggested that each Province clearly affirm that confirmation be shown as not a rite of admission to Communion.

---

8 World Council of Churches. *Baptism, Eucharist and Ministry*. Faith and Order Paper No. 111. Geneva: World Council of Churches, 1982.

The Anglican Consultative Council in 1984 had asked Provinces to consider and study the issue of admitting children to Communion prior to confirmation. By 1987 a number of Provinces had begun the admission of baptized children, including Australia, Brazil, Liberia, New Zealand, Scotland, Southern Africa, Canada and the USA. England was in a process of discussing the issue, and Central Africa had run a pilot scheme but decided not to change its practice. The 1987 meeting discussed the Boston consultation and questioned some of its assumptions. One was that potentially candidates would lack a public affirmation of their faith. Another was to ask if it was implicit to have a tight baptismal policy arising out of the Boston approach, and it questioned if the effect would be to reduce the frequency of confirmation. It asked if there was a danger of unworthily receiving Communion. The questions asked were somewhat muddled this last one in particular seemingly wanting to say that there were disciplinary requirements even on children who have not 'reached the years of discretion'. Clearly modern theories of faith development had not touched the ACC 7. The most bizarre of the questions was 'does not the limitation of the sacrament of initiation to water baptism reduce the full character of the sacrament?' This is bizarre from a scriptural perspective. There is no discussion in the Bible of 'the sacrament of initiation', there is simply baptism. Confirmation did not come to exist for a number of centuries. So what is this 'sacrament of initiation'? The questions however do show some resistance to the growing trend that had occurred. The ACC resolution encouraged the sharing of experience between Provinces on the admission of baptized children to Communion.

The 1988 Lambeth Conference reaffirmed the value of infant baptism but accepted the BEM criticism of indiscriminate baptism. It recommended that the text of the Boston statement be circulated in the Communion. It recognized that different patterns were developing over admission to Communion. It also recognized that a new pattern had developed concerning the baptism of adults, namely that adult baptism was combined with confirmation as a single rite over which the bishop presides. Finally, it recommended experiments in the reaffirmation of baptismal vows. Resolution 69 asked that Provinces report to the ACC on their experience of admission of those baptized but unconfirmed to Holy Communion.

IALC 4 Toronto 1991

A significant point in the development of Anglican views of initiation was the IALC in 1991. This picked up and expanded the agenda of the first IALC on children and Communion and considered a whole range of issues throughout the Communion. The fruit of this was gathered together in the book *Growing in Newness of Life*.[9] While an IALC has no authority it is influential as a document to be read within the Provinces, but it is also influential because those involved have roles in teaching liturgy and the liturgical commissions. There were representatives from 22 different Provinces at Toronto and thus it was a significant gathering of Anglican minds.

---

9 Holeton, D., ed. *Growing in Newness of Life: Christian Initiation in Anglicanism Today: Papers from the Fourth International Anglican Liturgical Consultation, Toronto, 1991*. Toronto: Anglican Book Centre, 1993.

The consultation produced seven principles of Christian initiation which are worth quoting in full.

1. The renewal of baptismal practice is an integral part of mission and evangelism. Liturgical texts must point beyond the life of the church to God's mission in the world.
2. Baptism is for people of all ages, both adults and infants. Baptism is administered after preparation and instruction of the candidates, or where they are unable to answer for themselves, of their parent(s) or guardian(s).
3. Baptism is complete sacramental initiation and leads to participation in the Eucharist. Confirmation and other rites of affirmation have a continuing pastoral role in the renewal of faith among the baptised but are in no way to be seen as a completion of baptism or as necessary for admission to Communion.
4. The catechumenate is a model for preparation and formation for baptism. We recognise that its constituent liturgical rites may vary in different cultural contexts.
5. Whatever language is used in the rest of the baptismal rite, both the profession of faith and the baptismal formula should continue to name God as Father, Son, and Holy Spirit.
6. Baptism once received is unrepeatable and any rites of renewal must avoid being misconstrued as re-baptism.
7. The pastoral rite of confirmation may be delegated by the bishop to a presbyter.

This is perhaps the fullest setting out of an agenda for liturgical reform. It starts from the principal of baptism as complete initiation, but also includes other key issues. It begins with the integral connection between baptism and mission, an element missed in much of the discussion so far. It includes aspects that were perhaps already accepted in some places, one rite of baptism for both adults and infants, and admitting the baptized to Communion. It returns to consider the catechumenate as an important part of a missiological approach, while recognizing the need for local variation. It resists the changing of the baptismal formula in a feminist direction, something that Rome has also spoken on, seeing Creator, Redeemer and Sustainer as inadequate and invalid language. While allowing rites of renewal, it discourages confusing them with re-baptism, a pastoral problem in some Provinces. Finally, in considering the nature of confirmation, it recognizes that this is not essentially an episcopal rite. This last point has perhaps been the most controversial, but it has to be recognized that in some Anglican Provinces, notably in uniting churches the possibility of a presbyteral confirmation exists, and in ecumenical full communion agreements e.g. the Porvoo Communion, there is acceptance of presbyteral confirmation.

The more detailed recommendations expand some of these points. In seeing confirmation as a pastoral rite of importance for those who are baptized as infants, it suggests that confirmation following an adult baptism is unnecessary, the point being that an infant professes their faith at confirmation while an adult has done it at their baptism. One aspect of the relationship with baptism and mission is the catechumenate which it sees as a community-based pattern of Christian formation. The report wants the local church to grasp the idea that it is a baptizing community. The catechumenate provides one approach, and the report sees this process as liturgically marked in four stages, enquiry, formation, immediate preparation and post-baptismal reflection. The report also suggests different aspects of renewing the baptismal faith, thus it sees the need for a rite of renewal, and reception from other churches, rites of reconciliation of the lapsed, and the restoration of the penitent, all as a part of baptismal renewal.

The report also suggests a number of elements for the baptismal liturgy.

1. Presentation of the candidates.
2. Renunciation of evil.
3. Prayer over the water.
4. Profession of Christian faith.
5. Administration of water.
6. Post-baptismal ceremonies, including ones from local culture.

It suggests that the rite be the same for adults and infants with minor modification for the latter.

This is perhaps the most thoroughgoing set of recommendations for liturgical reform within the Anglican Communion. Very few Provinces have implemented all of the recommendations, but it stands as a high point of the new theology and practice of Christian initiation. While some Provinces have implemented the recommendations in part, others continue to stay with the traditional practice. The Toronto IALC set out the clearest case so far for baptismal renewal.

1991–2016

The 1998 Lambeth conference commended the study of IALC documents but did not comment on baptism itself. There have been, however, in this period further important ecumenical documents.

Conversations Around the World 2000–2005 is the fruit of Anglican–Baptist dialogue.[10] The section on a process of initiation, paragraphs 42–43, wanted to see initiation as involving a number of elements, baptism, profession of faith, Christian instruction, membership of the church, welcome at the table. This recognition of initiation as a wider thing enables each church to see that all of these steps are important, but the order of them in the life of a disciple varies in each church. The dialogue had difficulty with the language of sacramental initiation complete in baptism, because this seemed to undermine the possibility of looking at initiation in this wider way. It particularly referred to the Toronto statement, in a footnote, as problematic. It wants to see confirmation as a part of initiation and suggested:

while baptized but not yet confirmed infants need not be excluded from the eucharist, this should not be taken to imply that initiation had been completed even by participating in the eucharist for the first time, if confirmation had not yet taken place.[11]

---

10 The Anglican Consultative Council and the Baptist World Alliance. *Conversations around the World 2000 – 2005*. London: The Anglican Communion Office, 2005.

11 Ibid., p. 47.

This is a clumsy and muddled piece of reasoning, which does not grasp the nature of baptism as explained by Toronto. Part of the issue seems to be that Baptists want to make clear that there needs to be a profession of faith. Toronto is suggesting the same thing too with confirmation, as that profession for those who have been baptized as infants. Part of the issue is in the use of the word initiation. It is not always used in exactly the same way, and is relatively new in sacramental theology. In Anglican–Baptist dialogue, it has a very wide usage. Often in some Anglican circles it has a narrower role, mostly to bolster up a doctrine for confirmation. Baptism and Eucharist are the sacraments of the Christian church. While there may be a process of initiation looked at from a broader perspective, there is no sacrament of initiation divided into various parts.

One Baptism: Towards Mutual Recognition 2011 is a study document of the World Council of Churches.[12] While not as influential as BEM it continues to operate with the same assumption that baptism admits the candidate to Holy Communion. It recognizes a considerable time of liturgical renewal and notes the development of a single rite for adults and infants, and the growing use of oil as a sign of the Spirit. The report suggests that a recognition of each other's baptism is the step to welcoming people to the table.

Thus while ecumenical dialogue may require clarification of some Anglican developments, the work of the World Council of Churches encourages a Toronto approach to baptism. Further work with Baptists would be helpful in order to clarify the misapprehensions in the report.

Conclusion

The long-running debate in Anglicanism around baptism has theologically come from the wrong assertion of Mason in 1891 that baptism and confirmation can only be regarded as forming together one sacrament. This was discredited in his own day, and is clearly wrong from the perspective of biblical theology (confirmation not being discussed in the Scriptures) and classical Anglican theology where confirmation is not regarded as a dominical sacrament. The resurrection of this view by Dix was roundly refuted by Lampe and Dunn exposing the lack of a sound patristic and biblical basis for such assertions. It is however a feature of Anglicanism that such views from time to time reassert themselves even if completely discredited.

In the absence of such a two-stage theory there have been two alternate options. One is to continue the traditional pattern of infant baptism, confirmation and Holy Communion. In this pattern, confirmation can be seen as the point of profession of the baptismal covenant for oneself, a prayer of blessing by the bishop as leader of the church and an admission to Holy Communion. Some Provinces continue in this traditional practice. It does not however answer the questions that have been raised about the implications of this for the meaning of baptism in general and adult baptism in particular.

The other alternative has been to baptize children, admit them to Communion later and then confirm at a later date. This would appear to be the new pattern that has been adopted by a number of Provinces. However, it would also appear that where this has

---

12 World Council of Churches. *One Baptism: Towards Mutual Recognition: A Study Text.* Faith and Order Paper No. 210. Geneva, Switzerland: World Council of Churches, 2011.

happened confirmation has withered away. In New Zealand, confirmation has come to be a rare event, and its increase recently has been due to the migration of people from Provinces with a traditional pattern, and the enduring nature of confirmation in private boarding schools. Some of those who have been receiving Communion from their baptism as an infant cannot see the point of confirmation. Each Sunday at the Eucharist they profess their faith and renew their baptismal covenant. Is this not sufficient in itself?

While these two approaches to baptismal incorporation into the church exist within the Anglican Communion at the same time, Toronto was right in pointing back to the key relationship between baptism and mission. While some Provinces like England are seeing a decline in infant baptism, at the same time there is an increase in adult baptism. This has led to the building of baptisteries that enable the full submersion of the candidate underwater. In some parts of the Communion adult baptisms are more in number than infant baptisms. The renewal of baptism within Anglicanism is not complete. There continues to need to be the sharing of practice between Provinces.

2. Provincial Baptismal Texts

The baptismal texts of the Anglican Communion show a considerable variety on a number of issues, but also a conservatism in terms of elements included and development of the received tradition. This may well be because baptism has a theological priority and thus caution is exercised in liturgical practice. It is also true that baptism is significant ecumenically and therefore creativity that might be found in pastoral rites is tempered by ecumenical considerations with regard to baptism. Various ecumenical documents such as *Baptism, Eucharist and Ministry*[13] not only comment on the theology but also on the elements of a baptismal rite. The Inter Anglican Toronto Statement of 1991 also discussed elements of the rite.[14] Thus ecumenical and liturgical considerations combine with inherited tradition to produce conservatism in the texts of the Anglican Communion. In order to look at those texts, I want to discuss them in a particular way: first to discuss context, then elements, then issues of order, inculturation and questions of reading.

Context of texts

There are a whole range of issues related to the context of baptismal texts. Biblical studies has introduced us to literary readings of Bible stories, and the same issues can be applied to a baptismal liturgy. One area to investigate is what may be called the authorial intended context. We can see in the work of Cranmer, his intended context was one where children were baptized and there were virtually no adult baptisms. Mission was intergenerational. Thus the service was completely directed to the baptism of children. However, there is also a practitioner actual context and this varies. It may be that in some places Cranmer's context is still similar in that virtually the whole population is baptized, as happens in parts of Africa. In this situation an infant baptism service fits with the practitioner context. However, in many other places the practitioner context has changed and this has required rewriting baptismal liturgies. It can be seen that the authorial intended context of some of the baptismal liturgies is still that where children are the intended recipients. Thus in some places there is only a service for children (e.g. Seychelles), or there is the older position where there is a separate additional service for adults (e.g. Portugal). Many other places have a more mixed economy with one service for both adults and children (e.g. Canada, Nigeria and Kenya).

---

13 World Council of Churches. *Baptism, Eucharist and Ministry*. Faith and Order Paper 111. Geneva: World Council of Churches, 1982.

14 Holeton, D.R. *Growing in Newness of Life: Christian Initiation in Anglicanism Today*. Toronto: Anglican Book Centre, 1993.

A second contextual issue is on a theological level. Does the practical context drive the theology of the rite or does that come from biblical and theological sources? This may seem a somewhat artificial question, but it raises considerable ecumenical issues around the theology of baptism. It is often said that Anglicans baptize children, as if this is their only way of baptism. In fact, all Anglicans baptize both adults and infants. The liturgical question is, do you work from the dominant practice of the baptism of infants to the liturgical text, as was the case of the reformers, or do you make adult baptism the theological norm? In 1958 the Church of England declared that 'in the New Testament adult baptism is the norm'.[15] The archetypal service is of adult baptism and confirmation. Infant baptism is a separate service derived from the archetype. This type of thinking is now quite widespread in the Anglican Communion and is liturgically expressed in a combined service of baptism of adults and infants. Ecumenically this is a significant development in repairing bridges with anti-paedobaptist churches; previous generations confused the issue by appearing to make infant baptism the theological norm. This switch has not occurred in all Provinces of the Anglican Communion, but there is a trend in this direction. It was probably hastened in the liturgical movement by the text of Hippolytus, where adults and children are baptized together, and the perceived ecumenical benefits.

Elements

It is now pertinent to look at the liturgical elements of the baptismal services. Here it can be seen that there is a strong consistency of elements within the services, even if there is significant variation in order. This creates a problem for discussing the elements as it may appear that my ordering of them is prioritizing a particular theory. This I want to try and avoid, as clearly there is Provincial diversity which rightly leads to discussion about the meaning of the rite.

A second consideration to do with the elements concerns their prioritization. The work of the Lutheran World Federation in discussing the issues of worship and culture encourages a distinction between ecumenical essentials, the ordo and in this case Anglican norms.[16] Such a typology might be further developed by having another category, recent developments. The latter could include new elements of the service that have become common in the Provinces but are clearly recent in their inclusion. They can either be completely new elements for pastoral reasons, or ancient elements reintroduced. All this can be compounded by questions of inculturation and the reception by dynamic equivalence of cultural elements into the services in particular Provinces. Within that somewhat complex structure I would like to suggest that the following table maps the elements within contemporary baptismal liturgical texts.

---

15 Liturgical Commission. *Baptism and Confirmation*. London: SPCK, 1960, p. x.
16 Wilkey, G. V. ed. *Worship and Culture: Foreign Country or Homeland*. Grand Rapids: Eerdmans, 2014.

Figure 2.1 Elements of the baptismal liturgy

Essential ordo	Anglican ordo	Recent developments
		Presentation of candidates
		Promises (of parents)
Ministry of the Word		
	Renunciation and decision	
		Deliverance
		Covenant commitment
	Profession of faith (Apostles Creed)	
	Blessing of water	
		Blessing of oil
Baptism		
	Secondary symbol (signing with cross)	Anointing, clothing, light
		Welcome
	Lord's prayer	
	Intercessions	
		Renewal of vows
	Confirmation	
		Anointing
		Reception reaffirmation
		Eucharist
	Conditional baptism	
	Emergency baptism	

This classification, and clearly there could be much discussion about which elements are in which column, includes 21 elements in the baptismal liturgy.

The presentation of the candidates seems to be a sensible pastoral introduction in the service. It may have arisen in a unified rite of baptism and confirmation because of the need for the candidates to be introduced to the bishop. It is also useful as a way of introducing the candidates to the congregation. However, this also raises the question why it is a necessity. In the past where the social context was the village a presentation of the candidates may not have been necessary as everyone knew everyone. In the present urban setting this may not be so. However, from a catechumenal prospective it might be that the presentation of the candidates could and should occur prior to the baptism by some weeks, and that the candidates should have been prayed for by name in the intercessions prior to the baptismal service. So the introduction of the presentation is both pastorally helpful and at the same time questions pastoral practice.

While some sort of promise of the parents was included in 1662, in some places there has been a tendency to increase these promises (these promises may also be made by adult candidates). The danger is that the impression given is that faith in the candidate is irrelevant and that the issue is of faith in the parents (cf. the Church of North India and the Church of South India). This to me seems to have given a prioritization of the theology of infant baptism as context and needs to be tempered by a theological norm of adult baptism. The question of the faith of the candidate is not irrelevant and traditional notions of proxy faith or of family faith while logically complex do still include a notion that the candidate is making a profession.

We come to the more centrally Anglican (and shared with other churches) element of renunciation and decision. First, it should be said that there is not a universal in the order of these elements, or the inclusion of both. Second, with regard to renunciation the tradition is of the world, the flesh and the Devil, although the latter may be increased in places where traditional religion may be seen to include superstitious practices, and in other places decreased where the renunciation is of evil rather than evil personified. It would seem that while renunciation is perhaps an Anglican norm the exact content and development of it could be an issue for inculturation. The third issue is concerning the part of this complex which I have called here the decision. There is a question within Anglican liturgy as to what this part is trying to achieve. If it is viewed as a profession of faith, then it seems to repeat a further element using the Apostles Creed. In some Provinces (Uganda, Kenya, Southern Africa) the decision has been removed, as it has become redundant as a profession. If, however, it is more to be seen as a decision, then it nuances profession of faith between elements of will and elements of belief. Thus the distinction becomes between one of asking the candidate 'Will you follow Christ?' and then 'Who is the Christ you follow?' Labelling the second element 'the decision' seems to clarify this distinction.

While in the past 'lesser exorcisms' have been a part of baptism, this has not been a part of Anglican baptismal renewal, save in Spain. However, in some places (England, Ireland and Southern Africa) prayers of protection are included in the rites often following the renunciations.

Some Provinces (e.g. The Episcopal Church) include a commitment from the candidates. This may be a series of questions about their intended behaviour with regard to church in the world. In a few Provinces this occurs early in the service, but in other Provinces it is late after baptism. There is a question here as to the extent to which this is a repetition of the renunciation and decision or a further development of it. The question also arises whether sufficient catechesis has occurred before baptism and if so why this might be required to be expressed in the service. Bryan Spinks has seen this a undermining baptismal grace.

The profession of faith is universal to Anglican baptism, although the location of this element varies and this will be discussed later. Anglicans primarily use the Apostles Creed in their profession of faith, although some Provinces (e.g. Wales) have used shorter question and answer statements. The Apostles Creed may be recited in one large block (e.g. Uganda) or may be divided into questions and answers (e.g. Philippines). The Creed may be recited by the candidates only (e.g. Australia) or in some Provinces it is recited by the whole congregation who are renewing their baptismal vows alongside the candidates (e.g. England). The ecumenical significance of this Creed might suggest that an Anglican norm should be that it is at least one option.

While there was a blessing of the water in 1549, it was reshaped to a blessing of the candidate in the 1552 Book of Common Prayer, however, it has been an Anglican norm to have a prayer over the water since 1662. The title for this prayer varies, some emphasizing thanksgiving and others emphasizing blessing. This indicates a distinction in language found even in the New Testament between thanksgiving and blessing. The content of the prayers is remarkably similar although some Provinces have gone in for alternative prayers. The Church of England is one of few Provinces that has provided seasonal prayers and recently short prayers. While clearly the content of the prayer is determined by biblical theology, there ought to be more possibility of inculturation in this prayer both in form and content (cf. Kenya).

In a few Provinces provision is made for the blessing of oil (e.g. The Episcopal Church and Uganda). This is usually in a Provincial context where anointing at baptism has become a possibility. Many Provinces now have services of the blessings of oil during holy week (e.g. England), and the suggestion of this is that oil of anointing is usually blessed by the bishop but it is not essential that it be so.

The primary symbol of the rite is the baptism in water. This itself contains certain elements of diversity. In terms of the words used, the majority of Provinces use the Western formal, 'N I baptize you in the name of the Father, and of the Son, and of the Holy Spirit'. Some places allow as an alternative the passive form, 'N is baptized', and in Sri Lanka this is the only form that is allowed, recalling the possible apostolic foundation of the church there by St Thomas. There is also a variant on the Western form 'N I baptize you in the name of God, the Father, the Son and the Holy Spirit' as in the Church of North India. The pouring of water is a common form for the use of the element, although it should be said that rubrics increasingly encourage copious use of water, allowing full immersion, the use of rivers or the sea. In places where adult baptism is becoming more common, or even is more frequent than infant baptism, the provision of large baptismal baths sufficient for immersing adults is also increasingly common, but may not be indicated in the rubrics.

An Anglican norm is for secondary symbolism in the signing of the cross. This was much debated in the post-Reformation and the post-restoration periods, but Anglicans have continued to defend the use of secondary symbols. A complex set of theological statements are often used with the signing of the cross based on traditional themes, although in some places there is no response (e.g. Ireland). A few places have moved the signing with the cross before baptism. In the Church of England this was to eliminate a local theology that viewed the signing with water as the essence of baptism. This location then picks up the signing as a catechumenal rite. In the Church of North India this secondary symbolism does not exist. In the majority the signing of the cross continues.

In some Provinces there is a proliferation of secondary symbols. These may include anointing, clothing and the giving of light (e.g. Nigeria, Bangladesh). Clothing can be a practical aspect where adults, or infants, have been fully immersed and need to replace their wet garments. In some places there is a vestige of this in the custom of a baptismal garment for children in white (a christening robe). In many Provinces there is the giving of a candle to express the light of Christ (e.g. South East Asia, Canada). This can be immediately after the baptism or later in the service as a missional element (e.g. England). In some Provinces words about light are used but it is not clear that a candle is given (e.g. Australia). In other places where candles are not readily available the giving of lamps may occur, clearly an issue of dynamic equivalence (e.g. Sri Lanka). Questions of anointing will be addressed later.

A more recent introduction is that of the welcome describing the implications of baptism. In some places it is supplemented by a statement of admission to Holy Communion (e.g. Kenya, Portugal). Again this would appear to be an organic development of the liturgy.

The prayers in the service are often included with an obvious inclusion of the Lord's Prayer and various intercessions. These can be in a variety of forms both as collects and as litanies. Candidates and their families are clear objects of prayer, but there may be a variety of other issues.

Anglicans have regarded confirmation as of great significance, although see the discussion in the previous chapter as to the changing theology of confirmation. 1662 included in confirmation the renewal of baptismal vows and in some places this has been expanded prior to the confirmation (e.g. England).

The confirmation itself remains quite stable in terms of a prayer bringing out the sevenfold gifts of the Spirit and a prayer by the bishop over the candidates with the laying on of the right hand. However, it has to be acknowledged that it is clear in some ecumenical contexts that there may be presbyteral confirmation (e.g. Church of North India, Church of South India). The rubrics of some Provinces influenced by liturgical renewal (e.g. Scotland) suggest that there may be the possibility of presbyteral confirmation.

In light of the Toronto Statement many Provinces are introducing rites of reception and reaffirmation (e.g. Canada, Australia). In the context of a baptism with Eucharist these are often performed by the bishop, although it is not universal that these newer additions are an episcopal rite.

Increasingly the baptismal liturgy is set within the context of a Eucharist. In practice this may not always be so but the authorial intended context is clearly eucharistic. There are still a number of Provinces that write baptismal services in the context of an office (e.g. Church of South India, Kenya).

Increasingly Anglicans use oil within their baptismal liturgies (e.g. The Episcopal Church, Scotland, England). Most commonly this is an option added to the sign of the cross after baptism. In some cases chrismation has replaced the traditional words of renunciation, often referring to the seal of the Spirit (e.g. The Episcopal Church). It is the oil of chrism that is used in a post-baptismal context. This is complicated when baptism and confirmation are combined, and where chrism will be used at confirmation. The authorial intention of the text in most cases would seem to be that chrism is then reserved to confirmation. Only a couple of Provinces follow the 1549 approach of separating the laying on of hands and anointing (e.g. Scotland, Southern Africa). A number of Provinces consecrate three oils during holy week. The Church of England and the Church in Wales are the few that actually give directions for the oil of catechumens. In this case the oil of catechumens is to be used before baptism and chrism is used after. The use of oil is complex in the patristic period and study of that period has influenced making it complex in Anglicanism today.

Questions of order

The ordering of various elements of the baptismal rites indicates the diversity of liturgical theology and practice in Anglicanism. It has already been discussed in the previous chapter concerning the place of confirmation and the Eucharist. There are questions around the place of profession (using the Apostles Creed) and baptism and some fundamental questions about the place of commitments.

With regard to the question of profession, three positions seem to be held. In many Provinces the profession comes after renunciation and decision and prior to the blessing of water and baptism (e.g. Nigeria, Chile). Thus one can see two liturgical units: renunciation – decision – profession; blessing of water – baptism. Other Provinces wish to put the profession as close to the application of water as possible and thus divide the blessing of water from the baptism (e.g. Sri Lanka, Ireland). Some Provinces put the profession at the end of the service (e.g. New Zealand and Japan). To many this will seem an unusual order, but the theory is of belonging before believing. In New Zealand this was sufficiently questioned to produce a modification to the rite to allow an alternative putting profession before baptism. The weight of tradition and ecumenical consensus would suggest that this is the correct order.

Asking for increasing commitment before baptism does seem to raise theological questions as to the nature of grace within the service. Bryan Spinks has commended those Provinces which put commitment to a way of life after baptism as expressing the priority of grace to enable such commitments to occur over against a more Pelagian approach.[17] The critique is thus that the commitment in baptism should follow a logical sacramental principle i.e. the grace of baptism is required to enable one to fulfil baptismal commitments.

A further theological question might arise associated with this through the labelling by some Provinces of a section prior to baptism as the baptismal covenant (e.g. The Episcopal Church). This might seem to suggest that our commitments are fundamental to the covenant rather than God's grace. However, the reintroduction of this concept of covenant is to be welcomed, not least as it was central to Anglican discussion of baptism from the time of Elizabeth to its gradual decline with the development of Tractarian theology. All Provinces might want to reconsider baptism within biblical concept of covenant and thus its implications for the ordering of the texts.

Inculturation

The history of baptism is one of inculturation by the proliferation of secondary symbols used to illustrate aspects of the service. This process can be seen with the substitution of different types of light appropriate to the local culture e.g. candles being substituted with lamps as in India. However, there is a certain conservatism in the texts that are used. This is perhaps natural in a dominical sacrament as compared to more pastoral rites.

The Church of Ceylon is perhaps one of the more notable exceptions where permissive rubrics allow the option of including more Sri Lankan customs to enter the

---

17 Spinks, B. *Reformation and Modern Rituals and Theologies of Baptism: From Luther to Contemporary Practices*. Aldershot: Ashgate, 2006, pp. 172–183.

rite, including oiling the body, striking with an ekel[18] and marking with a sandalwood cross. Later there is a possibility of a threefold circumambulation around the font and the cutting of the hair. Pots of water are passed round to renew baptismal vows. Sri Lanka shows how customs from local traditions may be incorporated and enrich the liturgy.

A different type of inculturation is tried in Spain. Here the Mozarabic tradition is drawn on rather than the Sarum tradition. This tradition has a theology of baptism more based in new life than death and resurrection. It is a different type of inculturation drawing inspiration from an ancient local tradition. Such an inculturation requires serious study of the tradition to see how it may be adapted to present use.

Ecumenical contexts require new rites. Organic unity in India led the way to different baptismal traditions being incorporated into one church, with a certain amount of pastoral flexibility. A different model is show in the Joint Liturgical Group's confirmation rite used widely in Ecumenical Partnerships where members are multipally confirmed in the service. In theory it might look odd; in practice it makes sense.

In terms of inculturation permissive rubrics would seem to be the way forward and with consideration of a more local set of secondary symbols.

Reading the text

There is considerable diversity in the provision of baptismal liturgies. The contrast may be made between the Church of England whose *Common Worship: Christian Initiation Book* is 377 pages long contrasted with the neighbouring Province, the Scottish Episcopal Church, whose *Holy Baptism 2006* is 16 pages. The Church of England not only has the most complicated baptismal liturgies of the whole of the Anglican Communion, with more alternatives than any Provinces, it all so has more paraliturgical elements in the form of introductions, commentary, indexes, notes, lectionaries and copyright information. All of this is a major development from the inclusion of only text and rubrics.

The baptismal liturgy contains large elements of intertextuality, the Anglican tradition being that prayers should reflect biblical theology, not least in their allusions to the biblical texts. This can be particularly seen in collects at the beginning of the service and in the blessing of the water. As yet the hermeneutical issues (which allusion is in and which allusion is out) have yet to be fully discussed, and then there is the further question of the issues that shape this decision. Clearly compared to some of the patristic hymns on baptism, for example in the hymns of Saint Ephraim, a narrow selection of texts is being used and a limited typology.

In terms of para text there is increasingly use of white space, and not a simple filling of the page with words. This makes the text easier to read both by the leader and the congregation. Page numbers, paragraph numbers and headings are common in many of the services. Paragraph headings are increasingly common although at times it is not clear as to the hierarchy of subheadings (and in the following texts some decisions have had to be made by the editor as to whether something is a heading or subheading). Most services include rubrics for the direction of the service and some notes as well.

---

18 An ekel is a type of cane.

These may be quite extensive (e.g. Brazil) and almost all of them include directions for conditional baptism and emergency baptism.

All of these changes in the textual layout of a book or service are there to help the words flow into worship, and perhaps this spiritual development is most important. Baptism is not about getting our child 'done' but about the inclusion of new people into the worshipping community of God. This worship needs to overflow in both directions, upwards towards God and outwards towards the surrounding community. Thus then the people of God are showing themselves to be a royal priesthood and thus participating in the mission of God revealed in baptism.

Conclusion

While this chapter may seem to have stressed diversity, there is in fact quite a considerable unity in Anglican baptismal rites as expressed in Figure 2.1. This ordo is shared between many of the Anglican Provinces and would be overlapping with the ordo of other denominations. This is to be expected in a baptismal rite as it is an aspect of us being 'one' as in the prayer of our Lord Jesus Christ. While Anglicans are discussing the nature of baptism and confirmation, which can be seen in the variation of the different texts, the wider ecumenical issues are rarely touched on in texts and may be found more in policy documents. However, these ecumenical issues are influenced by the texts that Provinces produce. Baptismal liturgical renewal in terms of text needs to go hand-in-hand with the ecumenical implications of one baptism.

B. Britain and Ireland (with Spain and Portugal)

3. The Church of England

Christianity came to England in Roman times; the first recorded martyr being St Alban who died in 304. St Augustine became the first Archbishop of Canterbury in 597. He was the head of a mission from Rome, although there were already Christians in the northern part of the country. The uniting of the two strands came in 664/5 at the Synod of Whitby. The Church of England continued as a part of the Western Church until the Reformation. The break with Rome was made by Henry VIII. But the reformation of the church began in the reign of his son Edward VI with the guidance of Archbishop Thomas Cranmer who produced the first reformed Book of Common Prayer in 1549 and another in 1552. In the Commonwealth period the prayer book was abolished. However it was restored in 1662. This continued to be the worship book of the Church of England until liturgical revision after the Second World War.

The current provision of the Church of England is twofold, first that of the *Book of Common Prayer*[19] and *Common Worship: Christian Initiation* (2006). Jagger included *Series 2 Baptism and Confirmation*.[20] In 1997 *Series 3 Initiation Services* was published, and in 1980 was included in a revised form in the *Alternative Service Book*. The ASB material was produced around an archetypal rite of baptism and confirmation at Holy Communion. Some of the very popular ASB material was included in Common Worship, particularly the alternative forms of decision and profession of faith, due to requests from the parishes.

The first Common Worship texts *Common Worship: Initiation Services* came out in 1998. Amendments to the service were made in 2000, and in 2005, and further provision has been made, 2015. *Common Worship: Christian Initiation* (2006) added material including catechumenal provision called 'Rites supporting disciples on the way of Christ', and services of reconciliation and restoration, recovering baptismal grace. The Common Worship material also includes various rites of affirmation of baptismal faith and reception into the Church of England; as well as a rite for first Communion, and thanksgiving for the gift of a child.

The 1998 volume includes a commentary by the Liturgical Commission, and the 2006 volume a second version of this commentary. A comparison of the two reveals the complex picture in the Church of England where no one policy has been fully pursued and so a variety of different approaches subsist next to one another. On the one hand

19 J 22–33.
20 J 138–147.

the provision of a service of holy baptism in the context of Holy Communion seems to suggest that the baptized are by baptism communicant, which might be reinforced by the provision of a service of first Communion. On the other hand, the canons and rubrics of the Church of England still require the baptized to be confirmed. Similarly, while the second commentary denies that chrismation by a presbyter after baptism is the equivalent to confirmation, the policy is still to admit people from Orthodox and Oriental churches on the basis of their baptism and chrismation.

There has been considerable debate over matters of initiation in the Church of England. This has been influenced by traditional patterns inherited from the Book of Common Prayer. Tractarian two-stage views of baptism and confirmation coincide with more recent views of 'sacramental initiation complete in baptism' as perhaps best shown in the 1971 Ely report, and the 1991 Toronto statement of the International Anglican Liturgical Consultation. The ins and outs of this debate are too complex to include in the introduction to the services.

Common Worship: Christian Initiation is a 377-page book. Of necessity this chapter is a considerable reduction of the material. The catechumenal material has been omitted for lack of space, and the reconciliation material is omitted as going beyond the purview of this book. The aim here has been to provide the text of holy baptism (within Holy Communion) and holy baptism and confirmation (within Holy Communion). These two services form the primary text from which a vast number of permutations are developed within different types of services. There is still considerable use of 'Baptism apart from a Celebration of Holy Communion' as an afternoon stand-alone service on Sunday. This volume also includes provision for emergency baptism and conditional baptism. The notes for emergency baptism say that in the case of an infant who dies without being baptized, the questions of ultimate salvation or the provision of a Christian funeral do not depend upon baptism.

Common Worship includes a rite for the 'Affirmation of baptismal faith' this is a pastoral rite for those who have been previously initiated but have a new faith experience. This can be conducted by a presbyter and includes a laying of a hand on the candidate with the words 'N, may God renew his life within you ...'. The rite for 'Reception into the Church of England' may also be conducted by a presbyter unless the person so received is a minister or priest in which case it is conducted by the bishop. The inclusion of these rites alongside the catechumenal material can be seen in part as the implementation of the Toronto IALC.

COMMON WORSHIP: CHRISTIAN INITIATION (2006)

HOLY BAPTISM

PREPARATION

THE GREETING

1 The grace of our Lord Jesus Christ, the love of God and
the fellowship of the Holy Spirit be with you all
and also with you.

2 *Words of welcome or introduction may be said.*

INTRODUCTION

3 *The president may use these or other words*
Our Lord Jesus Christ has told us
that to enter the kingdom of heaven
we must be born again of water and the Spirit,
and has given us baptism as the sign and seal of this new birth.
Here we are washed by the Holy Spirit and made clean.
Here we are clothed with Christ,
dying to sin that we may live his risen life.
As children of God, we have a new dignity
and God calls us to fullness of life.

4 *The Gloria in excelsis may be used*

THE COLLECT

5 Heavenly Father,
by the power of your Holy Spirit
you give to your faithful people new life in the water of baptism.
Guide and strengthen us by the same Spirit,
that we who are born again may serve you in faith and love,
and grow into the full stature of your Son, Jesus Christ,
who is alive and reigns with you in the unity of the Holy Spirit
now and for ever.
Amen.

THE LITURGY OF THE WORD

⟦Three readings as per the eucharistic provision.⟧

THE LITURGY OF BAPTISM

PRESENTATION OF THE CANDIDATES

6 *The candidates may be presented to the congregation. Where appropriate, they may be
presented by their godparents or sponsors.*

7 *The president asks those candidates for baptism who are able to answer for themselves*
Do you wish to be baptized?
I do.

8 *Testimony by the candidate(s) may follow*

9   *The president addresses the whole congregation*
Faith is the gift of God to his people.
In baptism the Lord is adding to our number those whom he is calling.
People of God, will you welcome *these children/candidates* and uphold *them* in *their* new life in Christ?
With the help of God, we will.

10   *At the baptism of children, the president then says to the parents and godparents*
Parents and godparents, the Church receives *these children* with joy.
Today we are trusting God for *their* growth in faith.
Will you pray for *them*, draw *them* by your example into the community of faith and walk with *them* in the way of Christ?
With the help of God, we will.

In baptism *these children* begin *their* journey in faith.
You speak for *them* today.
Will you care for *them*, and help *them* to take *their* place within the life and worship of Christ's Church?
With the help of God, we will.

THE DECISION

11   *A large candle may be lit. The president addresses the candidates directly, or through their parents, godparents and sponsors. [The candle may be the paschal candle. Alternative forms are provided for the decision.]*
In baptism, God calls us out of darkness into his marvellous light.
To follow Christ means dying to sin and rising to new life with him.
Therefore I ask:

Do you reject the devil and all rebellion against God?
I reject them.

Do you renounce the deceit and corruption of evil?
I renounce them.

Do you repent of the sins that separate us from God and neighbour?
I repent of them.

Do you turn to Christ as Saviour?
I turn to Christ.

Do you submit to Christ as Lord?
I submit to Christ.

Do you come to Christ, the way, the truth and the life?
I come to Christ

12   *Where there are strong pastoral reasons, the alternative form of the Decision may be used.*

SIGNING WITH THE CROSS

13   *The president or another minister makes the sign of the cross on the forehead of each candidate, saying [The oil of catechumens may be used here.]*
Christ claims you for his own
Receive the sign of his cross.

14   *The president may invite parents, godparents and sponsors to sign the candidates with the cross. When all the candidates have been signed, the president says*
Do not be ashamed to confess the faith of Christ crucified.
**Fight valiantly as a disciple of Christ
against sin, the world and the devil,
and remain faithful to Christ to the end of your life.**

15   May almighty God deliver you from the powers of darkness,
restore in you the image of his glory,
and lead you in the light and obedience of Christ. **Amen.**

PRAYER OVER THE WATER

The ministers and candidates gather at the baptismal font. A canticle, psalm, hymn or litany may be used.

The president stands before the water of baptism and says [optional seasonal, short and responsive forms are provided]

16   Praise God who made heaven and earth,
who keeps his promise for ever.

Let us give thanks to the Lord our God.
It is right to give thanks and praise.

We thank you, almighty God, for the gift of water
to sustain, refresh and cleanse all life.
Over water the Holy Spirit moved in the beginning of creation.
Through water you led the children of Israel
from slavery in Egypt to freedom in the Promised Land.
In water your Son Jesus received the baptism of John
and was anointed by the Holy Spirit as the Messiah, the Christ,
to lead us from the death of sin to newness of life.
We thank you, Father, for the water of baptism.
In it we are buried with Christ in his death.
By it we share in his resurrection.
Through it we are reborn by the Holy Spirit.
Therefore, in joyful obedience to your Son,
we baptize into his fellowship those who come to him in faith.
Now sanctify this water that, by the power of your Holy Spirit,
they may be cleansed from sin and born again.
Renewed in your image, may they walk by the light of faith
and continue for ever in the risen life of Jesus Christ our Lord;
to whom with you and the Holy Spirit
be all honour and glory, now and for ever.
Amen.

PROFESSION OF FAITH

The president addresses the congregation

17   Brothers and sisters, I ask you to profess together with these candidates the faith of the Church.

[Question and answer Apostles' Creed **CF2a**]

18   *Where there are strong pastoral reasons the alternative Profession of Faith may be used*

19   *If the candidate(s) can answer for themselves, the president may say to each one*
     N, is this your faith?
     Each candidate answers in their own words, or
     This is my faith

20   *The president or another minister dips each candidate in water, or pours water on them,*
     saying
     N, I baptize you in the name of the Father, and of the Son, and of the Holy Spirit.
     Amen.

21   *If the newly baptized are clothed with a white robe, a hymn or song may be used, and then*
     a minister may say
     You have been clothed with Christ.
     As many as are baptized into Christ have put on Christ.

22   *If those who have been baptized were not signed with the cross immediately after the*
     Decision, the president signs each one now.

23   *The president says* ⟦The oil of chrism may be used here.⟧
     May God, who has received you by baptism into his Church,
     pour upon you the riches of his grace,
     that within the company of Christ's pilgrim people
     you may daily be renewed by his anointing Spirit,
     and come to the inheritance of the saints in glory.
     Amen.

24   *The president and those who have been baptized may return from the font.*

COMMISSION

   Either

25a *Where the newly baptized are unable to answer for themselves, a minister addresses the*
     congregation, parents and godparents, using these or similar words

   We have brought *these children* to baptism knowing that Jesus died and rose again for
   them and trusting in the promise that God hears and answers prayer. We have prayed
   that in Jesus Christ *they* will know the forgiveness of *their* sins and the new life of the
   Spirit.

   As *they* grow up, *they* will need the help and encouragement of the Christian
   community, so that *they* may learn to know God in public worship and private
   prayer, follow Jesus Christ in the life of faith, serve *their* neighbour after the example
   of Christ, and in due course come to confirmation.

   As part of the Church of Christ, we all have a duty to support *them* by prayer,
   example and teaching. As *their* parents and godparents, you have the prime
   responsibility for guiding and helping *them* in *their* early years. This is a demanding
   task for which you will need the help and grace of God. Therefore let us now pray for
   grace in guiding *these children* in the way of faith.

   One or more of the following prayers may be used

   Faithful and loving God,
   bless those who care for *these children*
   and grant *them* your gifts of love, wisdom and faith.
   Pour upon *them* your healing and reconciling love,
   and protect *their* home from all evil.

Fill *them* with the light of your presence
and establish *them* in the joy of your kingdom,
through Jesus Christ our Lord.
Amen.

God of grace and life,
in your love you have given us
a place among your people;
keep us faithful to our baptism,
and prepare us for that glorious day
when the whole creation will be made perfect
in your Son our Saviour Jesus Christ.
Amen.

These words may be added
N and N,
today God has touched you with his love
and given you a place among his people.
God promises to be with you
in joy and in sorrow,
to be your guide in life,
and to bring you safely to heaven.
In baptism God invites you on a life-long journey.
Together with all God's people
you must explore the way of Jesus
and grow in friendship with God,
in love for his people,
and in serving others.
With us you will listen to the word of God
and receive the gifts of God.

or

25b *Here or at the beginning of the Sending Out, a minister may say to the newly baptized who
are able to answer for themselves*
Those who are baptized are called to worship and serve God.

Will you continue in the apostles' teaching and fellowship, in the breaking of bread,
and in the prayers?
With the help of God, I will.

Will you persevere in resisting evil, and, whenever you fall into sin, repent and return
to the Lord?
With the help of God, I will.

Will you proclaim by word and example the good news of God in Christ?
With the help of God, I will.

Will you seek and serve Christ in all people, loving your neighbour as yourself?
With the help of God, I will.

Will you acknowledge Christ's authority over human society, by prayer for the world
and its leaders, by defending the weak, and by seeking peace and justice?
With the help of God, I will.

May Christ dwell in your heart(s) through faith, that you may be rooted and
grounded in love and bring forth the fruit of the Spirit
Amen.

26 *PRAYERS OF INTERCESSION*
    [[An intercession is provided; alternatives may be used.]]

THE WELCOME AND PEACE

27 There is one Lord, one faith, one baptism: N and N, by one Spirit we are all baptized
    into one body.
    **We welcome you into the fellowship of faith; we are children of the same heavenly
    Father; we welcome you.**

28 *The congregation may greet the newly baptized.*

29 *The president introduces the Peace* [[Words are provided but not particularly baptismal.]]

30 **THE LITURGY OF THE EUCHARIST**

    [[As per normal eucharistic service.]]

31 *This short Proper Preface may be used*
    And now we give you thanks
    because by water and the Holy Spirit
    you have made us a holy people in Jesus Christ our Lord;
    you raise us to new life in him
    and renew in us the image of your glory

PRAYER AFTER COMMUNION

32 *The authorized Post Communion of the Day, or a seasonal form, or the following is used*
    Eternal God, our beginning and our end,
    preserve in your people the new life of baptism;
    as Christ receives us on earth,
    so may he guide us through the trials of this world
    and enfold us in the joy of heaven,
    where you live and reign,
    one God for ever and ever.
    Amen.

THE SENDING OUT

33 *Words to the newly baptized who answer for themselves may be used here if not done before*

THE BLESSING

34 *The president may use a seasonal blessing, or another suitable blessing, or*
    The God of all grace,
    who called you to his eternal glory in Christ Jesus,
    establish, strengthen and settle you in the faith;
    and the blessing of God almighty,
    the Father, the Son, and the Holy Spirit,
    be among you and remain with you always.
    Amen.

GIVING OF A LIGHTED CANDLE

35 *The president or another person may give each of the newly baptized a lighted candle.
    These may be lit from the candle used at the Decision.*

36 *When all the newly baptized have received a candle, the president says*
    God has delivered us from the dominion of darkness
    and has given us a place with the saints in light

37   You have received the light of Christ;
     walk in this light all the days of your life.
     Shine as a light in the world
     to the glory of God the Father.

THE DISMISSAL

38   Go in the light and peace of Christ (Alleluia, alleluia).
     Thanks be to God (Alleluia, alleluia).

HOLY BAPTISM AND CONFIRMATION

⟦The main rite provided for confirmation is holy baptism and confirmation in
Holy Communion service. This repeats much of what is above and so the distinctive
confirmation elements are set out below.⟧

PREPARATION

THE GREETING

1   *The bishop greets the people using these or other suitable words*
    Blessed be God, Father, Son and Holy Spirit.
    Blessed be his kingdom, now and for ever. Amen.

    From Easter Day to Pentecost this acclamation follows
    Alleluia. Christ is risen.
    He is risen indeed. Alleluia.

2   There is one body and one spirit.
    There is one hope to which we were called;
    one Lord, one faith, one baptism,
    one God and Father of all.

    Peace be with you
    and also with you.

3   The bishop may introduce the service.

⟦4 The Gloria may now be used, the collect is as 5 above.⟧

THE LITURGY OF THE WORD

⟦5 Three readings and a sermon as normal eucharistic liturgy.⟧

PRESENTATION OF CANDIDATES

⟦6 As 7 above for baptismal candidates.⟧

7   *The bishop asks the candidates for confirmation who have been baptized (together with*
    those who wish to affirm their baptismal faith and/or those who are to be received into the
    communion of the Church of England)
    Have you been baptized in the name of the Father, and of the Son, and of the
    Holy Spirit?
    I have.

    The bishop asks all the candidates
    Are you ready with your own mouth and from your own heart to affirm your faith in
    Jesus Christ?
    I am.

8   *Testimony by the candidates may follow.*

9   *The bishop addresses the whole congregation*
    Faith is the gift of God to his people.
    In baptism the Lord is adding to our number
    those whom he is calling.
    People of God, will you welcome these candidates
    and uphold them in their life in Christ?
    With the help of God, we will.

    *If children are to be baptized, the questions to parents and godparents in the services of
    Holy Baptism are used.*

THE DECISION

〚10 All candidates are asked the decision as 11 above.〛

SIGNING WITH THE CROSS

〚11 Baptismal candidates are signed with the cross as 13, 14, 15 above. Oil of catechumens
    may be used.〛
    Or, when there are no candidates for baptism, he may say
    May God, who has given you the desire to follow Christ,
    give you strength to continue in the Way.
    Amen.

PRAYER OVER THE WATER

〚12 All candidates stand at the font and prayer is said as 16 above.〛

PROFESSION OF FAITH

〚13 The bishop leads the profession as 17 above.〛

BAPTISM

〚14 Those to be baptized, as 19–23 above, chrism is not used here.〛

〚15 The service includes here the declarations for those for affirmation of faith and reception.〛

16   *The candidates for confirmation who have previously been baptized may come forward to
    the font and sign themselves with water, or the bishop may sprinkle them.*
    The bishop says
    Almighty God,
    we thank you for our fellowship in the household of faith
    with all who have been baptized into your name.
    Keep us faithful to our baptism,
    and so make us ready for that day
    when the whole creation shall be made perfect in your Son,
    our Saviour Jesus Christ.
    Amen.

17   *The bishop and the candidates gather at the place of confirmation.*

CONFIRMATION

18   *The bishop stands before those who are to be confirmed, and says*
    Our help is in the name of the Lord
    who has made heaven and earth.
    Blessed be the name of the Lord
    now and for ever. Amen.

19   *The bishop extends his hands towards those to be confirmed and says*
    Almighty and ever-living God,
    you have given these your servants new birth
    in baptism by water and the Spirit,
    and have forgiven them all their sins.
    Let your Holy Spirit rest upon them:
    the Spirit of wisdom and understanding;
    the Spirit of counsel and inward strength;
    the Spirit of knowledge and true godliness;
    and let their delight be in the fear of the Lord.
    Amen.

20   *The bishop addresses each candidate by name*
    N, God has called you by name and made you his own.

21   *He then lays his hand on the head of each, saying*
    Confirm, O Lord, your servant with your Holy Spirit.
    Amen.
    ⟦Chrism may be used in confirmation.⟧

22   *The bishop invites the congregation to pray for all those on whom hands have been laid.* **CF5**

⟦23 Affirmation and reception may happen here.⟧

COMMISSION

⟦24 As 25b above.⟧

PRAYERS OF INTERCESSION

⟦25 As above.⟧
    The welcome and peace

⟦26 The welcome as 27 and 28 above.⟧

27   *The bishop introduces the Peace in these or other suitable words.*
    God has made us one in Christ.
    He has set his seal upon us
    and, as a pledge of what is to come,
    has given the Spirit to dwell in our hearts

⟦28 The service continues with the Eucharist.⟧

29   *This short Proper Preface may be used*
    And now we give you thanks
    because by water and the Holy Spirit
    you have made us a holy people in Jesus Christ our Lord,
    you raise us to new life in him
    and renew in us the image of your glory

PRAYER AFTER COMMUNION

30   God of mercy,
    By whose grace alone we are accepted and equipped for your service:
    stir up in us the gifts of your Holy Spirit
    and make us worthy of our calling;
    that we may bring forth the fruit of the Spirit
    in love and joy and peace;
    through Jesus Christ our Lord.

THE BLESSING

31 *The giving of a lighted candle*
  [As 35–38 above.]

SEASONAL PROVISIONS

[A considerable amount of alternative seasonal provision is given covering the areas, introduction, acclamation at the blessing of light, collect, Bible reading and psalms, Gospel acclamation, prayer over the water, introduction to intercessions (confirmation), prayers of intercession, introduction to the peace, eucharistic prefaces, post-communion prayer and blessing. Three seasons are provided for, Epiphany/Baptism of Christ/Trinity, Easter/Pentecost and all Saints Day until Advent. What are included here are the prayers over the water.]

EPIPHANY/BAPTISM OF CHRIST/TRINITY

PRAYER OVER THE WATER

1a Praise God who made heaven and earth,
  who keeps his promise for ever.

  Let us give thanks to the Lord our God.
  It is right to give thanks and praise.

  Father, we give you thanks and praise
  for your gift of water in creation;
  for your Spirit, sweeping over the waters,
  bringing light and life;
  for your Son Jesus Christ our Lord,
  baptized in the river Jordan.
  We bless you for your new creation,
  brought to birth by water and the Spirit,
  and for your grace bestowed upon us your children,
  washing away our sins.
  May your holy and life-giving Spirit
  move upon these waters.
  Restore through them the beauty of your creation,
  and bring those who are baptized
  to new birth in the family of your Church.
  Drown sin in the waters of judgement,
  anoint your children with power from on high,
  and make them one with Christ
  in the freedom of your kingdom.
  For all might, majesty, dominion and power are yours,
  now and for ever.
  Alleluia. Amen.

1b *Or a responsive form.*
  Praise God who made heaven and earth,
  who keeps his promise for ever.

  Let us give thanks to the Lord our God.
  It is right to give thanks and praise.

  Father, for your gift of water in creation,
  we give you thanks and praise.

For your Spirit, sweeping over the waters,
bringing light and life,
We give you thanks and praise.

For your Son Jesus Christ our Lord,
baptized in the river Jordan,
We give you thanks and praise.
For your new creation,
brought to birth by water and the Spirit,
We give you thanks and praise.

For your grace bestowed upon us your children,
washing away our sins,
We give you thanks and praise.

Father, accept our sacrifice of praise;
may your holy and life-giving Spirit
move upon these waters.
Lord, receive our prayer.

Restore through them the beauty of your creation,
and bring those who are baptized
to new birth in the family of your Church.
Lord, receive our prayer.

Drown sin in the waters of judgement,
anoint your children with power from on high,
and make them one with Christ
in the freedom of your kingdom.
Lord, receive our prayer.

For all might, majesty, dominion and power are yours,
now and for ever.
Alleluia. Amen.

EASTER/PENTECOST

PRAYER OVER THE WATER

2 *The bracketed refrain **Saving God, give us** life is optional. If it is used, it may be said or*
sung by all.
*The first phrase **Saving God** (italicized) may be said or sung by a deacon or other minister.*

Praise God who made heaven and earth,
Who keeps his promise for ever.

Let us give thanks to the Lord our God.
It is right to give him thanks and praise.

Almighty God, whose Son Jesus Christ
was baptized in the river Jordan,
we thank you for the gift of water
to cleanse us and revive us.
[*Saving God,*
Give us life.]

We thank you that through the waters of the Red Sea
you led your people out of slavery
to freedom in the Promised Land.

[*Saving God,*
Give us life.]

We thank you that through the deep waters of death
you brought your Son,
and raised him to life in triumph.
[*Saving God,*
Give us life.]

Bless this water, that your servants who are washed in it
may be made one with Christ in his death and in his resurrection,
to be cleansed and delivered from all sin.
[*Saving God,*
Give us life.]

Send your Holy Spirit upon them,
bring them to new birth in the household of faith
and raise them with Christ to full and eternal life;
for all might, majesty, authority and power are yours,
now and for ever. Amen.
[*Saving God,*
Give us life.]

ALL SAINTS DAY UNTIL ADVENT

PRAYER OVER THE WATER

3 Praise God who made heaven and earth,
   Who keeps his promise for ever.

Let us give thanks to the Lord our God.
It is right to give thanks and praise.

Lord of the heavens,
we bless your name for all your servants
who have been a sign of your grace through the ages.
[*Hope of the saints,*
make known your glory.]

You delivered Noah from the waters of destruction;
you divided the waters of the sea,
and by the hand of Moses
you led your people from slavery
into the Promised Land.
[*Hope of the saints,*
make known your glory.]

You made a new covenant in the blood of your Son,
that all who confess his name
may, by the Holy Spirit,
enter the covenant of grace,
receive a pledge of the kingdom of heaven,
and share in the divine nature.
[*Hope of the saints,*
make known your glory.]

Fill these waters, we pray, with the power of that same Spirit,
that all who enter them may be reborn

and rise from the grave
to new life in Christ.
[*Hope of the saints,*
make known your glory.]

As the apostles and prophets, the confessors and martyrs,
faithfully served you in their generation,
may we be built into an eternal dwelling for you,
through Jesus Christ our Lord,
to whom with you and the Holy Spirit
be honour and glory, now and for ever. Amen.
[*Hope of the saints,*
make known your glory.]

ALTERNATIVE FORM OF THE DECISION

4   *Where there are strong pastoral reasons, the following may be used in place of the
Decision in the service of Holy Baptism and at other Initiation services.
The president addresses the candidates directly, or through their parents, godparents and
sponsors*

Therefore I ask:
Do you turn to Christ?
I turn to Christ.

Do you repent of your sins?
I repent of my sins.

Do you renounce evil?
I renounce evil.

ALTERNATIVE FORM OF PROFESSION OF FAITH

5   *Where there are strong pastoral reasons, the following may be used in place of the
Profession of Faith in the service of Holy Baptism.
The president says*
Let us affirm, together with these who are being baptized, our common faith in Jesus
Christ.

Do you believe and trust in God the Father,
source of all being and life,
the one for whom we exist?
I believe and trust in him.

Do you believe and trust in God the Son,
who took our human nature,
died for us and rose again?
I believe and trust in him.

Do you believe and trust in God the Holy Spirit,
who gives life to the people of God
and makes Christ known in the world?
I believe and trust in him.

This is the faith of the Church.
This is our faith.
We believe and trust in one God,
Father, Son and Holy Spirit.

ADDITIONAL BAPTISMAL TEXTS IN ACCESSIBLE LANGUAGE (2015)

SHORT FORM OF PRAYER OVER THE WATER

⟦One of the alternative texts is given here.⟧

6 Loving Father,
we thank you for your servant Moses,
who led your people through the waters of the Red Sea
to freedom in the Promised Land.
We thank you for your Son Jesus, who has passed through the deep waters of death
and opened for all the way of salvation.
Now send your Spirit, that those who are washed in this water
may die with Christ and rise with him, to find true freedom as your children,
alive in Christ for ever. **Amen.**

4. The Scottish Episcopal Church

Christianity came to Scotland with Ninian (d. 432) and later with Columba who worked at Iona from 563. The Scottish church grew as an independent church in an independent kingdom. In 1560 the Scottish Parliament rejected the authority of the Pope and a long debate continued between favouring Presbyterian polity and episcopacy. In 1690 William of Orange established Presbyterian polity in Scotland; from 1712 a legal Episcopal Church was tolerated. In 1784 the Scottish bishops consecrated Samuel Seabury for Connecticut in the newly formed United States of America. The church took on new life in the nineteenth century with the repeal of penal laws. The Scottish Episcopal Church has its own traditions with regard to baptismal rites, particularly the use of chrism at confirmation.

The Scottish Episcopal Church was much influenced by the 1968 Lambeth Conference which encouraged alternative lines of experimentation: first to separate admission to Holy Communion and confirmation, and thus to have an admission to Holy Communion sometime after the baptism of an infant; second to administer infant baptism and confirmation together followed by admission to Holy Communion at an early age (Lambeth 1968). The Scottish Episcopal Church passed a resolution in its Synod to the effect that infants were fully initiated. This has led to a long process of helping parishes develop this understanding, and a process of liturgical and canonical revision in order to make that clear. This was further strengthened by the IALC consultations in Boston (1985) and Toronto (1991). The 2006 rites of *Holy Baptism* and *Affirmation of Holy Baptism* make clear that the fundamental sacramental rite is baptism and that any subsequent ceremony is a rekindling of that which was begun in baptism. The Affirmation service says that wherever possible the bishop presides, implying that there might be circumstances in which the rite would be presided over by a presbyter.

The 1929 Scottish Prayer Book is still occasionally used in Scotland,[21] and a revised rite infant baptism was introduced in 1967.[22] A new service of baptism was introduced in 1973 but was rejected by the Provincial Synod. The 2006 services are the product of a considerable work of renewal on the meaning of baptism. This included the changing of Canon Law. The amended Canon 25 of 2005 states clearly, 'The Sacrament of Baptism is the full rite of initiation into the Church, and no further sacramental rite shall be required of any person seeking admission to Holy Communion'.

---

21 J 61–66.
22 J 134–137.

The Rite is intended for use within the Eucharist, following the gospel.
Whenever possible the Bishop presides.

1   *INTRODUCTION*

The president says
Blessed be God,
the Father of our Lord Jesus Christ,
by whose great mercy we have been born anew to a living hope
through the resurrection of Jesus Christ from the dead.

2   *GOD'S CALL*

The president addresses the candidate(s) or, at the baptism of infants, those who are
presenting the candidate(s)

2A   *Either*

God is love. God gives us life. In Christ God reaches out to us. In baptism God calls
us to respond.

Do you accept this call?
I hear and accept God's call.
I ask for baptism.

or

2B   *Presenters*
We hear and accept God's call to N.
We ask for baptism.

The president addresses the rest of the congregation
God calls the Church to reflect Christ's glory, in baptism to declare his new life, in
fellowship and mission to share it.
Do you accept this call?
We hear and accept God's call.

or

The apostle Peter proclaimed God's call when he urged his hearers:
'Repent and be baptised, every one of you, in the name of Jesus Christ for the
forgiveness of your sins, and you will receive the gift of the Holy Spirit. For the
promise is to you and to your children, and to all who are far away, everyone whom
the Lord our God may call.' *Acts 2.38–40*
Do you accept this call?

I hear and accept God's call.
I ask for baptism.

or

Presenters
We hear and accept God's call to N.
We ask for baptism.

The president addresses the rest of the congregation
Our Lord Jesus Christ said to his disciples: 'All authority in heaven and on earth has
been given to me. Go therefore and make disciples of all nations, baptising them in
the name of the Father and of the Son and of the Holy Spirit, and teaching them to
obey everything that I have commanded you.' *Matthew 28.18–20*

Do you accept this call?
All **We hear and accept God's call**

3   *TURNING TO CHRIST*

The president addresses the candidate(s) or, at the baptism of infants, those who are presenting the candidate(s)

Either

The Christian life means turning from evil and turning to Christ.
Standing now with Christ, do you renounce evil?
I renounce evil.

Seeking now to follow him, do you turn to Christ?
I turn to Christ.

or

The Christian life means turning from evil and turning to Christ.
Do you renounce evil?
I renounce evil.

Do you repent of sin?
I repent of sin.

Do you turn to Christ?
I turn to Christ.

Will you follow Christ?
I will follow Christ.

4   *PROFESSION OF FAITH*

Either

4A   *PROFESSION OF FAITH (LONGER FORM)*

The president addresses the whole congregation
⟦Question and answer Apostles' Creed **CF2b**⟧

The president addresses the candidate(s) or, at the baptism of infants, those who are presenting the candidate(s)
This is the faith of the Church.
This is our faith.
We believe in one God, Father, Son and Holy Spirit.
Amen.

or

4B   *PROFESSION OF FAITH (SHORTER FORM)*

Either

The president addresses the whole congregation
Do you believe in God the Father, who made the world?
I believe.

Do you believe in God the Son, who redeemed humanity?
I believe.

Do you believe in God the Holy Spirit, who gives life to God's people?
I believe.

The president addresses the candidate(s)
This is the faith of the Church.
This is our faith.
We believe in one God,
Father, Son and Holy Spirit.
Amen.

or

The president addresses the whole congregation
Do you believe in God the Creator, who made the world?
I believe.

Do you believe in God the Saviour, who redeemed humanity?
I believe.

Do you believe in God the Sanctifier, who gives life to God's people?
I believe.

The president addresses the candidate(s)
This is the faith of the Church.
This is our faith.
We believe in one God,
Creator, Saviour and Sanctifier.
Amen.

5 **COMMITMENT TO CHRISTIAN LIFE**

Either

The president addresses the candidate(s)
N., as a disciple of Christ will you continue in the Apostles' teaching and fellowship, in the breaking of bread and in the prayers?
With the help of God, I will.

or

At the baptism of infants the president addresses those who are presenting the candidate(s)
NN., as those who will love and care for N., will you continue in the Apostles' teaching and fellowship, in the breaking of bread and in the prayers?
With the help of God, I will.

The president then continues
Will you proclaim the good news by word and deed, serving Christ in all people?
With the help of God, I will.
Will you work for justice and peace, honouring God in all Creation?
With the help of God, I will.

The president addresses the whole congregation
This is the task of the Church.
This is our task: to live and work for the kingdom of God.

6 **THE BAPTISMAL PRAYER**

Water is poured into the Font. The president says
Holy God, well-spring of life,
in your love and justice,
you use the gift of water to declare your saving power.
In the beginning your Spirit moved over the face of the waters.

By the gentle dew, the steady rain,
you nourish and give increase to all that grows;
you make the desert a watered garden.
You command the wildness of the waves;
when the storm rages you calm our fear;
in the stillness you lead us to a deeper faith.
In the life-giving rivers and the rainbow
Israel discerned your mercy.
You divided the Red Sea
to let them pass from slavery in Egypt
to freedom in the Promised Land.
In the waters of Jordan
penitents found forgiveness in the baptism of John.
There, Jesus your beloved child
was anointed with the Holy Spirit,
that he might bring us
to the glorious liberty of the children of God.
Send upon this water and upon your people [*or* upon N.)
your holy, life-giving Spirit.

Bring those who are baptised in this water
with Christ through the waters of death,
to be one with him in his resurrection.
Sustain your people by your Spirit
to be hope and strength to the world.

Through Jesus Christ, our Lord,
to whom with you and the Holy Spirit
be honour and glory, now and for ever. **Amen.**

7   *THE BAPTISM*

The president immerses the candidate in the water, or pours the water upon the
candidate, saying
N., I baptise you in the name of the Father and of the Son and of the Holy Spirit.
Amen.

8   *ANOINTING AND LAYING-ON OF HANDS*

The president anoints the candidate upon the forehead, making the sign of the Cross with
the Oil of Chrism, and saying
N., you are sealed by the Holy Spirit in Baptism and marked as Christ's own for ever.
Amen.

The president lays hands on the candidate's head, saying
May the Spirit of God be in you,
wisdom and understanding keep you,
the power of God encircle you,
and God's truth lead you into freedom. **Amen.**

9   *GIVING OF LIGHT*

A lighted candle is given as the president says
N., the light of Christ
scatter the darkness from your heart and mind.
Christ go before you to guide your steps.

Christ be within you to kindle your vision.
Christ shine from you to give joy to the world.

10 *WELCOME*

The president addresses the candidate(s)
N., God has received you by baptism into the Church.
We welcome you.
We will care for you.
We will share our faith with you.

The Eucharist continues with the Peace
Renewed in the Spirit, we meet in Christ's name;
Let us share his peace.

⟦The book now includes orders for baptism outside the Eucharist and emergency baptism.⟧

AFFIRMATION OF HOLY BAPTISM 2006
FOR CONFIRMATION AND RENEWAL

The Rite is intended for use at the Eucharist following the Gospel.
Whenever possible the Bishop presides.

1 *INTRODUCTION*

The president says
Blessed be God,
the Father of our Lord Jesus Christ,
by whose great mercy we have been born anew to a living hope
through the resurrection of Jesus Christ from the dead.

2 *PRESENTATION OF THE CANDIDATE(S)*

The candidate(s) is/are introduced to the congregation by name.
The president may use these or similar words
Our brother/sister N. has come
to make a deeper commitment
to our Lord Jesus Christ
by renewing his/her baptismal promises and affirming his/her faith.
We pray for him/her and for ourselves.

3 *PRAYER*

Eternal God, who at the baptism of Jesus
revealed him to be your Son,
anointing him with the Holy Spirit:
keep your people, born of water and the Spirit,
faithful to their calling;
through Jesus Christ our Lord,
who lives and reigns with you and the Holy Spirit,
one God, now and for ever.
Amen.

4 *TURNING TO CHRIST*

The president addresses the candidate(s).

Either

The Christian life means turning from evil and turning to Christ.
Standing now with Christ, do you renounce evil?
I renounce evil.

Seeking now to follow him, do you turn to Christ?
I turn to Christ.

or

The Christian life means turning from evil and turning to Christ.
Do you renounce evil?
I renounce evil.

Do you repent of sin?
I repent of sin.

Do you turn to Christ?
I turn to Christ.

Will you follow Christ?
I will follow Christ.

5 *PROFESSION OF FAITH*

The president addresses the whole congregation

⟦Question and answer Apostles' Creed **CF2b**⟧

The president addresses the candidate(s)
This is the faith of the Church.
This is our faith. We believe in one God,
Father, Son and Holy Spirit.
Amen.

6 *COMMITMENT TO CHRISTIAN LIFE*

The president addresses the candidate(s)
N., as a disciple of Christ will you continue in the Apostles' teaching and fellowship,
in the breaking of bread, and in the prayers?
With the help of God, I will.

Will you proclaim the good news by word and deed, serving Christ in all people?
With the help of God, I will.

Will you work for justice and peace, honouring God in all Creation?
With the help of God, I will.

The president addresses the whole congregation
This is the task of the Church.
This is our task;
to live and work for the kingdom of God.

7 *THE LAYING-ON OF HANDS*

The president says
God of mercy and love,
new birth by water and the Spirit is your gift,
a gift none can take away;
grant that your servants may grow
into the fullness of the stature of Christ.
Fill them with the joy of your presence.
Increase in them the fruit of your Spirit:
the spirit of wisdom and understanding,
the spirit of love, patience and gentleness,
the spirit of wonder and true holiness.

The president lays hands on each candidate in silence, and then says
Come, Creator Spirit,
rekindle in N. your gifts of grace,
to love and serve as a disciple of Christ.
Amen.

Renew her/his life in Christ
and bring to completion
all that your calling has begun.
Amen.

*Either continuing the laying-on of hands, or anointing the candidate
with the Oil of Chrism, the president says*
Empower your disciple, N.,
to bring life to the world.
Amen.

*At the conclusion of the laying-on of hands for all of the candidates,
the president says*
Living God, sustain all your people
to be hope and strength to the world;
    through Jesus Christ, our Lord,
    to whom with you and the Holy Spirit
    be honour and glory, now and for ever.
    Amen.

8 *The Eucharist continues with the Peace*
Renewed in the Spirit, we meet in Christ's name;
    Let us share his peace.

AFTER COMMUNION THIS THANKSGIVING AND SENDING MAY BE USED

THANKSGIVING AND SENDING

The President addresses the congregation
The light of Christ is within you. Shine as a light in the world.
As the seed grows secretly in the earth,
    As the yeast rises in the dough,
    May the power of God be at work in us.
    Like a city on a hill,
    Like a lamp in the darkness,
    May we witness to the glory of the kingdom.

The Liturgy concludes with the Blessing and Dismissal.

5. The Church in Wales

The Church in Wales traces its roots to Christianity in the Roman Empire, and later the Celtic saints e.g. Dewi (St David d. 589). The Normans conquered Wales in a series of wars in the thirteenth century, and the Welsh Church came under the jurisdiction of the Archbishop of Canterbury. The Welsh Church accepted the Reformation as a part of ecclesiastical changes in England and Wales (the Tudors being in origin Welsh), and continued united to Canterbury until after the First World War. In 1920 the church was disestablished and became a separate Province in the Anglican Communion.

In 1968 new forms of baptism and confirmation were introduced.[23] Presently the Church in Wales has two forms of official liturgy. One is *The Book of Common Prayer* 1984 which is in more traditional language, and includes a service of the public baptism of infants, the private baptism of infants, the baptism of adults, thanksgiving for the birth and adoption of a child, and the order of confirmation.[24]

New modern language services, *Services for Christian Initiation*, were produced in 2006. There are two major orders in this book, one for the public baptism of infants, and another for baptism and confirmation. However, each of these major sections has a series of appendices with further important rites. The public baptism of infants includes an appendix with emergency baptism, lay baptism, the welcome of infants in church who were privately baptized and a welcome for those preparing for the baptism of their children. Baptism and confirmation has in the appendices emergency baptism, mission and welcome of candidates for baptism and confirmation, the formal passing on of the Apostles Creed, a series of intercessions for the candidates, a commitment to Christian life in service with an affirmation of faith, and a celebration after an initiation service outside the parish.

The new services therefore not only cover the traditional pattern of baptism and confirmation, but also include catechumenal material. In 2016 the Bishops of Wales announced in a pastoral letter that everyone who has been baptized can participate fully in Holy Communion.

---

23 J 148–154.
24 G 1984/1.

THE BOOK OF COMMON PRAYER 1984

PUBLIC BAPTISM OF INFANTS COMMONLY CALLED CHRISTENING

⟦1 The service begins with a series of notes setting the service in context.⟧

PUBLIC BAPTISM OF INFANTS

THE MINISTRY OF THE WORD

2 *For use when Holy Baptism is administered other than at the Holy Eucharist or Morning or Evening Prayer.*
In the Name of the Father, and of the Son, and of the Holy Spirit. **Amen.**

3 Let us pray.
Almighty God, our heavenly Father, who in every generation bestows new sons and daughters upon thy Church: grant that these infants may be born anew of water and of the Holy Spirit; that, daily increasing in the knowledge and love of thee, they may be numbered among the children of thine adoption; through Jesus Christ our Lord, who lives and reigns with thee and the Holy Spirit, one God, world without end. **Amen.**

⟦4 Some lessons are given when administered outside of morning prayer or Eucharist: Romans 6.3–11; Galatians 4.4–7; Colossians 3.1–4; Psalm 1; Psalm 36.5–10; Matthew 28.18–21; Mark 1.1–11; John 3.1–5. A sermon is preached.⟧

THE APOSTLES' CREED

⟦5 Traditional Apostles' Creed BCP CF1b⟧

THE INTRODUCTION

6 *At the time appointed for the Baptism, the parents and godparents with the child shall come to the Font and the Priest meets them there and says to them:*
What do you, in the name of this child, ask of the Church of God?
We ask for Holy Baptism.

Why do you ask for Holy Baptism?
That this child may be made a Christian.

7 *The Priest says:*
You have brought *this child* here to be baptized. Our Saviour Christ says, No one can enter into the kingdom of God unless he is born again of water and of the Holy Spirit. In Baptism our heavenly Father will make this *child a member* of Christ, the child of God, and an *inheritor* of the kingdom of heaven. You must see that he is brought up to worship with the Church and that he is taught the Creed, the Lord's Prayer, and the Ten Commandments, and is instructed in the Church Catechism. You are to take care also that he is brought to the Bishop to be confirmed, that, strengthened by the Holy Spirit, he may devoutly and regularly receive Holy Communion and serve God faithfully in the fellowship of his Church. Will you pray for him and help him to keep the promises you will make on his behalf?
I will, by the help of God.

8 *Then shall the Priest and People say this prayer:*
Almighty God, our heavenly Father; look mercifully upon *this child*; **give** *him* **thy Holy Spirit that** *he* **may be born again; deliver** *him* **from the dominion of evil, and receive** *him* **into the family of Christ's Church; through Jesus Christ our Lord. Amen.**

9 *The Priest blesses the water.*
We give thanks to thee, O Lord, Holy Father, Almighty, Everlasting God, because thou hast appointed the Water of Baptism for the regeneration of mankind through thy beloved Son; who at his baptism in the river Jordan was anointed with the Holy Spirit; and after his saving Death and mighty Resurrection commanded his Apostles to go and make disciples of all nations, baptizing them in the Name of the Father and of the Son and of the Holy Spirit. Hear, therefore, the prayers of thy Church; sanctify this water for the mystical washing away of sin, and grant that this child, now to be baptized therein, may receive the fullness of thy grace. and ever remain among thy faithful and elect children. Through Jesus Christ our Lord, to whom with thee in the unity of the Holy Spirit, be all honour and glory, world without end. **Amen.**

THE PROMISES

10 *The Priest asks these questions which the parents and godparents answer on behalf of the child.*
Do you renounce the works of the devil, the vain glory of the world, and all sinful desires?
I renounce them all.

Do you believe and trust in God the Father, who made you and all the world; and in his Son Jesus Christ, who redeemed you and all mankind; and in the Holy Spirit, who sanctifies you and all the elect people of God?
I do so believe and trust.

Will you obediently keep all the days of your life?
I will, the Lord being my helper.

THE BAPTISM

11 *The Priest takes the child in his arms or by the hand and says:*
Name this child.

12 *The godparents name the child and the Priest pours water three times on him or dips him three times in the water, saying:*
N. I baptize you in the Name of the Father, and of the Son, and of the Holy Spirit. Amen.
The Priest gives the child back to one of the godparents.

THE SIGNING WITH THE CROSS

13 *The Priest makes the sign of the Cross on the child's forehead, saying:*
This child has now been made a member of Christ's flock. Therefore we sign him + with the sign of the Cross's, in token that he shall not be ashamed to confess the faith of Christ crucified, and manfully to fight under his banner against sin, the world, and the devil; and to continue Christ's faithful soldier and servant unto his life's end. **Amen.**

14 *The Priest may put a white vesture upon the child, saying:*
We place this white vesture upon this child, as a token of the innocence bestowed upon him by God's grace in this holy Sacrament of Baptism.

15   *He may give a lighted candle to one of the godparents, saying:*
      We give this lighted candle to this child as a sign of the light of Christ and of the grace
      of Baptism.

THE THANKSGIVING

16   *The Priest says:*
      Now that *this child* is by Baptism born again and grafted into the Body of Christ,
      which is his Church; let us thank God for these benefits, and together pray that *this
      child* may lead the rest of *his life* according to this beginning.

⟦17   The Lord's Prayer CF4c.⟧

18   We thank thee heavenly Father, that it has pleased thee to bestow on this child new
      birth by thy Holy Spirit, to receive him for thine own child by adoption, and to make
      him a member of thy holy Church and an inheritor of thine everlasting Kingdom;
      through Jesus Christ our Lord, to whom with thee in the unity of the Holy Spirit, be
      all honour and glory, world without end. **Amen.**

      This prayer may follow:

19   Almighty God our heavenly Father, whose dearly beloved Son Jesus Christ shared
      with the Blessed Virgin Mary and Saint Joseph the life of an earthly home at
      Nazareth: bless we beseech thee the home of this child, and give such grace and
      wisdom to all who have the care of him, that by their word and good example he may
      learn truly to know and love thee; through the same thy Son Jesus Christ our Saviour.
      Amen.

20   *When Baptism is administered as a separate service, the Priest says:*
      The blessing of God Almighty, the Father, the Son, and the Holy Spirit, be upon you,
      and remain with you always. **Amen.**

21   *Immediately after the service the Priest shall enter the customary record in the baptismal
      register of the parish.*

⟦22   Directions are given for a private baptism that shall only be in emergency. Directions are
      also given for baptism by a lay person. Directions are then given for the bringing of a
      privately baptized infant to church, including conditional baptism.⟧

BAPTISM OF ADULTS

⟦1   Various directions are given for the service.⟧

THE MINISTRY OF THE WORD

2   *For use when Holy Baptism is administered other than at the Holy Eucharist or Morning
      or Evening Prayer.*
      In the Name of the Father, and of the Son, and of the Holy Spirit. **Amen.**

3   Let us pray.
      Almighty God, our heavenly Father, who in every generation bestows new sons and
      daughters upon thy Church: grant that these thy servants may be born anew of water
      and of the Holy Spirit; that, daily increasing in the knowledge and love of thee, they
      may be numbered among the children of thine adoption; through Jesus Christ our
      Lord, who lives and reigns with thee and the Holy Spirit, one God, world without
      end. **Amen.**

⟦4 The readings are Romans 6.3–11; Galatians 4.4–7; Col. 3.1–4: Ps 1; Ps 36.5–10; Mat 28.18–20; Mark 1.1–11; John 3.1–5⟧. *A sermon.*

THE APOSTLES' CREED

⟦5 Traditional Apostles' Creed BCP CF1b⟧

THE INTRODUCTION

6 *The candidates and their sponsors come to the Font and the Priest meets them there and says:*
What do you ask of the Church of God?
I ask for Holy Baptism.

7 God wills all men to be saved from the sin which defiles our human nature and to be delivered from the power of evil. Our Saviour Christ says, No one can enter into the kingdom of God unless he is born again of water and of the Holy Spirit. Let us therefore pray that in Baptism you may be born again and be made living members of Christ's Church.

8 **Almighty and immortal God, the helper of all who come to thee; look mercifully upon these persons, give them thy Holy Spirit that they may be born again; deliver them from the dominion of evil, and receive them into the family of Christ's Church; through Jesus Christ our Lord. Amen.**

9 *The Priest blesses the water.*
We give thanks to thee, O Lord, Holy Father, Almighty, Everlasting God, because thou hast appointed the Water of Baptism for the regeneration of mankind through thy beloved Son; who at his baptism in the river Jordan was anointed with the Holy Spirit; and after his saving Death and mighty Resurrection commanded his Apostles to go and make disciples of all nations, baptizing them in the Name of the Father and of the Son and of the Holy Spirit.

Hear, therefore, the prayers of thy Church; sanctify this Water for the mystical washing away of sin, and grant that these persons, now to be baptized therein, may receive the fullness of thy grace, and ever remain among thy faithful and elect children.

Through Jesus Christ our Lord, to whom with thee in the unity of the Holy Spirit, be all honour and glory, world without end. **Amen.**

THE PROMISES

10 *The Priest puts these questions to the candidates:*
Do you renounce the works of the devil, the vain glory of the world, and all sinful desires?
I renounce them all.

Do you believe and trust in God the Father, who made you and all the world; and in his Son Jesus Christ, who redeemed you and all mankind; and in the Holy Spirit, who sanctifies you and all the elect people of God?
I do so believe and trust.

Will you obediently keep God's holy will and commandments all the days of your life?
I will, the Lord being my helper.

THE BAPTISM

11 *The Priest takes each candidate by the right hand and, after asking the sponsors the name, pours water on him three times, or dips him three times in the water, saying:*
N. I baptize you in the Name of the Father, and of the Son, and of the Holy Spirit. Amen.

THE SIGNING WITH THE CROSS

12 *The Priest makes the sign of the Cross on the forehead of each of those baptized, saying:*
You have now been made a member of Christ's flock. Therefore we sign you + with the sign of the Cross, in token that you shall not be ashamed to confess the faith of Christ crucified, and manfully to fight under his banner against sin, the world, and the devil; and to continue Christ's faithful soldier and servant unto your life's end. **Amen.**

13 *If the Priest and the person baptized so desire, the Priest may put a white vesture upon him, saying:*
We place this white vesture upon you as a token of the innocence bestowed upon you by God's grace in this holy Sacrament of Baptism.

14 *He may give him a lighted candle, saying:*
Receive this lighted candle as a sign of the light of Christ and of the grace of Baptism.

THE THANKSGIVING

15 Now that these persons are by Baptism born again and grafted into the Body of Christ, which is his Church; let us thank God for these benefits, and together pray that they may lead the rest of their lives according to this beginning.

⟦16 The Lord's Prayer CF4c⟧

17 *This prayer may follow:*
Grant, O Lord, that as we are baptised into the death of thy blessed Son our Saviour Jesus Christ, so by continual mortify our corrupt affections we may be buried with him; and that through the grave, and gate of death, we may pass to our joy resurrection; for his merits, who died, and was buried, and rose again for us, thy Son Jesus Christ our Lord. **Amen.**

18 *When Baptism is administered as a separate service, the Priest says:*
The blessing of God Almighty, the Father, the Son, and the Holy Spirit, be upon you, and remain with you always. **Amen.**

19 *Immediately after the service, the Priest shall enter the customary record in the baptismal register of the parish.*

THE ORDER OF CONFIRMATION

⟦1 Notes and directions for the service.⟧

2 *All who are to be confirmed stand before the Bishop, the congregation being seated, and the Minister presents them to him, saying:*
Reverend Father in God, I present unto you these persons that they may be confirmed.

The Bishop:
Do you assure me that they have all been baptized and properly instructed?

The Minister:
I do so assure you.

3   *The Bishop says to the candidates:*
Beloved, in order that this congregation may know that you firmly intend to confess
the faith of Christ crucified and to fight manfully under his banner, and in order
that you may always remember what your calling is and how greatly you need the
continual help of the Holy Spirit, the Church requires that before you are confirmed
you shall publicly declare that you are bound to believe and to do all those things to
which Holy Baptism has pledged you.

Are you willing to do this?
I am willing.

THE RENEWAL OF THE BAPTISMAL VOWS

4   *The Bishop continues, the candidates still standing:*
Do you renounce the works of the devil, the vain glory of the world, and all sinful
desires?
I renounce them all.
Do you believe and trust in God the Father, who made you and all the world; and in
his Son Jesus Christ, who redeemed you and all mankind; and in the Holy Spirit, who
sanctifies you and all the elect people of God?
I do so believe and trust.
Will you obediently keep God's holy will and commandments all the days of your
life?
I will, the Lord being my helper.

THE CONFIRMATION

5   *Here may be sung the hymn VENI, CREATOR SPIRITUS or there may be silent prayer,
after which the Bishop begins the Confirmation saying:*

6   The Lord be with you;
And with your spirit.

Our help is in the Name of the Lord;
Who hath made heaven and earth.

Blessed be the Name of the Lord;
Henceforth world without end.

Let us pray.
Almighty and everliving God, who has been pleased regenerate these thy servants by
water and the Holy Spirit, I the forgiveness of all their sins: strengthen them, O Lord,
with thy Holy Spirit, and daily increase in them thy sevenfold gifts grace, the spirit of
wisdom and understanding; the spirit counsel and might; the spirit of knowledge and
true godliness and fill them, O Lord, with the spirit of thy holy fear, now for ever;
through Jesus Christ thy Son, our Lord, who lives reigns with thee in the unity of the
same Spirit, one God, world without end. **Amen.**

7   *The candidates kneel in order before the Bishop, and the Bishop lays his hands upon the
head of each one, saying:*
Confirm, O Lord, this thy child (or this thy servant) with thy heavenly grace, that he
may continue thine for ever, and daily increase in thy Holy Spirit more and more,
until he come unto thy everlasting kingdom. *Amen.*

Let us pray.

[8   The Lord's Prayer CF4c]

9   Almighty and everliving God, we pray for these thy servants, upon whom, after the example of thy holy Apostles, we have now laid our hands. May thy fatherly hand ever be over them; may thy Holy Spirit ever be with them; and so lead them in the knowledge and obedience of thy Word, that in the end they may obtain everlasting life; through Jesus Christ our Lord. **Amen.**

10 O Lord Jesus Christ, who has given us the holy Sacrament of thy Body and Blood: grant that these thy servants, ever partaking thereof by faith with thanksgiving, may grow in thy likeness, and be strengthened to serve thee truly all the days of their life; who with the Father and the Holy Spirit lives and reigns, one God, world without end. **Amen.**

11 The blessing of God Almighty, the Father, the Son, and the Holy Spirit, be upon you, and remain with you always. **Amen.**

⟦12 Further directions.⟧

SERVICES FOR CHRISTIAN INITIATION 2006

AN ORDER FOR THE PUBLIC BAPTISM OF INFANTS

THE GATHERING

⟦1   Welcome and liturgical greeting.⟧

2   *The minister may introduce the service with one of the following.*

Either

2a Our Lord Jesus Christ commanded, 'Go and make disciples of all nations, baptizing them in the Name of the Father, and of the Son, and of the Holy Spirit.'
Thanks be to God.

or

2b We were buried with Christ through baptism into his death, that just as Christ was raised from the dead by the glory of the Father, so we should walk in newness of life.
Thanks be to God.

or

2c When Christ was baptized in the Jordan, the Spirit descended like a dove and the Father spoke, saying, 'You are my beloved Son in whom I am well pleased.'
Thanks be to God.

3   *The minister then addresses the parents*
What do you ask of the Church of God?
We ask that this child may be baptized.
What name have you given your child?
The parents tell the minister the child's name.

The minister continues

4   The baptism of its new members is an occasion of great joy for the Christian Church. By water and the Spirit, we are reborn as God's children, and are made followers of Christ, members of his body, the Church, and inheritors of the kingdom of heaven. Will you accept these things for N? **We will.**

In asking for N to be baptized, you are accepting the responsibility of bringing *him/her* up as a Christian. In caring for *him/her*, will you help *him/her* to keep God's commandments by loving God and neighbour as Christ has taught us? Will you pray for *him/her*, and draw *him/her* by your own example into the community of faith? **With the help of God, we will.**

5 *The minister addresses the godparents*
Will you support and help N's parents in doing these things?
With the help of God, we will.

6 *The minister addresses the whole congregation*
Will you welcome N and do your best to uphold *him/her*
in *his/her* life in Christ?
With the help of God, we will.

7 Heavenly Father,
by the power of your Holy Spirit
you give to your faithful people
new life in the water of baptism:
guide and strengthen us by the same Spirit,
that we who are born again may serve you in faith and love
and grow into the full stature of your Son Jesus Christ,
who is alive and reigns with you and the Holy Spirit,
one God, now and for ever.
Amen.

THE PROCLAMATION OF THE WORD

⟦8–9 Readings are provided. A sermon is preached.⟧

THE LITURGY OF BAPTISM

THE DECISION

10 *The minister addresses the parents and godparents*
You have declared your wish for N to be baptized. We therefore now invite you to respond to Christ's call.

Do you turn to Christ?
I turn to Christ.
Do you repent of your sins?
I repent of my sins.
Do you renounce evil?
I renounce evil.

11 Almighty Father, you sent your Son into the world to destroy the powers of darkness. Hear our prayer for these children: deliver them from evil, give them light and joy and fill them with your Holy Spirit, through Jesus Christ our Lord. **Amen.**

12 *If the oil of catechumens is used, each child who is to be baptized may be anointed with it either at this point or while being signed with the cross.*

THE SIGNING WITH THE CROSS

13 By his cross and precious blood, our Lord Jesus Christ has redeemed the world. He has told us that, if any want to become his followers, they must deny themselves, take up their cross and follow him day by day.
The sign of the cross is made on the forehead of each child who is to be baptized.
N, I sign you with the sign of the cross and claim you for our Saviour Jesus Christ.

When all the children to be baptized have been signed with the cross, the minister continues

Never be ashamed to confess the faith of Christ crucified.
Fight valiantly against sin, the world and the devil,
and remain faithful to Christ to the end of your life. Amen.

THE PROFESSION OF FAITH

14 *At the font, the minister addresses the parents and godparents*
We invite you now to profess the Christian faith.

Do you believe in God the Father, the Creator of all?
I believe and trust in God the Father.
Do you believe in his Son Jesus Christ, the Saviour of the world?
I believe and trust in God the Son.
Do you believe in the Holy Spirit, the Lord, the Giver of life?
I believe and trust in God the Holy Spirit.

The minister addresses the congregation

15 This is the faith of the Church.
This is our faith. We believe and trust in one God, Father, Son and Holy Spirit.

THE BLESSING OF THE BAPTISMAL WATER

Either

16a We give thanks to you, O God:
we bless your holy name.
For your gift of water to nourish and sustain all life:
we give you thanks and praise.
Through the waters of the sea you led the children of Israel from slavery to freedom:
we give you thanks and praise.
At his baptism, your Son Jesus was anointed with the Holy Spirit:
we give you thanks and praise.
Through the power of that same Spirit, sanctify this water that your children who are washed in it may be united with Christ in his death and resurrection.
Cleanse and deliver them from all sin; bring them to new birth in the family of your Church and make them inheritors of your kingdom:
through Jesus Christ our Lord whom, by the power of the Spirit, you raised to live with you for ever and ever. **Amen.**

or

16b Praise God who made heaven and earth:
who keeps his promise for ever.
Heavenly Father, we thank you for your love in creation and for the gift of water to sustain, cleanse and refresh all living creatures.
We thank you for the covenant you made with your people of old: you led them through the sea from slavery to freedom.
We thank you that, in the waters of the Jordan, your Son Jesus was baptized by John and anointed with the Holy Spirit.
By his death on the cross and his resurrection, he has brought us forgiveness and set us free.
We thank you that in the waters of baptism you cleanse us from sin, renew us by your Spirit and raise us to new life. Sanctify this water so that your children who are washed in it may be made one with Christ.

In fulfilment of your promise, anoint them with your Holy Spirit, bring them to new birth in the family of your Church and give them a share in your kingdom:
through Jesus Christ our Lord whom, by the power of the Spirit, you raised to live with you for ever and ever. **Amen.**

THE BAPTISM

17　*The minister baptizes each child, saying*
N, I baptize you in the Name of the Father, and of the Son, and of the Holy Spirit. **Amen.**

18　*The minister may anoint each child on the crown of the head with chrism, saying*
May God, who has received you by baptism into his Church, pour upon you the riches of his grace. As Christ was anointed priest, prophet and king, may you daily be conformed to his image. **Amen.**

19　*The minister or a member of the congregation may clothe each of the newly baptized children in a white garment, saying*
You have been clothed with Christ and raised to new life in him.

THE GIVING OF THE LIGHT

20　*The minister or a member of the congregation may give a lighted candle to each of the newly baptized.*
You have received the light of Christ; walk in this light all the days of your life.
Shine as a light in the world to the glory of God the Father.

〚21　The service continues with the peace. Proper prefaces are given for the Eucharist. Prayers are provided where there is no Eucharist. The candle may be given at the dismissal.〛

AN ORDER FOR BAPTISM WITH CONFIRMATION

THE GATHERING

〚1　Liturgical greeting.〛

2　*The bishop may introduce the service with one of the following.*

Either

Our Lord Jesus Christ commanded, 'Go and make disciples of all nations, baptizing them in the Name of the Father, and of the Son, and of the Holy Spirit.'
Thanks be to God.

or

We were buried with Christ through baptism into his death, that just as Christ was raised from the dead by the glory of the Father, so we should walk in newness of life.
Thanks be to God.

or

When Christ was baptized in the Jordan, the Spirit descended like a dove and the Father spoke, saying, 'You are my beloved Son in whom I am well pleased.'
Thanks be to God.

3　*The candidates stand with their sponsors in front of the bishop. The person appointed may first name the candidates.*
Reverend Father in God, I present to you *these persons* that *they* may be *baptized and confirmed.*

4   *The bishop asks the candidates for baptism and confirmation*
    Is it your wish to be baptized and confirmed?
    It is.
    The bishop asks the candidates for confirmation
    Is it your wish to be confirmed?
    It is.

5   *The bishop asks the congregation*
    Will you welcome these candidates for *baptism and confirmation* and do your best to
    uphold them in their life in Christ?
    With the help of God, we will.

6   *The bishop addresses the congregation in these or similar words*
    In the sacrament of Baptism our heavenly Father sets his people free from the power
    of sin and death by uniting us to the death and resurrection of our Lord Jesus Christ.
    By water and the Holy Spirit we are reborn the children of God and inheritors of the
    kingdom of heaven. All who are baptized into Christ are members of the Church,
    the Body of Christ, where we grow in grace and daily increase in faith, love and
    obedience to the will of God.

7   Heavenly Father,
    by the power of your Holy Spirit
    you give to your faithful people
    new life in the water of baptism:
    guide and strengthen us by the same Spirit,
    that we who are born again may serve you in faith and love
    and grow into the full stature of your Son Jesus Christ,
    who is alive and reigns with you and the Holy Spirit,
    one God, now and for ever. **Amen.**

THE PROCLAMATION OF THE WORD

⟦8–9 Readings and a sermon.⟧

THE LITURGY OF BAPTISM AND CONFIRMATION

THE DECISION

10 *The bishop addresses the candidates and their sponsors* You have declared your wish
    to be *baptized and confirmed (and for these children/this child to be baptized).* We
    therefore now invite you to respond to Christ's call.

    Do you turn to Christ?
    I turn to Christ.
    Do you repent of your sins?
    I repent of my sins.
    Do you renounce evil?
    I renounce evil.

11 *The bishop says to those who are to be baptized*
    May God, who has called you out of darkness into light, restore you in the image of
    his glory and lead you in the way of Christ. **Amen.**

12 *If the oil of catechumens is used, the candidates for baptism may be anointed with it either
    at this point or while they are being signed with the cross.*

THE SIGNING WITH THE CROSS

13 *The bishop continues*
By his cross and precious blood, our Lord Jesus Christ has redeemed the world. He has told us that, if any want to become his followers, they must deny themselves, take up their cross and follow him day by day.

The sign of the cross is made on the forehead of each one who is to be baptized.
N, I sign you with the sign of the cross and claim you for our Saviour Jesus Christ.
When all the candidates for baptism have been signed with the cross, the bishop continues

Never be ashamed to confess the faith of Christ crucified.
Fight valiantly against sin, the world and the devil,
and remain faithful to Christ to the end of your life. Amen.

THE PROFESSION OF FAITH

14 *At the font, the bishop addresses the candidates and their sponsors*
We invite you now to profess the Christian faith.

Do you believe in God the Father, the Creator of all?
I believe and trust in God the Father.
Do you believe in his Son Jesus Christ, the Saviour of the world?
I believe and trust in God the Son.
Do you believe in the Holy Spirit, the Lord, the Giver of life?
I believe and trust in God the Holy Spirit.

15 *The bishop addresses the congregation*
This is the faith of the Church.
This is our faith. We believe and trust in one God, Father, Son and Holy Spirit.

THE BLESSING OF THE BAPTISMAL WATER

16 *The bishop uses one of these forms.*
Either

16a We give thanks to you, O God:
we bless your holy name.
For your gift of water to nourish and sustain all life,
we give you thanks and praise.
Through the waters of the sea
you led the children of Israel from slavery to freedom:
we give you thanks and praise.
At his baptism,
your Son Jesus was anointed with the Holy Spirit:
we give you thanks and praise.
Through the power of that same Spirit, sanctify this water that your children who are washed in it may be united with Christ in his death and resurrection.
Cleanse and deliver them from all sin; bring them to new birth in the family of your Church and make them inheritors of your kingdom:
through Jesus Christ our Lord
whom, by the power of the Spirit,
you raised to live with you
all
Amen.

or

16b Praise God who made heaven and earth:
who keeps his promise for ever.
Heavenly Father, we thank you for your love in creation and for the gift of water to
sustain, cleanse and refresh all living creatures.
We thank you for the covenant you made with your people of old: you led them
through the sea from slavery to freedom.
We thank you that, in the waters of the Jordan, your Son Jesus was baptized by John
and anointed with the Holy Spirit.
By his death on the cross and his resurrection, he has brought us forgiveness and set
us free.
We thank you that in the waters of baptism you cleanse us from sin, renew us by your
Spirit and raise us to new life.
Sanctify this water so that your children who are washed in it may be made one with
Christ.
In fulfilment of your promise, anoint them with your Holy Spirit, bring them to new
birth in the family of your Church and give them a share in your kingdom:
through Jesus Christ our Lord whom, by the power of the Spirit, you raised to live
with you for ever and ever. **Amen.**

THE BAPTISM

17 *The bishop baptizes each candidate, saying*
N, I baptize you in the Name of the Father, and of the Son, and of the Holy Spirit.
Amen.

18 *Any small children who have been baptized but are not to be confirmed on this occasion
may be anointed on the crown of the head with chrism by the bishop, who says*
May God, who has received you by baptism into his Church, pour upon you the
riches of his grace. As Christ was anointed priest, prophet and king, may you daily be
conformed to his image. **Amen.**

19 *The bishop or a member of the congregation may clothe each of the newly baptized in a
white garment, saying*
You have been clothed with Christ and raised to new life in him.

THE GIVING OF THE LIGHT

20 *The bishop or a member of the congregation may give a lighted candle to each of the
newly baptized.*
You have received the light of Christ; walk in this light all the days of your life.
Shine as a light in the world to the glory of God the Father.

THE CONFIRMATION

21 *The bishop, standing, extends his hands towards the candidates for confirmation and says*
Almighty and everlasting God,
you have given your *servants* new birth
in baptism by water and the Holy Spirit,
and have forgiven *them* all *their* sins.
Pour out your Holy Spirit upon *them*:
the Spirit of wisdom and understanding;
the Spirit of counsel and inward strength;
the Spirit of knowledge and true godliness;
and let *their* delight be in the fear of the Lord. **Amen.**

22 *The bishop addresses each candidate by name*

N, God has called you by name and made you his own.

23 *The bishop lays his right hand on the head of each candidate, saying*

Either

23a Confirm, O Lord, your *servant/child* with your heavenly grace and anoint *him/her* with your Holy Spirit; empower *him/her* for your service and keep *him/her* in eternal life. **Amen.**

or

23b Confirm, Lord, your servant N with your heavenly grace, that *he/she* may continue yours for ever, and daily increase in your Holy Spirit more and more until *he/she* comes to your everlasting kingdom. **Amen.**

⟦The service continues with the peace, eucharistic propers, blessing, prayers when there is no Eucharist and the option of giving the candle at the dismissal.⟧

6. The Church of Ireland

Christianity came to Ireland in the fifth century, with the mission of Patrick traditionally dated at 430. In the seventh century it developed its own character. The Anglo-Norman invasion led to the church being organized a similar way as in England. At the Reformation the church followed a similar pattern to England, but many people remained Roman Catholic. In 1869 the church was disestablished and in 1871 it was founded as an independent Anglican Church.

The Book of Common Prayer 2004 of the Church of Ireland contains two orders of services of baptism and confirmation. The first order is in traditional language and comes from the 1926 *Book of Common Prayer*.[25] This in itself is a revision of the English 1662 service. The services included in the 2004 edition are those of baptism and confirmation. In practice these are rarely used.

The modern language services represent the fruit of a number of years of development of modern language baptismal services. Holy Baptism 1969 was a radically new service pioneering modern language in Irish liturgy.[26] This was incorporated into a collection of modern language services, *Revised Services* 1973. The *Alternative Prayer Book* 1984 included a service for the baptism of children. *Confirmation* 1987 added to the new services. *Alternative Occasional Services* 1993 continued the development of thinking with a service of 'Baptism, Confirmation and First Communion', an alternative form of confirmation, renewal of baptismal vows, the thanksgiving for the birth of a child and a thanksgiving after the adoption.

Christian Initiation 2 in the 2004 book includes: a service of 'holy baptism' which is both for adults and children; a service of holy baptism in the context of morning or evening prayer; an order for receiving into the congregation those privately baptized; the order of confirmation; seasonal variations for baptismal seasons; readings and psalms for Christian initiation; an outline order for baptism, confirmation and Holy Communion; thanksgiving after the birth of a child and thanksgiving after adoption.

The Church of Ireland normally expects those who are to receive Communion to have been confirmed.

---

25 J 39–44.
26 J 155–162.

HOLY BAPTISM 2

[[Pastoral Introduction]]

THE GATHERING OF GOD'S PEOPLE

[[1 Greeting]]

2 Our Lord Jesus Christ has told us
   that to enter the kingdom of heaven
   we must be born again of water and the Spirit,
   and has given us baptism as the sign and seal of this new birth.
   Here we are washed by the Holy Spirit and made clean.
   Here we are clothed with Christ,
   dying to sin that we may live his risen life.
   As children of God, we have a new dignity and
   God calls us to fullness of life.

[[3–5 Kyrie, confession, Gloria, Collect]]

PROCLAIMING AND RECEIVING THE WORD

[[6–9 Readings, hymn, gospel, sermon]]

THE PRESENTATION

10 *The presiding minister invites the candidates and their sponsors to stand in view of
    the congregation.*
    *The presiding minister invites the sponsors of baptismal candidates to present the
    candidates.*
    We welcome those who come to be baptized. I invite *their* sponsors to present
    them now.

11 *We present ... to be baptized.*

12 *The presiding minister says to the sponsors of those unable to answer for themselves*
    Parents and godparents, will you accept the responsibilities placed upon you in
    bringing ... for baptism and answer on their behalf?
    By your own prayers and example, by your teaching and love, will you encourage
    them in the life and faith of the Christian Community?
    With the help of God, we will.
    In baptism these *children* begin their journey in faith.
    You speak for *them* today.
    Will you care for *them*, and help them to take *their* place within the life and worship
    of Christ's Church?
    With the help of God, we will.

THE DECISION

13 *At this point testimony may be given by one or more of the candidates.*

14 *The presiding minister says to the candidates able to answer for themselves, and to the
    sponsors of other candidates*
    In baptism, God calls us from darkness to his marvellous light.
    To follow Christ means dying to sin and rising to new life with him. Therefore I ask:

Do you reject the devil and all proud rebellion against God?
I reject them.
Do you renounce the deceit and corruption of evil?
I renounce them.
Do you repent of the sins that separate us from God and neighbour?
I repent of them.
Do you turn to Christ as Saviour?
I turn to Christ.
Do you submit to Christ as Lord?
I submit to Christ.
Do you come to Christ, the Way, the Truth and the Life?
I come to Christ.

The presiding minister says to the congregation

15 You have heard these our brothers and sisters respond to Christ.
Will you support them in this calling?
We will support them.

16 *The presiding minister makes the sign of the cross on the forehead of each candidate for baptism, either here or after the baptism with water, saying*

17 Christ claims you for his own. Receive the sign of the cross.
Live as a disciple of Christ, fight the good fight, finish the race, keep the faith.
Confess Christ crucified, proclaim his resurrection,
look for his coming in glory.

18 May almighty God deliver you from the powers of darkness, restore in you the image of his glory, and lead you in the light and obedience of Christ. **Amen.**

19 *A hymn may be sung.*

THE BAPTISM

20 *The presiding minister and the candidates go to the place where the water for baptism is, and the presiding minister begins the thanksgiving prayer.*
Praise God who made heaven and earth.
Who keeps his promise for ever.
Let us give thanks to the Lord our God.
It is right to give our thanks and praise.

20a We give you thanks that at the beginning of creation your Holy Spirit moved upon the waters to bring forth light and life. With water you cleanse and replenish the earth; you nourish and sustain all living things.
Thanks be to God.
We give you thanks that through the waters of the Red Sea you led your people out of slavery into freedom, and brought them through the river Jordan to new life in the land of promise.
Thanks be to God.
We give you thanks for your Son Jesus Christ: for his baptism by John, for his anointing with the Holy Spirit.
Thanks be to God.
We give you thanks that through the deep waters of death Jesus delivered us from our sins and was raised to new life in triumph.
Thanks be to God.
We give you thanks for the grace of the Holy Spirit who forms us in the likeness of Christ and leads us to proclaim your Kingdom.

Thanks be to God.
And now we give you thanks that you have called *names/these your servants* to new birth in your Church through the waters of baptism. Pour out your Holy Spirit in blessing and sanctify this water so that *those* who *are* baptized in it may be made one with Christ in his death and resurrection. May *they* die to sin, rise to newness of life, and continue for ever in Jesus Christ our Lord, through whom we give you praise and honour in the unity of the Spirit, now and for ever. **Amen.**

or

20b We thank you, almighty God, for the gift of water to sustain, refresh and cleanse all life. Over water the Holy Spirit moved in the beginning of creation. Through water you led the children of Israel from slavery in Egypt to freedom in the Promised Land. In water your Son Jesus received the baptism of John and was anointed by the Holy Spirit as the Messiah, the Christ, to lead us from the death of sin to newness of life. We thank you, Father, for the water of baptism. In it we are buried with Christ in his death. By it we share in his resurrection. Through it we are reborn by the Holy Spirit. Therefore, in joyful obedience to your Son, we baptize into his fellowship those who come to him in faith. Now sanctify this water that, by the power of your Holy Spirit, *they* may be cleansed from sin and born again. Renewed in your image, may they walk by the light of faith and continue for ever in the risen life of Jesus Christ our Lord; to whom with you and the Holy Spirit be all honour and glory, now and for ever. **Amen.**

21 *The presiding minister shall ask the following question of each candidate for baptism, or, in the case of those unable to answer for themselves, the sponsors of each candidate:*
Do you believe and accept the Christian faith into which you are (... is) to be baptized?
I do.

22 *The presiding minister addresses the congregation.*
Brothers and sisters, I ask you to profess, together with *these* candidates the faith of the Church.
〚Question and answer Apostles' Creed **CF2a**〛

23 *The presiding minister baptizes by dipping the candidates in the water, or by pouring water over them, saying*
... , I baptize you in the name of the Father, and of the Son, and of the Holy Spirit. **Amen.**

〚24 Optional place for signing with the cross.〛

25 God has called you into his Church.
We therefore receive and welcome you
as a member with us of the body of Christ,
as a child of the one heavenly Father,
and as an inheritor of the kingdom of God.

〚26 Directions for the Eucharist.〛

THE DISMISSAL

God has delivered us from the dominion of darkness
and has given us a place with the saints in light.
You have received the light of Christ;
walk in this light all the days of your life.
Shine as a light in the world
to the glory of God the Father.

Go in peace to love and serve the Lord:
In the name of Christ. **Amen.**

[Notes on baptism including emergency and conditional baptism.]

CONFIRMATION 2

THE GATHERING OF GOD'S PEOPLE

[1 Greeting]

2 *The bishop may introduce the service with these or other suitable words:*
Brothers and sisters, we meet today to support and to pray for those who have been
baptized and instructed in the Christian faith and who now intend, in the presence
of God and of this congregation, to make the and is all there think promises of their
baptism their own. At the heart of this Confirmation service are two distinct, yet
related, acts of confirming. First the candidates will profess their faith in Christ,
confirming their desire to serve God throughout their lives, to turn to Christ and to
renounce all evil. Then, as bishop, I will lay my hand on them, praying that God's
Spirit will confirm, strengthen and guide them as they strive, each day of their lives,
to live up to the solemn commitment they will make today. It is our privilege and joy
as the people of God to hear the candidates' response to God's call and to renew our
own baptismal commitment to our Lord Jesus Christ. It will be our responsibility to
encourage the newly confirmed in their discipleship, so that the Christian family may
be built up, recognizing the diverse gifts of all its members. On this their Confirmation
day, let us pray in silence for ... so that, increasing in the Holy Spirit more and more,
they may experience God's wisdom and love for ever.

[3–5 Penitence – confession and absolution; Gloria]

6 *Collect*
Heavenly Father,
by water and the Holy Spirit
you give your faithful people new life:
Guide and strengthen us by that same Spirit
that we who are born again
may serve you in faith and love,
and grow into the full stature of your Son Jesus Christ,
who lives and reigns with you and the Holy Spirit,
one God, now and for ever. **Amen.**

PROCLAIMING AND RECEIVING THE WORD

[7–9 Readings, hymns, Gospel]

THE PRESENTATION

10 *The candidates are presented to the congregation.*
*Where appropriate, they are presented by their godparents or sponsors and the bishop may
say*
Who presents these persons for confirmation?
We do.

11 *The bishop asks the candidates*
Have you been baptized in the name of the Father,
and of the Son, and of the Holy Spirit?
I have.
Are you ready with your own mouth and from your own heart
to affirm your faith in Jesus Christ?
I am.

12 *The bishop asks the clergy who have been responsible for pastoral care of the candidates*
Have these persons been carefully prepared in their understanding of the
Christian faith?
I believe they have.

13 *Testimony by the candidates may follow.*

THE DECISION

14 *The bishop says to the candidates*
In baptism, God calls us from darkness to his marvellous light. To follow Christ
means dying to sin and rising to new life with him. Therefore I ask:

Do you reject the devil and all proud rebellion against God?
I reject them.
Do you renounce the deceit and corruption of evil?
I renounce them.
Do you repent of the sins that separate us from God and neighbour?
I repent of them.

Do you turn to Christ as Saviour?
I turn to Christ.
Do you submit to Christ as Lord?
I submit to Christ.
Do you come to Christ, the Way, the Truth and the Life?
I come to Christ.

15 *The bishop says to the congregation*
You have heard these our brothers and sisters respond to Christ.
Will you support them in this calling?

The congregation answers
We will support them.

THE PROFESSION OF FAITH

16 *The bishop asks the candidates*
Do you ... believe and accept the Christian faith into which you are baptized?
I do.

17 *The bishop addresses the congregation*
Brothers and sisters, I ask you to profess together with *these candidates*
the faith of the Church.

⟦Question and answer Apostles' Creed **CF2a**⟧

18 *The bishop and the candidates gather at the place of confirmation.*
A hymn, psalm, canticle or a litany may be used.

THE CONFIRMATION

19 *The bishop says*
Our help is in the name of the Lord
who made heaven and earth.
Blessed be the name of the Lord
now, and for ever. Amen.

Silence

20 Almighty and everliving God,
whose Son Jesus Christ was crucified and rose again
to break the power of sin and death:
We give you thanks and praise for the gift of your Holy Spirit
by whom your servants have been born again
and made your children.
Grant that in the power of the same Holy Spirit
they may continue to grow
in the knowledge and likeness of Christ;
increase in them your gracious gifts,
the spirit of wisdom and understanding,
the spirit of right judgment and inward strength,
the spirit of knowledge and godly living;
and fill them, O Lord, with the spirit of reverence for you.

21 *Those who are to be confirmed kneel before the bishop,*
who lays a hand upon each of them saying
Confirm ..., O Lord, with your heavenly grace,
that *he/she* may continue to be yours for ever,
and daily increase in your Holy Spirit more and more
until *he/she* comes to your eternal kingdom.

And each one of them answers **Amen.**

22 *Those receiving the laying on of hands for reaffirmation*
kneel before the bishop, who lays a hand upon each of them saying
..., may the Holy Spirit
who has begun a good work in you
direct and uphold you
in the service of Christ and his kingdom.
God, the Father, the Son and the Holy Spirit,
bless, preserve and keep you. *Amen.*

23 *The bishop continues*
Heavenly Father,
we pray for your servants
upon whom we have now laid our hands,
after the example of the apostles,
to assure them by this sign
of your favour towards them.
May your fatherly hand ever be over them.
Let your Holy Spirit ever be with them.
Lead them to know and obey your word,
and keep them in eternal life;
through Jesus Christ our Lord. **Amen.**

THE COMMISSION

24 *The bishop may use this commission:*
Those who are baptized are called to worship and serve God.
Will you continue in the apostles' teaching and fellowship,
in the breaking of the bread, and in the prayers?
With the help of God, I will.

Will you persevere in resisting evil,
and, whenever you fall into sin, repent and return to the Lord?
With the help of God, I will.

Will you proclaim by word and example
the good news of God in Christ?
With the help of God, I will.

Will you seek and serve Christ in all people,
loving your neighbour as yourself?
With the help of God, I will.

⟦The service continues with directions for a Eucharist.⟧

7. The Lusitanian Church (Portugal)

Christianity came to the Iberian Peninsula in Roman times. The Portuguese church was able to show after the Council of Trent an independent liturgical tradition based on Braga. The English Book of Common Prayer was first translated into Portuguese in 1695 for the East Indies.[27] In the nineteenth century Anglican chaplaincies were opened in Lisbon. The declaration of papal infallibility led to concern by local Christians. By 1880 they had formed their own Synod and in 1882 produced their own liturgy. There was a revision of the liturgy in 1928.[28] The present liturgy of the church, *Liturgia da Igreja Lusitana*, was produced in 1991.[29]

LITURGY OF THE LUSITANIAN CHURCH 1991

〚Translated by Joseph Fernandes〛

THE BAPTISM OF CHILDREN

〚Introductory rubrics〛

INTRODUCTION

1   The Lord be with you.
    And also with you.

2   Holy Baptism is administered for children on the assumption that they will grow in the Church of Christ community that the Christian faith is taught to them, and that, been publicly confess this faith, will be confirmed by Bishop and admitted to Holy Communion.

3   *The minister, addressing in particular the parents and godparents of children to be baptized, says*
    So I ask you:
    Will you educate this child as a Christian, within the church family?
    Yes, to this we commit.

    Will you help this child to be regular in public worship and in private prayer, for your education, by your example and for your intercession for her?
    We will.
    Will you encourage this child to receive Holy Communion and confirmation?
    We will.

---

27 G 137: 1.
28 G 137: 8.
29 G 137: 13.

4 Heavenly Father,
   the baptism of your Son Jesus Christ in the Jordan,
   proclaimed Him as your only Son;
   grant that by your Spirit,
   this child is born again
   and a child is taken yours by adoption and grace.
   Through the same Jesus Christ our Lord. **Amen**

THE MINISTRY OF THE WORD

5 ⟦Three alternative readings are provided, and a sermon or this homily.⟧

6 God is the creator of all things, and by the birth of children, he gives to parents a share in the work and joy of creation. But we were born of earthly parents need to be born again. For in the Gospel Jesus tells us that unless one is born again, one will not enter the kingdom of God. And so God opens for us the way to a second birth, a new creation and to live in union with Him.

Baptism is the sign and seal of the new birth. In the Gospel of Matthew, we see the risen Jesus to order his apostles to make disciples of all nations, and everywhere to minister baptism, and in the Book of Acts, we hear of St. Peter preaching in these terms: 'Repent of evil and that each one is baptized in the name of the Lord Jesus Christ for the remission of sins, and ye shall receive the gift of the Holy Spirit of God for the promise is to you and to your children and to all that are far off as many as the Lord will call.' *(Acts 2.38)*

It was in obedience to this commandment we ourselves were baptized. Now – comforted by the example of Jesus, who Himself calls children, embraces and blesses them – we bring this child to baptism.

7 Therefore, recalling our own baptism, we pray for this child, saying together:
   Heavenly Father,
   in your love you have called us to know you,
   you called us to trust you,
   and united our lives to yours.
   Surround this child that your love;
   Take her in your arms and bless her;
   protects her from evil;
   fill her in your Holy Spirit;
   and welcomes her in the family of your Church;
   that they may accompany us on the path of Christ,
   and grow in the knowledge of your love. Amen.

THE DECISION

8 Those who bring children to baptism must declare their fidelity to Christ, and their abhorrence of evil. It is your duty to educate this child accordingly.
   So I ask the following questions which each must answer for yourselves and for this child.

9 Do you turn to Christ?
   I turn to Christ.
   Do you repent of your sins?
   I repent of my sins.
   Do you renounce evil?
   I renounce evil.

10 *The Minister may make silent sign of the cross on the child's forehead, and then says*
May Almighty God deliver you from the powers of darkness, and lead you in the light and obedience of Christ. **Amen.**

11 *A hymn or Psalm*

THE BAPTISM

12 Praise God who made heaven and earth,
who keeps his promise for ever.
Almighty God, whose Son Jesus Christ was baptized in the river Jordan:
we thank you for the gift of water to cleanse us and revive us;
we thank you that through the Waters of the Red Sea,
you led your people out of slavery
to freedom in the promised land;
we thank you that through the deep Waters of death
you brought your Son, and raised him to life in triumph.
Bless this water, that your *servants* who *are* washed in it
may be made one with Christ in his death and in his resurrection,
to be cleansed and delivered from all sin.
Send your Holy Spirit upon *them* to bring *them* to new birth in the family of
your Church,
and raise *them* with Christ to full and eternal life.
For all might, majesty, authority, and power are yours, now and forever. **Amen.**

13 You brought this child to baptism. You must now confess before God and his Church, Christian faith into which she is going to be baptized, and in which you will help her to grow. Therefore you must answer for yourselves and for this child.

14 ⟦Modern Question and Answer form from the ASB **CF3**⟧

15 This is the faith of the Church.
This is our faith.
We believe and trust in one God,
Father, Son, and Holy Spirit.

16 *Parents and godparents hold the child, and the minister baptizes he/her; He dips he/her three times in water or pours water three times on his/her head, while making mention of the Persons of the Trinity*
N, I baptize you in the name of the Father, and the Son, and of the Holy Spirit.

THE WELCOME INTO THE CHURCH

17 I sign you with the cross, the sign of Christ.

Never be ashamed to confess the faith of Christ crucified.
Fight, inspired by Christ,
sin and evil forces
and continues his faithful servant to the end of your life.

18 *A candle, then lit (from the paschal candle, if possible) is delivered to one of the godparents, with the following words*
Christ is our light. Through baptism into Christ, you passed from darkness to light.
Shine like a light in the world to the glory of God the Father.

19 *The minister, the parents and godparents, along with the child, move to the sanctuary, and all say the acclamation.*

20 We welcome you into the Lord's Family.
We are members together of the body of Christ;
we are children of the same heavenly Father;
we are inheritors together of the kingdom of God.
We welcome you.

PRAYERS

[[Four prayers based on ASB, 59, 60, 61 and Lord's Prayer.]]

21 Merciful Father,
we thank you for the gift of Holy Baptism;
grant that this child
worthily receives the blessings of your grace
and grow to the full stature of Christ your Son;
who lives and reigns with You and the Holy Spirit,
one God, now and forever. **Amen.**

22 Almighty God, Father of our Lord Jesus Christ, who gave us new life by water and
the Holy Spirit, and forgive us our sins, save us in your grace, now and forever.
Amen.

CONFIRMATION OF THOSE ALREADY BAPTISED

[[Three rubrics including permission to use oil.]]

PREPARATION

1 Heavenly Father,
by the power of your Holy Spirit
you gave to your faithful people
new life in the water of baptism.
Guide and strengthen us by that same Spirit,
that we who are born again
may serve you in faith and love,
and grow into the full stature of your Son Jesus Christ,
who is alive and reigns with you and the Holy Spirit,
one God now and forever. **Amen.**

MINISTRY OF THE WORD

2 [[Three lessons as ASB plus four possible psalms and a sermon.]]

3 *Veni Creator Spiritus*

Come, O Divine Creator
Come Holy Spirit of love;
Fill the souls of mortals
Fire and heavenly light.

Sublime gift of heaven above,
Source of life, eternal God,
Intercessor, consolation,
Extremely powerful anointing.

Promise made by Jesus.
Finger of the Father who leads us,
Your seven gifts come to endow us
In order to praise God

Lights up on us, pure splendour,
The holy flame of love;
Changes in triumphal virtues
Our personal weaknesses.

Defend us from Satan
With the power of your peace;
Our darkness lacerates us,
Illuminate our path.

The Father and the Son,
In between eternal love,
Rise to the high heavens for You
Our praise to the Triune God.

The Triune God, to Thee, Lord,
Glory, honour and praise forever. Amen.

RENEWAL OF BAPTISMAL VOWS

4 *The confirmands are standing before the Bishop, who tells them*
You came here to be confirmed. You are in the presence of God and his Church.
With your own mouth and all your heart, you must proclaim your faithfulness to
Christ and your rejection of all that is evil. So, I ask you:
Do you turn to Christ?
I turn to Christ.
Do you repent of your sins?
I repent of my sins.
Do you renounce evil?
I renounce evil.

5 You must now declare before God and his Church that you accept the Christian faith
into which you were baptize, and in which you will live and grow.

[Modern question form from the ASB **CF3**]

6 This is the faith of the Church.
This is our faith.
We believe and trust in one God,
Father, Son, and Holy Spirit.

CONFIRMATION

7 *The Bishop stands before those to be confirmed and says:*
Our help is in the name of the Lord
who has made heaven and earth.
Blessed be the name of the Lord
now and forever.

8 *The Bishop stretches out his hands towards them and says*
Almighty and ever/living God,
you have given your *servants* new birth in baptism by water and the Spirit,
and have forgiven them all their sins.

Let your Holy Spirit rest upon them:
the Spirit of wisdom and understanding;
the Spirit of counsel and inward strength;
the Spirit of knowledge and true godliness;
and let their delight be in the fear of the Lord.
Amen.

9　*The confirmands kneel before the Bishop. He may mark them on the forehead with the sign of the cross, using oil and saying*
N, I sign you to with the sign of the cross and I lay my hand upon you.

10　*Laying his hand upon the head of each, confirming the Bishop says*
Confirm, Lord, your servant N. with your Holy Spirit, and strengthen him for your service. **Amen.**

11　*After confirmation the Bishop says*
My children, now that you have been confirmed, I admit you full communion of Christ's Church, and urge the gifts that help you to live your Christian prayers and example.

12　Confirmation Prayer **CF5** said by all

13　[[Propers for the Eucharist and prayers of intercession.]]

BLESSING

14　*Bishop:*
Our help is in the name of the Lord
who made heaven and earth.
Blessed be the name of the Lord,
now and forever.
Go in peace to the world;
Fight with courage the good fight of faith,
Be joyful to the end of your pilgrimage.
And the blessing of God almighty,
the Father and the Son and the Holy Spirit,
be with you forever. **Amen.**

THE BAPTISM AND CONFIRMATION OF ADULTS

[[Rubrics saying the rite is celebrated in a Eucharist and uses the ministry of the word from confirmation.]]

BAPTISM

INTRODUCTION

1　*The minister, along with the people who will be baptized, their parents and godparents, are placed near the baptismal font*

2　Our Lord Jesus Christ, for the salvation of mankind, surrendered himself to death on the cross and rose again.
Baptism is the sacrament by which, by repentance and faith, we receive this salvation: we join with Christ in his death; we obtain the forgiveness of our sins; we are made members of his Body; and with Him we rise to new life in the Spirit.

In confirmation, through the imposition of the Bishop's hands, we are empowered with the power of the Spirit, to worship God, to witness to the Gospel and serve Christ.

THE RENUNCIATION

3 *The minister addresses the candidates, parents and godparents, omitting paragraphs that are not appropriate to the occasion.*
You who have come here for Baptism and Confirmation, you must declare your rejection of all that is evil.

You present these children for Baptism, you must promise to educate them to reject all that is bad. So you ought to answer for yourselves and for these children.

You who already have been baptized, and now have come to be confirmed, ought, in your own voice and with all your heart, declare your rejection of all that is evil.

4 *The minister asks the following questions*
Do you renounce all evil and wicked spirit forces, who rebel against God?
I renounce.
Do you renounce the evil powers of this world which corrupt and destroy God's creation?
I renounce.
Do you renounce all sinful desires that keep you from God's love?
I renounce.

5 *The minister says to the congregation*
Dear Brothers in Christ, pray for these people.
God of all mercy, welcome them. **Amen.**
Mortify their sinful desires. **Amen.**
Give them the life of your Spirit. **Amen.**
Help them to overcome the wicked. **Amen.**
Give them all the Christian virtues. **Amen.**
Guide them with your saints to glory everlasting. **Amen.**

6 *The minister, extending his hand over the candidate says*
May Almighty God free you from the powers of darkness and lead you to life and to the obedience of Christ. **Amen.**

THE BLESSING OF WATER

7 Almighty God whose Son Jesus Christ was baptized in the Jordan River;
we thank you for the gift of water which purifies and revives us;
thank you that, through the waters of the Red Sea, you led your people from slavery in Egypt the freedom of the Promised Land;
thank you because you brought your Son through the abyss of death, and in triumph rose again to life.
Bless this water, that your servants, purified in it, are united with Christ in his death and resurrection, and are cleansed and freed from all sin.
Send on them your Holy Spirit, so they have a new birth the family of your Church, and with Christ stand in the fullness of eternal life.
For the majesty and power, the authority and power are yours, now and forever.
Amen.

8 *Candidates, parents and godparents recite The Apostles' Creed*

〚The Apostles' Creed **CF1a**〛

9   You who are to be baptized in this faith, and you who are to be confirmed in it: is your will to live in obedience to God's laws, as loyal members of his church?
It is, so help me God.

Parents and godparents, is your will educate this child, by your example and teaching, to live in obedience to God's laws, as a loyal member of the Church?
It is, so help me God.

BAPTISM

10   *Each candidate is presented to the Minister by their parents or godparents.*
Reverend Father in God, meet N to be baptized.

11   *The minister baptizes the candidate, each dipping in water for three times, or by pouring water three times on his head. while making mention of the Persons of the Trinity*
N., I baptize you in the Name of the Father and of the Son and of the Holy Spirit.
Amen.

THE WELCOMING INTO THE CHURCH

12   *The minister makes the sign of the cross on the forehead of each of the newly baptized saying*
I sign you with the cross, the sign of Christ.
Then he adds
Never be ashamed to confess the faith of Christ crucified.
Combat, inspired by Christ, sin and evil forces,
and continue his faithful servant until the end of your life.

13   *A candle is lit from the Paschal candle and given to each newly baptized or their sponsor, with the words*
Christ is our light.
After this the minister adds
Through baptism into Christ, you passed from darkness to light.
Shine like a light in the world to the glory of God the Father.

14   *The congregation, representing the whole Church, welcomes the newly baptized*
God by baptism received you into his church.
We welcome you in the Lord's family:
We are with you members of the Body of Christ;
we are children of the same heavenly Father;
we are co-heirs of the Kingdom of God.
We give you welcome, brother/sister.

CONFIRMATION

15   *The Bishop is placed before them that will be confirmed and invites those present to pray.*

16   *Silence.*

17   *All sing a hymn of invocation of the Holy Spirit or*
VENI CREATOR SPIRITUS
⟦As in confirmation service above⟧

18   *The Bishop stands and says*
Our help is in the Name of the Lord,
who made heaven and earth.
Blessed be the Name of the Lord,
now and forever.

19   *The Bishop raises his hand in the direction of the confirmands and says:*
Almighty and eternal God, in baptism by water and the Spirit,
you gave this new birth unto thy servants, and forgave their sins.
Grant that your Spirit rest upon them: the Spirit of wisdom and understanding;
the Spirit of counsel and inward strength; the Spirit of knowledge and piety;
and that your joy may be in the fear of the Lord. **Amen.**

20   *The confirmands kneel before the Bishop.*
He may mark them on the forehead with the sign of the cross, using oil and saying
I sign you with the sign of the cross, and impose upon you my hand.

By laying his hand upon the head of each confirming the Bishop says
Confirm Lord your servant N. with your Holy Spirit, and strengthen him for your
service. Amen.

21   *After confirmation, the Bishop says*
My children, now that you have been confirmed, I admit you into the full communion
of Christ's Church, and urge the gifts that help you to live your Christian prayers and
example.

22   Confirmation prayer **CF5** said by all

⟦23   The rubrics give propers for the Eucharist including the blessing. There are directions
for conditional baptism, emergency baptism and the reception into baptism of those
previously baptized.⟧

8. The Spanish Reformed Episcopal Church

Christianity in Spain may have existed from apostolic times; in Romans St Paul shows an intention to visit Spain. Spain had its own liturgical tradition, the Mozarabic rite, before the later adoption of the Roman rite. The Spanish Reformed Episcopal Church grew up as a result of dissatisfaction with Vatican 1. In 1894 Bishop Cabrera was consecrated as the first bishop. Close links were kept with the Church of Ireland. In 1980 the church was received into the Anglican Communion and became extra Provincial to Canterbury. A liturgy was authorized by the Synod of 1889 with Mozarabic elements in it.[30] A translation of this, by R. Stewart Clough, was arranged in 1889 by Lord Plunket, Archbishop of Dublin, who had a strong interest in the church. There are presently two liturgies used by the church: the *Oficios Divinos* (1975) and *Orden del Bautismo*. The confirmation service is from the older book in a shortened version, and is almost identical to that of the 1889 prayer book; the translation below adapts the Clough translation. The new baptismal order is very close to Mozarabic baptism.[31]

ORDER OF BAPTISM FOR CELEBRATION IN ANY SEASON

[Translated by Andii Bowsher]

1   *The child is brought to the priest to be exorcised. The priest breaths three times on the child's face reciting this exorcism:*
I exorcise you, unearthly spirit, enemy of humankind, by God the Almighty Father who made the heavens, and the earth and the sea and all that is in them, and by Jesus Christ his Son and by the Holy Spirit. All diabolical hosts, every power of the adversary, every violent shaking of the enemy, every dark and turbulent spirit be eradicated and flee from this created being so that s/he may be made a temple of the living God through the remission of all sins. By the justification of our Lord and Saviour Jesus Christ who comes to judge the world with fire. **Amen.**

2   *Making the sign of the cross on the child's forehead, the name is given in the course of this exorcism. After asking what is the name of the child, the priest says to him/her:*
Receive the sign of the cross: follow God's precepts. Today you are reborn by the word of God, grow strong in spiritual light. Leaving behind error and darkness, enter the temple of the living God and joyfully know that the cords of death have let you go. Let Almighty God who made the bodies of human beings live in your senses and convert them into a dwelling-place for the divine spirit. Fear then the divine decrees and await the coming of our only-begotten Saviour who was born of a virgin and

---

30 G 162: 13.
31 See Whitaker, E.C. and Johnson, M.E. *Documents of the Baptismal Liturgy*, 3rd edn. London: SPCK, 2003 (1960), pp. 164–172.

conceived by the infusion of the Holy Spirit. By his light you are illumined, by his virtue you are strengthened, with his sign you are marked on the forehead so that by Him you merit [to be brought to] the grace of baptism. Therefore, I place on you this sign in the name of the Father and of the Son and of the Holy Spirit. Who reign for ever and ever. **Amen.**

3   *After the priest says this exorcism, s/he turns towards the east.*
Remember Satan that, for you, condemnation will remain. Flee and withdraw confounded when you see the person that my God and Lord has dignified to call by his grace; if you leave falsely, the same Christ has prepared judgement for you. You will render an account before the living God and you will not be able to make use of the vessel which God himself has marked with his sign. This I affirm in the name of the Father, the Son and the Holy Spirit, to whom belongs this sign and whose name knows no defeat.

4   *Then the priest anoints with blessed oil the child's mouth and ears, saying:*
Open, open up with the Holy Spirit, open with sweet scent. The Spirit has done all things well, making the deaf hear and the mute speak.

5   *Then the priest lays hands upon the child, saying:*
Blessed be the Lord God of Israel, who visits redemption upon his people, and raises us with his dwelling to salvation. Before your coming in glory, you sent the spirit and virtue of Elijah to your servant John so that he might prepare your paths, giving your people knowledge of salvation by the forgiveness of their sins and by the revelation of your name; so that the unfaithful might be led into the wisdom of the just; so that he might prepare for you a perfect people by the enfolding of your mercy. His voice is heard crying out: 'Prepare the way of the Lord, make his paths straight'.
Here, Lord, we present ourselves also, following humbly the commandments of your majesty; we prepare the path so that we might lead your people as a deer thirstily seeks out water. Now you, Lord, cancelling our iniquity and covering our sins according to your covenant, will bring us to the Promised Land which flows with milk and honey. You are the Lamb of God who takes away the sin of the world. You caused the children of God to know you. You were anointed by the Father with the oil of gladness above all your brothers and sisters. Lord, infuse into these people the grace of your blessing, and keep them from falling back into their former sins. Wash them by your blessing in founts of water; may they be reborn in the Holy Spirit and see Jerusalem, your eternal altar, cover them with the shadow of the most high. Blessed be Mother Church, for God glorified his servants with goodness and his reign will have no end. **Amen.**

6   *Having laid on hands, The priest will recite the creed to the end, saying:*
Do you believe in God...?

7   *Having said it all, the priest goes to the baptismal font, and breathes on it three times repeating this exorcism, facing towards the east:*
Away, unearthly spirit, away from all those to whom our faith will serve as sacrament. Do not look for guilt of crime, you who recognise the power of the Lord. The power of the minister gives dignity to the ministry, but not by trusting in their own merits but because God has said it. For the God of all of us summons you, creature of water. Keeping your ordinary form, do not hold back from giving yourself over to the service necessary to please God. Put far from yourself all communion with demons and every sign of iniquity. Charged with God's precepts, eliminate every stain of unearthly spirits. Thus having received the grace of sanctification you will make innocent before our God those who come into you laden with sin. Amen. By our living Lord Jesus Christ.

8 *After the priest says this blessing of the font in the manner usually said in the mass:*
Heavenly water be sanctified by the word of God; be sanctified water of Christ, trodden by uncountable feet, unfathomed by the multitude of mountains, unshakable even though struck by rocks, scattered through the world but always united. You hold the world firm and support the weight of the mountains but you do not sink. You are in the most high heaven stretched out throughout the globe and cleanse it all, yet nothing cleanses you. You held yourself back when the Hebrews escaped and again flowed over the furious pursuing enemy hosts. You are one and the same: salvation for the faithful and castigator of sinners. You were behind the rock struck by Moses and could not remain hidden when commanded by majestic command. Nurtured by clouds, in pleasing rain you nourish the trees. You lead arid bodies to saving grace, and the sea extends itself towards life. You break out of secret places bringing fertile essences so that the dry earth does not fail to produce abundant harvests. You hold the beginning and the end yet God has laid it down that we do not know when the end is to come.

Now you, almighty Lord, full of virtue, while we set out the merits of water and proclaim its distinguished works, lift up your favour upon the guilty and help the captives with your constant pity. You return to us what Adam lost in paradise, what his wife gave up, what the intemperance of voracious gluttony threw away. Give us the drink of salvation so that the indigestible corruption of mortals and ancient wickedness may be broken down by the divine antidote. Cleanse the gluttony of the untended earth. Pull down the wall of paradise, pressed upon by the boundaries of fire. Let the ways to your flowering field be open for those who return. Let them receive the image of God once lost through the deceptions of the serpent. Let them abandon through the purity of this water every crime contracted through the serpent's perversion of truth. May they be raised to repose, receive your pardon and, renewed by mystic waters, know that they are redeemed and born again. **Amen.**

9 *Then the priest makes the sign of the cross with blessed oil on the forehead or in the font where the baptism is to take place, saying:*
In the name of the Father and of the Son and of the Holy Spirit, who reigns through all the ages. **Amen.**

10 *After the mixing of the oil and water, the priest says this blessing:*
Although we are unclean through the filthiness of our crimes, and our consciences prick us because of our evil deeds, humbly we kneel before you to request and make supplication that by your mercy you help us with good will showing us grace and favour, bless these waters with the sanctifying oil that they may receive your virtue; infuse into them from your heavenly throne grace and holiness. May those who go into these waters while we invoke the name of the Holy Trinity be cleansed of original sin and pardoned with perpetual blessing so that washed of their vices and confirmed with spiritual gifts they may be written into the Book of Life. Thus regenerated, may they attain new life and leave behind the old, and by the laying on of hands receive the Holy Spirit. May they be freed from present sins and gain eternal riches and be made happy by your constant and perpetual help. Amen. You live and reign in Trinity ever one God for ever and ever.

11 *Then, whoever is holding the child, hands her/him naked to the priest who asks:*
Do you renounce, child of God, the devil and all his angels? *Yes, I renounce them.*
And his works? *Yes, I renounce them.*
And his power? *Yes, I renounce them.*
What is your name? *The child's name is given*
Do you believe in God almighty? *Yes, I do believe.*

And in Jesus Christ his only-begotten Son, our Lord? *Yes, I do believe.*
And in the Holy Spirit? *Yes, I do believe.*

12 I baptise you in the name of the Father and of the Son and of the Holy Spirit so that you might have eternal life.

13 *Baptised, the child, is taken towards the priest by the one who has taken her/him from the font, and holds the child in their right arm, clothed and with head uncovered. The priest chrismates the child making the sign of the cross on the forehead saying:*
This is the sign of eternal life, that God has given to those who believe in God through Jesus Christ his Son. **Amen.**

14 *Having done that, s/he once again lays a hand on the child and says:*
O God: you conferred upon the sacrament of regeneration the union of the Holy Spirit and water so that those who receive it may have been washed and confirmed by its benefits! By the water the filth of sin is removed and the grace of the sacrament is infused, but in addition you set out that the unction of chrism be added to Holy Baptism. So that we might follow your precepts, we ask and beg that you infuse your Holy Spirit into these your servants. **Amen.**

Give them the spirit of wisdom and understanding. **Amen.**
Give them the spirit of counsel and endurance. **Amen.**
Give them the spirit of knowledge and piety. **Amen.**

Fill them with holy respect so that, as they are inspired to obey your precepts, the may receive the power of your gifts. Thus, confirmed in the name of the Trinity and by the mediation of Christ and his anointing, they might merit being made Christians.

15 *After the priest covers the head of the baptised children and goes on to give them communion.*

16 *Three days after the baptism, the children are brought again to the priest so that s/he might give them the blessing of white clothing or gowns.*
Lord Jesus Christ, Redeemer of the world who was born truly human from true humanity by the will of the Father: confirm these your servants whom you have signed with your name and washed with sacred water; by your spirit may they live in fullness as you have filled them and redeemed them with your body and blood. May these sacraments that they have received for newness of life obtain for them ceaseless salvation so that they might securely reach the reward of your blessedness. **Amen.**

17 *After this the Lord's Prayer is not said, only the blessing:*
The Lord Jesus Christ who washed you in water from his side and redeemed your with the spilling of his blood, strengthen you with the grace of the redemption that you have received. **Amen.**

May he bring you to the heavenly kingdom for which you have been born again by water and the Holy Spirit. **Amen.**

May the one who brought you to know the holy faith, confer on you perfection in your deeds and fullness of godly love. **Amen.**

18 *Having said this, the priest takes their white garments and returns to the usual place.*

THE ORDER OF CONFIRMATION (1975 SHORTENED)

⟦Translated by R.S. Clough (1899) adapted by Phillip Tovey⟧

1 *After the hymn, all that and then to be confirmed being placed standing and in order before the Bishop, the Minister shall present them, saying:*

2 Reverend Father in Christ, I present to you these persons, in order that they, making a public confession of the Christian faith, may be confirmed by you, and admitted to the Holy Communion.

3 *Bishop* May the Holy Spirit come upon them, and the power of the Most High, guard them from all sin.

4 *After which, the Bishop may give an address, if he deem it convenient so to do.*

   The address ended, the Bishop shall say:

5 Do you here in the presence of God, and of the church, and of your own free will renew the solemn profession made in your name at your baptism, confirming the same in your own persons, and promising, with the assistance of God's grace, to believe and to do all things which your Godparents acknowledged that you were bound to perform?
   I desire so to do.

6 Make, one of you, this ratification in an audible voice.
   We renew and confirm the profession of our baptism. We renounce the devil and all his works, the vain pomp and the glory of the world, with all its concupiscence, and the sinful desires of the flesh. We promise, with the help of divine grace, to live and die in the face of Jesus Christ, and to keep the commandments of God all the days of our life.

7 Is this the promise of every one of you before God, and his church?
   Each one shall answer: **Yes.**

8 God Almighty who has given to you the will to make this promise, grant you also grace and strength to keep it; through Jesus Christ our Lord. **Amen.**

9 Our help is in the name of the Lord.
   Who has made heaven and earth.
   Blessed be the name of the Lord.
   From this time forth and for evermore.
   Hear, O Lord, our prayer.
   And let our cry come unto you.

10 *Bishop* O Almighty and everlasting God, who vouchsafes to the regenerate the pardon of all their sins, and grace whereby to persevere in your love and obedience; strengthen, we beseech you, these your servants with the Holy Spirit is the Comforter, and daily increase in them the manifold gifts of your grace; the spirit of wisdom and understanding; the spirit of counsel and ghostly strength; the spirit of knowledge and true godliness; and fill them, O Lord, with the spirit of your holy fear, now and for ever. **Amen.**
   Through your mercy, O our God, who are blessed, and lives and governs all things, world without end. **Amen.**

11 *The candidates kneel before the bishop and he lays his hand on each one.*

⟦12 Confirmation prayer **CF5** in singular said by bishop.⟧

13   O Lord Jesus Christ, grant, we beseech you, that your servants, quickened by your Spirit, strengthened by your power, illuminated by your splendour, and filled with your grace, may walk day by day, leaning upon your divine help. Grant them O Lord, a lively faith, a perfect love, and true humility. Grant that they may be in them simple affection, strong patients, persevering obedience, a perpetual peace, a pure mind, a bright and clean part, a firm will, a holy conscience, sincere repentance, spiritual strength, and understand life; so that after they have fought a good fight, manfully finished the course, and faithfully kept their faith, they may receive the crown of righteousness, which you will give in that day to all who love your coming. **Amen.**

14   Graciously look upon all of us, all and young, and vouchsafe, we beseech you, to direct, sanctify, and govern, both our hearts and bodies, in the ways of your laws, and in the works of your commandments; that, through your most mighty protection both here and ever, we may be preserved in body and soul, in the name and through the merits of and Lord and saviour Jesus Christ. **Amen.**

15   *The candidates receive a New Testament.*

C. North America

9. The Anglican Church of Canada

Christianity came to Canada with the French and British settlement. In 1534 Jacques Cartier arrived under the commission of the king of France. What became Canada was already known to fishermen; this marked the beginning of settlement. In 1576 Martin Frobisher made expeditions to find the Northwest Passage. Frobisher had a chaplain with him and celebrated Holy Communion, the first recorded Anglican service in Canada. As people settled, services were led by lay people in the scattered communities. From 1698 SPCK supported mission work in Canada later assisted by SPG. In 1787 Charles Inglis was appointed the first Bishop in Canada after the American Revolutionary War. Canada became a Confederation in 1867, and in 1893 the church became a separate Province.

Worship in Canada was at first with the Book of Common Prayer (1662). This was revised to *Common Prayer Canada* in 1918[32] and then again in 1959.[33] The *Book of Alternative Services* was authorized in 1985 and includes the archetypal service of baptism in the Holy Communion for adults and infants. This enables full sacramental initiation and confirmation, reaffirmation and reception. Children receive Communion from their baptism and supplementary baptismal resources exist online for catechumenal approaches and for the restoration of the lapsed. The following is the main service from the BAS.

THE BOOK OF ALTERNATIVE SERVICES 1985

HOLY BAPTISM

THE GATHERING OF THE COMMUNITY

1a *All stand. The presiding celebrant greets the community.*
The grace of our Lord Jesus Christ, and the love of God, and the fellowship of the Holy Spirit, be with you all. **And also with you.**

1b *Or from Easter Day through the Day of Pentecost,*
Alleluia! Christ is risen.
The Lord is risen indeed. Alleluia!
May his grace and peace be with you.
May he fill our hearts with joy.

---

32 G 1922: 1–7, J 34–38.
33 G 1959: 2–3 and in French 36/77, J 86–94.

2 *The celebrant then continues,*
There is one body and one Spirit,
There is one hope in God's call to us;
One Lord, one faith, one baptism,
One God and Father of all.

3 *The Collect of the Day*

THE PROCLAMATION OF THE WORD

⟦4 Readings, psalms and sermon.⟧

PRESENTATION AND EXAMINATION OF THE CANDIDATES

5 *The celebrant says,*
The candidate(s) for Holy Baptism will now be presented.

ADULTS AND OLDER CHILDREN

6 *Candidates able to answer for themselves are presented by their parents and sponsors as follows:*
I present N to receive the sacrament of baptism.

The celebrant asks each candidate when presented,
Do you desire to be baptized?
I do.

INFANTS AND YOUNGER CHILDREN

7 *Then the candidates unable to answer for themselves are presented individually by their parents and sponsors as follows:*
I present N to receive the sacrament of baptism.

When all have been presented the celebrant asks the parents and sponsors,
Will you be responsible for seeing that the child you present is nurtured in the faith and life of the Christian community?
I will, with God's help.

Celebrant Will you by your prayers and witness help this child to grow into the full stature of Christ?
I will, with God's help.

8 *Then the celebrant asks the following questions of the candidates who can speak for themselves, and of the parents and sponsors who speak on behalf of the infants and younger children.*
Do you renounce Satan and all the spiritual forces of wickedness that rebel against God?
I renounce them.
Do you renounce the evil powers of this world which corrupt and destroy the creatures of God?
I renounce them.
Do you renounce all sinful desires that draw you from the love of God?
I renounce them.
Do you turn to Jesus Christ and accept him as your Saviour?
I do.
Do you put your whole trust in his grace and love?
I do.
Do you promise to obey him as your Lord?
I do.

9 *When there are others to be presented, the bishop says,*
The other candidate(s) will now be presented.
Presenters I present *these persons* for Confirmation.
or I present *these persons* to be received into this Communion.
or I present *these persons* who *desire* to reaffirm *their* baptismal vows.

The bishop asks the candidates,
Do you reaffirm your renunciation of evil?
I do.
Do you renew your commitment to Jesus Christ?
I do.
Do you put your whole trust in his grace and love?
I do, and with God's grace I will follow him as my Saviour and Lord.

10 *After all have been presented, the celebrant addresses the congregation, saying,*
Will you who witness these vows do all in your power to support *these persons* in *their* life in Christ? **We will.**

PRAYERS FOR THE CANDIDATES

⟦11 A short litany.⟧

THE CELEBRATION OF BAPTISM

THANKSGIVING OVER THE WATER

12a *The celebrant blesses the water, using one of the following forms.*
The Lord be with you.
And also with you.
Let us give thanks to the Lord our God.
It is right to give our thanks and praise.
We give you thanks, almighty God and Father, for by the gift of water you nourish and sustain all living things.
Blessed be God for ever.
We give you thanks that through the waters of the Red Sea, you led your people out of slavery to freedom in the promised land.
Blessed be God for ever.
We give you thanks for sending your Son Jesus. For us he was baptized by John in the river Jordan. For us he was anointed as Christ by your Holy Spirit. For us he suffered the baptism of his own death and resurrection, setting us free from the bondage of sin and death, and opening to us the joy and freedom of everlasting life.
Blessed be God for ever.
We give you thanks for your Holy Spirit who teaches us and leads us into all truth, filling us with his gifts so that we might proclaim the gospel to all nations and serve you as a royal priesthood.
Blessed be God for ever.
We give you thanks for you have called *N* to new life through the waters of baptism. Now sanctify this water, that your servants who are washed in it may be made one with Christ in his death and resurrection, to be cleansed and delivered from all sin. Anoint them with your Holy Spirit and bring them to new birth in the family of your Church, that they may become inheritors of your glorious kingdom.
We give you praise and honour and worship through your Son Jesus Christ our Lord, in the unity of the Holy Spirit, now and for ever.
Blessed are you, our strength and song, and our salvation.

or the following:

12b The Lord be with you.
  And also with you.
  Let us give thanks to the Lord our God.
  It is right to give our thanks and praise.
  We thank you, Almighty God, for the gift of water. Over water the Holy Spirit
  moved in the beginning of creation. Through water you led the children of Israel
  out of their bondage in Egypt into the land of promise. In water your Son Jesus
  received the baptism of John and was anointed by the Holy Spirit as the Messiah, the
  Christ, to lead us, through his death and resurrection, from the bondage of sin into
  everlasting life.

  We thank you, Father, for the water of baptism. In it we are buried with Christ in his
  death. By it we share in his resurrection. Through it we are reborn by the Holy Spirit.
  Therefore in joyful obedience to your Son, we bring into his fellowship those who
  come to him in faith, baptizing them in the name of the Father, and of the Son, and of
  the Holy Spirit.
  Now sanctify this water by the power of your Holy Spirit, that those who are here
  cleansed from sin and born again, may continue for ever in the risen life of Jesus
  Christ our Saviour.
  To him, to you, and to the Holy Spirit, be all honour and glory, now and for ever.
  Amen.

  The celebrant then says these or similar words.
  Let us join with those who are committing themselves to Christ and renew our own
  baptismal covenant.

THE BAPTISMAL COVENANT

⟦13 Question and answer Apostles' Creed **CF2b**⟧

14 Will you continue in the apostles' teaching and fellowship, in the breaking of bread,
  and in the prayers?
  I will, with God's help.
  Will you persevere in resisting evil and, whenever you fall into sin, repent and return
  to the Lord?
  I will, with God's help.
  Will you proclaim by word and example the good news of God in Christ?
  I will, with God's help.
  Will you seek and serve Christ in all persons, loving
  your neighbour as yourself?
  I will, with God's help.
  Will you strive for justice and peace among all people, and respect the dignity of every
  human being?
  I will, with God's help.

THE BAPTISM

15 *Each candidate is presented by name to the celebrant, or to an assisting priest or deacon,
  who then immerses, or pours water upon, the candidates, saying,*

  N, I baptize you in the name of the Father, and of the Son, and of the Holy Spirit.
  Amen.

16 *The celebrant makes the sign of the cross on the forehead of each one (using chrism if desired) saying to each,*
I sign you with the cross, and mark you as Christ's own for ever.

17 *The celebrant, at a place in the full sight of the congregation, prays over the newly baptized, saying,*
Heavenly Father,
we thank you that by water and the Holy Spirit
you have bestowed upon *these* your *servants*
the forgiveness of sin,
and have raised *them* to the new life of grace.
Sustain *them*, O Lord, in your Holy Spirit.
Give *them* an inquiring and discerning heart,
the courage to will and to persevere,
a spirit to know and to love you,
and the gift of joy and wonder
in all your works. **Amen.**

THE GIVING OF THE LIGHT

18 *One of the ministers may then give to each of the newly baptized a lighted candle, saying,*
Receive the light of Christ,
to show that you have passed from darkness to light.

Let your light so shine before others
that they may see your good works
and glorify your Father in heaven.

19 Let us welcome the newly baptized.
We receive you into the household of God.
Confess the faith of Christ crucified,
proclaim his resurrection,
and share with us in his eternal priesthood.

AT CONFIRMATION, RECEPTION, OR REAFFIRMATION

20 *The bishop says to the congregation,*
Let us now pray for *these persons* who have renewed *their* commitment to Christ.

21 *Silence may be kept.*

22 *Then the bishop says,*
Almighty God, we thank you that by the death and
resurrection of your Son Jesus Christ you have overcome sin
and brought us to yourself, and that by the sealing of your
Holy Spirit you have bound us to your service. Renew in *these*
your *servants* the covenant you made with *them* at *their* baptism.
Send *them* forth in the power of that Spirit to perform the
service you set before *them*; through Jesus Christ your Son our
Lord, who lives and reigns with you and the Holy Spirit, one
God, now and for ever. **Amen.**

The bishop lays his hand upon each one and says,

FOR CONFIRMATION

23a Strengthen, O Lord, your servant N with your Holy Spirit;
empower *him/her* for your service; and sustain *him/her* all the days of *his/her* life.
Amen.

or this:

23b Confirmation prayer **CF5** in singular

FOR RECEPTION

24 N, we recognize you as a member of the one holy catholic and apostolic Church, and
we receive you into the fellowship of this Communion. God, the Father, Son, and
Holy Spirit, bless, preserve, and keep you. **Amen.**

FOR REAFFIRMATION

25 N, may the Holy Spirit, who has begun a good work in you, direct and uphold you in
the service of Christ and his kingdom.
Amen.

26 *Then the bishop says,*
Almighty and everliving God, let your fatherly hand ever be
over *these* your *servants*; let your Holy Spirit ever be with *them*;
and so lead *them* in the knowledge and obedience of your
word, that *they* may serve you in this life, and dwell with you
in the life to come; through Jesus Christ our Lord. **Amen.**

THE PEACE

⟦27 The service continues with the peace and Eucharist.⟧

10. The Episcopal Church (The United States of America and provinces outside the USA)

Christianity came to what became the United States with European settlement. Different colonies reflected different traditions. Jamestown in Virginia became a royal colony in 1607 and Holy Communion was celebrated according to Anglican rites. The Pilgrim Fathers settled in New England in 1620 bringing the Puritan tradition. Anglican ministry was supported by the SPG, who ministered to settlers, slaves and Native Americans. The American Revolution brought great change to the colonies, and in 1783 Samuel Seabury was elected by the clergy as Bishop of Connecticut. He was consecrated in Aberdeen in 1784. Local Conventions were followed by the first General Convention of 1785. The process began of creating a new prayer book. A proposed version appeared in 1786 and the first American prayer book was published in 1789.[34] Numerous minor amendments were made to the prayer book between 1789 and 1871.[35] Then two major revisions were made in 1892[36] and 1928.[37]

The current rites of the Episcopal Church are from the 1979 *Book of Common Prayer*.[38] Considerable discussion occurred over the baptism service and its theology. The present text points the church strongly in the direction of sacramental initiation being completed in baptism. This is symbolized in the chrismation of the candidate immediately after baptism. The steps towards the new service included *Prayer Book Studies 18* and *Prayer Book Studies 26* which moved away from the theology of Gregory Dix on baptism and confirmation and towards the new pattern. This new theology is expressed in the introduction to the service in this way: 'Holy Baptism is full initiation by water and the Holy Spirit into Christ's Body the Church.' The service of holy baptism is a separate section in the ordering of the book, while confirmation is a subsection of pastoral offices. This indicates the theological trend in the Episcopal Church. The renewal of baptismal vows is included within the Easter vigil.

The 1970 General Convention allowed children to be admitted to Communion before confirmation. No service of first Communion was provided as baptism was regarded as performing this function. *The Book of Occasional Services* (1988) includes a number of services relating to the catechumenate and services for reaffirmation of the baptismal covenant in different contexts. It also includes prayers for the consecration of chrism.

---

34 G 1790: 13.
35 G 1871: 17.
36 G 1892: 4&5.
37 G 1928: 5–11, J 54–60.
38 G 1979: 1.

HOLY BAPTISM

⟦1 Introduction called Concerning the Service.⟧

2   *A hymn, psalm, or anthem may be sung.*

3a Blessed be God: Father, Son, and Holy Spirit.
   And blessed be his kingdom, now and for ever. Amen.

3b *In place of the above, from Easter Day through the Day of Pentecost*
   Alleluia. Christ is risen.
   The Lord is risen indeed. Alleluia.

3c *In Lent and on other penitential occasions*
   Bless the Lord who forgives all our sins;
   His mercy endures for ever.

4   *The Celebrant then continues*
   There is one Body and one Spirit;
   There is one hope in God's call to us;
   One Lord, one Faith, one Baptism;
   One God and Father of all.

5   The Lord be with you.
   And also with you.

   Let us pray.

THE COLLECT OF THE DAY

⟦6 The Lessons and sermon as in the Eucharist.⟧

PRESENTATION AND EXAMINATION OF THE CANDIDATES

7   The Candidate(s) for Holy Baptism will now be presented.

ADULTS AND OLDER CHILDREN

8   *The candidates who are able to answer for themselves are presented individually by their Sponsors, as follows*

   Sponsor   I present N. to receive the Sacrament of Baptism.
   Do you desire to be baptized?
   I do.

INFANTS AND YOUNGER CHILDREN

9   *Then the candidates unable to answer for themselves are presented individually by their Parents and Godparents, as follows*

   Parents and Godparents
   I present N. to receive the Sacrament of Baptism.

   When all have been presented the Celebrant asks the parents and godparents
   Will you be responsible for seeing that the child you present is brought up in the Christian faith and life?
   I will, with God's help.

Celebrant

Will you by your prayers and witness help this child to grow into the full stature of Christ?

I will, with God's help.

10   *Then the Celebrant asks the following questions of the candidates who can speak for themselves, and of the parents and godparents who speak on behalf of the infants and younger children*

Do you renounce Satan and all the spiritual forces of wickedness that rebel against God?

I renounce them.

Do you renounce the evil powers of this world which corrupt and destroy the creatures of God?

I renounce them.

Do you renounce all sinful desires that draw you from the love of God?

I renounce them.

Do you turn to Jesus Christ and accept him as your Savior?

I do.

Do you put your whole trust in his grace and love?

I do.

Do you promise to follow and obey him as your Lord?

I do.

11   *When there are others to be presented, the Bishop says*

The other Candidate(s) will now be presented.

I present *these persons* for Confirmation.

or I present *these persons* to be received into this Communion.

or I present *these persons* who *desire* to reaffirm their baptismal vows.

12   *The Bishop asks the candidates*

Do you reaffirm your renunciation of evil?

I do.

Do you renew your commitment to Jesus Christ?

I do, and with God's grace I will follow him as my Savior and Lord.

13   *After all have been presented, the Celebrant addresses the congregation, saying*

Will you who witness these vows do all in your power to support *these persons* in *their* life in Christ?

We will.

14   *The Celebrant then says these or similar words*

Let us join with *those* who are committing *themselves* to Christ and renew our own baptismal covenant.

THE BAPTISMAL COVENANT

〚13   Question and answer Apostles' Creed **CF2b**〛

14   Will you continue in the apostles' teaching and fellowship, in the breaking of bread, and in the prayers?

I will, with God's help.

Will you persevere in resisting evil, and, whenever you fall into sin, repent and return to the Lord?

I will, with God's help.

Will you proclaim by word and example the Good News of God in Christ?
I will, with God's help.

Will you seek and serve Christ in all persons, loving your neighbor as yourself?
I will, with God's help.

Will you strive for justice and peace among all people, and respect the dignity of every human being?
I will, with God's help.

PRAYERS FOR THE CANDIDATES

15 *The Celebrant then says to the congregation*
Let us now pray for *these persons* who *are* to receive the Sacrament of new birth [and for those (this person) who *have* renewed *their* commitment to Christ.]

16 *A Person appointed leads the following petitions*

Leader Deliver *them*, O Lord, from the way of sin and death.
Lord, hear our prayer.

Leader Open *their hearts* to your grace and truth.
Lord, hear our prayer.

Leader Fill *them* with your holy and lifegiving Spirit.
Lord, hear our prayer.

Leader Keep *them* in the faith and communion of your holy Church.
Lord, hear our prayer.

Leader Teach *them* to love others in the power of the Spirit.
Lord, hear our prayer.

Leader Send *them* into the world in witness to your love.
Lord, hear our prayer.

Leader Bring *them* to the fullness of your peace and glory.
Lord, hear our prayer.

Grant, O Lord, that all who are baptized into the death of Jesus Christ your Son may live in the power of his resurrection and look for him to come again in glory; who lives and reigns now and for ever. ***Amen.***

THANKSGIVING OVER THE WATER

17 The Lord be with you.
And also with you.

Let us give thanks to the Lord our God.
It is right to give him thanks and praise.

We thank you, Almighty God, for the gift of water. Over it the Holy Spirit moved in the beginning of creation. Through it you led the children of Israel out of their bondage in Egypt into the land of promise. In it your Son Jesus received the baptism of John and was anointed by the Holy Spirit as the Messiah, the Christ, to lead us, through his death and resurrection, from the bondage of sin into everlasting life.

We thank you, Father, for the water of Baptism. In it we are buried with Christ in his death. By it we share in his resurrection. Through it we are reborn by the Holy Spirit. Therefore in joyful obedience to your Son, we bring into his fellowship those who come to him in faith, baptizing them in the Name of the Father, and of the Son, and of the Holy Spirit.

At the following words, the Celebrant touches the water
Now sanctify this water, we pray you, by the power of your Holy Spirit, that those who here are cleansed from sin and born again may continue for ever in the risen life of Jesus Christ our Savior.

To him, to you, and to the Holy Spirit, be all honor and glory, now and for ever. **Amen.**

CONSECRATION OF THE CHRISM

18   *The Bishop may then consecrate oil of Chrism, placing a hand on the vessel of oil, and saying*
Eternal Father, whose blessed Son was anointed by the Holy Spirit to be the Savior and servant of all, we pray you to consecrate this oil, that those who are sealed with it may share in the royal priesthood of Jesus Christ; who lives and reigns with you and the Holy Spirit, for ever and ever. **Amen.**

THE BAPTISM

19   *Each candidate is presented by name to the Celebrant, or to an assisting priest or deacon, who then immerses, or pours water upon, the candidate, saying*
N., I baptize you in the Name of the Father, and of the Son, and of the Holy Spirit. Amen.

When this action has been completed for all candidates, the Bishop or Priest, at a place in full sight of the congregation, prays over them, saying

20   Let us pray.
Heavenly Father, we thank you that by water and the Holy Spirit you have bestowed upon *these* your servants the forgiveness of sin, and have raised *them* to the new life of grace. Sustain *them,* O Lord, in your Holy Spirit. Give *them* an inquiring and discerning heart, the courage to will and to persevere, a spirit to know and to love you, and the gift of joy and wonder in all your works. **Amen.**

21   *Then the Bishop or Priest places a hand on the person's head, marking on the forehead the sign of the cross [using Chrism if desired] and saying to each one*
N., you are sealed by the Holy Spirit in Baptism and marked as Christ's own for ever. **Amen.**

Or this action may be done immediately after the administration of the water and before the preceding prayer.

22   *When all have been baptized, the Celebrant says*
Let us welcome the newly baptized.

23   *Celebrant and People*
We receive you into the household of God.
Confess the faith of Christ crucified, proclaim his resurrection,
and share with us in his eternal priesthood.

24   *If Confirmation, Reception, or the Reaffirmation of Baptismal Vows is not to follow, the Peace is now exchanged*

AT CONFIRMATION, RECEPTION, OR REAFFIRMATION

25   *The Bishop says to the congregation*
Let us now pray for *these persons* who have renewed *their* commitment to Christ.

Silence may be kept.

26 Almighty God, we thank you that by the death and resurrection of your Son Jesus Christ you have overcome sin and brought us to yourself, and that by the sealing of your Holy Spirit you have bound us to your service. Renew in *these* your *servants* the covenant you made with *them* at *their* Baptism. Send *them* forth in the power of that Spirit to perform the service you set before *them*; through Jesus Christ your Son our Lord, who lives and reigns with you and the Holy Spirit, one God, now and for ever. **Amen.**

FOR CONFIRMATION

27 *The Bishop lays hands upon each one and says*

28a Strengthen, O Lord, your servant N. with your Holy Spirit; empower *him* for your service; and sustain *him* all the days of *his* life. **Amen.**

or this

⟦28b Confirmation Prayer **CF5** in singular.⟧

FOR RECEPTION

29 N., we recognize you as a member of the one holy catholic and apostolic Church, and we receive you into the fellowship of this Communion. God, the Father, Son, and Holy Spirit, bless, preserve, and keep you. **Amen.**

FOR REAFFIRMATION

30 N., may the Holy Spirit, who has begun a good work in you, direct and uphold you in the service of Christ and his kingdom. **Amen.**

31 *Then the Bishop says*
Almighty and everliving God, let your fatherly hand ever be over *these* your *servants*; let your Holy Spirit ever be with *them*; and so lead *them* in the knowledge and obedience of your Word, that *they* may serve you in this life, and dwell with you in the life to come; through Jesus Christ our Lord. **Amen.**

32 *The Peace is then exchanged*

⟦33 The directions say the preface of baptism should be used at the Eucharist.⟧

⟦34 There are directions for a non-eucharistic service and for conditional and emergency baptism.⟧

D. Central and South America

11. The Anglican Churches of Mexico, the Central American Region, Cuba, Bermuda and the Falklands

The Mexican Episcopal Church or Church of Jesus began with those who separated from Rome in the nineteenth century. In 1875 it entered into communion with the Protestant Episcopal Church and had its own liturgy *The Book of Provisional Offices* from 1894.[39] This book included offices for the baptism of children and for confirmation. From 1906 to 1995 the Mexican Episcopal Church was a part of PECUSA and used the Spanish translation of American rites. In 1995 the Mexican Episcopal Church became a separate Province within the Anglican Communion. The 1979 American baptismal rites in Spanish remain in use in Mexico.[40]

The Anglican Church of the Central American region became a Province in 1998. It continues to use the Spanish translation of the Episcopal Church's 1979 liturgy.

The Diocese of Cuba is extra-provincial and also uses the Spanish translation of the Episcopal baptismal rites.

The Anglican Church of Bermuda and the church in the Falkland Islands are extra provincial to Canterbury and use Church of England liturgy.

39 G 162/14.
40 G 162/20.

12. The Church in the Province of the West Indies

Christianity came to the West Indies with the settlements of the Spanish in the late fifteenth century. The islands were then divided between rivals, first the French, then the Dutch and finally the British. Cromwell sent commissioners to Barbados who banned the use of the prayer book. At the Restoration the 1662 Book of Common Prayer began to be used. Technically a part of the Diocese of London, there was little episcopal influence in the islands and in 1720 the jurisdiction was denied, the governor in effect operating as ordinary. As a part of the abolition of slavery the government appointed two bishops in 1824 for the religious instruction of the former slaves. They embarked upon a course of the provision of places for worship and education.

The Church in the Province of the West Indies came into being in 1883. For a long time it continued to use the Book of Common Prayer 1662. Liturgical revision began in the 1960s with *Order of Baptism and Confirmation 1964*, that was used by permission of each bishop.[41] In the 1980s a series of booklets was produced as liturgical revision quickened, e.g. *Liturgical Texts of Holy Baptism (Infants), Confirmation, and Adult Initiation –Baptism, Confirmation and Eucharist 1989*. This was the precursor to the 1995 *Book of Common Prayer*.[42]

THE BOOK OF COMMON PRAYER 1995

HOLY BAPTISM (INFANTS)

1   *One of the following Sentences shall be said by the minister.*

⟦1 Peter 1.3–5; John 3.5; Romans 6.4 written in full.⟧

THE GREETING

2   Blessed be God, Father, Son and Holy Spirit.
    Alleluia! Alleluia!
    And blessed be His Kingdom now and forever. Amen.
    Alleluia! Alleluia!

3   In Holy Baptism, the Church proclaims the Good News of Our incorporation into the Kingdom of God, a Kingdom which Jesus Christ, our Incarnate Lord, inaugurated by His life of perfect trust and obedience to the Father. By the power of the Holy Spirit, He brought into being a people for His own possession, which people we are. By the power of the Holy Spirit, we are united with Christ in Holy Baptism, sharing not only in His death but also in His resurrection, becoming God's children by adoption and

---

41 J 103–112.
42 G 1995/1.

grace, thus changing our created nature so deeply that the Holy Scripture says that in Baptism we are born again.

4 Let us therefore pray that those who have come for Baptism may receive, in this Holy Sacrament, that blessing which by nature they cannot have, that they may be made living members of the Church, which is the Body of Christ, and so be set free from the bondage of sin.

5 The Lord be with you.
And also with you.

6 Let us pray.
Heavenly Father, by the power of your Holy Spirit you gave to your children new life through the water of Baptism: Grant that this child *(these children)* raised to new life in Christ, may serve you in faith and love and may grow into the full stature of your Son Jesus Christ, who lives and reigns with you and the Holy Spirit, one God, now and forever. **Amen.**

THE PROCLAMATION OF THE WORD

⟦7 Readings, Gospel and sermon.⟧

THE PRESENTATION

8 *The minister shall invite the parents and godparents of the children who have been brought for Baptism to come forward using the following or other appropriate words.*
Let all Parents and Godparents who have brought children to be baptized now come forward.

Why do you present these children *(this child)* for Baptism?

8a *Either:*
We present these children (this child) for Baptism in order that they (he/she) may be incorporated into Christ, our Incarnate Lord.

8b *Or:*
We present these children (this child) for Baptism in order that they (he/she) may be made living members of the Church which is the Body of Christ.

9 Parents and Godparents, the children *(child)* whom you have brought for Baptism will, by reason of their *(his/her)* infancy, depend on your help and encouragement to grow in the knowledge, reverence and service of Almighty God, our Heavenly Father. You must remember, that it is also your duty to see that they *(he/she)* are *(is)* instructed in the good news of God's Salvation in Christ, the Church's Creeds and Catechism and all other things which a Christian ought to know, believe and practice as a member of the family of God.
As they *(he/she)* grow(s) up, they *(he/she)* will also need the help and encouragement of that family, so that they *(he/she)* learn(s) to be faithful in public worship and private prayer, to live by love and trust in God, and in due course to come to receive the laying on of the hands by the Bishop in Confirmation.

Will you give that help and encouragement by your prayers, by your example, and by your teaching?
I will do so, the Lord being my helper.

Will you do all in your power to see that these children *(this child)* are *(is)* brought to the Bishop to be confirmed by him and to receive the Body and Blood of our Lord and Saviour Jesus Christ in the Holy Communion?
I will do so, the Lord being my helper.

THE BAPTISMAL VOWS

10 Therefore I ask these questions which you must answer for yourself and for these children *(this child)* whom you have brought for Baptism.

Do you turn to Jesus Christ and accept Him as your Saviour?
I turn and accept Him.
Do you put your whole trust in His grace and love?
I so put my trust.
Do you promise to love God and obey Him as your Lord?
I promise.

Do you renounce Satan and all the spiritual forces of wickedness?
I do
Do you renounce injustice and all the evil powers of the world?
I do.
Do you reject sin so as to live in the freedom of God's children?
I do.

11 Let us pray

Heavenly Father, in your love you have called us to know you, led us to trust you, and united our life with yours: Surround these children *(this child)* with your love; protect them *(him/her)* from evil; sustain and guide them *(him/her)* by your Holy Spirit, and receive them *(him/her)* into the family of your Church; that they *(he/she)* may walk with us in the way of Christ and grow in the knowledge of your love. **Amen.**

Heavenly Father and giver of all grace, we ask your blessing on those who are about to be baptized and made heirs of your Heavenly Kingdom, that through the prayers, the teaching, the example, and the sharing in the life of those who love and care for them, they may grow up in the faith of Christ crucified and in the fellowship of His Church, to serve you faithfully all the days of their life; through Jesus Christ our Lord. **Amen.**

THE BLESSING OF THE WATER

12 The Lord be with you.
And also with you.
Let us give thanks to the Lord our God.
It is right to give God thanks and praise

We thank you Heavenly Father for the gift of water; over it your Holy Spirit moved in the beginning of creation; through it you led the children of Israel out of the bondage of Egypt; in it your Son Jesus received the Baptism of John and was anointed by the Holy Spirit; fulfilling His Ministry by the offering of Himself on the Cross, blood and water flowed from His side.

We thank you Heavenly Father because you have appointed the water of Baptism for the regeneration of all people, through Jesus Christ your Son. In joyful obedience to Him, we make disciples of all nations and baptize them in the name of the Father, and of the Son, and of the Holy Spirit.

Now therefore sanctify this water by the same Holy Spirit, and grant that all who are baptized in it may be united with Christ, forgiven in Him, set free from the bondage of sin and raised with Christ to eternal life.

By Him, and with Him, and in Him, in the unity of the Holy Spirit all honour and glory are yours, Almighty Father, now and forever. **Amen.**

THE PROFESSION OF FAITH

13 You have brought these children to Baptism. Will you now declare before God and His Church the Christian Faith into which these children are to be baptized and in which you will help them live and grow?
I will.

The Minister says to the congregation:

14 My brothers and sisters in Christ, let us join with those who are committing themselves to Christ and renew our Baptismal commitment.

⟦Question and answer Apostles' Creed **CF2b**.⟧

15 This is the faith of the Church.
This is our faith. We believe and trust in one God, Father, Son and Holy Spirit. (Alleluia! Alleluia!)

THE BAPTISM

16 Name this child.
*N_*

17 *The Minister then baptizes the candidates. He immerses each child in the water or pours water on (his/her) head, addressing (him/her) by name.*
N_ I baptize you in the name of the Father, and of the Son and of the Holy Spirit.
Amen.

18 *The Minister then makes the sign of the cross saying:*
God has united you to Himself and received you into His family the Church. I sign you with the cross, the sign of Christ. Do not be ashamed to confess the faith of Christ crucified. Fight valiantly against all evil and continue Christ's faithful servant to the end of your life.

19 *The Minister or another person may give a lighted candle to the parents or godparents of each child, saying:*
God has rescued us from the power of darkness and brought us into the Kingdom of His beloved Son. Receive this light and walk as a child of light.
Let your light so shine among men, that they may see your good works and give glory to your Father in heaven.

WELCOME

20 My brothers and sisters in Christ, let us welcome the newly baptized!
We welcome you into the Lord's family. We are members together of Christ, children of the same heavenly Father and inheritors together of His kingdom.

21 *A form of intercession and the Act of Penitence may follow. The Eucharist continues with The Peace.*

22 *In place of the usual Post-Communion prayer the bishop or priest says the following:*
Most merciful Father, we thank you for feeding us with the body and blood of your Son Jesus Christ, for adopting us as your own children, for incorporating us into your Holy Church, and for making us worthy to share in the inheritance of your saints in light; through Jesus Christ your Son our Lord, who lives and reigns with you and the Holy Spirit, one God for ever and ever. Amen.

⟦Directions and prayers are provided for where there is no eucharist.⟧

CONFIRMATION

THE SENTENCES

1 *One or more of the following shall be said by the Bishop*
[John 14.15–17; II Corinthians 13.14; Ephesians 4.4–6; Acts 1.8]

THE GREETING

2 Blessed be God, Father, Son and Holy Spirit.
Alleluia! Alleluia!
And blessed be His Kingdom now and for ever. Amen.
Alleluia! Alleluia!

THE DECLARATION

3 In Baptism we became members of Christ, children of the Heavenly Father, inheritors together of the Kingdom. This was the work of God who adopted us as His children and made us members of the family of God. We are to continue to grow in grace and in faith, to worship with the family and to respond to the living Word.

Through the laying on of hands in Confirmation, the indwelling Spirit enlightens, frees, transforms and sanctifies those who in Baptism were made God's children. Let us therefore pray that those who now come for Confirmation may be strengthened by the power of the Holy Spirit; and that they may live in righteousness and true holiness all their days.

4 The Lord be with you.
And also with you

5 Let us pray
Grant, Almighty God, that we, who have been redeemed from the old life of sin by our baptism into the death and resurrection of your Son Jesus Christ, may be renewed in your Holy Spirit, and live in righteousness and true holiness; through Jesus Christ our lord, who lives and reigns with you and the Holy Spirit, one God, now and for ever. **Amen.**

6 *Then shall follow the collect of the day*

THE PROCLAMATION OF THE WORD

[7 Reading(s), Gospel, sermon]

THE PRESENTATION AND EXAMINATION

8 *Reverend Father in God, I present unto you these persons who desire to reaffirm their baptismal vows.*

Have you examined them and found them ready and desirous to be confirmed?
I have examined them and found them so to be.

The Bishop then addresses the confirmands

9 You who have come to be confirmed must now renew the solemn promise and vow that you made or was made in your name at your baptism, and must pledge to believe and to do all those things which you or your Parents and Godparents then undertook.

Do you declare and promise that you will, with the help of God, live your life in the faith of Christ into which you were baptized?
I do.

Do you commit yourself in love to God, Father, Son and Holy Spirit?
I do.

Will you continue in the Apostles' teaching and fellowship, in the breaking of bread and in prayer?
I will.

Will you persevere in resisting evil and repent whenever you fall into sin?
I will.

Will you be a witness in your daily life to God's saving work in Christ?
I will.

Will you seek and serve Christ by loving your neighbour as yourself remembering that every person is loved and valued by God?
I will.

Do you put your whole trust in His grace and love?
I do, and with God's help I will follow Christ as my Saviour and Lord.

10   *The Bishop then addresses the congregation*
Will you who witness these vows do all in your power to support these persons in their life in Christ?
We will.

THE PROFESSION OF FAITH

11   Let us join with those who are to be confirmed in the profession of our Faith.

⟦Apostles Creed **CF1a**⟧

12   *The Act of Penitence may follow. All may kneel to say or sing the 'Veni Creator Spiritus' or some other hymn to the Holy Spirit.*

PRAYER FOR THE CONFIRMANDS

13   Let us pray for these persons to be confirmed, and for all the baptized everywhere.

The Bishop or a person appointed leads the following litany.
That they may be filled with your Holy and life-giving Spirit.
Lord in your mercy;
Hear our prayer.

That the Holy Spirit may open their hearts to your grace and truth.
Lord in your mercy;
Hear our prayer.

That they may be redeemed from all evil and rescued from the way of sin and death.
Lord in your mercy;
Hear our prayer.

That they may be kept in the faith and communion of your Holy Church.
Lord in your mercy;
Hear our prayer.

That they may go out into the world to witness to your love and transforming power.
Lord in your mercy;
Hear our prayer.

That they be brought to the fullness of your peace and glory.
Lord in your mercy;
Hear our prayer.

Silence may be kept.

14 *Then the Bishop says the following, stretching out his hands towards the confirmands, all kneeling.*
Father, in your Son Jesus Christ you have given to these your servants new birth in baptism by water and the Holy Spirit, and have given the forgiveness of all their sins. Let your Holy Spirit strengthen them now:
The Spirit of wisdom and understanding;
The Spirit of counsel and inward strength;
The Spirit of knowledge and true godliness;
The Spirit of reverence and true religion;
and graft in their hearts the love of your most Holy Name:
Through Jesus Christ our Lord who lives and reigns with you and the same Holy Spirit, one God now and for ever. **Amen.**

THE CONFIRMATION

15 *Then all of them in order, kneeling before the Bishop, he shall lay his hand upon the head of each of them saying:*

15a Confirm O Lord your servant N_ with your heavenly grace that *he/she* may continue yours for ever, and daily increase in your Holy Spirit more and more until *he/she* comes to your everlasting kingdom.

or

15b Strengthen O Lord your servant N_ with your Holy Spirit that *he/she* may continue yours forever, and daily increase your Holy Spirit more and more until *he/she* comes to your eternal kingdom.

And each one answers:
Amen.

16 *The Bishop may sign each one on the forehead with the Holy Chrism saying:*
The seal of the Spirit, the promise of the Father.

FOR RECEPTION

17 N_, we recognize you as a member of the one holy catholic and apostolic church, and we receive you into the fellowship of this Communion. God, the Father, Son, and Holy Spirit, bless, preserve, and keep you. **Amen.**

FOR REAFFIRMATION

18 N_, may the Holy Spirit, who has begun a good work in you, direct and uphold you in the service of Christ and his kingdom. **Amen.**

19 *The Bishop concludes with this prayer.*
Almighty and everliving God we pray for these your servants upon whom after the example of your Holy Apostles we have now laid our hands. Let your fatherly hand ever be over them, let your Holy Spirit ever be with them and so lead them in the knowledge and obedience of your word that they may faithfully serve you in this life and dwell with you in the life to come through Jesus Christ our Lord. **Amen.**

〚20 The peace and directions for the Eucharist.〛

13. The Episcopal Anglican Church of Brazil

Christianity came to Brazil with Portuguese colonisation beginning in 1500. An exception to the prohibition of Protestants was made in 1810, where chapels for British citizens of the Church of England were allowed to be built, providing they did not look like churches. These congregations lacked a mission outlook and the roots of the present church are seen more in a surprise act of God. The Theological Seminary of Virginia, at the time a place of missionary zeal, sent a couple of missionaries to Brazil in 1889. In this movement can be seen the origins of the Brazilian church, as they and successor missionaries engaged in evangelisation and church planting. The church was seen as a missionary district of the Episcopal Church, and the first Brazilian Bishop was consecrated in 1940.

Brazil became a Province in 1964, inheriting a Portuguese translation of the current American texts.[43] In 1967 a revision of American texts began. In 1988 *Livro de Oração Comum* became the official prayer book.[44] This includes two rites, the office of the sacrament of holy baptism, and confirmation. However, the rite of confirmation is separated from baptism by being in a section called 'pastoral offices'. In 2015 a new service book was produced *Livro de Oração Comum*. This includes a section of liturgies of initiation comprising of, holy baptism, confirmation and reception, and a joint celebration of baptism and confirmation and reception. Directions are included on conditional and emergency baptism.

LIVRO DO ORAÇÃO COMUM 2015

〚Translated by Joseph Fernandes〛

〚Extensive rubrics and directions〛

HOLY BAPTISM

LITURGY OF THE WORD

PREPARATION

1 Blessed be God: Father, Son and Holy Spirit. *or* Blessed be the Holy Trinity, one God.
   Blessed be his kingdom, now and forever. Amen.
   Blessed be God,
   and Father of our Lord Jesus Christ.

---

43 G 137/10.
44 G 137/12.

By his mercy born again,
for a lifetime of love and hope.
Through the resurrection of Jesus Christ,
and by making the waters of baptism.

CALL FOR CELEBRATION

2   Our Lord Jesus Christ taught us
that to enter the Kingdom of Heaven
we must be born again, in the water and the Spirit,
and he gave us baptism as a sign and seal this new birth
Through baptism, the Holy Spirit washes and cleanses.
Through baptism, we put on Christ,
dying to sin and attaining his risen life.
As sons and daughters of God, we have new dignity
and God calls us to the fullness of life.

KYRIE ELEISON

3   **Lord, have mercy on us.**   *or*   Kyrie Eleison
Christ, have mercy on us.   Christe Eleison
Lord, have mercy on us ...   Kyrie Eleison

GLORIA IN EXCELSIS

〚4   The Gloria is said or sung.〛

COLLECT OF THE DAY

5   The Lord be with you.   *or*   The Lord is here
And also with you.   **Your Spirit is with us.**

Let us pray.
Loving God,
that by our baptism
into the death and resurrection of your Son Jesus Christ,
you rescued us from the dominion of sin,
grant that we may live as new creatures
in righteousness and holiness all the days of our life.
Through Jesus Christ our Lord,
who lives and reigns with you and the Holy Spirit,
one God, now and forever.
Amen.

〚6   Two or three readings and a sermon.〛

WELCOME

7   This is the house of God. Receive our welcome!
We bring this child (person) to be received into the Church through Baptism.

8   Do you know what Holy Baptism means?
I know that, through Baptism, we are born spiritually, we join the community of believers and become forever, sons and daughters of God and disciples of Christ.
Have you thought about the commitment you assume, to accept the call of the Lord Jesus Christ?
I'm aware of the need to fulfil my part in the mission entrusted to the People of God.

9 Do you renounce evil and all the powers that rebel against God, corrupt and destroy the creatures and separate us from the love of God?
Yes! I renounce them.
Do you accept Jesus Christ as your Saviour?
Yes! Jesus Christ is my Saviour.
Do you deposit your trust in his grace and love?
Yes! I trust in the Lord.
Do you promise to follow and obey Jesus Christ as your Lord?
Yes! I promise.

10 Do you believe in all the articles of the Christian faith contained in the Creed of the Apostles?
Yes! I believe.
Do you promise to make this child (children)/person(s) live out the principles of the Christian faith, and thus when prepared be presented to the Bishop for Confirmation?
Yes! I promise.
Come, then, my brothers and my sisters, the people of this community rejoice with you, to be renewed by the receipt of this child (children)/person (s) who joins our fellowship by the bond of faith at the service of God.

BAPTISMAL COVENANT

11 Let us unite with these people and, with them, renew the vows of our Baptismal Covenant.

[Question and answer Apostles' Creed **CF2b**]

12 Will you continue in the apostles' teaching and fellowship, in the breaking of bread, and in the prayers?
With the help of God, I will.
Will you persevere in resisting evil, and if you fall into sin, repent and return to the Lord?
With the help of God, I will.
Will you proclaim by word and example the good news of the Kingdom of God?
With the help of God, I will.

INTERCESSIONS

13 The good will of our eternal Father is infinite. Let us pray for this child (children)/person(s) for our lives and for our God.
Deliver us, Lord, the way of sin and death.
Lord, hear our prayer.
Open our hearts to your grace and truth.
Lord, hear our prayer.
Fill in your holy and life-giving Spirit.
Lord, hear our prayer.
Keep us in the faith and communion of your holy Church.
Lord, hear our prayer.
Teach us how to love others in the power of the Spirit.
Lord, hear our prayer.
Send us into the world to witness your love.
Lord, hear our prayer.
Leads us to the fullness of your peace and glory.
Lord, hear our prayer.

14   Source of eternal life, grant,
      by thy Holy Spirit,
      new birth to all people
      passing through the waters of baptism.
      That they may get to know you better in the Church of your family.
      Help them in their new lives resist evil in order to continually grow in grace of our
      Lord Jesus Christ.
      Amen.

BLESSING OF THE WATER

15   The Lord is here   *or*   The Lord be with you
      His Spirit is with us.   **And also with you**

      Lift up our hearts
      We lift them up to the Lord.

      Let us give thanks to God.
      It is right and just.
      We thank you, almighty God, for the gift of water
      Over water the Holy Spirit moved in the beginning of creation;
      through water you led the children of Israel
      from slavery in Egypt to freedom in the Promised Land;
      in water your Son Jesus received the baptism of John
      and was revealed by the Holy Spirit as your Son, the Christ,
      and lead us through his death and resurrection,
      from the slavery of sin to Eternal life.
      We thank you, Father, for the water of Baptism;
      in it we follow Christ in his death,
      by it we share in his resurrection,
      and are reborn in the Holy Spirit.
      So, obedient to the command of your Son,
      we bring to his community
      all the people who come to him with faith,
      to baptize them.
      Now sanctify this water + that, by the power of your Holy Spirit,
      they may be cleansed and reborn in Christ,
      receive remission from sin
      and remain forever in the risen life
      of Jesus Christ
      our Saviour,
      to whom with you and the Holy Spirit
      be all honour and glory, now and for ever.
      Amen.

BAPTISM

16   What is the name given to this child/person?

17   N, I baptize you in the name of the Father, and of the Son, and of the Holy Spirit.
      Amen.

18   N, in Baptism you are sealed by the Holy Spirit with the sign of the Cross. + Christ
      claims you for his own. **Amen.**

19 I give you this Light, as a testimony that you have passed from darkness to light. Shine as a light in the world to the glory of God the Father.

20 Let us greet this child (children) person (persons) as a new member of the Body of Christ by saying:
Today God received you in his Church through Baptism;
we happily become the Lord's family.
We are members of the Body of Christ,
we are sons and daughters of the same Heavenly Father,
we are citizens of God's kingdom.
We confess our faith in the crucified Christ,
we proclaim his resurrection and we share in his eternal priesthood.

THE LORD'S PRAYER

21 As Christ the Saviour taught us, we join in prayer:

⟦The Lord's Prayer **CF4a**⟧

CONCLUDING PRAYERS

22 Lord Jesus Christ,
you take N
in the arms of your mercy and make him/her/them living member(s) of your Church:
give him/her/them Grace, we beg you,
to grow in your faith,
obeying your Word and
persevering in your love;
so that, strengthened by thy Holy Spirit,
they resist temptations, overcome evil,
rejoice with you in life that there is to come,
by your merits, O merciful Savior,
who with the Father and the Holy Spirit, live and reign as one God, for ever and ever.
Amen.

23 With all our heart we thank thee,
merciful God, for all that,
by your Holy Spirit,
you have deigned to give to N
receiving him/her/them, by adoption, in your family,
integrating them in your Holy Church,
making him/her/them heir(s) of your Eternal Kingdom;
through Christ, our Lord.

⟦24 The sharing of the peace, Eucharist and post communion prayers.⟧

BLESSING

25 O God of all grace,
who called us to his tender glory in Christ Jesus,
strengthen us, secure us and protect us in his faith;
and the blessing of almighty God, Father, Son and Holy Spirit,
be among us,
and remain with us forever.
Amen.

26 God delivered us from the valley of the shadow of death and prepared for us a special place, with all the saints.
You received the light of Christ, walk in that light as long as long as you live.
We live as light in this world reflecting the glory of our God.
We leave in the light of Christ. (Alleluia!)
Thanks be to God. (Alleluia!)

CONFIRMATION AND RECEPTION

LITURGY OF THE WORD

PREPARATION

1 *All the people remain standing, if possible, and the Bishop proclaims:*
Blessed be God: Father, Son and Holy Spirit *or* Blessed be the Holy Trinity, one God.
Blessed be his kingdom, now and forever. Amen.

2 God is love, God gives us life.
We love because God first loved us.
In baptism, God declared that love;
and today, invites us to affirm it.

CALL FOR CELEBRATION

3 This/these person (s) came here in order to establish a deeper commitment with our Lord Jesus Christ, renewing their baptismal vows. We are here to testify, pray and support this/these person (s) in their calling.

⟦4 Kyrie and Gloria.⟧

COLLECT

5 The Lord be with you.   *or*   The Lord is here.
And also with you   *or*   **Your Spirit is with us.**

God faithful, grant that we,
who were rescued from the dominion of sin by our baptism
in the death and resurrection of your Son Jesus Christ,
We have the renewal, by your Holy Spirit
and live in righteousness and true holiness;
through Jesus Christ our Lord,
who lives and reigns with you and the Holy Spirit,
one God, now and forever. **Amen.**

⟦6 Readings and sermon.⟧

LITURGY OF CONFIRMATION AND RECEPTION

WELCOME

7 *The person (s) is (are) to be confirmed and/or received and their proposer (s), move forward and remain standing in front of the Bishop. The proposer(s) say in unison:*
Reverend Father (Mother) in God, this/these person (s) here is (are) to be confirmed *and/or*
received in the communion of this Church.

8   *The Bishop asks those who will be confirmed:*
You are in God's presence and this congregation, to renew the solemn promise and vow you made or was made for you, in Baptism, therefore:
Do you reaffirm the renunciation of evil?
Yes! We reaffirm.
Do you renew your commitment to Jesus Christ?
Yes! And by the grace of God we will follow him as Lord and Savior.
Do you believe that this Church is part the true Church, One, Holy, Catholic and Apostolic Church of Christ?
Yes! We believe.
Do you promise to be faithful to the teaching, discipline and worship of this Church?
Yes! We promise.

9   *The Bishop asks the congregation:*
And you who are witnesses of these vows, will you do everything in your power to encourage this/these people in your life in Christ?
We will, with God's help.

BAPTISMAL PROFESSION

10   Let us unite with these people and with them, renew the vows of our Baptismal Covenant.

⟦Question and answer Apostles Creed **CF2b**⟧

11   Will you persevere in the doctrine of the apostles, in fellowship, in the breaking of bread and prayer?
I will, with God's help.
Will you continue resisting evil and, if you fall into sin, always seek, in repentance, forgiveness from the Lord?
I will, with God's help.
Will you proclaim through word and example, the good news of God's Kingdom?
I will, with God's help.
Will you endeavor to teach, baptize and nurture new faithful people into the fold of Christ?
I will, with God's help.
Will you seek to respond to human needs with love, serving Christ in every person?
I will, with God's help.
Will you seek to transform unjust structures of society, defying all sorts of violence, respecting the dignity of every human person and seeking peace and reconciliation?
I will, with God's help.
Will you fight to safeguard the integrity of creation?
I will, with God's help.

INTERCESSIONS

12   *Keep a few moments of silence. The person administering says:*
The good will of our Heavenly Father is infinite.
Let us pray for this/these person (s)
who came to reaffirm their commitment to Christ.

Keep up a few moments of silence.

Free us, O Lord, the way of sin and death.
Lord, hear our prayer.
Open your hearts to your grace and truth.
Lord, hear our prayer.

Fill us with your holy and life-giving Spirit.
Lord, hear our prayer.
Keep us in the faith and fellowship of your Church.
Lord, hear our prayer.
Teach us how to love others in the power of the Spirit.
Lord, hear our prayer.
Send us to the world, to witness your love.
Lord, hear our prayer.
Carry us to the fullness of your peace and glory.
Lord, hear our prayer.

13 *The Bishop concludes with the following prayer:*
Gracious God,
we thank you because,
through the death and resurrection of your Son Jesus Christ,
you conquered death and sin
and brought us to life with you,
and because by the anointing of the Holy Spirit,
you committed us to your service.
Renew in these thy servants and handmaids
the covenant you made at baptism.
Send these people, in the power of the same Spirit,
to do the work that you have prepared for them,
through Jesus Christ your Son, our Lord,
who lives and reigns with you and the Holy Spirit,
one God, now and forever. **Amen.**

CONFIRMATION

14 *The Bishop imposes his hand on each person saying:*
Strengthen, O Lord, thy son/daughter N with thy Holy Spirit;
Give him/her power to serve you and sustains him/her all the days of his/her life.
Amen.

   or

Protect, O God, thy son/daughter N with your heavenly grace,
in order to continue to be yours forever;
and day by day increasingly grow in your Holy Spirit,
until it comes to your everlasting kingdom. **Amen.**

RECEPTION

15 *The Bishop taking the right hand of each person will say:*
N, I admit you to the communion of this Church.
With joy, we receive you in our midst.
The peace of the Lord be always with you.
In the name of the Father and of the Son and of the Holy Spirit. **Amen.**

16 *If there is the celebration of Holy Communion, the Lord's Prayer is omitted*

THE LORD'S PRAYER

17 As Christ the Savior taught us, so we pray:
   ⟦The Lord's Prayer **CF4a**⟧

18 *If there is a Eucharist, the following closing prayer can be omitted:*

CLOSING PRAYER

19 Everlasting God,
We pray thy hand is always extended
on these your sons and daughters;
granting them continuously, your Holy Spirit,
so that they remain in the knowledge
and obedience of your Word,
to serve you in this life
and dwell with you in the life to come,
through Jesus Christ our Lord. **Amen.**

[20 Directions for the peace and on receiving communion.]

POST-COMMUNION

21 Living God,
we have sought to be strengthened
in the sacred mysteries
the Body and Blood of our Lord,
we pray that you may sustain us,
so that we are strength and hope to the world,
and fulfil our baptismal promises
and the Gospel of our Lord Jesus Christ,
who lives and reigns with you and the Holy Spirit,
now and forever. **Amen.**

BLESSING

22 *The Bishop, gives this or another blessing.*
God of all grace,
who called us to His eternal glory in Christ Jesus
strengthen us, steady us and protect us in faith;
and the blessing of God omnipotent,
Father, Son and Holy Spirit,
be with us, and abide with us forever. **Amen.**

FAREWELL

23 *It is the privilege of the Deacon, when present, to do the farewell:*
The light of Christ is in you. Shine as light in this world.
As the seed grows on the ground,
and yeast gives life to the bread,
may the power of God work in us:
as a city on the hill,
as a lamp in the darkness.
Let us be witnesses to the light of the Kingdom!
We depart in the light of Christ. (Hallelujah!)
Thanks be to God. (Hallelujah!)

14. The Province of the Southern Cone of South America

Christianity came to the Southern Cone with the Spanish colonization. Anglicans came through the influence of Captain Alan Gardiner (d. 1851) who longed for missionary work in Patagonia and effectively developed the South American Missionary Society. It was supplemented by the development from the mid-1820s of chaplaincies in the main towns. Outreach began to the Spanish population and to various indigenous tribes. In 1869 a bishop of the Falkland Islands was consecrated to oversee the missionary work in South America. Gradually there was a division of the work resulting in the Province being formed in 1983. It inherited various translations of Anglican rites into Spanish and Indian languages.[45] Its constitution recognized liturgical diversity in the Province with the bishop responsible for keeping worship within Anglican norms. The 1966 Sao Paulo Report encouraged liturgical inculturation.

The 1973 *Libro de Oracion Comun y Manual de la Iglesia Anglicana*,[46] originally of the Diocese of Chile, is still used today in some dioceses as their official prayer book. There is a long section at the end of the service called Notes which deals with two issues. One is to do with infant baptism and faith, recognizing that some people have problems when they have been baptized as a child in a context with minimal faith. While teaching that normally baptism is not repeated, the note does seem to imply that it is possible to rebaptize people who have issues of conscience over their infant baptism. It uses Acts 19.5 – Paul baptizing the disciples of John the Baptist in the name of Jesus Christ – as a justification for more than one baptism. The second note is on the quantity of water, although immersion at any age is appropriate.

LIBRO DE ORACIÓN COMÚN Y MANUAL DE LA IGLESIA ANGLICANA 1973

[Translated by Andii Bowsher]

ORDER OF BAPTISM

1 *INTRODUCTION*

Baptism is the sacrament which the Lord has ordained as a symbol of the entry of a person into the family of God and into the Kingdom of Heaven.
This sign speaks not only of the grace of God freely offered to us but also of the desire of the candidate to be washed and cleaned to receive the blessings of forgiveness and of new life that are offered by the sacrifice of Jesus Christ his death on the cross.

---

45 G 88/1 Lengua, G 109/1 Wichi, G 194/1 Yaghan.
46 G 162/19.

The visible part of baptism does not have effective value by itself but with a true repentance and a lively faith, signifies the union of the believer with Christ in his death and resurrection. It also speaks to us of the washing away of sin and of the outpouring of the Holy Spirit who God offers to all those who believe in Jesus Christ. Baptism is for believers but also it is appropriate for their children because God makes his covenant in the Old Testament with Abraham and his children; and in the New Testament, Peter proclaimed the forgiveness of sin and the promise of the Holy Spirit for all those who believe and for their children.

2   THE WORD OF GOD

⟦One or more appropriate readings are suggested from a list of readings.⟧

3   PRESENTATION

The Candidates stand before the congregation and, in the case of children, also those who will speak on their behalf.
Minister: to the congregation.
It is my responsibility to present to you this person who professes a faith in Jesus Christ and desires baptism in the name of the Father, the Son and the Holy Spirit; and in front of all I wish to question them as to their profession of faith.

4   EXAMINATION

Minister: to the candidates and/or their sponsors.
All who wish to receive the sacrament of baptism because they receive Jesus Christ for forgiveness of sin and salvation of life, you must answer the following questions in the presence of God and of this congregation:

4a   RENUNCIATION OF SIN

Do you recognise that from birth you are a sinner and by nature you cannot please God?
Yes, I recognise it.
Do you repent of all your sins?
Yes, I repent of all (of them)
Do you renounce the works of the devil, the vain things of this world and all that is impure and carnal in your human nature?
Yes, I renounce all this.

4b   PROFESSION OF FAITH

I require that you repeat with the rest of the congregation the Christian faith in the words of the Apostles' Creed.
All stand.
⟦The Apostles' Creed **CF1a**⟧
The congregation sit.
Do you believe in this faith?
Yes, I believe in this faith.
Do you trust in Jesus Christ, in the Son of God as your Saviour and Lord?
Yes, in Him I trust.

4c   PROMISES

Will you follow obediently the holy will of God and fulfil his commands to walk in them all the days of your life?
This I will do, with the help of the Lord.

If there are children to baptise, the minister continues thus:

You have made these promises in your own name and on behalf of *this child*. Now it is necessary to recognise the great responsibility which you have to help to nurture this child so that s/he understands and appreciates the significance of what we have done today. Therefore, I ask you:

Will you nurture *this child* in a Christian home and in the fear of God, giving him/her a wholesome example and discipline your own life so as to cause no stumbling in her/his life?
This I will do, with the help of the Lord.
Will you pray for her/him faithfully?
This I will do, with the help of God.
Will you teach him/her to pray, to read the Bible and to follow the Christian faith, guiding him/her into the Church of Christ so that s/he comes to personally know and trust in Jesus Christ and so prepare him/her for confirmation of the promises that you have made on his/her behalf in his/her own name?
This I will do, with the help of the Lord.

Let us pray to the Lord for his grace to fulfil these promises and so receive his blessing.
Oh heavenly Father who have given us the privilege and the responsibility to care for children in the unity of the family, and have said to us by your Son Jesus Christ that you are always disposed to receive them; give, we ask, to these people the grace to keep the promises made in the name of this child that s/he may come to a full knowledge of God through Jesus Christ our Saviour. Amen.

5   *BAPTISM*

Eternal and almighty God whose Son left us his command to make disciples baptising them in the name of the Father, the Son and the Holy Spirit, we ask your grace for this *your servant* that we are to baptise in your name. Make holy this water for the symbolic taking away of her/his sin and the pouring out of the Holy Spirit so that s/he may remain always among the number of your chosen people through Jesus Christ our Lord. **Amen.**

For a child: N, Son/Daughter of the Covenant
For an adult: N, Son/Daughter of the Covenant and Believer in the Promise

I baptise you in the name of the Father, the Son and the Holy Spirit.

6   *RECEPTION*

We receive this person with pleasure as a *brother/sister* in the Church of Christ.

I sign you with the sign of the cross to show that you do not need to be ashamed to confess faith in Christ crucified, that you are a soldier to fight valiantly beneath his banner against sin, the world and the devil and that you must continue as a faithful servant of Christ until your life's end.

In the case of adults, if the Bishop is present, Confirmation can follow from paragraph 5 or if the minister believes that it is convenient, the confirmation can take place on another occasion after further instruction and preparation.

7   *PRAYERS*

Let us give thanks to God for the increase in the family of Christ, joining in the family prayer:

[The Lord's Prayer **CF4a**]

We give thanks, Oh Heavenly Father, that your promises are for us and for our children and that you receive *this person* into your family as your own adopted child, Humbly we ask that, obeying your word and renewed by your Holy Spirit, s/he might grow in likeness to Jesus Christ and remain always in the company of your Church for the glory of your name. **Amen.**

The Minister or other invited members may add further intercessions here.

8   **SERMON**

Hymn

9   **BLESSING**

May the God of peace who raised from the dead our Lord Jesus Christ the great shepherd of the sheep by the blood of the eternal covenant, make you apt in every good work that you may do his will, doing in you what is agreeable before him, through Jesus Christ to whom be the glory for all ages. **Amen.**

ORDER OF CONFIRMATION

1   *INTRODUCTION*

Confirmation is a rite of great antiquity in the church, preserved for good order in the congregation. It is an occasion when the candidates can publicly confirm their baptismal promises. At the same time, it is the traditional service to admit members into full communion in our Church. In the Holy Scriptures, the laying-on of hands has various meaning: some of which are important in our service of confirmation. Often in the biblical story, this act shows a spirit of love and sympathy among all those who participate and it is associated with prayer for some special blessing for those who receive the laying-on of hands. Some were healed of their illnesses; others received the Holy Spirit and his gifts. On various occasions, it signified receiving a special commission in the work of the Lord and an expression of fuller participation in the life of the Church. It is our desire even today, that the time of confirmation might be an opportunity to give public witness to the faith and to receive a special blessing of the Holy Spirit and to make a greater commitment to the service of Jesus Christ.

2   *THE WORD OF GOD*

Let us hear now the Word of the Lord.
〖These readings are suggested, Jn. 3.1–8; Act. 8.14–24; Act. 19.1–7; Gal. 5.16–25.〗

3   *PRESENTATION*

Lord Bishop, it is my pleasure, in the name of the Church, to present to you *these candidates* for confirmation. *All are* baptised and born again by the Spirit of God. They have received instruction in the Christian faith and desire to be full members in our company participating with us in the Lord's Supper and in the whole life of the Church.

4   *EXAMINATION*

Bishop: Those who are going to be confirmed must declare their loyalty to Christ and their rejection of all that is sinful; to this end, in the presence of God and of this congregation, I ask of each one of you.

4a   *RENUNCIATION OF SIN*

Do you recognise that from birth you were a sinner and that your human nature cannot please God?

Yes: I recognise it.
Do you repent of all your sins?
Yes, I repent of all of them.
Do you renounce the works of the devil, the vain things of the world and all that is impure and carnal in your human nature?
Yes, I renounce all of this.

4b PROFESSION OF FAITH

I require that you repeat together with the congregation, the Christian faith in the words of the Apostles' Creed.

[The Apostles' Creed, **CF1a**. The congregation sit.]

Do you believe in this faith?
Yes, I believe in this faith.
Do you trust in Jesus Christ, the Son of God as your Saviour and your Lord?
Yes, in Him I trust.

4c PROMISES

Will you obediently do the holy will of God and fulfil his commandments and walk in them all the days of your life?
This I will do with the help of the Lord.

5 **CONFIRMATION**

The minister presents the candidates to the Bishop who lays his hand upon them as they kneel before him.
Defend, Oh Lord, your servant …. with your heavenly grace that s/he may continue yours for ever and that day by day s/he may grow in your Holy spirit, more and more, until s/he comes into your eternal kingdom.

6 **RECEPTION**

We receive *these brothers* as *participants* with us in the work of Christ and in the company of the Church.

7 **PRAYERS**

[The Lord's Prayer **CF4a**]

Bishop: Almighty and eternal God, we make our humble supplications to you for your servants upon whom, according to scriptural custom, we have laid our hands in order to assure them by that sign, of your favour and goodness to them. May your paternal hand be always with hem; strengthen them always with the body and blood of your Son; and thus lead them in the knowledge of your Word that they may enter into your eternal glory, through the same Christ our Lord. **Amen.**

Here the minister or other invited members can add other intercessions.

Hymn.

8 **SERMON**

Hymn

9 **BLESSING**

And to Him who is powerful to keep you from falling, and to present you without stain before his glory with great joy, to the only wise God, our Saviour, be glory and majesty, rule and power now and for all ages. **Amen.**

E. Africa and the Middle East

15. The Anglican Church of Kenya

In 1842 Johann Krapf, a German in the employ of the Church Mission Society (CMS), came to settle on the coast of East Africa. While there were Portuguese trading forts along the coast, Christianity had yet to penetrate the interior, which was the vision of Krapf taken up by CMS. The mission was interested in both evangelization and opposition to the slave trade. In 1895 Kenya became a British protectorate. The mission work developed with the translation of the Book of Common Prayer into the vernacular.[47] In 1960 the present church became a part of the Province of East Africa, and in 1970 became an independent Province.

The new prayer book for the Anglican Church in Kenya, *Our Modern Services* 2002, owes much of its existence to the vision of Archbishop David Gitari and the team of liturgical leaders that he fostered. There is rich provision for baptism within the book and a clear development of baptismal approaches in the Province. Previously the church had been very loyal to the Book of Common Prayer 1662 translated into many vernacular languages. *Modern English Services* 1975 was based on the English Book of Common Prayer but in modern English, and was used in schools, colleges and English-speaking congregations. *Modern Services* 1991 was a booklet precursor to the 2002 book with baptism, admission, and confirmation and commissioning. The pattern in *Our Modern Services* for a child who is baptized is that at the age of nine to ten, after instruction, they will be admitted to Holy Communion by their local minister. After the age of 12, and after further instruction, they may come to the bishop for confirmation and commissioning.

Our Modern Services contains: a service of baptism, conditional baptism, emergency baptism, admission to Holy Communion, a revised catechism, confirmation and commissioning for service and witness, and a service of admitting Christians from other churches. It also has separate from this baptismal material a service of thanksgiving after childbirth.

---

47 G 80: 1–6 Kikuyu, G 92: 1–3 Luo.

SERVICE OF BAPTISM

[[The notes say that this is a complete service in itself and should normally be in the Sunday service. The service is for both adult and infant baptism. When adults are baptized, children over 19, they should also be admitted to Holy Communion in the service. Adult candidates need to be presented to the bishop for confirmation.]]

ORDER OF SERVICE

1 The Lord be with you.
   And also with you.

2 Have these children been baptised in water in the name of the Father, Son, and the Holy Spirit? *No.*
   Have you been baptised in the name of the Father, Son, and the Holy Spirit? *No.*

3 [[Mark 1.4–5; Acts 2.38]] So as we come to this service of baptism, let us reverently confess our sins to Almighty God.

4 **Almighty God, Creator of all, you marvellously made us in your image; but we have corrupted ourselves and damaged your likeness by rejecting your love and letting our neighbours. We have done wrong and neglected to do right. We are sincerely sorry and heartily repent of our sins. Cleanse us and forgive us by the sacrifice of your son; remake us and lead us by your spirit the comforter. We ask this through Jesus Christ our Lord. Amen.**

5 Almighty God, whose steadfast love is as great as the heavens are high above the Earth, remove your sins from you as far as the East is from the West, strengthen your life in his kingdom and keep you upright to the last day; through Jesus Christ our merciful high priest. **Amen.**

[[6 Prayer for day and hymn.]]

MINISTRY OF THE WORD

[[7 Reading(s), Gospel, notices, hymn, sermon.]]

EXHORTATION ON BAPTISM

8 Brothers and sisters in Christ, in the Gospel of John, Jesus tells us, 'no one can enter the kingdom of God unless he is born of water and spirit'. Because all of us have been born with the sinful nature and continually sin in many ways, we need to be born again. Baptism is the outward sign of this new birth whereby we are united with Christ in his death on the cross for the forgiveness of sins and his resurrection to new life. In St Matthew's gospel Jesus commanded his disciples to go and make disciples of all the nations, baptising them in the name of the Father, Son, and the Holy Spirit. In the same way Peter after preaching the gospel on the day of Pentecost said, "repent and be baptised in the name of Jesus Christ for the forgiveness of sins and you shall receive the gift of the holy spirit. For the promise is to you and your children and all that are faraway, everyone whom the Lord calls him".

It is therefore in obedience to Christ's command that we ourselves have been baptised and these people will be baptised today so let us thank the Lord for our baptism and pray for these candidates as they now go to be baptised.

9   Almighty Father we thank you for calling us to know you and to put our trust in you through your son, Jesus Christ our saviour. Deepen our knowledge and strengthen our faith in you. Pour out your spirit on these people that they may be born again of water and spirit and added to the family of your church; through Jesus Christ the pioneer of our salvation.

PRESENTATION OF CANDIDATES

⟦10   The candidates are presented by an instructor, but if the baptizer is the instructor this section is omitted.⟧

The candidates, parents and godparents stand:
Instructor: **I present these candidates for baptism.**

Have you sufficiently prepared these candidates for baptism?
Instructor: **Yes, I have sufficiently taught them the Christian faith and found them fit and ready for baptism.**

Have you sufficiently prepared the parents and godparents for the vows they are about to take on behalf of these children?
Instructor: **Yes I have.**

COMMITMENT

11   The Bible tells us that when the Philippian jailer was saved, 'he and all his family were baptised'. The Anglican Church baptises children who are not able to answer for themselves on the basis of the faith and repentance of their parents and godparents and on the understanding that they will be brought up as Christians in the Fellowship of the church. We therefore ask you to commit yourself to this responsibility by answering these questions.

Are you prepared to take baptismal vows on behalf of these children?
I am.
Will you teach these children the Christian faith by your word and example?
I will.
Will you guide and encourage these children in Christian living?
I will.
Will you pray for them regularly and bring them to Sunday worship?
I will.
As soon as they are sufficiently prepared and ready, will you bring them for confirmation?
I will.

12   *An adult candidate may be given an opportunity to give a brief testimony.*

BAPTISMAL VOWS

13   *A candle may be lit for every candidate.*

14   You have come here to be baptised. You should therefore answer sincerely before God and this congregation are questions which I now put to you.

Do you turn to Christ?
I turn to Christ.
Do you repent of all your sins?
I repent of all my sins.
Do you renounce Satan, all his works and all the evil powers of this world?
I renounce them all.

Do you renounce the desires of your sinful nature and all forms of idolatry?
I renounce them all

Do you believe and trust in God the Father who made the world?
I believe and trust in him.
Do you believe and trust in his Son Jesus Christ who redeemed humankind?
I believe and trust in him.
Do you believe and trust in his Holy Spirit who gives life to the people of God?
I believe and trust in him.

THANKSGIVING OVER WATER

15 O give thanks to the Lord for he is good;
For his steadfast love endures forever.
For the blessing of water;
We thank you Lord.
For your son Jesus Christ who was himself baptised in the river Jordan;
We thank you Lord.

Hear our prayers as we obey your Son's command to go and baptise in the name of the Father, Son, and the Holy Spirit;
Hear us O Lord
Sanctify this water for baptising your servants;
Sanctify.
Bless those who are to be baptised in it.
Bless them.
May they be cleansed from all their sins.
Be cleansed.
May they be united with Christ in his death and resurrection;
Be united.
May they be born again by the spirit to eternal life;
Be born again.
May they be joined into the fellowship of the body of Christ.
Be joined.
Christ has defeated Satan and all evil powers!
Alleluia!

BAPTISM

16 Name this person.

17 *The minister immerses the candidate or pours water on the candidate's head, saying:*
NN, I baptise you in the name of the Father, Son, and the Holy Spirit. **Amen.**

SIGN OF THE CROSS

18 *The minister marks each candidate with the sign of the cross saying:*
Since you have passed from death to new life in Christ I mark you with the sign of the cross. **Amen.**

Ululations may be made and choruses sung after all the candidates have been baptised.

ANOINTING (OPTIONAL)

19 I anoint you in the name of the anointed one.

WELCOME

20 We welcome you into the body of Christ: you are a new creation, the old has passed away, the new has come.
Do not be ashamed to confess the faith of Christ crucified. Fight bravely under his banner against sin, the world and the devil, and continue his faithful soldier and servants to the ends of your lives. Amen.

21 *The adult candidates, who have just been baptised, stand.*
We were all baptised by one spirit,
into one body.

We who are many are one body,
for we share one bread.

Let us then welcome these are brothers and sisters as fellow partakers of the Lord's Supper.
We welcome you to share with us the Lord's Supper. Happy are those invited to the marriage feast of the lamb. Alleluia.

[The peace is now shared. Instructions are given if the service is to include communion or if it ends here.]

CONFIRMATION AND COMMISSIONING FOR SERVICE AND WITNESS

[The notes say this is to be included in a service of Holy Communion. It is for those 12 years or older who have been instructed, baptized and admitted to Communion. It is conducted by the bishop.]

ORDER OF SERVICE

1 *Hymn*

CALL TO WORSHIP

2 The Lord be with you:
and also with you

The earth is the Lord's and all that is in it:
Let the heavens rejoice and the earth be glad.
Our help this in the name of the Lord:
who made heaven and earth.
I was glad when they said to me:
let us go to the house of the Lord.
Praise the Lord.
The name of the Lord be praised.

Heavenly Father, by the power of your Holy Spirit you give to your faithful people new life in the water of baptism.
You commission them to serve you in the world.
Guide and strengthen us by that same Spirit, that we who are born again may serve you in faith and love and grow into the full stature of your son Jesus Christ, who is alive and reigns with you and the Holy Spirit,
one God now and for ever. Amen.

PRESENTATION

3   *Minister, sponsors and parents together say:*
Father in God, we bring you these candidates who have been baptised, that you may confirm and commission them for service and witness to Christ and his church.

Take care that these people you have presented to us have been instructed, and that they fully understand their baptismal vows and are willing to serve Christ and his church.
We have instructed and examine them and find them worthy.

4   Let us pray for these candidates that God may help them so that they may fulfil the vows that they just made before God and his congregation.

Almighty God, you give gifts to humankind, and appoint someone to the apostles, prophets, evangelists, pastors and teachers, to prepare all God's people for the work of Christian service in order to build the body of Christ; we now pray for these your servants who have come to be confirmed and commissioned. Grant men's sincerity of heart that they may fulfil the promises they are about to make. Fill them with the truth of your doctrine and close them with holiness of life that by word and good example they may faithfully serve you to the glory of your name; through our saviour Jesus Christ. **Amen.**

MINISTRY OF THE WORD

⟦5   Readings, hymn and sermon.⟧

MAKING OF THE PROMISES

6   You stand in the presence of God and his Church; with your own mouth and from your own heart you must declare your allegiance to Christ and your rejection of all that is evil. Therefore I ask these questions:

Do you turn to Christ?
I turn to Christ.
Do you repent of all your sins?
I repent of all my sins.
Do you renounce Satan, all his works and all the evil powers of this world?
I renounce them all.
Do you renounce the desires of your sinful nature and all forms of idolatry?
I renounce them all

7   I now call upon you to declare before God and his Church that you accept the Christian faith into which you were baptised, and in which you live, grow and serve.

Do you believe and trust in God the Father, who made this world?
I believe and trust in him.
Do you believe and trust in his Son Jesus Christ who redeemed humankind?
I believe and trust in him.
Do you believe and trust in his Holy Spirit who gives life to the people of God?
I believe and trust in him.

8   This is the faith of the church.
This is our faith.
We believe and trust in one God,
Father, Son and Holy Spirit

⟦The bishop continues either with the next section and/or the section after.⟧

9a So that all may know your intention and resolve, I ask you:

Will you be willing to tell your neighbours about the love of Christ?
I will.
Will you pray and support your church, the bishops, clergy and all the other church workers?
I will do so, God being my helper.
Will you read the Bible regularly and fashion your life after it?
I will diligently do so.
Will you endeavour to meet with other Christians for fellowship and stir up the gift of God that is in you?
I will endeavour to do so.
Will you make every effort to attend Sunday worship and in particular the celebration of Holy Communion?
I will do so.
Will you pursue justice, truth and reconciliation of God's people?
I will do so whenever opportunities arise.

Will you endeavour to feed the hungry, give water to the thirsty, welcome the needy, clothe the naked, visit the sick and those in prison?
I will do so with the help of God.
Will you support and pray for the lonely, the orphans, widows and all the voiceless?
I will support and pray for them.
Will you endeavour to be a good steward of God's creation and care for the environment?
I will endeavour to do so.
Will you be a faithful citizen of your nation, and regularly pray for its leaders?
I will.
Will you be alert and watchful, and firmly resist your enemy the devil?
I will do so with the help of God.

or/and

9b So that all may know your intention and resolve, what is your pledge?

I, about to be commissioned for service and witness to Christ and his church, to pledge to keep and walk in God's commandments all the days of my life, and to read the Bible and pray regularly. I pledge to proclaim Christ in season and out of season, to obey him and to live in the fellowship of all true believers throughout the world. I pledge to be active in the church, to give to the work of the church, to help the needy, support the poor, and to be a good steward of all that the Lord gives me. I pledge to uphold truth and justice, and to seek reconciliation among all people; Christ being my helper.

10 Do you who are gathered here agree that these people be confirmed and commissioned for the mission of Christ and his church?
We agree.

CONFIRMATION

11 *The Bishop stretches out his hand over the candidates and says:*
The Lord says: 'you are my witnesses, and my servants whom I have chosen.'
We are indeed.
Give thanks to the Lord and call upon his name.
I will thank him, praise him and call upon his name always.

12 *The Bishop lays hands on the head of each candidate saying:*
Strengthen, O Lord, your servant N with your Holy Spirit. Empower *him* for your service and sustain *him* all the days of his life. **Amen.**

COMMISSIONING

13 *All candidates stand and face the congregation and the Bishop stretches his hands over them and says:*
Now that you have been confirmed, I commission you to go into the world. This is your mission:
where there is hatred, so love.
Where there is injury, pardon.
Where there is doubt, faith.
Where there is despair, hope.
Where there is darkness, light.
Where there is sadness, joy.

O Divine Master,
Grant that they may not so much seek
to be consoled, as to console;
to be understood, as to understand;
to be loved, as the love.
For it is in giving that we receive,
it is in hardening that we are pardoned,
it is in dying that we are born to eternal life. **Amen.**

14 **O Lord, without whom our labour is lost; we beseech you to prosper all works in your church undertaken according to your holy will. Grant your work as a pure intention, the patient faith, sufficient success on earth, and the blessedness of serving you in heaven; through Jesus Christ our Lord. Amen.**

15 On behalf of the Anglican communicants in this parish of..., and in the diocese of..., and the Anglican Church of Kenya and the entire Anglican Communion throughout the world, I welcome you to become full communicants and commissioners for Christ in the Anglican Church, in the name of the Father, Son, and Holy Spirit. **Amen.**

16 Will you welcome and support these whom we have confirmed and commissioned into the service and witness of Christ and his church?
In the name of Christ we welcome them and pledge support.

〚17 The service continues with the peace, greetings, a hymn and Holy Communion.〛

16. The Church of the Province of Uganda

Christianity came to Uganda in 1877 following its 'discovery' by English explorers. In 1884 the Diocese of Eastern Equatorial Africa was formed, and in 1897 this was divided to form the Diocese of Uganda. This has subsequently been divided such that there are now 34 dioceses. The Church of Uganda has been significantly influenced by the East African Revival movement.

The early missionaries translated the Bible and the Book of Common Prayer into various languages, the first being Luganda portions from 1879.[48] Thus most of the worship of the church is in vernacular languages in the towns and villages scattered across the country. This tends to be the 1662 Prayer Book with occasionally additions from the 1928 Prayer Book of England depending upon when the last translation was made. In places where worship is in English – colleges, schools and some churches – English-language services are found in the book *Come and Worship*, which was first produced in 1980 and revised in 2009. The 1980 services followed closely the Book of Common Prayer in modern English. The 2009 revision has moved away from the Prayer Book, revising services to be appropriate for today.

The 2009 revision has one service of baptism, for adults and infants, unlike the Prayer Book. There is no service of confirmation, but then this is not a full prayer book but a set of services commonly used when worshipping in English.

In 2013 a *Book of Common Worship* was produced by the Bishop Ticker School of Divinity in thanksgiving for their centenary. It would appear that this is used alongside the other services. In it there is a new service of baptism with instructions for conditional and emergency baptism. There is a separate service for reception and reaffirmation of baptismal vows, led by an archdeacon, but no service of confirmation. This is not to suggest that confirmation is ceasing; the canons of the church make clear that all baptized Anglicans must be confirmed. The canons also provide for a catechumenate. Thus bishops still spend their time confirming in large numbers.

COME AND WORSHIP (REVISED) 2009

ORDER OF SERVICE FOR BAPTISM FOR ALL AGES

1 *This Order of Service begins as in Morning and Evening Prayer to the end of the second reading. However, proper Psalms, readings, sentence and collect may be used instead of those of the day*

---

48 G 38:1.

2 2nd Lesson

Reader: This is the word of the Lord
Thanks be to God.

3 *Announcements (and notices)*

4 *Hymn*

All stand

5 Christ has died:
Christ. is risen:
Christ will come again.

Alleluia! Christ is alive.

The Lord is loving to everyone:
and his mercy is all over his works.

6 Dear friends, all people are born with a sinful nature; and our Saviour Christ has said that no one can enter the Kingdom of God unless they are born again through water and the Holy Spirit. So let us pray to God the Father, through our Lord Jesus Christ, that by his great mercy he will give to *these children [and persons]* what they cannot have by birth; that they may be baptised with water and the Holy Spirit, and enter and become active *members* of Christ's holy Church.

THE DUTIES OF PARENTS AND GOD PARENTS

7 Infants are baptised on the understanding that they will be brought up as Christians within the family of the Church.
As they grow up, they need the help and encouragement of that family, so that they learn to be faithful in public worship and private prayer, come to confirmation and continue to like as God wishes.
Parents and God parents, *the children [and person]* whom you have brought for baptism *depend* chiefly on you for the help and encouragement they need. Are you willing to give it to them by your prayers, by your example, and by your teaching?
I am willing.

8 *And if the persons are old enough to understand, the priest speaks to one of them in these or similar words*
N, When you are baptised, you become a *member* of a new family. God takes you for his own *child,* and all Christian people will be your brothers and sisters.

THE DECISION

9 *The parents and God parents remain standing. The rest sit. Then the priest addresses the parents and God parents*
Dear friends, you have brought *these children* here to be baptised. You must promise to God on *their* behalf, until *they* grow up and make the promises for themselves, that they will reject evil and fight against it to follow Christ. Therefore I ask these questions which you must answer for yourselves and for these children.

And/or the following words to the adults to be baptised
Dear *friends,* you have come seeking Holy baptism. Therefore you, *yourselves* must promise before your witnesses and this congregation, that you will reject evil and fight against it to follow Christ. Therefore I ask these questions which you must answer for yourselves.

Do you turn to Christ?
I turn to Christ.
Do you repent of your sins?
I repent of my sins.
Do you renounce evil?
I renounce evil in the name of the Father, the Son and the Holy Spirit.

10 May the almighty God pardon and deliver you from the powers of darkness, and lead you in the light and obedience of Christ. **Amen.**

11 *All those previously baptised can renew their vows through saying this creed.*

THE APOSTLES CREED
[The Apostles' Creed **CF1a**]

12 *A hymn or Psalm may be sung*

THE BAPTISM

13 *The priest stands before the water of baptism and say*
Almighty God, your Son Jesus Christ was baptised in the river Jordan:
we thank you for the gift of water to cleanse us and revive us;
we thank you that through the Red Sea, you led your people out of slavery to freedom in the promised land;
we thank you that through death you brought your Son, and raised him to life.
Bless this water in the name of the Father, the Son and the Holy Spirit,
that your *servants* who *are* washed in it may experience with Christ, his death, and resurrection, to be cleansed and delivered from all sin.
By this water and the Holy Spirit may *they* be born again into new life,
adopted as your own, and received into the fellowship of your Church. **Amen.**

14 Do you believe and trust in God the Father, who created the world?
I believe and trust in him.

Do you believe and trust in his Son Jesus Christ, who redeemed mankind?
I believe and trust in him.

Do you believe and trust in his Holy Spirit, the giver of life?
I believe and trust in him.

15 *The parents and God parents being present with each child (or adult candidate for baptism). the priest baptises him/her. He dips him/her in the water or pours water on him/her addressing him/her by name*
N, I baptize you in the name of the Father, and of the Son, and of the Holy Spirit.
Sponsors: **Amen.**

16 *The priest makes. THE SIGN OF THE CROSS on the forehead of each candidate, saying to each*
I sign you with the cross, the sign of Christ.

After the signing of each or all, he says:
Do not be ashamed to confess the faith of Christ crucified.
Fight valiantly under the banner of Christ against sin, the world and the devil, and continue his faithful *soldier(s)* and *servant(s)* to the end of *your life/lives.*

17 *The priest or other person may give to a parent or God parent for each candidate A LIGHTED CANDLE, saying to each*
Receive this light.

And when a candle has been given to each one, he says:
This is to show that you have passed from darkness to light.
Shine as a light in the world to the glory of God the Father.

THE WELCOME

18 *The priest and the congregation, representing the whole Church, welcome the newly baptised*
God has received you by baptism into his Church.
We welcome you into the Lord's Family.
We are members together of the body of Christ;
We are children of the same heavenly Father;
We are inheritors together of the Kingdom of God.
We welcome you.

THE PRAYERS

19 *All kneel. These prayers may be omitted*
Heavenly Father, bless and give the parents of these children (persons) the Spirit of wisdom and love, that their homes may reflect the joy of your eternal kingdom.
Amen.

Almighty God, we thank you for our fellowship in the household of faith with all those who have been baptised in your name. Keep us faithful to our baptism and in the knowledge of your Son and our Saviour Jesus Christ. **Amen.**

20 *Hymn/chorus*
Continue service as in Morning and Evening Prayer from sermon

BOOK OF COMMON WORSHIP (2013)

THE HOLY BAPTISM

1 *The Priest welcomes the congregation, saying*
I welcome and greet you all in the name of the Father, and of the Son, and of the Holy Spirit as we come to baptise our children. Baptism is an initiation into God's family, and is a voluntary response to His invitation to His redemptive plan for us through His Son Jesus Christ.
This sacrament calls for clear and careful guidance by the whole body of Christ. It is the entry point into the covenant of the mysteries of God's abundant and immeasurable love for us. We therefore gather here as happy witnesses to an act of grace for these people now being presented for baptism. As a community, every child born to us is often welcomed with great joy. Greater joy then should be now as a community of believers to receive and dedicate these children to their Creator as He continues to unfold blessings to them. Our role as a community and church should be to nurture them into a community that we all can be proud of. Greater demand on this role is even mare on the role of the parents and godparents.

2 *All join in the following prayer:*
O God of all creation and designer of order: You and Your Son Jesus Christ, together with Your Holy Spirit, are present with us now. We pray that you cause increased awareness of Your expectations of us in regard to the act of baptism, and what it means for our church and community. Enable us a genuine commitment to actualise this sacrament into a process of good upbringing of our children, for God seeks godly offspring. *Malachi 2.15*

Good Lord, you are Father both to adults and infants: grant us the adults ability and responsible parenting for our children according to the guidance to Your Holy Spirit. Grant us our prayer, the name of our Lord and Saviour Jesus Christ. Amen.

3 *Celebration in Christian hymns, songs, and dance; at most, three as the candidates for baptism are ushered into the church.*

THE MINISTRY OF THE WORD OF GOD

⟦4 One or two lessons as appointed and a sermon.⟧

PRESENTATION AND EXAMINATION OF CANDIDATES

5 *The Priest then asks the following questions of the parents and godparents who have gathered at the font, or candidates for baptism if they can answer for themselves:*
Parents and godparents, the candidates you have brought for baptism depend on you for their spiritual growth. Do you commit yourselves to guide them in the ways of God and have to have faith in Him?
I do.
Do you repent of your sins?
I repent of my sins.
Do you renounce evil?
I renounce evil.

6 *All join in the Apostles' Creed*
⟦ The Apostles' Creed **CF1a**⟧

7 God is the creator of all things, and through the birth of children, gives parents a share in the work and the delight of creation. However, birth in the flesh is inadequate until birth in the Spirit is done, which leads to renewal in godliness. Baptism is the sign and the seal of this new birth. In Christ's Great Commission, His disciples were under command to make disciples of all nations, and to baptise people everywhere. St Peter talks of repentance and baptism in the name of Christ, which leads to forgiveness of sin and receiving the Holy Spirit. The promise is for parents and their children called of God by His Son, Jesus Christ. *Acts 2.38*

8 We want to thank God for this gracious gift, as we bring these candidates to share in that promise of God.
Heavenly Father, in Your love, You have called us to know You and trust You. You have united our life with Yours. Surround these children with Your love, shield them against evil, fill them with Your Holy Spirit, and receive them into the family of your church militant, that they may walk with us in the way of Christ while growing in the knowledge of Your love.

BLESSING OF THE WATER AND THE OIL

9 Almighty God and our divine Father, thank You for the gift of water. The Holy Spirit moved over the surface of the water at the time of Creation. Through water, You led the children of Israel out of bondage in Egypt, to the land of promise and blessing. In water, Your Son Jesus Christ received the baptism of John, and You declared Him Your Son. Your Son's experience in birth, work, death, resurrection, and ascension remains the indisputable basis of our faith. Thank You for this water for baptism. In it, we are buried with Christ in His death; by it, we share in His resurrection; through it, we are born of the Holy Spirit.
Now sanctify this water in the name of the Father, and of the Son, and of the Holy Spirit. May all who are cleansed from sin and born again continue to grow in the amazing grace of our Lord and Saviour Jesus Christ.

10   We bless this oil, which will be used as a sign of the cross, in the name of the Father, and of the Son, and of the Holy Spirit.

THE BAPTISM

11   Has this person been baptised?
No.

The parents and godparents then present the candidate to be baptised, saying together
I present N. to receive the Sacrament of Baptism.

Each candidate is presented by name to the Officiant, who then pours water on the candidate or immerses in the three-fold administration, saying

13   N, I baptise you in the name of the Father, and of the Son, and of the Holy Spirit.

⟦14   Directions for conditional baptism.⟧

15   *The Officiant then makes a sign of the cross on the forehead of each one baptised, saying*
N, I sign you with a cross, the sign of Christ.

After the signing of every candidate, the Priest says:
Do not be ashamed to confess the faith of Christ crucified.

16   Heavenly Father, we thank You that by water and the Holy Spirit You have bestowed upon these Your children the forgiveness of sin, and have raised them to the new life of grace. Sustain them, O Lord, in Your Holy Spirit. Give them an inquiring and discerning heart, the courage to will and to persevere, a spirit to know and to love You, and the gift of joy and wonder in all Your works. **Amen.**

THE GIVING OF THE LIGHT

17   N, receive the light of Christ to show that you have passed from darkness to light.
Let your light so shine before others that they may see your good works and glorify your Father in heaven.

THE WELCOME

18   Let us welcome the newly baptised.
We welcome and receive you into the household of God. Confess the faith of Christ crucified, proclaim His resurrection, and share with us in His eternal priesthood.

⟦19   The Lord's Prayer **CF4b**⟧

THANKSGIVING AND OFFERTORY

20   *As parents and godparents move forward for thanksgiving, the Offertory is collected from the congregation.*
Almighty God, we thank You for Your Holy Scripture and Your call to each of us. In every age, You have spoken through prophets. We also thank You that over the years, we have heard You speak to us through the preaching of Your Word in this place, and have also witnessed the increase of believers through the sacrament of baptism. Today, we thank You for our children's baptism, a holy sacrament that adds to the heritage of our church's mission of God's salvation for us all. We offer our gratitude for all this, through Jesus Christ our Lord. Amen.

21   We thank You, Lord God our Creator, for the gift of parenthood, and we delight in the gift of children that You create through us. Thank You for Your own Son Jesus Christ, who heads the church that we belong to. We give you thanks for the baptism today, and we pray for special inspiration and commitment on the part of parents and godparents for proper parenting of our children. We lift them in this prayer to

bless their hands and labour and to meet the needs of our children, so they can grow up happy, faithful, and responsible citizens. Bless their future, now and in eternity, to your honour and glory, in the name of Jesus Christ Our Lord and Saviour. Amen.

22 *An appropriate hymn or chorus may be sung.*

GIVING OF CERTIFICATES

23 *The Priest then presents the baptism certificates to the parents and godparents.*

DEDICATION

24 **Almighty God, we thank You for our fellowship in the household of faith with all those who have been baptised in Your name. We dedicate our lives to You, and we ask You to keep us faithful to our baptism, and so make us ready for that day when the whole creation shall be made perfect in Your Son, our Saviour and Lord, Jesus Christ. Amen.**

25 *If Holy Communion, Form 3 is to be celebrated, then the Peace follows before the celebration of the Eucharist.*

BENEDICTION

26 You are all children of God through faith in Christ Jesus, for all of you who were baptised into Christ have clothed yourselves with Christ. There is neither Jew nor Greek, slave nor free, male nor female, for you are all one in Christ Jesus. If you belong to Christ, then you are Abraham's seed, and heirs according to the promise. *Galatians 3.26–28*

27 May the blessing of God Almighty, the Father, the Son, and the Holy Spirit, be with you and remain with you always. Amen.

RECESSIONAL HYMN

28 *The procession walks out in reverse order of the procession.*

DISMISSAL

29 Go in peace to shine as a light in the world.
    To the glory of God. Amen.

30 *When applicable, the congregation may then share a meal.*

17. The Province of the Anglican Church of Rwanda

Rwanda had been a part of the Belgian Empire with Roman Catholic missions bringing the gospel. In 1914 and 1916 two CMS doctors explored Rwanda and started a mission hospital in 1925. The East African revival led to enormous church growth. In 1965 the first Rwandan bishop was elected, and in 1992 Rwanda became a separate Province.

Early translation of the Book of Common Prayer was a part of the mission.[49] The present prayer book, *Igitabo Cy'Amasengesho*, was produced in 1967, revised in 1973 and is now in its eighth edition. It follows closely the 1662 Book of Common Prayer having services of infant baptism, adult baptism and confirmation, and has added a service for those transferring from the Roman Catholic Church.

IGTABL CY'AMESENGESHO

PRAYER BOOK 1973

⟦Translated by Stephen Nshimye⟧

BAPTIZING CHILDREN

⟦1 Rubrics⟧

2 *The pastor will go ahead and say:*
Dear brethren, we know that the human nature is sin-driven and our Lord Jesus Christ said that we cannot enter the kingdom of God if we are not born by water and the Holy Spirit; I beseech you to pray to God our father through the name of Jesus Christ so that by his infinite mercy he forgives these children of the original sin through baptism in water and the Holy Spirit in order that they enter the church of Jesus and they become its vital organs.

3 *Then the pastor says:*
Let's pray
Almighty eternal God, by your infinite mercy long ago you sent Noah and his family into the Ark and you saved them from the flood, you also guided Israelites through the red sea, this beckoned your holy baptism; and when your beloved son was baptized in Jordan river he blessed water to wash away sins. So we beseech you by your infinite mercy, wash and bless these children with the Holy Spirit, save them of your anger, let them enter the Ark, it is the church of Christ, so they go through the hardships of the Earth beholding what we believe, happy of the faith they have,

---

49 G 142: 1.

witnessing love, so they go in the kingdom of everlasting life and with you reign your throne perpetually; in the name of Jesus Christ we pray. **Amen!**

Almighty eternal God savior of those who call upon you, redeemer of those who seek their refuge in you, you give Life to those who believe in you, you resurrect the dead, so we pray for these children that, as they have come for your holy baptism, they be born again by the Holy Spirit and their sins be forgiven.
Lord, receive them, as you promised by the words of your beloved son, when he said: 'Ask and it shall be given you; seek and ye shall find; knock and it shall be opened unto you.'
So we who asked please give us, we who sought let us find, those who knocked open for them, so that these children be blessed with your spiritual washing in order that they can enter your kingdom on the day of judgement, as you promised through Jesus Christ our king. **Amen!**

4   *All people stand up and the pastor says:*
Listen to the holy gospel according to Saint Mark 10.13–16
⟦ Mark 10.13–16⟧

5   *When the pastor has finished reading the scripture he will go ahead and explain in the following way*:
Beloved brethren you have understood from the scripture how Jesus recommended that young children be brought unto him, and how he advised disciples to emulate young children for they are innocent. You have noticed that he loved young children such that he took them up in his arms, put his hands upon them, and blessed them. Therefore, don't hesitate, rather confidently believe that he will kindly accept these children and that he will grace them with everlasting life, and make them inheritors of his eternal rule. Since we believe that our Father in heaven loves young children and assists them as his Son Jesus established it; and we strongly believe that God supports our act of love, of bringing these young children to receive the holy baptism; let us pray devotedly and kindheartedly.

Almighty and everlasting God, our Father in heaven, we humbly thank you that you called us to know your mercy and believe in you, so we beseech you, increase our knowledge of your mercy and strengthen our faith in you, forever and ever. Also give these children your Holy Spirit, so that they are born again, and become heirs of your never-ending salvation. We pray in the name of Jesus Christ our king, who stays with you, and who reigns with you and the Holy Spirit. **Amen!**

6   *Then the pastor will explain to the Godparents saying:*
Dear Godparents you have brought these children to be baptized and you have asked our Lord Jesus Christ to accept them and save them from sin, purify them with the Holy Spirit and lead them to the kingdom of heaven and give them everlasting life. You have also heard that our Lord Jesus Christ in the gospel promised to do everything you ask Him, and he will not fail to do what he promised. Therefore, as Jesus promised, you Godparents need to swear to these children that until they grow old enough and believe by themselves to do away with the devil and all of his evil deeds, and continue to believe in the holy gospel of God, and observe his commandments.

7   *Biological parents and Godparents stand up and swear to children before the congregation.*
You as Godfather/Godmother, do you promise to teach this child to do away with the devil and all his evil deeds, useless worldly glory and respect, fake promises of the devil, and lust, so that he/she may not do them neither be driven by them?

I agree to all of that and promise to realize my duties.

8   *Pastor:* Do you promise to facilitate this child to believe in God our father, the creator of heaven and earth; and Jesus Christ his only son our Lord? Who was conceived by the Holy Spirit and born of the Virgin Mary? Who suffered under Pontius Pilate, who was crucified, died, and was buried; who descended to hell and that the third day he rose again from the dead. That he ascended to heaven and he is seated at the right hand of God the father almighty?

Do you promise to facilitate this child to believe that from there our Lord Jesus will come to judge the living and the dead?

Dear Godfather/Godmother do you promise to facilitate this child to believe in the Holy Spirit, the holy Catholic Church of all Christians, the communion of saints, the forgiveness of sins, the resurrection of the body, and the everlasting life?

I agree to all of that and promise to realize my duties.

9   Do you promise to assist this child in how to pray and follow the will of God, and act accordingly till he dies?

Will you teach him/her to attend the holy mass to learn the Bible until he/she grows old enough and believe by himself/herself?

Will you also teach him/her to read the Holy Scripture and sing for our Father in Heaven?

I agree to all of that and promise to realize my duties.

10 On behalf of this child do you want him/her to be baptized?

It is what we want.

11 *When the pastor has finished asking the above questions he goes on and prays like this:*
Merciful God, accept that Adam's sin-driven nature dies in these children, so that the nature of the new creature is resurrected in them. **Amen!**

Accept that their bodily desires die so that they long for your will. **Amen!**

Give them power to overcome the devil, worldliness, and their evil-bound nature. **Amen!**

We ask you to give them ability to behave like residents of heaven so that they obtain your reward, Lord of glory Eternal God, ruler of everything forever and ever. **Amen!**

12 Almighty everlasting God, we thank you because your beloved son Jesus Christ shed water and blood from his left rib so that our sins are forgiven, he gave his disciples the mission to preach all nations, and baptize in the name of the Father, the Son and of the Holy Spirit; so we beseech you to listen to the prayers of the congregation here present: bless this water so that it cleanses sins; and accept that these children who came to be baptized in this water be filled with your mercy, and remain in your chosen flock, in the name of Jesus Christ we pray. **Amen!**

13 *Then the pastor holds a baby and tells Godparents the following words:*
Give a name to this child.

14 *The pastor says the name Godparents told him and pours water on the head of that child saying:*
N I baptize you in the name of the Father, of the Son and of the Holy Spirit. **Amen!**

15 *The pastor then says:*
We have received this child in the church of the flock of Jesus Christ, we are now placing on him/her the sign of the cross to ascertain that from now on, he/she will not shy away from witnessing his/her belief in resurrected Christ and that he/she will fight bravely under the flag of Jesus fighting against sins, the world, and the devil, remain a faithful servant of Christ till he/she dies. **Amen!**

16   *Thereafter the pastor says these words:*
Beloved brethren, now that these children have been granted a new birth, and grafted in the body of the church of Jesus Christ, let us thank God for those blessings. United in faith, let us pray requesting God to sustain this faith our children have now so that they endure temptations till the moment of death.

17   *All of them say 'the prayer of our Lord' with everybody kneeling.*
[The Lord's Prayer **CF4a**]

18   *Then the pastor says:*
Our merciful father, we thank you because you promised our children to be born again by your Holy Spirit, and you received them in your holy church. As baptism is a sign meaning that we died to sin, and buried with Christ, we beseech you that these children die to sin and rise again to live a sin-free life. We pray to you that these children be buried with Christ and rise again with him. So that on the day of judgement they inherit your everlasting reign with all the flock of your holy church.
Amen!

19   *Biological parents and Godparents stand up and the pastor says:*
Now that you, parents of these children have avowed on their behalf that they will do away with the Devil, and his evil deeds, that they will believe in God, and work for Him. You have to know that it is your responsibility to ensure that these children are well taught, and when they reach the reasoning age and come to know this wonderful oath you took on their behalf, you need to confirm and witness what you said here today. And so that they understand very well what we believe, you (Godparents and biological parents) have to ensure that these children come to church to listen to scriptures especially that they learn our belief, the prayer of our lord, the Ten Commandments in their mother tongue, and everything a Christian should know and believe in order that their lives be good. Also be courageous to bring them up and teach them the Christian charisma.
Besides that, always remember that baptism reminds us of our belief and prompts us to follow the footsteps of our saviour Jesus Christ, and as he died for us and rose again from the dead we also have to die to sin, do away with our bad habits and eradicate our lust then rise again to live a perfect life and develop a good character of obeying God.

20   *The pastor again says:*
We call you to bring these children to the bishop so that he puts his hands on them after they have been taught the belief of disciples, the prayer of our lord, and the Ten Commandments, together with the catechism, and everything required of candidates for confirmation.

BAPTIZING ADULTS

[1   Rubrics]

2   Most beloved brothers and sisters, we know that the human nature longs for sin, and whatever is begot by flesh is flesh; and those who are led by that nature cannot please to God, they often rather make sins of different kinds. We also know that our savior Christ said that we cannot enter the kingdom of God unless we are born again by God the father, the Son and the Holy Spirit. That is why I beseech you to ask God the Father through the name of our Lord Jesus Christ, to give these people what their human nature cannot give them, and that they be baptized by Water and the Holy Spirit so that they enter the holy church of God and become an integral part of it.

3   *The pastor will then say:*
Let's pray
Everybody kneels
Almighty eternal God, by your infinite mercy long ago you sent Noah and his family
into the Ark and you saved them from the flood, you also guided Israelites through
the red sea, this beckoned your holy baptism; and when your beloved son was
baptized in Jordan river he blessed water to wash away sins. So we beseech you by
your infinite mercy, wash and bless these people with the Holy Spirit, save them from
your anger, let them enter the Ark, it is the church of Christ, so they go through the
hardships of the world, holding to what we believe, happy in the faith they have,
witnessing by love, they enter the kingdom of everlasting life, and with you reign on
your throne forever, in the name of Jesus Christ we pray. **Amen!**

Almighty eternal God and savior of those who call upon you, redeemer of those who
seek their refuge in you, you give Life to those who believe in you, you resurrect the
dead, so we pray for these people that, as they have come for your holy baptism, they
be born again by the Holy Spirit and their sins be forgiven.
Lord, receive them, as you promised by the words of your beloved son, when he said:
'Ask and it shall be given you; seek and ye shall find; knock and it shall be opened
unto you'.
So we who asked please give us, we who sought let us find, those who knocked open
for them, so that these people be blessed with your spiritual washing in order that
they can enter your kingdom on the day of judgement, as you promised through Jesus
Christ our king. **Amen!**

4   *All people stand up and the pastor says*:
Listen to the Holy Gospel according to Saint John, chapter 3.1–8.
⟦Reading John 3.1–8⟧

5   *After reading the scripture the pastor explains like this*:
Brothers and sisters, you have heard from the scripture what our savior said that no
one can see the kingdom of God unless they are born again. You understand that if
possible everybody should receive this sacrament. Also when we read in the gospel
of Saint Mark we see that when Jesus was about to ascend to heaven he commanded
his disciples to go to all nations and teach the holy gospel to all people. He said that
those who believe and get baptized will be saved and those who don't believe will be
condemned. These words show us the importance of baptism.
This is the reason why the time Saint Peter started preaching the gospel, people asked
him together with other disciples: 'Brethren what can we do?' He answered them:
'repent your sins and everybody amongst you gets baptized in the name of Jesus
Christ to have your sins forgiven then receive the gift of the Holy Spirit' because this
is the vow for you and your children, in addition to that our Lord will call people
from afar to receive this gift beyond compare. He continued to explain to them
saying: 'save yourselves from the people who disregard what our savior died for.'
Also Saint Peter in his second epistle asserted that baptism cleanses our sins but it is
not meant to wash away dirt on our outer body. He added that baptism is based on
the vow of God the Father to give us a righteous heart by saving us with the help of
the resurrection of Jesus Christ.
Do not hesitate then, rather believe that Christ has graciously received these people
who honestly repented their sins and came to him after trusting in him and believing
that their sins were forgiven, that they were given the Holy Spirit and the blessing of
everlasting life. Jesus has as well granted them heritage to his never-ending reign.

Therefore, as we have believed that our Father in heaven always does good to these people as confirmed by Jesus Christ his Son, let us humbly thank him:

6 Almighty everlasting God, our Father in heaven, we humbly thank you for the fact that you called us to know your amazing grace, so that we trust in you. Increase that knowledge in us and strengthen our faith all the time and give these people your holy blessing so that they are born again and inherit your eternal salvation. In the name of our Lord Jesus Christ we pray. **Amen!**

7 *Therefore the pastor tells candidates for baptism this*:
Brothers and sisters who came to seek Holy Baptism, you have understood that this congregation prayed so that our Lord Jesus Christ receives you, blesses you, and sets you free from your sins, so that you enter the kingdom of heaven when you die, and that he gives you everlasting life. And you have understood from his holy gospel that he promised to give us everything we ask him, and what he promised will absolutely come true. Thus, as Jesus promised, you too need to avow in the presence of your Godparents and the congregation here present, that you will do away with the Devil and his evil customs, and promise to continue beholding the Holy Scriptures and comply with his sacraments.

8 *The pastor asks these questions to each of the candidates for baptism:*
From now on, will you do away with the Devil, run away from worldly glory, mundane fame, and lust so that they do not subjugate you.
Yes, I will do away with all of that.

9 Do you believe in God the Father, the creator of heaven and earth; and our Lord Jesus Christ his only Son? Who was conceived by the Holy Spirit and born of the Virgin Mary? Who suffered under Pontius Pilate, who was crucified, died, and was buried; who descended to hell and that the third day he rose again from the dead. That he ascended to heaven and he is seated at the right hand of God the father almighty? Do you believe that from there our Lord Jesus will come to judge the living and the dead? Do you believe in the Holy Spirit, the holy Catholic Church of all Christians, the communion of saints, the forgiveness of sins, the resurrection of the body, and the everlasting life?
Yes, I do believe in all of that.

10 You too, do you want to be baptized in this faith?
It is what I want.
Do you promise to do the will of God and comply with his commandments throughout your lifetime?
With God as my guide I will try.

11 *When the pastor has finished asking questions, he prays like this*:
Merciful God, accept that Adam's sin-driven nature dies in these people, so that the nature of the new creature is resurrected in them. **Amen!**
Accept that their bodily desires die so that they long for your will. **Amen!**
Give them power to overcome the devil, worldly belongings and their evil-bound nature. **Amen!**
We ask you to give them ability to behave like residents of heaven so that they obtain your reward, Lord of glory Eternal God, ruler of everything forever and ever. **Amen!**

12 Almighty everlasting God, we thank you because your beloved son Jesus Christ shed water and blood from his left rib so that our sins are forgiven, he gave his disciple the mission to preach all nations, and baptize in the name of the Father, the Son and of the Holy Spirit; so we beseech you to listen to the prayers of the congregation here present: bless this water so that it cleanses sins; and accept that these people

who came to be baptized in this water be filled with your mercy, and remain in your chosen flock, in the name of Jesus Christ we pray. **Amen!**

13 *Then the pastor takes hold of a catechumen and tells Godparents the following words*:
Give a name to this person.

14 *The pastor says the name Godparents told him/her and pours water on the head of that person saying*:
N I baptize you in the name of the Father, of the Son and of the Holy Spirit. **Amen!**

15 *The pastor then says*:
We have received this person in the church of the flock of Jesus Christ, we are now placing on him/her the sign of the cross to make sure that from now on, he/she will not shy away from witnessing his/her belief in resurrected Christ and that he/she will fight bravely under the flag of Jesus fighting against sins, the world, and the devil, remain a faithful servant of Christ till he/she dies. **Amen!**

16 *Thereafter the pastor says these words*:
Beloved brothers and sisters, now that these people have been granted a new birth, and grafted in the body of the church of Jesus Christ, let us thank God for those blessings. United in faith, let us pray requesting God to sustain this faith our brothers and sisters have now so that they endure temptations till the moment of death.

17 *After everybody went down on their knees, all of them say "the prayer of our Lord".*
[Lord's Prayer said by congregation **CF4a**]

18 *Then the pastor says*:
Our merciful Father, we thank you because you promised these people to be born again by your Holy Spirit, and you received them in your holy church. As baptism is a sign meaning that we died to sin, and buried with Christ, we beseech you that these people die to sin and rise again to live a sin-free life. We pray to you that these people be buried with Christ and rise again with him. So that on the day of judgement they inherit your everlasting reign with all the flock of your holy church. **Amen!**

19 *The whole congregation stands up and the pastor explains to the Godparents*:
Now that these people have sworn to do away with the Devil, and his evil deeds, to believe in God, and work for Him, you should remember that it is your duty to remind them the oath they have just taken before the congregation, and especially before you, carefully chosen Godparents. Also remember to encourage these people to learn Holy Scriptures, so that they grow up in the grace of God and know more about our Lord Jesus Christ, this will help them to obey God, and live on earth a perfect life full of humility.

20 *The pastor tells people who have just been baptized*:
You too, who are wearing Christ thanks to baptism, now that you are children of God, and children of the Light since you believe in Christ, you have to know that it is your duty to behave righteously as Christians and children of the Light. Constantly remember that baptism reminds us our belief then we walk in the footsteps of our Lord Jesus Christ, as he died for us and rose from the dead for us, we too the baptized should die to sin and rise again to live a righteous life. By so doing we can overcome our lust and behold the good manners of acting in accordance with God.

21 *It is very important for every grown up baptized not to delay, rather rush for confirmation by the bishop for him/her to be allowed for Holy Communion.*

18. The Anglican Church of Burundi

What is now Burundi was occupied by the Belgians in 1916. They brought with them French-speaking Roman Catholic missionaries. CMS brought the first Anglican missionaries in 1935. The East African revival led to rapid growth in the Anglican Church. The first Bishop for Burundi was consecrated in 1965 and the church became an independent Province in 1992, when it separated from Uganda.

Translation of the Book of Common Prayer into Kirundi was part of the mission's work.[50] For a while the church used a 1991 translation of the Church of England *Alternative Service Book* in French and Kirundi. The present prayer book *Igitabo C'Amasengesho* dates from 2012. The baptism service is very close to the English 1662 but combines the baptism of adults and children into one service.

IGITABO C'AMASENGESHO 2012

[Translated by John Niyondiko]

THE BAPTISM

[1 Directions on godparents for children and adults. A direction to enquire if already baptized.]

2 Brothers and sisters, since all people are born with a sinful nature, and since our Lord Jesus Christ said that if a person is not born of water and the Spirit, he will not enter the Kingdom of God, therefore, I plead with you to ask God our Father, because of our Lord Jesus Christ, to give these children (people) in his great mercy, what their nature cannot give them; that they be baptized with water and the Holy Spirit, for them to be accepted in the Holy Church of Christ, and become members of his body.

3 Let us pray:
Almighty and Eternal God, you who saved your servant Noah and his household, rescuing them in the boat so that they did not die of the flood; and you who led the children of Israel into the red sea. This is for us a sign of your holy baptism. You also cleansed the water for it to be a sign of how you wash sins, when your beloved son Jesus Christ was baptized in the Jordan River. We ask you, because of your unfailing love to have mercy on these children (people). Wash their sins; sanctify them with your Holy Spirit. Save them from all that could bring upon them your wrath, for them to be welcomed in that boat which is the Church of Christ. We pray that they will be strengthened by their faith, be glad in the hope of what is to come, that they be rooted into love, so that they can overcome the trials in this world, and be able to get in the place of eternal life to live eternally with you. We pray this in the name of our Lord Jesus Christ our Lord. **Amen.**

---

50 G 143: 1.

4 Almighty God, Eternal, Rescuer of the miserable, Helper of those who look for
   refuge in you, you who give life to those who trust in you, you who raise the dead:
   we pray for these people who have come to be baptized your holy baptism, so that
   you give them seal of the second birth by the Spirit, which is the forgiveness of their
   sins. Receive them as you promised in the words of your well beloved Son who said:
   'Ask, you will receive, search and you will find; knock and it will be open for you.' So,
   we are asking, give us, we are seeking, let us get, we are knocking, open the door for
   us. Bless and cleanse these children (people) in the way of heaven, so they will go into
   your unending kingdom, which you have promised through Jesus Christ, our Lord.
   Amen.

5 *All people should stand up and the Gospel should be read. If there are children to be
   baptized, the reading should be from Mark 10.13.*
   Listen to the Gospel according to Saint Mark in chapter 10, from verse 13:
   ⟦Mark 10.13–16⟧

6 *The pastor continues saying:*
   Sisters and brothers, you heard from that gospel the words of our Saviour Christ, how
   he said that they bring to him small children, and that he rebuked those who wanted
   to forbid them from coming to him; also he summoned all people to be holy as little
   children. And you saw how he showed his love with what he did, laying on them his
   hands and blessing them. Therefore, do not doubt but believe that he receives these
   children with compassion; that he receives them with loving hands and that he will
   give them a blessing of eternal life, giving them the gift of his eternal kingdom. So,
   let us assuredly know that our heavenly father is pleased with being merciful to these
   children as it has been told to us by his Son Jesus Christ: and we do not doubt that he
   accepted with compassion this tradition of bringing little children to be baptized of
   his holy baptism.

7 *When there are adults who are to be baptized, the passage to be read should be John 3.1–
   8. The whole congregation standing up:*
   Listen to the words of the Gospel according to Saint John, in the third chapter, from
   verse one: ⟦John 3.1–8⟧

8 *The pastor continues by reading these words:*
   Sisters and brothers, you heard from this good news the words of our Saviour Jesus
   Christ, when he said this: 'Except a man is born again, he cannot see the kingdom
   of God.' These words show us that this sacrament is for all people, if possible.
   Also, as we read in the last chapter of the Gospel according to Mark, our Lord,
   before ascending to heaven, commanded his disciples in these words: 'Go into all
   the countries, preach the Good News to all. Those who will believe and be baptized
   will be saved, but those who will not believe will be condemned.' These words point
   directly to the importance of baptism. Likewise, when Saint Peter, the apostle of
   Christ, preached at the beginning of his evangelistic ministry, many people were
   pierced in their hearts and asked him and other apostles: 'brothers, what should we
   do? Peter replied: each of you must repent of your sins and return to God, and be
   baptized in the name of Jesus Christ for the forgiveness of sins. Then you will receive
   the gift of the Holy Spirit. For this promise is yours and your children and even to
   the Gentiles – all who have been called by the Lord our God. He continued for a long
   time, strongly urging all his listeners to save themselves from this crooked generation.'
   This Apostle said even elsewhere that the baptism which saves us is not the one which
   removes the stain of the body. It is rather a covenant between God and a pure heart.
   This baptism saves us by the resurrection of our Jesus Christ. Let us kneel down and
   praise him with faith and honor.

9 Let's pray.
   Almighty God, Eternal, our heavenly Father, in humility, we thank you that you even called us to know your grace and have faith in you. Multiply that knowledge in us and let us always have that faith. Give these children (these people) your Holy Spirit, for them to be ascertained that they are born again, and they will become heirs of the eternal salvation, by our Lord Jesus Christ. Amen.

10 *If there are children to be baptized, their godparents stand up and the pastor speaks to them in these words:*
   Brothers and sisters, you brought these children here to be baptized; and you are asking our Lord Jesus to receive them and to give them deposit guaranteeing their salvation from their sins, and to cleanse them with the Holy Spirit, and to give them the Kingdom of heaven and eternal life. You also heard that our Lord Jesus Christ promised in the Scripture to give us all we ask for and he will fulfil his promise. Therefore, these children must make vows. But, before they are grown up and make vows themselves, you are to do this on their behalf, that they will abandon Satan and all his works, and that they will always believe the Holy Scriptures, and obey his commands.

11 Now I ask you, on the behalf of these children, do you abandon Satan and all his works, and the desires of this world and its pride and its lusts of the lust of the flesh? Do you accept not to follow his ways and not to live according to his standards?
   I will not obey him.

12 On his behalf do you believe the Almighty God our heavenly Father, the creator of heaven and earth, and Jesus Christ his only son and our Lord?
   Do you believe on his behalf that the Virgin Mary conceived by the power of the Holy Spirit and gave birth to Jesus Christ. And that he was delivered to Pontius Pilate, suffered, was crucified on the cross, died, was buried among the dead. That he rose again on the third day, and that he ascended back to heaven and is seated at the right of God our heavenly Father, the Almighty. That he will come back at the end of the world to judge the living and the dead.
   On his behalf, do you also believe in the Holy Spirit. Do you believe on his behalf that there is one Catholic Church of all believers, and the (Holy) good relations between believers, the forgiveness of sins, the resurrection of the body, and eternal life after death?
   I do believe all that on his behalf.

13 You want him to be baptized, don't you?
   That is what I want for him.

14 Do you promise on his behalf that he will obey God's commands and what He likes, so that he will walk in that all the days of his life?
   I promise that on his behalf.

15 *When there are adults who are to be baptized, the pastor will address them in these words:*
   Brothers and sisters, you came here wanting to receive the sacrament of a holy baptism; you heard that we prayed to our Lord Jesus Christ to accept to receive you, to bless you, free you from sins, to give you the kingdom of heaven and eternal life. You also heard that our Lord Jesus Christ promised in his holy word to give us what we asked. He will himself fulfil his promise. Therefore, since he has promised that, you have to promise before these witnesses and before all these people that you abandon Satan and his works, and that you will always believe in the holy word of God, and that you will obey all his commandments.

16   *The pastor asks each one of them:*
Do you abandon Satan and all his works, and the desires of this world and its pride and its lusts of the lust of the flesh? Do you confess that you will not follow that, that you will not be ruled by them?
I reject doing all of that.

17   Do you believe in God our almighty Father, the creator of heaven and earth, and Jesus Christ his only begotten son, our Lord. Do you believe he was delivered to Pontius Pilate, that he suffered, was crucified on the cross, that he died, he was buried, went among the dead. And that he rose again on the third day, ascended to heaven? And that he is sited at the right hand of God our almighty Father. And that he will come back at the end of the world to judge those who will be still alive and those who will be dead. Do you believe in the Holy Spirit? Do you believe that there is one Catholic Church of all believers, and a holy unity of believers, and the forgiveness of sins, the resurrection of the body, and eternal life after death?
I believe all that.

18   Do you want to be baptized, do you believe that?
That is what I want.

19   Will you obey God's holy commands and what he likes? Will you walk according to them all your days of your life?
I will try, helped by God.

20   Gracious God, we ask you to remove the nature of Adam from these children (these people) so that they get a new nature. **Amen.**
We ask you to take away all the sinful desires of the flesh in order to bear all the fruit of the Holy Spirit. **Amen.**
Give them the power to fight and overcome the devil and the world and the body. **Amen.**
Give all these people we bring to you the good conduct which is from heaven. May they be given the eternal gift, in your grace, eternal blessed Lord God who reign over everything forever. **Amen.**

BLESSING OF THE WATER

21   Almighty God, Eternal, when your beloved Son died on the Cross for us to be forgiven our sins, he shed his blood and water from his side; and he gave a command to his disciples to go into the world, teach people, to baptize them in the name of the father, and the Son, and the Holy Spirit. We humbly ask you to hear the prayer of your church. Sanctify this water; make it a sign of the spiritual water that removes sins. Fill these children (people) who are going to be baptized with your grace, and give them to always be counted among the number of your elected children. We pray this in the name of Jesus Christ, our Lord. **Amen.**

22   *The pastor takes a child in his hands and tells the witnesses (godfathers/godmothers):* Give this child a name.

23   *Then, calling the child by that name, he baptizes him/her by saying:*
… I baptize you in the name of the Father, and the Son and the Holy Spirit. **Amen.**

24   *If it is an adult who is being baptized, the pastor will hold his right hand and ask him/her the name, and baptize him using the above same words.*

25   *The pastor goes on with these words:*
We receive this person in the congregation of the flock of Christ, and we put on him the sign of the cross, that means that from now on he will not be ashamed to confess that he/she believes in Jesus Crucified on the cross, and that he will always

fight victoriously, following the flag of Jesus Christ; that he will fight sins, the world and Satan; and that they will always be faithful soldiers of Jesus Christ all their lives. **Amen.**

26 *If there are people from other denominations who want to become members of the church, the pastor receives them using prayers provided elsewhere.*

27 *After baptizing all of them and receiving the new people in the church, the pastor says:*
Brothers and sisters, beloved ones, since these children (people) have received the sign of the second birth, and since they have been received in the church of Christ, let us praise God the almighty for that, and let us pray to him with one heart, so that they will always stay in the way of the Lord as we have helped them to start with it.

28 *All kneeling down pray together:* ⟦The Lord's Prayer **CF4a**⟧

29 *And the pastor prays with these words:*
We thank you, our gracious Father that you accepted to give these children (people) the mark (sign) of the second birth by the Holy Spirit, and to make them your children, and to receive them in your holy Church; and as baptism is sign of dying to sins and to be buried with Christ, we plead with you to give these children (these people) to crucify their old self, to die to sins, and live in righteousness. We thank you that they are given the seal of being united with the death of your son, that they will rise with him so that they will inherit your unending kingdom with him with all the members of your holy Church. We pray this in the name of Jesus Christ our Lord. **Amen.**

30 *The (godparents – witnesses) and parents of children stand up, and the pastor gives them advice saying:*
You godparents and parents of these children, since you have promised on their behalf that they will abandon the works of Satan and believe in God and obey him, you also have to always remember that it is your responsibility to teach these children when they will be able to understand, that what you have done on their behalf is very important. Make sure that they come to church to learn. In addition to all of that, make sure they will be taught the Apostles' Creed and the Lord's prayer, and the ten commandments, and the catechism, together with all a believer must know in their Christian life, what we have vowed in our Christian life, which is to imitate Christ and to be like him. And as he died and rose again on our behalf, us who have been baptized, we must die to sin and rise again for righteousness. May we therefore overcome all our sinful desires, and always live godly lives and fear God. After they will have been taught the Apostles' Creed, the Lord's Prayer, the catechism, and every other prerequisite for confirmation, make sure these children will be brought to the Bishop for the laying of hands.

31 *All those in the church stand up while those who have just been received in the church and those who have just been baptized are sitting down. The pastor gives advice as follow:*
These people have vowed before you that they abandon Satan and all his works; they have promised to fear and serve him. Remember always that it is your duty to remind them their commitment and their promise they have made before you, especially you the witnesses. Also, you must always encourage them to learn the holy Word of God, so they will grow in the grace of God and in the knowledge of our Lord Jesus Christ, live in this world fearing God, in holiness and being watchful everyday.

32 *After these have sat down, those who have been received in the church and those who have been baptized stand up and the pastor tells them:*
And you who have put on Christ in the baptism, since you have become children of God and of light because of your faith in Jesus Christ, know that it is your

responsibility to live a life worthy of Christians and children of light. Remember always that baptism is an external sign of what we confess and believe, which is to follow the example our Saviour Christ gave us, and to be like him. As he died and rose again for us we who have been baptized, we have to die to sin and rise up for righteousness. Let us be always like that, overcoming every kind of evil desire, gaining always the good behaviour of fearing God. May the grace of our Lord Jesus Christ, and the love of God, and the unity of the Holy Spirit, be with you all, forever more. Amen.

B. CONFIRMATION

1   *The pastor asks those who have come to be confirmed to stand up on a line before the Bishop seated in his seat near the holy altar. He presents them to the Bishop saying:*
Our father in the Lord, I am bringing to you these people for you lay your hands on them, to be confirmed in their Christian life.

2   *The Bishop:* We advise you not to bring to us anyone before you have verified that they are of good conduct, living out the teaching of the Holy Scriptures; that they know to pray the Lord's Prayer; that they are able to testify the Apostles' Creed; that they know the commandments of God and live according to them; that they know the reason of our faith.
Pastor: I have been teaching them and trying to check on them concerning all you have said. I have also enquired from others about them. Now, I certify that they are ready.

3   *Bishop:* You want them to be confirmed, and to be allowed to take part at the table of the Lord?
Pastor: That is what I want for them.

4   *Then these words should be read by the Bishop or someone appointed by him. He should lay his hands on them. They should stay up until the Lord's Prayer is prayed.*

5   Listen to the word of God written in the Acts of the Apostles 8.14–17.
⟦Reading of Acts 8.14–17.⟧

6   *The pastor asks those who have been brought to be confirmed to stand up on a line in front of the Bishop seated in his chair, near the Holy Table. The pastor introduces them to the Bishop saying:*
They had been baptized only in the name of the Lord Jesus. And those apostles laid their hands on them, and they were given the Holy Spirit.

7   *This should then be read:* What the church wants is that those who will be confirmed will be more confirmed spiritually. This is the reason why it has been decided that those who are brought to be confirmed must be able to profess the Apostles' Creed, and pray the Lord's Prayer, and know the Ten Commandments. Moreover, those who want to be confirmed have to be able to answer to the questions from the catechism. This law of the church is very good, and it must be obeyed so that people who have been baptized being children after they have grown up and been mature, and known what their witnesses promised when they were baptized, they will confess it by themselves and make the vows themselves. Therefore, everyone who wants to be confirmed, you must testify before this congregation that you will always trust in Jesus Christ, and obey the commandments of God, following his will. You have to also accept that you will continue to fulfill what you have promised at the time of your baptism.

8   *The Bishop asks those who were baptized being adults:* You who were baptized being adults, before God and before this church, do you accept to recommit yourself to what you have promised when you were baptized and that you will continue being faithful to your vows?
Yes indeed, I make the vow again.

9   *The Bishop asks to those who were baptized when they were children, (their godparents standing by them to support them), saying:*
And you who were baptized when you were still children, I ask you: Before God and before this congregation, do you accept to make again the vow that your witnesses vowed on your behalf when you were baptized? Do accept to do it as they promised at that time?
I accept it, I make the vow myself.

10 *The godparents leave those they were holding and go back to their seats as the program continues as follow.*

11 *The Bishop should ask all of them this:*
I ask you all: do you reject Satan and all his works, and the pleasures of this world, and its lusts, and the desires of the flesh, do you accept to not follow those things nor to be ruled by those things?
I reject all of that.

12 *Bishop:* Do you believe in our Almighty God Father, the Creator of heaven and earth? Do you also believe in Jesus Christ, His only Son, our Saviour? Do you believe in also the Holy Spirit, our help?
I believe all of that.

13 *Bishop:* Will you obey the holy commands of God and all he loves? Will you live in them all the days of your life?
I will try to do it helped by God.

14 *The Bishop:* Our rescue is found in God
Who created the heaven and the earth.
Bishop: May the name of God be praised.
From now and for ever.
Bishop: Lord, listen to what we ask you.
May our cry reach you.

15 Let us pray.
Almighty and Eternal God, we thank you for accepting to give your servants a new birth by water and the Holy Spirit. You forgave all their sins. Strengthen them with your Holy Spirit our help, and we pray that you will always bestow them the gifts of your grace. Give them the spirit of wisdom and understanding, the spirit of unity and of strength, the spirit of knowing and truly fearing the Lord. Also O Lord, fill them with the spirit of giving you glory because of your holiness, from now till when they will enter in your unending Kingdom. **Amen.**

16 *The Bishop while laying his hands on them says:* Lord God, strengthen your servant, and keep him always in your heavenly grace. Amen. May he continually be yours for ever; and may he always grow in the grace of your Holy Spirit, until when you will come in your eternal Kingdom. **Amen.**

17 *The Bishop then says:* May the Lord be with you.
and also with your spirit.

18 Let's pray together
〖Lord's Prayer **CF4a**〗

19 Almighty and eternal God, we thank you that it is you who give us to love and to do good and what pleases you. We bow down before you to plead with you on the behalf of these servants of yours; we lay hands on them as your apostles did. We ask for that sign which will show them that you love them, and that it pleases you to do good for them. Keep them always with your hand, as a parent watches over his children. May the Holy Spirit be with them all the time, and may you always lead them to the knowledge and obedience of your word, so that they will attain eternal life. We pray that by our Lord Jesus Christ, the Eternal One who is reigning with the Holy Spirit; you are one God, forever and ever. **Amen.**

20 Almighty Lord, Eternal God, we ask you to lead and to take control over our hearts and our bodies; give us to follow the way of your commandments, to do all you have commended us, so that your power will keep our bodies and hearts every day. We pray this in the name of our Lord Jesus Christ, our Saviour. **Amen.**

21 May the blessing of the Almighty, our Father and the Son, and the Holy Spirit, be in you, with you, everyday. **Amen.**

19. The Anglican Church of Tanzania

Johann Krapf visited Zanzibar in 1844 (at the time ruled by the Sultan of Oman, later a British protectorate), before moving on to Mombasa. The expedition of Speke and Burton in 1876 led to CMS mission stations following the route into the interior. In 1886 Tanzania became a German colony and at the end of the First World War it was transferred to the British. A diocese for East Equatorial Africa was started in 1884, and through division in 1899, and then again in 1927 the Diocese of Central Tanganyika was formed. Meanwhile, the Universities' Mission to Central Africa (UMCA) approached from the south and arrived in Zanzibar in 1864. Diocese of Zanzibar was started in 1892. In 1960 the dioceses formed a part of the Province of East Africa, and in 1978 the Province of Tanzania was formed.

Early mission work concentrated on translation of the prayer book into the vernacular languages and particularly Swahili in the CMS areas.[51] The UMCA developed their own liturgy, partially to stabilize the ever-changing opinion of Anglo-Catholic worship.[52] There was an attempt to produce a united liturgy for five denominations published in 1966 but the proposed union failed. Work on a Tanzanian liturgy began in 1972, was initially authorized in 1973 and finally published in 1979. Further revision led to the production of the present book, the 1995 *Kitabu Cha Sala Kanisa La Jimbo La Tanzania*. This book contains a service for the baptism of adults, the baptism of children (both of which have a common beginning) and confirmation.

KITABU CHA SALA KANISA LA JIMBO LA TANZANIA 1995

⟦Translated by Bridget Lane and Ian Tarrant⟧

BOOK OF PRAYER
CHURCH OF THE PROVINCE OF TANZANIA

HOLY BAPTISM

⟦1 Rubrics to direct the service including immersion as preferred mode and readings.⟧

BAPTISM OF ADULTS

2 *The Minister says*:
   Beloved brothers and sisters, because everyone is born sinful they are unable to please God, without being born again by water and the Holy Spirit; I beseech you to ask God the Father through the Name of our Lord Jesus Christ, to grant these people that

---

51 G 165: 1 Central Dialect, 166: 1–2 Zanzibar Dialect.
52 G 166: 4.

which they are unable to obtain through human nature: to be baptised by water and the Holy Spirit, and to be welcomed into God's Holy Church and to be made living members of Christ.

3 Let us pray
Almighty and eternal God, who by your many mercies rescued Noah and his family in the ark so that they did not perish in the water; and safely brought the children of Israel, your people, through the Red Sea, so making plain to us from long ago your holy Baptism: again, through the Baptism of your beloved Son, Jesus Christ in the river Jordan, you sanctified water for the mystical washing of sins: We beg you, by your great mercies, look on these your servants; wash them and cleanse them by your Holy Spirit, so that they being saved from your anger, may be welcomed into the ark of Christ's Church; and being steadfast in faith, and rejoicing in hope, they may be established in love; and after passing through the perturbations of this troubled world, may reach the land of eternal life, and there reign together with you. Through Jesus Christ our Lord. **Amen.**

4 *The Minister says to those who are to be baptised:*
Beloved, you have come here desiring holy baptism. Therefore, you must confess, before these your witnesses, and all these who are present here, that you will continue to reject Satan and all his works, that you will always believe the Holy Word of God, and hold fast in obedience to his commandments.
I ask each one of you:
Do you reject Satan and all his works, the world's unseemly ostentation and pleasures, its immoral desires of all kinds, and the evil lusts of the body that you will neither follow nor be guided by them?
I reject them all.

5 In whom do you believe?
At this point all who are to be baptised confess the Apostles Creed. [[CF1a]]

6 Do you want to be baptised into this Faith?
Yes, I do.
Will you hold fast in obedience to the commandments of God and follow his will?
Yes, I will so do, with God's help.

7 *All Christians stand.*
Then the Minister asks them:
Will you who are witnesses to these promises, make every effort to be a good example by your lives so that these people may grow in Christ?
Yes, we will so do, with God's help.

PURIFICATION OF THE WATER

Responses:

8 O God of mercy, your beloved Son Jesus Christ, by his baptism in the River Jordan, made himself one with us who are sinful, revealing to us our true humanity, grant that the first Adam who is in these people may be buried, so that the new man may be seen. **Amen.**
Grant that all wrong desires may die in them and the things of the Spirit may live and grow in them. **Amen.**
Grant that they may have the power and strength to triumph over Satan, the world and the body. **Amen.**
Grant that all who have been set apart for the work of our service may be clothed with heavenly goodness, that they may obtain an eternal reward, by your mercy, holy Lord God, Who lives and reigns over all, for ever and ever. **Amen.**

9   *And then the Minister will say or sing:*
    May the Lord be with you:
    And with your spirit.
    Lift up your hearts:
    We lift them up to the Lord.
    And let us thank the Lord our God:
    It is right and it is our duty.
    It is indeed fitting, right and also our duty that we should thank you, holy Lord, Almighty Father, and eternal God. Because from his side your beloved Son, Jesus Christ, gave water and blood for the forgiveness of our sins; he commissioned his disciples to go and teach all nations and to baptise them in the Name of the Father and the Son and the Holy Spirit.
    We entreat you, look on the prayers of your people here present; sanctify + this water for the mystery of the washing of sins; grant that these people who will be baptised in it may receive your abundant grace that they may continue in the number of your chosen children. Through Him, our Lord Jesus Christ your Son: who lives and reigns with you eternally in unity with the Holy Spirit, God, for ever and ever. **Amen.**

10   *All sit, apart from those to be baptised and their sponsors.*

11   The Minister will invite all who are ready to be baptised one by one and their sponsors who should not be fewer than two, and to ask the names in which he will be baptised; then he will sprinkle water on his head (or immerse him), saying:

12   (Name) I baptise you in the Name of the Father and the Son and the Holy Spirit. Amen.

13   Our Lord Jesus Christ has received you into his flock, I put the sign of the cross + on you (*at this point the Minister makes the sign of the cross on the forehead*) to show that you should not be ashamed to confess the faith of Christ who was crucified for your sake; that you may be Christ's servant and faithful witness until the end of your life. Amen.

14   *Where it is the custom for those who are baptised to be given the token of white robes and a candle, the following order of service should be used:*
    He has clothed us with the robes of salvation:
    He has covered us with the robes of righteousness.
    Giving the token of the white robe:
    Receive this robe, symbol of the purity of your spirit, and preserve this purity until the mercy seat of our Lord Jesus Christ that you may obtain eternal life. **Amen.**

15   All glorify the Father
    Let your light shine before all people; that they may see your good works.
    And glorify our Father who is in heaven.
    Giving him a candle
    Receive this candle, its light is a symbol of the grace of your baptism; keep all God's commandments, so that when the Lord comes you may be acceptable to him, and welcomed together with his saints into the eternal kingdom. Amen.

16   *Afterwards the Minister says:*
    Beloved brothers and sisters, because these people have been born again and brought into Christ's body, which is his Church, let us thank Almighty God for these good things which he has given them; and with one mind, let us pray that they will live from now on in the way that they have begun today.

17 Let us pray
We give you our heartfelt thanks, O merciful Father; because it pleased you that these people should be born again by your Holy Spirit and that you chose them to be your children and to bring them into your holy Church. We humbly beseech you, grant that they may be dead to the things of sin, alive to the things of righteousness; and having shared in the death of your Son, grant that they may share in his resurrection; until at the end they inherit your eternal kingdom, together with the chosen of your holy church, through Christ our Lord. **Amen.**

18 *Then the Minister tells those who have been baptised:*
And you who are clothed with Christ now through Baptism, because you have been made children of God and of light, through faith in Jesus Christ, it is your duty not to be ashamed to confess the faith of Christ crucified; but being under his banner, bravely fight against sin, the world and Satan; and continue to be Christ's faithful soldiers and servants until the end of your lives, through Christ our Lord. **Amen.**

19 *The Lord's prayer.*
[[**CF4a**]]

20 *The Minister gives the Blessing.*

THE BAPTISM OF YOUNG CHILDREN

Introduction

1 *The Minister says:*
Beloved brothers and sisters because all are born in sin and are unable to please God, unless they are born again of water and the Holy Spirit, I humbly beg you to ask God the Father in the Name of our Lord Jesus Christ, that he may grant these children what they are unable to obtain through human nature; that is to be baptised in water and the Holy Spirit and to be welcomed into God's holy Church of God, and to be made living members of Christ.

2 Let us pray
Almighty and eternal God, who by your many mercies saved Noah and his family in the ark from drowning; and safely brought the children of Israel, your people, through the Red Sea, so showing us your Holy Baptism; again through the Baptism of your beloved Son Jesus Christ in the River Jordan, you purified the water for the mystery of washing sins: We beg you by your great mercy, look on these your children: wash them and sanctify them by your Holy Spirit, so that they being saved from your anger, may be welcomed into the ark of Christ's Church: and being steadfast in faith, and rejoicing in hope, they may be established in love, and after passing through the restlessness of this troubled world, may reach the land of eternal life and there reign together with you, through Jesus Christ our Lord. **Amen.**

3 *Then the Minister says to the sponsors and parents:*
Beloved, you have come here desiring holy baptism for these children. So you must, on their behalf, promise before all these who are present, that they will reject Satan and all his works, always believe God's Holy Word, and obediently keep his commandments.

4 *Afterwards the Minister questions the sponsors:*
Do you reject Satan and all his works?
I reject Satan and all his works.
Do you reject the pleasures and ostentation of the world?
I reject the pleasures and ostentation of the world.

Do you reject the immoral lusts of the body?
I reject the immoral lusts of the body.

5   *At this point, the sponsors and those who are baptised, say the Apostles Creed. After the Creed, all turn toward the font, then he asks the sponsors:*

6   Do you want to be baptised into this faith?
Yes, I do.
Will you obey God's commands and do his will?
Yes, I will do this with God's help.

7   *Then the Minister asks all present:*
Do you who witness these promises, promise to be good examples by your lives so that these children may grow in Christ?
Yes, we will do this with God's help.

8   *There where it customary, the Minister may say:*
I order you, Satan, in the Name of the Father and Son and Holy Spirit, depart from these children, because our Lord Jesus Christ has invited them to his holy baptism and made them members of his body. So, O accursed spirits, know the judgement which was recorded, and do not dare to ill-treat these children who Christ has redeemed by his precious blood and chosen to come into his family through this his baptism.

9   *Then the Minister marks each one with the sign of the cross on the forehead, with the oil of salvation.*
May the cross of Christ be always between you and Satan; And you, my child, fight bravely against him until the end of your life.

BLESSING OF THE WATER

10   O God of mercy, your beloved Son Jesus Christ, by his baptism in the River Jordan, made himself one with us who are sinful, revealing to us our true humanity: Grant that the first Adam who is in these people may be buried, and the new person appear. **Amen.**
Grant that all immoral desires may die in them, and that the things of the Spirit may live and grow in them. **Amen.**
Grant that they may have the power and strength to triumph over Satan, the world and the body. **Amen.**
Grant that all who have been set apart for our work and service may be clothed with heavenly goodness, that they may obtain the eternal reward, through your mercy, holy Lord God, who lives and reigns over all, for ever and ever. **Amen.**

11   *The Minister then says or sings:*
May the Lord remain with you.
And also with your spirit.
Lift up your hearts;
We lift them up to the Lord.
And let us give thanks to our Lord God;
It is right and also our duty.
It is indeed proper, right and our duty to give you thanks holy Lord, Almighty Father, and eternal God,
Because your beloved Son, Jesus Christ, offered from his holy side water and blood for the forgiveness of our sins; he instructed his disciples to go and teach all nations, and to baptise them in the Name of the Father and the Son and the Holy Spirit.
We entreat you, look on the prayers of your people here present; sanctify + this water for the mystical washing of sins, grant that these children who will be baptised with it

may receive your grace in abundance, and may continue in the number of your chosen children. Through Him, our Lord Jesus Christ your Son; Who lives and reigns together with you, in the unity of the Holy Spirit, God eternal for ever and ever. **Amen.**

12 *Then one of the sponsors brings a child and the Minister baptises the child by sprinkling water on his head three times:*
(Name) I baptise you in the Name of the Father and the Son and the Holy Spirit. Amen.

13 Our Lord Jesus Christ has received you into his flock, I put the sign of the cross + on you so that you may not be ashamed to confess the faith of Christ, crucified for your sake; be a faithful servant and witness of Christ until the end of your life. **Amen.**

14 *If those who have been baptised are to receive the sign of the white robe and candle, the following order should be used:*
He has clothed us with robes of salvation;
He has covered with robes of righteousness.
He gives them the robe.
Receive this robe, symbol of the purity of your spirit, and preserve this purity until the mercy seat of our Lord Jesus Christ so that you may obtain eternal life. **Amen.**

15 Let your light shine before all (people); that they may see your good works.
And glorify our Father who is in heaven.
He gives him a candle.
Receive this candle, its light is a symbol of the grace of your baptism; keep all God's commandments, so that when the Lord comes you will be acceptable to him, and welcomed together with his saints into the eternal kingdom. **Amen.**

16 *Then the Minister says:*
Beloved brothers and sisters, because these children have been born again, and brought into Christ's body, that is his Church, let us thank Almighty God for these good things which he has given them; and united let us pray that these children may live from now as they have begun today.

17 Let us pray
We thank you from our heart, O merciful Father, because it pleased you that these children be born again by your Holy Spirit, and that you chose them to be your children and to bring them into your holy Church. And we humbly beseech you, grant that they may be dead to the things of sin and alive to the things of righteousness; and as they have already shared in the death of your Son, grant that they may share in his resurrection; until at the end, they may inherit your eternal kingdom, together with the chosen of your holy Church, through Jesus Christ our Lord. **Amen.**

18 *The Minister then warns the sponsors with these words:*
Because this child has promised through the lips of you his sponsors, to reject Satan and all his works, and to believe God and to serve him; so you must remember that it is your responsibility to see that this child is taught, once he is old enough to learn, how he confessed and made a solemn vow and promise through your lips. Also let him learn the Creed, the Lord's Prayer, the Ten Commandments and all other things which a Christian should know and believe for his spiritual life; and may this child understand the Christian worship and conduct. When this child reaches the age of reason, let him be brought to the Bishop so that he can be confirmed.

19 The Lord's prayer.
[[CF4a]]

20 *The Minister gives the Blessing.*

[[Rubrics about baptism of the sick and what to do on recovery.]]

CONFIRMATION

[[1 Rubrics about catechesis and the normal context being a Eucharist.]]

Prayer

2 O God, you taught the hearts of believers by the light of the Holy Spirit; grant that by this Spirit we may know all things with understanding; and always rejoice in his holy comfort. Through our Lord Jesus Christ your Son; who lives and reigns together with you in the unity of the Holy Spirit, eternal God, for ever and ever. **Amen.**

[[3 Readings.]]

Presenting those who will be confirmed.

4 *While a hymn or Psalm is sung, the Priest stands in front of those who will be confirmed, facing the altar. The Bishop sits on his chair in front of the Altar, facing the congregation.*

5 *Then the Priest says:*
Father in God, I bring you these people here present so that they may be confirmed through the laying on of hands.
Bishop: Tell me, have you tested them and examined their Christian lives, and their understanding of the Church's teachings, and do you affirm that they are worthy of the laying on of hands?
Priest: I have tested them, and also examined them, and I affirm that they are worthy of the laying on of hands.

6 *Then the Bishops asks those who are to confirmed:*
You who are here in the presence of God and this congregation, are you ready to affirm for yours those promises and vows made at the time of your baptism?
We are ready.
Tell me, do you affirm that you reject Satan and all his works, worldly pleasures, its ostentation and the wrongful desires of the body.
I reject Satan and all his works, worldly pleasures, its ostentation and the wrongful desires of the body.

7 Tell me, do you promise to fellowship with your fellow Christians in worship and frequently receive Holy Communion.
I will so do with God's help.
Tell me, will you willingly continue to be Christ's faithful soldiers and servants, by reading the Word of God, through a life of prayer and witnessing to others about the Christian faith?
I will so do with God's help.
Tell me, will you work hard to be faithful stewards of Christ by giving your life and wealth for the work of the Church and the extension of God's kingdom?
I will so do with God's help.
In whom do you believe?

8 I believe in God Father Almighty *(Here each one recites the Apostles Creed)*
[[CF1a]]

9 *Then all Christians present stand: and the Bishop asks them:*
You who witness these promises, will you make every effort to be a good example by your lives, so as to help these who are being confirmed now, that throughout their lives they may continue to grow in their faith and in serving Christ?
We will indeed do this with God's help.

The congregation sits.

10 *The Bishop stands and stretches out his hands to them in Confirmation, and says:*
May the Holy Spirit descend on you, and his power. May he who is high up keep you safe from all sin. **Amen.**

11 *Afterwards he continues:*
The Name of the Lord be praised;
From today and for ever.
Our help is in the Name of the Lord;
Who made heaven and land.
O Lord hear our prayer;
May our cry reach you.
May the Lord remain with you;
And with your spirit.

12 *Bishop:* Let us pray
Almighty God who lives for ever, it pleased you that these your servants should be born again by water and the Holy Spirit, and to give them forgiveness of all their sins: We beseech you strengthen them by the Holy Spirit, the Comforter; daily increase in them the gifts of your grace. **Amen.**
Spirit of wisdom and understanding: **Amen.**
Spirit of counsel and inner strength: **Amen.**
Spirit of knowledge and godliness: **Amen.**
Fill them with the spirit of your holy reverence, this day and always, through Christ our Lord. **Amen.**

13 *If it is the custom to anoint with oil, the following order of service should be used:*
Let us pray
O Lord, give them your strength which overcame our enemy by whom you suffered and were crucified, may they be given with us the sign of the cross, set them apart to be yours for ever; being anointed with oil on their face, fill their hearts with the Holy Spirit; so that they may obtain eternal life, You who live and reign, God, for ever and ever. **Amen.**

14a *Then when the Bishop reaches each one (his sponsor places his right hand on the right shoulder of the one who he is sponsoring), he places his hand on his head saying:*
(Name) I put the sign of the cross on you; I place my hands on you that you may be made strong by the Holy Spirit. In the Name of the Father and the Son and the Holy Spirit. **Amen.**

or

14b *Where the custom of anointing with oil is not used, the following order of service should be followed. Those to be confirmed kneel. The bishop places hands on each head saying:*
O Lord, keep this your servant in your heavenly grace that he may continue yours for ever: and may he grow more and more each day in the Holy Spirit until he reaches the eternal kingdom. **Amen.**

15 *The Bishop then says:*
The peace of the Lord remain with you always;
And also with your spirit.

16 Let us pray

Almighty God who lives for ever, who gives us a heart to want and do what is good, and at to please you who are Holy: We ask that these your servants, on whom we have just now laid hands according to what was done by your holy apostles; so that by this sign (token) to give them the certainty of the favour of your grace and goodness towards them. Your hand, O Lord, be on them continually, your Holy Spirit be with them always, lead them to know and obey your holy Word, so that at the end they may obtain eternal life. Through our Lord Jesus Christ your Son, who lives and reigns together with you, in the unity of the Holy Spirit, God, for ever and ever. **Amen.**

17 *Then the Bishop faces those who have been confirmed and blesses them:*

May Almighty God, Father and Son and Holy Spirit, bless you. Amen.

20. The Church in the Province of the Indian Ocean

Christianity came to the islands of Madagascar, Mauritius and the Seychelles by the Roman Catholic Church and with French colonization. In 1810 the British captured Mauritius and began to send Anglican chaplains. Missionaries arrived in Mauritius in the 1830s, the Seychelles in 1840s and Madagascar in 1864. The Diocese of Mauritius was established in 1854. In 1973 the Province of the Indian Ocean was formed. Two of the dioceses are rather remote from the others and there are a variety of liturgies.

The Province has a diversity of liturgical practice. The five dioceses in Madagascar use a version of the Book of Common Prayer translated into Malagasy, *Ny Boky Fivavahana*.[53] There have been a number of editions of this prayer book, the present one dating from 1976, with reprints. The Diocese of the Seychelles produced a *Service Book* in 1997 in English, French and Creole. The Diocese of Mauritius produced *Liturgie pour L'initiation Chrétienne* (2012) which is their contemporary version of baptism and confirmation.

DIOCESE OF THE SEYCHELLES

SERVICE BOOK 1997

BAPTISM SERVICE FOR CHILDREN

1   Children who are too young to profess the Christian faith are baptised on the understanding that they are brought up as Christians within the family of the Church. As they grow up, they need the help and encouragement of that family, so that they learn to be faithful in public worship and private prayer, to live and trust in God and come to confirmation.

  Parents and godparents, the children whom you have brought for baptism depend(s) chiefly on you for the help and encouragement they need(s). Are you willing to give it to them by your prayers, by your example, and by your teaching?
  I am willing.

2   Heavenly Father, grant that by your Holy Spirit, these children may be born again and brought to know you in the family of your Church; that in newness of life, they may overcome evil and grow in grace until their lives' end; through Jesus Christ, our Lord; **Amen.**

---

53 G 95: 9.

THE DECISION

3 Those who bring children to be baptised must affirm their allegiance to Christ and their rejection of all that is evil. It is your duty to bring up these children to fight against evil and to follow Christ. Therefore I ask:
Do you turn to Christ?
I turn to Christ.
Do you repent of your sins?
I repent of my sins.
Do you renounce evil?
I renounce evil.

THE BLESSING OF THE WATER

4 We give thanks to you, Almighty Father, everlasting God, through your most dearly beloved Son, Jesus Christ, our Lord. By his death and resurrection you have broken the power of evil, and by your sending of the Spirit, you have made us new people in the family of your Church; Bless we pray you this water, that all who are baptised in it may be born again in Christ; that being baptised into his death and receiving forgiveness of all their sins, *they* may know the power of his resurrection and may walk in newness of life; through Jesus Christ our Lord. **Amen.**

THE BAPTISM

5 You have brought *these children* to baptism. You must now declare before God and his Church the Christian faith into which *they are* to be baptised and in which you will help them to grow.

〚Modern question form from ASB **CF3**〛

6 N ..., I baptise you in the name of the Father, and of the Son, and of the Holy Spirit. Amen.

7 I sign you with the cross, the sign of Christ.
Do not be ashamed to confess the faith of Christ crucified.
Fight manfully under his banner against sin, the world and the devil and continue his faithful soldier and servant to the end of your life.

8 Receive this light.
This is to show that you have passed from darkness to light.
Shine as a light in the world to the glory of God the Father.

9 God has received you by baptism into his Church:
We welcome you into the Lord's family
as fellow members of the Body of Christ,
as children of the same heavenly Father,
as inheritors with us of the Kingdom of God.

10 Lord God, our Father, we thank you that by your Holy Spirit *these children* have been born again into new life, adopted for your own, and received into the fellowship of your Church: grant that they may grow in the faith into which *they have* been baptised, that they may profess it for *themselves* when *they come* to be confirmed, and that all things belonging to the Spirit may live and grow in *them*, through Jesus Christ our Lord. **Amen.**

Heavenly Father, we pray for the parents and godparents of *these children*, give them the spirit of wisdom and love, that their homes may reflect the joy of your eternal Kingdom. **Amen.**

DIOCESE OF MAURITIUS

LITURGY FOR CHRISTIAN INITIATION 2012

BAPTISM AND CONFIRMATION

⟦Translated by Damian Scragg and Phillip Tovey⟧

FORM 1

RENUNCIATION OF SATAN AND ACCEPTANCE OF CHRIST

1 For salvation of the world, Christ, our saviour died on the cross, and was resurrected from the dead. Baptism is the external sign by which we receive the benefits which he did for us: we are united in his death, we receive the forgiveness of sins, we are raised with Christ for the new life in the Spirit.

BAPTISM OF INFANTS

2 You are asking for baptism of this child; you will have to educate them to resist sin and follow Christ.

BAPTISM AND/OR CONFIRMATION OF ADULTS

3 You who have come to receive the sacraments of baptism and confirmation, you must confirm your faith to Christ and renounce all evil.

4 So I ask you these questions:
Do you renounce Satan and all rebellion against God?
Yes I renounce.
Do you renounce lust and corruption?
Yes I renounce.
Do you renounce the sin which separates us from God and our neighbours?
Yes I renounce.

Do you accept Christ the Saviour?
Yes I accept.
Do you accept Christ as Lord?
Yes I accept.
Do you come to Christ for life and freedom?
Yes I come to him.

PROFESSION OF FAITH

5 Beloved in Christ, let us profess together our faith with those going to be baptised and confirmed.

⟦Question and answer Apostles Creed **CF2b**. Adds to question 'and put your trust in him?'⟧

THE RITE OF BAPTISM

BLESSING OF WATER

6 Praise God who made heaven and earth.
We bless you Lord.
God your Son Jesus Christ was baptised in the waters of the Jordan, we bless you for the gift of water to cleanse and revive us.
We bless you Lord.

We thank you because through the waters of the red Sea, you have freed your people from slavery, to lead them to freedom in the Promised Land.
We bless you Lord.
We thank you because through the deep waters of death, you lead your son, and you raised him to life in glory.
We bless you Lord.
Bless this water that your servant who is baptised is united with Christ in his death and his resurrection, for purification and deliverance from all sin.
We bless you Lord.
Send your Holy Spirit on *him* lead *him* to the new birth in the family of your church, and raise *him* with Christ for the fullness of eternal life, for yours is the glory, the honour, and power for ever and ever. **Amen.**

THE BAPTISM

7 N I baptise you in the name of the Father, and of the Son and of the Holy Spirit. **Amen.**

SIGN OF THE CROSS

The priest marks the sign of the cross on the forehead of the child

8a Receive the cross, sign of Christ.
May Almighty God free you from the powers of darkness and lead you in the light and obedience of Christ.

8b Receive the cross: A welcoming sign showing the desire of God to reveal himself to you as a Father full of love; A sign of battle for the life which Jesus has won by his death and resurrection; The sign of the cross also shows our desire to learn to know God and grow gradually in the footsteps of his son Jesus Christ.
May Almighty God free you from the powers of darkness and lead you in the light and obedience of Christ.

THE SHINING LIGHT

9a I give you this light as sign that you have passed from darkness to light.
Shine as light in the world to the glory of God the Father.

9b Receive this flame a symbol of love and truth. Keep it alive in your hands radiant in your heart warm for everyone. May your light reflect the presence of God, shining with evidence that it is your light.

9c Receive this day this flame and allow it to spread. Keep it alive in your hands, radiant in your heart, warm for everyone. Be a child of the light. The fruit of the light is called love justice and truth. Thus your light shines as evidence to all, that in their prayer, thanking God that before their eyes is a reflection of his presence.

BLESSING

10 May Almighty God who was received you into his church, shower on you the riches of his grace by replenishing you daily by the spirit, and make you capable to have a part of the heritage of the saints in light.

WELCOME BY THE ASSEMBLY

11 God has received by baptism you into his church.
We welcome you in the family of the Lord. Together with you we are members of the body of Christ, children of the same Father, and inheritors of the kingdom of God.

RITE OF CONFIRMATION

THE INVOCATION OF THE SPIRIT

12 *Bishop*: Our salvation is in the name of the Lord
Who made heaven and earth.
Blessed be the name of the Lord
Now and forever.

13 God eternal and all-powerful here are your servants who you have born-again in
water and the holy spirit, and who you have pardoned from their sins; we beseech
you, strengthen them by the Holy Spirit the comforter; and increase in them every day
the seven gifts of the Holy Spirit, the spirit of wisdom and discernment, the spirit of
council and courage, the spirit of knowledge and benevolence and inspire them in the
fear of the Lord, now and always. **Amen.**

IMPOSITION OF HANDS

14 *Bishop*: N God has called you by name and made you his own, strengthen Lord your
servant with your Holy Spirit. *Amen*

15 Peace be with you
And with your spirit

CONCLUSION

16 *Bishop*: Beloved in Christ let us pray for these servants of God that they will be strong
in faith and love to witness to Christ in their life.
**Assist Lord these servants with your divine grace, so that they are yours for ever and
grow daily in the Holy Spirit, until they reach your eternal kingdom.**

17 *Bishop*: May the God of all grace, who in Jesus Christ call you to his eternal glory,
perfect you and strengthen you, and fortify you and making steadfast. And may the
blessing of God the Creator, Father, Son, and Holy Spirit, the always with you and in
you. **Amen.**

THE CELEBRATION OF BAPTISM

MODEL 2

1 *INTRODUCTION*

1.1 The duties of parents
Children who have not yet arrived at the age of reason and who are not able to
profess faith personally are baptised on the condition that they will be raised in the
faith to which they were baptised.
You are asking for this child to be baptised; you will have to educate them in the faith
so that by keeping the commandments they will love God and neighbour as Christ
taught us.
Are you willing to take this responsibility?

The sponsors (parents, godfathers and godmothers)
Yes we are.

1.2 The decision

Those who bring their children to baptism must affirm their commitment to Christ and renounce all evil. It's your duty to raise this child to fight against evil and follow Christ.

Therefore I ask you these questions, which you must respond for yourselves and for this infant.

Do you turn to Christ?

I turn to Christ.

Do you repent of your sins?

I repent of my sins.

Do you renounce evil?

I renounce evil.

2   *PRESENTATION*

Who presents this/these candidates for baptism?

We present N so that he/she receives the sacrament of baptism.

3   *BLESSING OF THE WATER*

Praise God who made heaven and earth

Who keeps his promise for ever.

God, your Son Jesus Christ was baptised in the water of the Jordan we bless you for the gift of water to purify us and to revive us. We thank you for by the crossing of the water of the Red Sea, you liberated your people from slavery, for the journey to liberty in the Promised Land. We thank you, for the journey through the deep waters of death, you led your Son, and you raised him in life for glory. Bless this water, so that your servant who is baptised will be united with Christ in his death and resurrection, to be purified and delivered from all sin. Send your Holy Spirit on him for the new birth in the family of your church and that he is raised with Christ for the fullness of eternal life for yours is the glory, the honour and the power for ever and ever. **Amen.**

4   *PROFESSION OF FAITH*

You have brought this child for baptism. In the presence of God and in his church, you must profess the faith into which he will be baptised. You must respond for yourself and for this child.

Do you believe in God the Father, who made heaven and earth and do you put your confidence in him?

I believe, and put my confidence in him.

Do you believe in Jesus Christ his only Son the saviour of all people?

I believe, and put my confidence in him.

Do you believe in the Holy Spirit who gives life to the people of God?

I believe, and put my confidence in him.

This is the faith of the church.

This is our faith: we believe in one God, Father, Son, and Holy Spirit, and we put our confidence in him.

5   *BAPTISM*

N, I baptise you in the name of the Father and of the Son and of the Holy Spirit.

In baptism you received the seal of the Holy Spirit and the mark of your belonging to Christ for ever. **Amen.**

6 SIGN OF THE CROSS

I mark you with the cross, sign of Christ. Do not be ashamed to confess the faith of Christ crucified.
Fight valiantly under his sign against sin, the world and the devil, and remain his faithful soldier and servant for all the days of your life.
May Almighty God deliver you from the powers of darkness and lead you in the light of Christ.

7 THE LIGHT

7.1 I give you this light a sign that you have passed from darkness to light.
Shine as a light in the world to the glory of God the Father.

7.2 Receive this light symbol of love and truth. Keep it alive in your hands, shining in your heart, warm for everyone. Let your light reflect the presence of God, shine with evidence and that it is the light for you.

7.3 Receive today this flame and make it spread. Keep it alive in your hands, radiant in your heart, warm for everyone. Be a child of light. The fruit of light is called Love, Justice and Truth. Thus let your light so shine that everyone, in their prayer will thank God for having before our eyes a reflection of his presence.

8 WELCOME

Through baptism God has received you in his church.
We welcome you in the family of the Lord. Together with you we are members of the body of Christ, children of the father and inheritors of the kingdom of God.

21. The Church of the Province of Central Africa

Christianity came to Central Africa with missionary explorers such as Dr Livingstone and the missionary work of the UMCA. The Province began in 1955. Currently the church does not have a Provincial liturgy as such; different dioceses and linguistic groups use different books. First the English Prayer Book was translated into various vernacular languages, probably with adaptions.[54] Of historic interest is the *Occasional Offices* (1956) with English rubrics and Nsenga text (spoken in Zambia, Zimbabwe and Mozambique) as there is a complex set of catechetical services including making of catechumens, anointing of catechumens and scrutinies, as well as baptism and confirmation. A Provincial Book of Common Prayer was produced in 1966. This used the South African 1954 baptismal services.[55]

The Provincial Book in English was translated into other languages. A Shona Prayer Book, *Buku Re Munamato Wevese*, has gone through numerous reprints since its publication in 1963, and was corrected in 1972.[56] Similarly the Chichewa version, *Mapemphero ndi Nyimbo za Eklezia*, was first published in 1971 and has gone through many editions.[57] In English-speaking congregations the use of Southern African services is common.

Jagger included the baptism of infants and confirmation from the South African 1954 services. The following is the Baptism of Adults from the Shona translation as used today.

BUKU RE MUNAMATO WEVESE 1963/1972

THE BOOK OF COMMON PRAYER

⟦Translated by Rainah Madzorera⟧

MUSHANDO WORUBABATIDZO KUNA AVO VANE MAKORE OUKURU
THE BAPTISM OF ADULTS

⟦1 Rubrics⟧

2 Dearly beloved, I beg you to call upon God the Father, through our Lord Jesus Christ, that of his unending goodness he will grant to these people the things which by birth they cannot have; that they may be baptized with Water and the Holy Spirit, and be received into Christ's holy Church, and be made living members of the church.

---

54 G 124: 1–2 Nsenga.
55 J 77–85.
56 G 180: 7.
57 G 127: 11.

3   *Then, with the people standing, the Priest says,*
    Let us pray.
    Almighty and everlasting God, who by the Baptism of your well-beloved Son Jesus
    Christ, in the river Jordan, you sanctified water for the mystical washing away of sin:
    mercifully look upon these people; wash them and sanctify them with the Holy Spirit,
    that they may be received into the ark of Christ's Church; and being steadfast in faith,
    joyful through hope, and rooted in love, may so pass the waves of this troublesome
    world, that finally they may come to the land of everlasting life, there to reign with
    You world without end; through Jesus Christ our Lord. **Amen.**

4   *After which he may also say this prayer.*
    Almighty and immortal God, the aid of all that are in need, the helper of all that come
    to You for succour, the life of them that believe, and the resurrection of the dead; We
    call upon You for these people, that as they come to Your Holy Baptism, they may
    be spiritually born again and receive remission of their sins. Receive them, O Lord,
    as You have promised through Your beloved Son, saying, 'Ask, and you will receive;
    seek, and you will find; knock, and it will be opened to you.' Therefore give us as
    we ask; let us who are seeking; open the gate unto us who knock; that these persons
    may enjoy the everlasting benediction of thy heavenly washing, and may come to the
    eternal kingdom which You have promised through Christ our Lord. **Amen.**

⟦5   Reading John 3.1–8⟧

THE PROMISES

6   Well-beloved, you have come here desiring to receive Holy Baptism, you have
    heard how the congregation has prayed, that our Lord Jesus Christ may receive you
    and bless you, to release you of your sins, to give you the kingdom of heaven, and
    everlasting life. You have heard also that our Lord Jesus Christ has promised in his
    holy word to grant all these things that we have asked for; which promise he, for his
    part, will most surely keep and do.
    Therefore you, on your part, must undertake to do these three things: first, that you
    will renounce the devil and all his works; secondly, that you will consistently believe
    God's holy word; and thirdly, that you will obediently keep his commandments.

7   Therefore I ask.

    Do you renounce the devil and all his works?
    I do.
    Do you renounce the vain pomp and glory of the world?
    I do.
    Do you renounce the carnal desires of the flesh?
    I do.

8   Do you believe in God the Father Almighty, Maker of Heaven and earth?
    I do.
    Do you believe in Jesus Christ his only Son our Lord, who was conceived by the Holy
    Spirit, born of the Virgin Mary, suffered under Pontius Pilate, Was crucified, died,
    and was buried, He descended into hell; the third day he rose again from the dead, He
    ascended into heaven, and is seated at the right hand of God the Father Almighty; and
    from there he will come to judge the living and the dead?
    I do.
    Do you believe in the Holy Spirit; the holy Catholic Church; the Communion of
    Saints; the Remission of sins; the Resurrection of the body; and life everlasting?
    I do.

9 Will you be baptized in this faith?
That is my desire.

Will you then obediently keep God's holy will and commandments, and follow them all the days of your life?
I will endeavour so to do, God being my helper.

10 *Then the Priest says,*
Merciful God, grant that the old Adam in in these people may be so buried, that the new person may be raised up in them. **Amen.**
Grant that all evil desires of the flesh may die in them, and that all things belonging to the Holy Spirit may live and grow in them. **Amen.**
Grant that they may have power and strength to win and triumph, over the devil, the world, and the flesh. **Amen.**
Grant that these who are being dedicated here to You by our office and ministry, may be endued with heavenly virtues, and everlastingly rewarded, through Your mercy, O blessed Lord God, who lives, and reigns forever. **Amen.**

THE BLESSING OF THE WATER

11 The Lord be with you.
And also with you.
Lift up your hearts.
We lift them up to the Lord.
Let us give thanks to the Lord.
It is right to do so.
It is right, and our bounden duty that we should give thanks to You, O Lord, Holy Father, Almighty, Everlasting God, for that Your most dearly beloved Son Jesus Christ, for the forgiveness of our sins, He shed blood and water from His precious side that our sins may be forgiven; and gave commandment to his disciples, that they should go teach all nations, and baptize them in the name of the Father, the Son, and the Holy Spirit. Regard, we beseech you, the supplications of your congregation; sanctify this water to the mystical washing away of sin; and grant that these persons, now to be baptized therein, may receive the fullness of your grace, and ever remain in the number of your faithful and chosen children: through Jesus Christ our Lord, to whom, with you, in the unity of the Holy Spirit, be all honour and glory, now and evermore. **Amen.**

THE BAPTISM

12 *Then the Priest shall take each person to be baptized by the right hand, and shall say the name; and then dip him in the water or poor water upon him, saying,*
N. I baptize you in the name of the Father, and of the Son, and of the Holy Spirit. **Amen.**

13 We receive this person into the congregation of Christ's flock, and do * sign him with the sign of the Cross, as a sign that shows hereafter he shall not be ashamed to confess the faith of Christ crucified, and strongly fight under his banner, against sin, the world, and the devil; and remain Christ's faithful soldier and servant to the end of his life. **Amen.**

* Here the priest shall make a cross upon the persons (child's) forehead.

14 *Then, if so desired, the priest shall put upon the person the white vesture, commonly called the Chrysom, saying,*

Take this white vesture as a token of the innocency bestowed upon you, and for a sign whereby you are admonished to give yourself to pureness of life that after this transitory life you may be a partaker of life everlasting.

15 *And shall give to him a lighted candle, saying,*

Receive the light of Christ, so that when the bridegroom comes, you may go forth with all the saints to meet him; and see that you keep the grace of your baptism.

THE THANKSGIVING

16 Dearly beloved brethren, now that these people are born again, and grafted into the body of Christ's Church, let us give thanks to Almighty God for these blessings and with one accord make our prayers to Him, that they may lead the rest of their lives according to this beginning.

17 *Here they say the Lord's Prayer together*

Our Father, which art in heaven…

18 We give you hearty thanks, most merciful Father, that it has pleased you to regenerate these people with your Holy Spirit, to receive them as your own children by adoption, and to make them members of your Holy Church. Grant, O Lord, that they, being buried with Christ by baptism, and made partakers of his death, may also be partakers of his resurrection; that serving you here in newness of life, they may finally, with the rest of your Holy Church, in your everlasting kingdom; through Christ our Lord. **Amen.**

19 *Then, all standing up, if there is no sermon, the priest shall use these to exhortations following; speaking to the witnesses first.*

Now that these people have promised in your presence to renounce the devil and all his works, to believe in God, and to serve him; you must remember, that it is your part and duty to remind them, about the solemn vow, promise, and profession they have made before this congregation, and especially before you their chosen witnesses. And you are also called upon to help them to use all diligence, to be rightly instructed in God's holy Word; that so they may grow in grace and in the knowledge of our Lord Jesus Christ, and live godly, righteously, and soberly in this present world.

20 *And then, speaking to the newly baptized people, he shall proceed, and say,*

And as for you, who have worn Christ in baptism, it is your part and duty also, being made the children of God and of the light, by faith in Jesus Christ, to walk worthily of your Christian calling, and as children of light; remembering always that baptism reminds us of our faith in Jesus Christ; to follow the accordingly your call to Christianity, as blessed children remembering all the time that Baptism reminds us of our faith that we follow our Saviour Christ, and make us like him, that as he died, and rose again for us; so should we, who are baptised, would be die from sin, and rise again in righteousness; continually mortifying all evil desires, and daily advancing in all virtue and godliness of living.

21 *If the baptism is not joined to another service, the priest shall pronounce this blessing, the people kneeling:*

The Lord bless you, and keep you: the Lord make his face shine upon you, and be gracious to you: the Lord lift up his countenance upon you, and give you peace, now and evermore. **Amen.**

⟦22 Rubrics that direct the candidate should be confirmed as soon as possible; and conditional baptism.⟧

22. The Church of the Province of Southern Africa

Because of its strategic position en route to India, Christianity came to South Africa with the Portuguese, but more importantly with the settlement by the Dutch East India Company. In 1795 the British arrived and in 1814 the first Church of England chapel was opened. In 1847 Robert Gray was consecrated as Bishop for the Diocese of South Africa. Grey was an orthodox high churchman (rather than Anglo-Catholic) and a pioneer in Anglican constitutions. The first Provincial synod was in 1870 and gradually there was a division of the dioceses. The work of Dr Livingstone encouraged the church to continuously push northwards. The church took a strong stance against apartheid, which colours the church today.

In the early period the Book of Common Prayer was used and translated into various vernaculars.[58] This was adapted to local culture and also to the later Tractarian movement. In 1954 *A Book of Common Prayer: South Africa* was published.[59] Later liturgical revision led to a period of liturgical development with proposed rites in 1967.[60] The result of this liturgical development was *An Anglican Prayer Book 1989*. The Province has agreed to embark on a further period of liturgical revision.

Southern Africa operates in 11 languages, using the approach of dynamic equivalence, the final translation of *An Anglican Prayer Book* being into Portuguese for Mozambique. Baptism and confirmation are seen as services appropriately performed within Holy Communion. The bishop is seen as the minister of baptism, but this is mostly delegated to the local priest. The archetypal service of baptism and confirmation is at the Eucharist. There is also provision for a separate service of infant baptism and confirmation. Associated services of conditional baptism, emergency baptism, reception, admission, renewal and admission of a catechumen are included in the book. The service below is that of the archetypal service.

---

58 G 182: 1 Tswana, G 193: 1 Xhosa, G 199: 1 Zulu.
59 G 1954/1, J 77–85.
60 J 113–124.

BAPTISM AND CONFIRMATION

⟦A pastoral introduction. General rubrics about the service, including that baptism and confirmation should be celebrated in the Eucharist with the bishop. Directions as to where to place the service in the Eucharist or in morning and evening prayer.⟧

THE SERVICE OF BAPTISM AND CONFIRMATION

THE INTRODUCTION

1 *After the sermon the Bishop addresses the people in these or similar words*
Our Lord Jesus Christ gave himself to death on the cross and was raised again for the salvation of humankind.
Baptism is the sacrament in which, by repentance and faith, we enter into this salvation: we are united with Christ in his death; we are granted the forgiveness of sins; we are made members of his body and we are raised with him to new life in the spirit.
In confirmation become to be filled, through the laying on of hands, with the power of the spirit for worship, witness and service.

THE RENUNCIATION

2 *The Bishop addresses the candidates, parents and godparents, omitting any paragraph not required.*
You, who have come for baptism and confirmation, must declare your rejection of all that is evil.
You, who present children to baptism, must promise to bring them up to reject all that is evil. You are to answer for yourselves and for your child.
You, who have already been baptised and have now come to be confirmed, must reject with your own lips and from your heart declare your rejection of all that is evil.

3 *The Bishop asks them*
Do you renounce the devil and all the spiritual forces of wickedness that rebel against God?
I renounce them.

Do you renounce the evil powers of this world which corrupt and destroy what God has created?
I renounce them.

Do you renounce all sinful desires that draw you from the love of God?
I renounce them.

4 *The Bishop says to the congregation*
Dear friends in Christ, let us pray for these persons

God of all mercy, look on them. **Amen.**
Put to death their sinful desires. **Amen.**
Grant them the life of your spirit. **Amen.**
Enable them to overcome the evil one. **Amen.**
Give them every Christian virtue. **Amen.**
Bring them with your saints to everlasting glory. **Amen.**

5 *The Bishop, who may stretch out his hand towards the candidates, says*
May Almighty God deliver you from the path of darkness and lead you into the light and obedience of Christ. **Amen.**

THE BLESSING OF THE WATER

6 *The Bishop together with the candidates and their sponsors and parents, stands before the water of baptism and says*
Praise God who made heaven and earth
who keeps his promise for ever

7 Almighty God, our heavenly Father whose Son our Lord Jesus Christ was baptized in the river Jordan:
we thank you for the gift of water to cleanse and revive us
we thank you that through the waters of the Red Sea You led your people out of slavery and bondage to freedom in the promised land:
we thank you that through the deep waters of death you brought your Son and raised him to life in triumph
Bless this water, that your servants who are washed in it may be made one with Christ in his death and in his resurrection, to be cleanse and delivered from all sin.
Send your Holy Spirit upon them to bring them to new birth in the family of your church, and raise them with Christ to full and eternal life.
For all light, Majesty, authority, and power are yours, now and forever. **Amen.**

THE ALLEGIANCE

8 *The Bishop addresses the candidates, parents and godparents, omitting any paragraph not required.*
You, who are to be baptised and confirmed, must now in allegiance to Christ declare before God and his church the Christian faith into which you are to be baptised, and in which you will live and grow.

Parents and godparents, you must now in allegiance to Christ declare before God and his church the Christian faith into which these children are to be baptised, and in which you will help them live and grow. You are to answer for yourselves and for your child.

You who have already been baptised and are to be confirmed, must now in allegiance to Christ declare before God and his church that you accept the Christian faith into which you were baptised and in which you will continue to live and grow.

9 ⟦Modern question form from ASB **CF3**⟧

10 This is the faith of the church.
This is our faith.
We believe and trust in one God
Father, Son, and Holy Spirit.

11 *To the candidates he says*
Will you, who are to be baptised into this faith, and will you, who are to be confirmed, lives in obedience to God's laws, as a loyal member of his church?
With God's help, I will.

12 *To the parents and godparents he says*
Parents and godparents, will you by your own example and teaching, bring up your child to live in obedience to God's laws, as a loyal member of his church?
With God's help, I will.

THE BAPTISM

13 *Each candidate is presented to the Bishop by his parent sponsor who says*
Reverend Father in God, I present you N to be baptised.

14 *The Bishop baptises the candidates, dipping each in the water three times, or pouring water on each three times, once at the mention of each Person of the Holy Trinity, and saying*
N I baptise you in the name of the Father, and of the Son, and of the Holy Spirit. **Amen.**

THE WELCOME

15 *The Bishop makes the sign of the cross on the forehead of each one who has been baptised saying*
I sign you with the cross, the sign of Christ.

Do not be ashamed to confess the faith of Christ crucified.
Fight valiantly under the banner of Christ against sin, the world and the devil and continue his faithful soldiers and servants to the end of your lives.

16 *A candle, lit from the Easter candle if possible, is given to each, or to the godparents, with the words*
Christ our light.

By baptism into Christ you pass from darkness to light.
Shine as a light in the world to the glory of God the Father.

17 God has received you by baptism into his Church:
We welcome you into the Lord's family
we are members together of the Body of Christ,
we are children of the same heavenly Father,
we are inheritors together of the Kingdom of God.
We welcome you.

THE CONFIRMATION
⟦The bishop calls to prayer, silence is kept. The hymn Veni Creator is sung.⟧

18 Our help is in the name of the Lord.
Who has made heaven and earth
Blessed be the name of the Lord
Now and for ever. Amen.

20 *The Bishop stretches out his hands towards those to be confirmed and says*
Almighty and everliving God,
you have given your servants new birth
in baptism by water and the Spirit,
and have forgiven them all their sins.
Let your Holy Spirit rest upon them,
the Spirit of wisdom and understanding
the Spirit of discernment and inner strength
the Spirit of knowledge and true godliness;
and fill them with the Spirit of the fear of the Lord,
now and for ever. **Amen.**

21 *The candidates kneel in order before the Bishop. The Bishop may sign them on the forehead, using at his discretion the Chrism, and many say*
N I sign you with the sign of the cross and I lay my hand upon you.

Or he may say
N I lay my hand upon you.

He lays his hand on their heads, saying
Lord, confirm and strengthen with your Holy Spirit this your child (N) and empower him for your service. Amen.

22 Confirmation Prayer **CF5** said by all.

23 *The Bishop says*
Heavenly Father, we pray for your servants upon whom we have now laid our hands. May your fatherly hand be ever over them, your Holy Spirit ever be with them. Sustain them continually with the body and blood of your Son, and so lead them in the knowledge and obedience of your word that in the end they may enjoy the fullness of eternal life; through Jesus Christ our Lord. **Amen.**

23. The Province of the Anglican Church of the Congo

Anglican Mission in the Congo began in 1896 through the Ugandan evangelist Apolo Kivebulaya. The centre of his work was around Boga in the Belgian Congo. Greater expansion throughout the country began in 1960, and in 1972 the Diocese of Boga Zaire was created. From 1973 to 1981 Anglicans were part of the *Eglise du Christ*, one of the three churches allowed by the government. In 1992 the church became a Province within the Anglican Communion.

A variety of service books have been used in tribal languages following the BCP 1662.[61] However, because of linguistic diversity Congo Swahili is used as the main prayer book. The first prayer book seems to have been produced in 1973, followed by the 1984 Prayer Book, both including services of baptism and confirmation. This led to the 1998 Prayer Book for Congo *Kitabu cha sala kwa watu wote*. The following is a translation of the 1998 service book, however it needs to be remembered that previous service books may be used alongside this according to availability.

KITABU CHA SALA KWA WATU WOTE 1998

⟦Translated by Bridget Lane and Ian Tarrant⟧

BAPTISM

TEACHING

1 Paul wrote: 'There is one Lord, one faith, one baptism.' *(Ephesians 4.5)* Baptism is one pillar of the unity among Christians. But often baptism has brought division between Christians of different churches. We need to study carefully the purpose of baptism, its significance and its methods.
   The purpose of baptism is to show who are members of the church. God alone sees inside people's hearts, and discerns how many are his. We humans are unable to do this, but to organize ourselves properly in service, we need a way of recognizing God's flock and separating it from those who are not his. Long ago, the Jews used circumcision as a sign of God's people; we Christians use baptism.

2 Baptism signifies the start of a new life: some think of it as being washed; others of being born anew like a child from the waters of its mother's womb; still others see entering the water and coming out again as resembling the burial and resurrection of the Lord Jesus.

---

61 G 5: 1–2 Alur, G 119: 1 Lingala.

3   There is not just one method of baptism: if we read the New Testament we
    understand there are different practices. Some people were baptised in rivers, others at
    home; some were baptised alone, others together with their family.

4   We Anglicans consider baptism in much water to be the same a baptism by sprinkling
    a small amount of water, and from long ago we have been permitted to baptize in
    both ways.

5   Also we agree to baptize the children of believers, because we understand that
    believers will teach our faith to their children, through their everyday words and
    actions.

INSTRUCTIONS

⟦6   Rubrics to conduct the service, conditional baptism, godparents, readings and
    reaffirmation of baptismal vows.⟧

BAPTISM

7   *The Minister greets the people and briefly explains the meaning of this service.*

8   *Psalm 34.1–8 or another psalm may be read or sung, or a hymn may be sung.*

9   *The priest says:* The Lord be with you
    And with your spirit.
    Let us pray
    Almighty God, through the baptism of Christ in the river Jordan, you declared him
    to be your only Son, accept that through this baptism, these your servants be made
    members of your body through the Holy Spirit, and that they may become children
    of the family of your Church, through your Son Jesus Christ, our Lord, who lives and
    reigns with you and the Holy Spirit,one God, for ever and ever. **Amen.**

10 *Two or three passages may be read.*

11 *Hymns may be sung between the readings, or Psalm 107.1–9 or another psalm may be
    read or sung.*

12 *The Minister may preach, or he may read the following words (in a previous note), or he
    may do both.*

13 *The Minister says:*
    God is the creator of all things, and through the birth of children, he gives parents the
    gift of participating in the work and joy of creation.
    But we who are born to earthly parents, need to be born again. For in the Gospel,
    Jesus tells us that: 'Unless a man is born again he cannot see the kingdom of God.'
    And so God gives us a way to be born again, and to be new creations and to have
    new life in unity with him. Baptism is a sign and seal of this new birth.
    In Matthew's Gospel we read about the risen Christ who instructed his followers:
    'Go therefore to all nations that you might make them my disciples, baptising them in
    the name of the Father and of the Son and of the Holy Spirit.'
    On the day of Pentecost, St Peter obeyed this command saying: 'Repent of your sins,
    and let each one of you be baptised in the name of Jesus Christ for the forgiveness of
    your sins, and you will receive the gift of God, the Holy Spirit. Because this promise
    has been given to you and to your children and to all who are far away, to all who
    will be called by our God.'

14 *A hymn may be sung. The priest stands near those who are to be baptised.*

15 *If children are to be baptised, the parents and godparents should stand in front of the priest. The priest says:*
It is the custom of a church in the Anglican Communion to accept for baptism those who are not old enough to confess their faith in Christ.
They are accepted because it is understood that they will be brought up as Christians in the family of the Church of Christ. That is to say they will be taught the Christian religion, and they will be encouraged to practise it in their life, until they stand before the Bishop for Confirmation and publicly declare the faith into which they were baptised.

16 *The priest says to the parents and godparents:*
Will you bring up these children as Christians, as you are able, within the family of the Church of Christ?
I will.
Will you help them to worship regularly in the Church, and to pray by themselves, and not just teaching them to live by faith in Christ, but you being models for them?
I will
Will you encourage them when the time is right to come for Confirmation and to receive Holy Communion?
I will.

17 *And if the child is old enough to understand, the priest will say this:* N, when you are baptised, you change and become a member of a new family. God will take you to be his child, and all Christians will be your brothers and your sisters.

18 *If children are to be baptised, the priest continues:*
Our Lord Jesus Christ embraced children, and blessed them saying, 'Let the children come to me and don't stop them, for the kingdom of God is for those who are like them. Truly I tell you this, anyone who does not receive the kingdom of God like a little child, cannot enter it at all.' *Mark 10.13–15*

So let us pray for these little ones who we are bringing for baptism in the name of our Lord, saying together:
Heavenly Father, accept that these children be born again by your Holy Spirit; and be brought to know you, in the family of your Church, in newness of life, overcoming evil, and growing in grace till the end of their life; through Jesus Christ our Lord. Amen.

19 *If adults are to be baptised, they should stand, and the priest says:*
Those who are to be baptised should confess with their mouth their belief in Christ and their rejection of all evil.

20 *The priest says to the godparents (and the parents of children if children are to be baptised):*
It is right that those who are bringing these to be baptised should confess with their mouth their belief in Christ, and their rejection of all evil. They should help them mature in faith, fight evil and follow Christ.

21 So I ask you:
Do you turn to Christ?
I turn to Christ.
Do you repent of your sins?
I repent of my sins.
Do you reject Satan's evil and the evil of others who rebel against God?
I reject their evil.
Do you reject the desires of the body which separate you from God?
I reject those desires.

22 *One or two of those who are to be baptised may give short testimonies about leaving sin and turning to Christ.*

23 *A hymn may be sung.*

24 *The priest, standing near the water for baptism says*: Let us pray.
We thank you, Almighty Father, eternal God, for your dearly loved Son, Jesus Christ, because through his death and resurrection, you have broken the power of evil, and in sending the Holy Spirit, you have made us new, in the Family of your Church.
Purify, we beseech you, this water, so that all those who are baptised in it, may be united with Christ in his death and resurrection; that being baptised into his death, and being given the forgiveness of all their sins, may know the power of his resurrection, and walk in newness of life.
Through your Son, Jesus Christ our Lord, through him and together with you and the Holy Spirit, glory is his and greatness and power and strength to all generations for ever and ever. **Amen.**

25 *If adults are to be baptised, the priest says to them*:
You have come here to be baptised. You stand before God, and before his Church. Now you must make your own confession of faith in Christ in which you will be baptised.

26 *The priest says to the godparents (and the parents of the children if children are to be baptised)*:
Godparents (and parents,) you have brought these candidates to be baptised, and you stand before God and before his Church. Now you must confess your Christian faith in which you were baptised.

Do you believe and trust in God the Father who made you and all creation?
I believe and trust in him.
Do you believe and trust in his Son Jesus Christ, who redeemed you and all people?
I believe and trust in him.
Do you believe and trust in his Holy Spirit, who purified you together with all God's people?
I believe and trust in him.

27 *The priest says to all*:
This is the faith of the church.
This is our faith.
We believe and trust in one God, Father, Son and Holy Spirit.

28 *Each person who is to be baptised should come to the place of Baptism, and the priest will ask his name, and place him in the water or sprinkle him with water, saying*:

29 N, I baptise you in the name of the Father, and of the Son and of the Holy Spirit. Amen.

30a *After baptising, the priest makes the sign of the cross on the face of each person, saying*:
I place on you the sign of the cross, the sign of Christ.
To each one, the priest says:
From now on do not be ashamed, to confess the faith of Christ who was crucified on the cross.

Fight bravely under his flag, to conquer sin, the world and Satan, and continue to be his soldier, and a faithful servant of Christ, until the end of your life. Amen.

30b *Or, after putting the sign of the cross on all (the candidates), he says*:
From now on do not be ashamed to confess the faith of Christ, who was crucified on the cross.

Fight bravely under his flag, to conquer sin, the world and Satan, and continue to be his soldier and faithful servants of Christ, until the end of your lives. Amen.

31 *The ministers and others return from the place of baptism, singing a hymn. All stand and say to those who have been baptised:*
God has received you through Baptism into his Church. And so we welcome you into the family of our Lord. You are members with us of the Body of Christ; you are offspring together with us of one Father in heaven; you are inheritors with us of the kingdom of God.

32 *If baptism is taking place during another service, go back now to that order of service. If the baptism service is being used on its own, the priest should say:*
Jesus taught us to call God our Father, and so in faith and hope we say:
[The Lord's Prayer **CF4a**]

33 *Priest:*
We praise you and thank you Father of mercy, that by your Holy Spirit you have made us your offspring, and also through baptism we begin a new life as members of your Church. Enable those who were baptised today to grow in faith in Christ; and we beseech you that, being filled with your Spirit, they may live in your service, and they may receive what you have promised; through Jesus Christ, our Lord. Amen.

34 *If children were baptised, the Priest says:*
Father in heaven, Lead and help the parents of these children, give them the Spirit of understanding and love, that their homes may be an example of your eternal kingdom, so that these children come to affirm their faith at the time of confirmation; through Jesus Christ our Lord. **Amen.**

35 *Offering hymn*

36 *If this is a Baptism service, other prayers may be said and the Priest may finish by saying:*

37 *The Blessing:*
The peace of God which passes all understanding...

38 *The Grace:*
The grace of our Lord Jesus Christ....

CONFIRMATION

IN OTHER WORDS LAYING HANDS ON THOSE WHO WERE BAPTISED AND WHO HAVE COME TO PRESENT THEMSELVES

TEACHING

1 From his baptism, a person is considered to be a member of the Church of Christ. So, what is the meaning of confirmation?

2 The Bishop conducts confirmation as the representative of the universal Church, a sign of the unity of Christians everywhere.

3 In front of the Bishop, a Christian affirms the faith of his baptism; if he was baptised when he was still a child, this part has even more meaning.

4 The Bishop places his hands on the Christian, praying that the power of the Holy Spirit will be increased in his life.

5 The Bishop will send the Christian to do the Lord's work on earth: he should not just be a (club) member but a representative of King Jesus.

⟦6 Instructions about the candidates. Directions for combining services. Readings for the service.⟧

CONFIRMATION

7 *After the Sermon, all stand to praise God and sing a hymn or read a Psalm, or these words from Psalm 139, 65 and 84*

8 Let us praise God!
Who gives grace and glory.
The Lord has searched for me and knows me.
He knows when I sit down and when I go out.
Our sins overwhelm us
But he cleanses our wrongdoings.
Happy are those who are called to him.
They will praise God for ever!
Better is one day in his courts
Than a thousand in the tent of evil.
The Lord God is the sun and a shield.
He gives grace and glory.
Alleluia!
Amen.

9 *Those who are to be confirmed should stand, and the parish Pastor stands with them in front of the Bishop, saying:*
Our Bishop, we welcome you on this day of great meaning. We bring before you these people, to affirm publicly their faith, to receive the laying on of hands and to be prayed for, so that they may be filled with the Holy Spirit and witness to Jesus in the world through their words and deeds.

Bishop: Have you made sure that they have been taught the Christian faith, as the church received it from the Apostles; and that each one is ready to serve God and his church until the end of their life?
Pastor: **Yes, they have been taught and they are ready.**

10 *Bishop:* I ask all of you who are gathered here: are you in agreement that these people receive the laying on of hands and be sent into the Lord's work?
Yes, we are.

11 *Bishop:* Let us pray.
Father in heaven, by the power of your Spirit you draw people to believe in you and to serve you, giving us different gifts to build your church. Today we pray for these your servants, who have grown in faith, and who desire to be filled with that Spirit: may they affirm their faith with sincerity, may they give themselves in joyful service, and may they attain the perfection of Christ, who lives and reigns with you and the Holy Spirit, One God, now and for ever. **Amen.**

12 *Those who are to receive the laying on of hands stand. The bishop says:*
Those who are to receive the laying on of hands should publicly affirm their faith in Christ and their rejection of all evil. And so I ask you:
Do you turn to Christ?
I turn to Christ.
Do you repent of your sins?
I repent of my sins.

Do you reject Satan's evil and the evil of all who rebel against God?
I reject their evil.
Do you reject the desires of the body which separate you from God?
I reject the desires of the body.

13 You stand before God and before his Church. Now you must affirm your Christian faith, the faith into which every Christian is baptised.
Do you believe and trust in God the Father who made you and all creation?
I believe and trust in him.
Do you believe and trust in his Son, Jesus Christ, who redeemed you and all people?
I believe and trust in him.
Do you believe and trust in his Holy Spirit, who purified you and all God's people?
I believe and trust in him.

14 *The Bishop addresses everyone:*
This is the faith of the church.
This is our faith.
We believe and trust in one God, Father, Son and Holy Spirit.

15 *Bishop:* So that everyone understands your intention to give your whole life to the Lord's service, I ask you:
Will you continue to study the Word of God, to live in unity with believers, to fellowship at the Lord's table, and to pray?
I will do this, with God's help.
Will you witness each day to the love of Jesus for your neighbour, by your words and actions?
I will do this, with God's help.
Will you pray for and support the Church, its bishops, priests and other servants?
I will do this, with God's help.
Will you try to satisfy the hungry and thirsty, to care for those who have no families and to welcome strangers?
I will do this, with God's help.
Will you be a faithful citizen of this nation, praying for its leaders, and seeking justice, truth and peace for all people, without tribalism or discrimination of any kind?
I will do this, with God's help.
Will you be a good steward of the world God created and maintain its splendour?
I will do this, with God's help.

16 *A hymn to invite the Holy Spirit (for example: Veni Creator).*

17 *Bishop:* We are not able to fulfil our duties without God's strength. Let us now pray for those who will receive the laying on of hands.
All kneel.
Almighty God, who lives for ever, who has granted that your servants be born again, of water and the Holy Spirit, and has forgiven them all their sins,
we beg you to give them the strength of the Holy Spirit, the Helper;
increase in them every day his many gifts of grace:
the Spirit of intelligence and understanding;
the Spirit of counsel and power;
the Spirit of wisdom and devotion;
and fill them, O Lord,
with the Spirit of your holy fear,
now and forever. **Amen.**

18 *Each one who is to receive the laying on of hands approaches the Holy Table and kneels. The Bishop places his hands on the head of each one, saying:*
O Lord, give the strength of your Holy Spirit to this your servant. **Amen.**

19 *The Bishop and all the congregation pray for those who have been confirmed:*
Keep, O Lord, these your servants, by your heavenly grace, so that they may remain yours for ever, and increase in your Holy Spirit until they arrive in your eternal kingdom. **Amen.**

20 *After all have received the laying on of hands, they stand. The Bishop says:*
Now I am sending you to serve the Lord in the world,
Where there is hatred, bring love.
Where there is anger, forgiveness.
Where there is division, unity.
Where there is doubt, faith.
Where there is discouragement, hope.
Where there is darkness, light.
Where there is sadness, joy.

21 Let us pray:
O holy Lord,
Give to these people:
that they may not seek to be comforted
more than to comfort others;
nor to be understood
more than to understand others;
nor to be loved
more than to love others.
For in giving, we receive;
in forgiving, we are forgiven;
in dying, we are born to eternal life.
Amen.

〚22 Rubrics about giving thanks, hymns and continuing with Holy Communion.〛

23 *And the final blessing should be this:*
Go into the world in peace;
be joyful,
hold on to what is good;
do not return evil for evil;
strengthen those who have no strength;
support the weak;
help those who have troubles of every kind;
honour everyone;
love and serve the Lord;
rejoicing through the power of the Holy Spirit.
And the blessing of Almighty God,
Father, and Son and Holy Spirit,
be with you and remain with you always. **Amen.**

24. The Church of Nigeria

In 1842 a CMS missionary travelled from Freetown to Nigeria and celebrated Holy Communion on Christmas Day. This is the point of the establishment of the Anglican Church in Nigeria. From the start Samuel Crowther was involved in the development of the mission and in 1864 (despite opposition from some missionaries) he was consecrated as the first African bishop and invited to the Lambeth Conference. In 1951 a Province of West Africa was inaugurated which included Nigeria, and in 1979 there was a division, Nigeria becoming an independent Province.

From the beginning, the Church of Nigeria used the Book of Common Prayer 1662 translated into the vernacular.[62] When the church became an autonomous Province it desired to have its own liturgy, which bore fruit in the 1996 Book of Common Prayer. This book contains a service of holy baptism which is intended to take place in the eucharistic celebration. A separate service of confirmation exists in the section for pastoral offices.

THE BOOK OF COMMON PRAYER OF THE CHURCH OF NIGERIA 1996

THE ORDER FOR HOLY BAPTISM

After the Ministry of the word, Churching or thanksgiving of women after child birth is conducted, then a hymn or psalm or lyrics may be sung and the people move to the font.

INTRODUCTION

1 Dear people of God, Baptism is the initiatory rite of the church into her membership. It is administered to both young and old, male and female. This is in obedience to the injunction of our Lord Jesus Christ that except one is born of water and the Spirit one cannot enter into the Kingdom of God. Since all who are born into sin are being regenerated through the sacrament of baptism, therefore all infants who are brought forth for baptism in faith by their Christian parents and sponsors, and adults who come into it through repentance and faith are thus made new creatures in Christ. By this sacrament of Baptism they are co-sharers of His death and resurrection and members of His everlasting kingdom.

PRESENTATION OF THE CANDIDATE(S)

2 *The candidates are presented by the Sponsors*
We/I present these candidates to receive the sacrament of Baptism and to be made members of Christ and His Church.

---

62 G 55–58: 1 Igbo, G 196: 1–6 Yoruba, G 49: 1–5 Hausa.

If the candidate is able to answer for himself or herself, the minister asks the candidate and in case of infants the parents and the Sponsors will answer on their behalf.
Do you desire to be baptized?
I do.

In case of an infant, the Priest asks the parents and sponsors
Will you take it as your responsibility to see that this child is brought up in the Christian faith and life?
I will, God being my Helper.
Will you visit the child frequently and see that he or she is brought to Church regularly?
I will, God being my Helper
Will you continually uphold the child in your prayers?
I will, God being my Helper.

RENUNCIATION OF SIN

3 *Having got all candidates presented, they will all renounce evil personally, and in case of infants, their sponsors and parents will do so on their behalf.*
To be baptized and become a member of Christ and His Church, you must declare your absolute allegiance to Christ and your total rejection of the devil and of all that is evil. Will you now declare this in the presence of God and members of His Church?
I renounce the devil and all his works.

Do you repent of your sins?
I do repent.

Do you renounce Satan and all the spiritual forces of wickedness that rebel against God?
I do renounce them.

Do you renounce the evil powers of this world which corrupt and destroy the creatures of God?
I do renounce them.

Do you renounce all sinful desires that draw you from the love of God?
I do renounce them.

PROFESSION OF THE CHRISTIAN FAITH

4 I now ask you all to be baptized to profess the Christian faith into which we are baptized, and in committing yourselves to serve the Lord.

Do you turn to Christ Jesus?
I do turn to Christ

Do you accept him as your Saviour and Lord?
I do accept him.

Do you put your whole trust in his grace and love?
I do put my trust in him.

Do you promise to follow and obey him as your Lord throughout your life?
I do so promise.

5 ⟦Question and answer Apostles' Creed **CF2b**⟧

6 This is the faith of the church.
This is our faith,
we believe and trust in one God,
Father, Son and Holy Spirit.

7   Will you, then love God with all your heart, with all your mind, and with all your strength, and your neighbour as yourself?
I will, God being my Helper.

Will you continue in the apostles teaching and fellowship, in the breaking of bread, and in the prayer?
I will, God being my Helper.

Will you persevere in resisting evil, and, whenever you fall into sin, repent and return to the Lord?
I will, God being my Helper.

Will you strive for justice and peace among all people, and respect the dignity of every human being?
I will, God being my helper.

PRAYERS FOR THE CANDIDATES

8   *Here one of the sponsors already appointed may read the litany.*
The Lord be with you.
And also with you.

Let us pray for the persons who are to receive the sacrament of new birth.

Lord have mercy upon us.
Christ have mercy upon us.
Lord have mercy upon us.

[9   The Lord's Prayer **CF4b**]

Redeem them, O Lord, from all evil and rescue them from the way of sin and death.
Lord hear our prayer.

Open their hearts to your grace and truth.
Lord hear our prayer.

Keep them in the faith and communion of your holy Church.
Lord hear our prayer.

Teach them to love others in the power of the Holy Spirit.
Lord hear our prayer.

Fill them with your holy and life-giving Spirit.
Lord hear our prayer.

Strengthen them as you are now sending them to witness to your love.
Lord hear our prayer

Bring them to the fullness of your peace and glory.
Lord hear our prayer.

Grant, O Lord,
that all who are baptized
into the death of Jesus Christ your Son
may live in the power of his resurrection
and look for his coming in glory,
who lives and reigns now and for ever. Amen.

10   *Hymn may be sung and any further preparation may be done here.*

BLESSING OF THE WATER

11 The Lord be with you.
And also with you.

Let us pray.
Almighty God, our heavenly Father whose Son our Lord Jesus Christ was baptized in the river Jordan:
We thank you for the gift of water to cleanse and revive us.
We thank you that through the waters of the Red Sea You led your people out of slavery and bondage to freedom in the promised land:
We thank you that through the deep waters of death you brought your Son and raised him to life in triumph.
We thank you, Father, for the water of Baptism. In it we are buried with Christ in his death; by it we share in His resurrection; through it we are reborn by the Holy Spirit.
Therefore in joyful obedience to your Son, we bring into his fellowship those who come to Him in faith, baptizing them in the Name of the Father, and of the Son and of the Holy Spirit.
(Here the priest touches the water)
Now Lord, sanctify this water, we pray you, by the power of your Holy Spirit, that those who here are baptized in it may be cleansed from their sins and being born again may continue for ever in the risen life of Jesus Christ our Lord and Saviour.
To the Father, Son and Holy Spirit, be all honour and glory, now and for ever. **Amen**

12 *Sponsors and/or Parents will present the candidates by names to the Priest who then immerses or generously pours water upon each candidate. Saying:*
N... I baptize you in the Name of the Father, and of the Son and of the Holy Spirit.
Amen.

13 *The Priest marks the sign of the cross on the forehead of the candidate (with chrism if so desired)*
I sign you with the cross and mark you as Christ's own forever. **Amen.**

14 *If so desired, the candidate will be worn with white dress (chrisom) by his or her sponsor, saying:*

14a Wear this garment as a token of your membership of the band of saints with purity of heart.
Blessed are the pure in heart for they shall see God.

or

14b We give this white vesture, for a token of the innocency bestowed upon you, and for a sign whereby you are admonished to give yourself to pureness of living, that after this transitory life, you may be partaker of the life everlasting. **Amen**

15 *Then one of the sponsors may give to the candidate a lighted candle, saying:*
Receive the light of Christ, to show that you have passed from darkness to light.
Shine as light in the world, to the glory of God the Father. *Amen.*

16 *Then the Priest and the people, standing, say to the newly baptized*
We welcome you into the body of Christ
Do not be ashamed to confess the faith of Christ
Fight valiantly under His banner
against sin, the world, and the devil,
and continue as his faithful soldier and servant
to the end of your life. Amen

⟦17 A rubric directs the peace and the Eucharist.⟧

AN ORDER FOR CONFIRMATION SERVICE
OR
SERVICE OF LAYING-ON HANDS BY THE BISHOP

After the ministry of the word, a hymn or psalm may be sung in the service begins with 'Presentation of Candidates'

PRESENTATION OF CANDIDATES

1 Reverend Father in God, I present to you these persons to receive the laying-on of hand.

2 Dearly beloved in the Lord, in ministering Confirmation the Church follows the example of the Apostles of Christ. For in the eighth chapter of the Acts of the Apostles, we thus read:

〚Acts 8.4–5; 12; 14–17〛

The Scripture here teaches us that a special gift of the Holy Spirit is bestowed through the laying-on of hands with prayer. And for as much as this gift comes, from God alone, let us who are here present pray to God Almighty, but he will strengthen with his Holy Spirit in Confirmation those who in Baptism were made his children.

You, then, who are to be confirmed must now declare before this congregation that you are steadfastly purposed, with the help of this gift, to lead your life in the faith of Christ and in obedience to God's will and commandments; and must openly acknowledge yourselves bound to fulfil the Christian duties to which your baptism has pledged you.

THE RENEWAL OF BAPTISMAL VOWS
The candidates stand before the Bishop and he addresses them:

3 You, who are to be confirmed, must renew the vows of your baptism, and first, with your own lips and from your heart you must declare your rejection of all that is evil. Do you here, in the presence of God, and of this congregation, renew the solemn promises and vows that you made all that were made in your name at baptism?

I do.

Do you renounce the devil and all the spiritual forces of wickedness that rebel against God?
I do renounce them.

Do you renounce the evil powers of this world which corrupt and destroy what God has created?
I do renounce them.

Do you renounce all sinful desires that draw you from the love of God?
I do renounce them.

4 Now, in allegiance to Christ, you must declare before guard and this congregation that you accept the Christian faith into which you are baptised and in which you will continue to live and grow.

〚Modern question form from ASB CF3〛

Will you live in obedience to God's laws, as a loyal member of this church?
With God's help, I will.

CONFIRMATION PROPER

5   Our help is in the name of the Lord.
Who has made heaven and earth
Blessed be the name of the Lord
Now and for ever. Amen.

6   *The Bishop stretches out his hands towards those to be confirmed and says*
Almighty and ever living God,
you have given your children new birth
in baptism by water and the Spirit,
and therefore given them all their sins.
Let your Holy Spirit rest upon them,
the spirit of wisdom and understanding
the spirit of counsel and inward strength
the spirit of knowledge and true godliness;
and let their delight the in the fear of the Lord,
through Jesus Christ our Lord. Amen.

7   *The candidates will come up very quietly in a continuous stream and kneel before the Bishop*

8   We lay our hands upon you. Be confirmed and strengthened with the Holy Spirit for his service. *Amen.*

9   Strengthen, O Lord, your servants with your Holy Spirit; empower them for your service; and sustain them all the days of their lives. *Amen.*

10   *When all have been confirmed the Bishop will lead the congregation in saying:*
〚Confirmation Prayer **CF5**, with 'these children of yours' rather than 'your servants'.〛

11   *The Bishop continues*
Heavenly Father, we pray for your children upon whom we have now laid our hands.
May your fatherly hand be ever over them, your Holy Spirit ever be with them.
Sustain them continually with the body and blood of your Son, and so lead them in the knowledge and obedience of your word that in the end they may enjoy the fullness of eternal life, through Jesus Christ our Lord. Amen.

〚12   Service resumes with the peace and Holy Communion. Prayers are provided for if there is no Communion.〛

25. The Episcopal Church of Jerusalem and the Middle East, The Church of the Province of West Africa, and The Province of the Episcopal Church of South Sudan and Sudan

A number of Provinces have a complex pattern of liturgies in some cases because there is no set Provincial liturgy, and in Sudan because of the recent warfare.

The Episcopal Church in Jerusalem and the Middle East

Jerusalem and the Middle East is the cradle of Christianity. The Anglican Jerusalem bishopric was founded in 1841 and became an archbishopric in 1957. The current shape of the Province came to be in 1976. Early work included translation of the Book of Common Prayer 1662 into Arabic.[63] There are also some unofficial Arabic translations of the Church of England ASB and Common Worship.

The Episcopal Church of Jerusalem and the Middle East does not have a Provincial liturgy. On their website a videoed service in Arabic of renewal of baptismal vows at the Jordan can be seen. In many congregations that are chaplaincies American or English liturgies are used. In Jerusalem the Arabic translation of the prayer book is used, and while there is some liturgical revival in Egypt it has as yet not touched baptismal rites, although Common Worship has been translated into Arabic.

The Church of the Province of West Africa

The Church of the Province of West Africa has no Provincial liturgy. The Province divided from Nigeria in 1979. There is considerable linguistic diversity in the Province both in the vernaculars and French and English. In some dioceses English and American liturgy is used; in Ghana there is a version of the English Book of Common Prayer.[64]

The Province of the Episcopal Church of South Sudan and Sudan

In 1976 the church became an independent Province and has suffered greatly from war. In theory the BCP 1662 remains the official services. The Province is considering a process of liturgical revision.

---

63 G 8: 1–11.
64 G 1960/2

F. Asia

26. The Church of Pakistan

According to *The Acts of Judas Thomas* the apostle Thomas may well have preached the gospel in what is now Pakistan before moving on to South India. Anglicanism came out first with chaplains of the East India Company. The company did not favour missionary work and a campaign in England caused a change in the 1813 charter to allow missionaries to work. Anglican mission societies then began a work which stretched across the whole of North India into present Pakistan. In 1813 the bishopric of Calcutta was founded, which included all of India. In 1833 the Diocese of Bombay was founded. In 1930 the Church of India, Burma and Ceylon became an independent Province in the Anglican Communion. This church added Pakistan to its title in 1947 after partition. The ecumenical movement led to the formation of the Church of Pakistan in 1978, a union of Anglicans, Church of Scotland, United Methodists and Lutherans.

Anglican missionaries translated the Book of Common Prayer into Urdu.[65] The Book of Common Prayer of the Church of India, Pakistan, Burma and Ceylon was also translated into Urdu.[66] Baptismal rites in this church date from 1951 and 1960.[67] The present prayer book, completely written in beautiful Urdu, dates from 1985, and then a second edition in 2005. It includes services of the baptism of children, the baptism of adults, and of confirmation.

COMMON PRAYER: CHURCH OF PAKISTAN (1985, 2005)

[Translated by Evelyn Bhajan and Augusten Masih]

LITURGY FOR INFANT BAPTISM

1   *A hymn may be sung. Parents (and Godparents) may bring their child near the baptismal font.*

2   *Presbyter:* Has this child been baptized or not?
    If the answer is in the negative the service may continue.

3   *Presbyter:* Our help is in the name of the Lord.
    Who made the heavens and the earth.

---

65 G 187: 1–29.
66 G 187: 30.
67 J 67–76, 95–102.

4 *Presbyter:* Praise be to God the Father of our Lord Jesus Christ, who has created us with great mercy to be born again for a new hope through Jesus Christ.

This promise is for you, and your children and all who are far away but whom God has called unto Him.

5 *Presbyter:* Dear friends, participants in the House of God, we have gathered here to baptize this child.

Our Lord Jesus Christ said, 'No one can enter the kingdom of God unless they are born of water and the Spirit.'

Therefore come let us hear those words which our Lord said to his disciples after he rose up from the dead.

'All authority in heaven and on earth has been given to me. Therefore go and make disciples of all nations, baptizing them in the name of the Father and of the Son and of the Holy Spirit, and teaching them to obey everything I have commanded you. And surely I am with you always, to the very end of the age.'

Whatever the Lord commanded his disciples then, we joyfully obey and do today. Our Lord has promised, 'Whoever believes and receives baptism, will be saved.'
Saint Paul says, 'For we were all baptized by one Spirit so as to form one body.'

6 *Presbyter should briefly explain about baptism or he should use the following words:*
Through baptism God unites us to the church which is the true grapevine. In this way we are born anew to become living members of his body. In baptism, god gives us a tangible sign and seal of the covenant of His grace. It is through that covenant that he makes us his children and cleanses us from our sins. He proclaims that we are His heirs and participants of everlasting life.

These little children and you belong to God. They are included in the household of believers through holy baptism, so that they may continue to grow as parts of the body of Christ and heirs of God's kingdom.

7 *Presbyter:* It is the duty and right of those who are presenting this child for baptism to confess obedience to Christ and renounce all evil. Therefore I ask:
Do you turn to the Lord Jesus Christ?
Yes [I turn to the Lord Jesus Christ].
Do you repent from your sins?
Yes [I repent of my sins].
Do you reject the Devil and every kind of idolatry and superstition?
Yes [I reject them].

8 *Presbyter:* It is the duty and right of those who have brought their children to be baptized that they proclaim the faith in which the children will be baptized before God and the congregation.
[All join in saying The Apostle's Creed **CF1a**]. **Amen.**

9 *Presbyter:* Do you want baptism in this faith?
Yes. This is my desire.
Will you fulfill God's will and obey His commands throughout your life?
Yes I will.

10 *Presbyter:* It is written in Mark 10.13–16
[Reading Mark 10.13–16].
Praise to you O Christ!

11 *Presbyter:* Lift up your hearts!
We lift them to the Lord.

Let us give thanks to the Lord our God.
It is right to give thanks and praise.
Presbyter: It is indeed right to give thanks and praise.
Grant O Lord that we may ever thank you because your Son Jesus Christ took on flesh, died for our sake and then rose up from the dead, and gave us this sacrament through which we are united with the church that is the body of Christ and called to die to sin and be raised up to life through righteousness.

Therefore with angels and archangels and with all the company of heaven, we proclaim your great and glorious name, forever praising you and saying,

Holy, holy, holy Lord, God of power and might

Heaven and earth are full of your glory. Hosanna in the highest.

Blessed is He who has come and is to come in the name of the Lord. Hosanna in the highest.

O Lord we beseech you to have mercy upon us and work through that which you commanded and we follow.

Through your Spirit bless us and this water. *(The minister places his hand on the font).* And grant that (this child) may be born again through water and the Holy Spirit and may forever be counted amongst your faithful people.
Amen.

Oh Holy Saviour, who took little children and blessed them. We request you to take [this child] and put your seal on him as your special possession, you who reign with the Father and the Holy Spirit, now and forever.
Amen.

12 *The child/ren are brought to the font one by one. The presbyter asks about each one:*
What is the name of this child?
Takes name except the family name and baptizes the child.

13 N I baptize you in the name of the Father, the Son and the Holy Spirit. The Lord bless you!

14 *If the Presbyter has still not taken the child in her/his arms, S/he should do so. And make the sign of the cross on the child's forehead.*
Receive the sign of the cross, which is a reminder that you now belong to the crucified and resurrected Christ and have been grafted in the body of Christ.

15 *When all have been baptized, the Presbyter will say the following:*
The Lord bless you and keep you. The Lord make His face to shine upon you, and be gracious to you; The Lord turn His face toward you and give you peace.

16 We welcome this child in the name God into the congregation of Christ's flock. May [this child] never shy away from but always proclaim Christ the crucified and may he/she valiantly fight sin, the world and the devil under Christ's flag and serve and follow him till death. **Amen.**

17 *The congregation stands.*
My brothers and sisters in faith, I submit this child whom we have accepted into the house of God today into your love and supervision. Will you with the help of God live a life that [this child] will grow in the knowledge and love God through Christ our Lord?
Yes with the help of God we will.

18   *The congregation sits and the Presbyter addresses the parents and god-parents:*
You who have brought [this child] for this holy Sacrament, do you promise that if
God grants you life you will do your best to fulfil all the responsibilities of parents
and God parents so that this child will be taught the Scriptures, and he/she will learn
and memorize the Creed, the Lord's Prayer and the Ten Commandments and the
Beatitudes, and that he/she will be trained and advised accordingly?
Yes, with the help of God we will.
Will you ensure that when he/she has received enough teaching that he/she will be
presented before the Bishop for confirmation, so that he/she may continue to remain
joined in the true grapevine as he/she has now been grafted into?
Yes, with the help of God we will.

19   Let us pray
All say the Lord's Prayer. [[CF4a]]

20   O God, you are merciful, and your promises are not only for us but also our children,
we pray that your Spirit may strengthen this child in such a way that he/she may
continue to take root in Christ and grow in love. He/she may be guided year by year
and grant that the time may come when he/she may approach the holy table and
partake of the body and blood of the Lord, and may fearlessly proclaim Christ before
others.
O Father, whose Son was raised in a family from Nazareth, we pray for the household
and parents of this child. Grant that his/her house may be filled with love, joy and
peace. And that his/her parents may be concerned about his/her needs. Grant that [the
child's] parents may through training and example enable him/her to grow in your
knowledge and obedience.
O gracious God, whose universal church believes in one Lord, one faith and one
baptism, grant that we may accept the Lordship of your Son Jesus Christ, may profess
that one true faith all our lives, and may love all those who have been baptized in
His name. In the name of the same Jesus Christ who with you O Father and the Holy
Spirit is praised and worshipped.
Amen.

LITURGY FOR ADULT BAPTISM

(A BAPTISM FOR THOSE CHILDREN WHO CAN SPEAK FOR THEMSELVES)

1   *A hymn may be sung.*

2   *The candidate(s) and their guarantors are invited to approach the font.*
Presbyter: Has this person (man or woman, boy or girl) been baptized or not?
If the answer is in the negative the service may continue.

3   *Presbyter:* Our help is in the name of the Lord.
Who made the heavens and the earth
Praise be to God the Father of our Lord Jesus Christ, who has created us anew by his
great mercy through the resurrection of Jesus Christ for a living hope.
Repent and be baptized, every one of you, in the name of Jesus Christ for the
forgiveness of your sins. And you will receive the gift of the Holy Spirit. The promise
is for you and your children and for all who are far off – for all whom the Lord our
God will call.

4   Dear friends, participants in the House of God, we have gathered here to baptize (this
person). Our Lord Jesus Christ said, 'No one can enter the kingdom of God unless

they are born of water and the Spirit.' Therefore come let us hear those words which our Lord said to his disciples after he rose up from the dead.

'All authority in heaven and on earth has been given to me. Therefore go and make disciples of all nations, baptizing them in the name of the Father and of the Son and of the Holy Spirit, and teaching them to obey everything I have commanded you. And surely I am with you always, to the very end of the age.'

Whatever the Lord commanded his disciples then; we joyfully obey and do today. Our Lord has promised, 'Whoever believes and receives baptism, will be saved.'

Saint Paul says, 'For we were all baptized by one Spirit so as to form one body.'

5 *Presbyter should briefly explain about baptism or he should use the following words:* Through baptism God fastens us to the church which is the true grapevine. In this way we are born anew to become living members of his body. In baptism, God gives us a tangible sign and seal of the covenant of His grace. It is through that covenant that he makes us his children and cleanses us from our sins. He proclaims that we are his heirs and participants of everlasting life.

6 *Presbyter:* You who are going to be baptized must confess obedience to Christ and renounce all evil. Therefore I ask:

Do you turn to the Lord Jesus Christ?

Yes [I turn to the Lord Jesus Christ].

Do you repent from your sins?

Yes [I repent of my sins].

Do you reject the Devil and every kind of idolatry and superstition?

Yes [I reject the Devil and every kind of idolatry and superstition].

7 You have come to receive baptism and you stand before the Lord and His congregation. You must proclaim the faith in which you will be baptized.

All candidates join in saying the Apostles' Creed. [[**CF1a**]] **Amen.**

8 You have come to be baptized and commit yourself to the Lord Jesus Christ so that you may serve by becoming a part of the congregation. Therefore I ask:

Do you promise to be God's faithful servants and witness? Will you attend the service regularly? Will you ardently serve the congregation? And will you gladly give offerings for godly work?

Yes. I promise.

9 It is written in John 3.1–8

[[Reading John 3.1–8]]

Praise to you O Christ!

10 Lift up your hearts!

We lift them to the Lord.

Let us give thanks to the Lord our God.

It is right to give thanks and praise.

It is indeed right to give thanks and praise. O Lord that we give you thanks at all times because your son Jesus Christ took our nature, died for our salvation and then rose up from the dead, and gave us this sacrament through which we are united with the church that is the body of Christ and called to die to sin and be raised up to life through righteousness.

Therefore with angels and archangels and with all the company of heaven, we proclaim your great and glorious name, forever praising you and saying,

Holy, holy, holy Lord, God of power and might

Heaven and earth are full of your glory. Hosanna in the highest.

Blessed is He who has come and is to come in the name of the Lord. Hosanna in the highest.

O Lord we beseech you to have mercy upon us and work through that which you commanded and we follow.

Through your Spirit bless us and this water. (The minister places his hand on the font). And grant that (this brother, this sister) may be born again through water and the Holy Spirit and may forever be counted amongst your faithful people, through Jesus Christ our Lord. **Amen.**

11 *Then the candidates may stand or kneel before the font one by one and the Presbyter may ask:*

What is his/her name?

A guarantor takes the name. It is possible that it may be a new name, therefore the Presbyter may repeat the name while baptizing.

13 N I baptize you in the name of the Father, the Son and the Holy Spirit. May the Lord bless you!

14 *Then the Presbyter should make the sign of the cross on the candidate's forehead.*

Receive the sign of the cross, which is a reminder that you now belong to the crucified and resurrected Christ and have been grafted in the body of Christ through the Holy Spirit.

15 *All the candidates must kneel before the font. A hymn should be sung for the blessing of the Holy Spirit. Meanwhile the Bishop may take a chair and sit before the candidates. The local Presbyter calls the candidates one by one and he/she comes and kneels before the Bishop's chair. The Bishop places both hands on the candidate's head and prays the following:*

16 *Bishop:* O Lord, by your heavenly grace strengthen your servant [Name] so that he/she may continue to be yours, and till he/she reaches your eternal kingdom may continue to receive your Holy Spirit daily.

The candidate and congregation may respond after every confirmation: **Amen**

17 *The candidates may return to their seats but remain standing.*

In the name of God we welcome you, who have been admitted in the congregation of the flock of Christ [and in the communion of His table]. Never shy away from confessing your faith in Christ crucified, and valiantly fight under his banner against sin, the world and the devil, and continue to serve and follow Him till death.

18 The Lord bless you and keep you. The Lord shine His face on you, and be gracious to you; The Lord turn His face toward you and give you peace. **Amen.**

Alternatively, the Priestly blessing may be sung or said collectively.

19 My fellow brothers and sisters in faith, I submit this person whom we have accepted into the house of God today into your love and supervision. Will you with the help of God live a life that [this person] will grow in the knowledge and love of God through Christ our Lord?

Yes, with the help of God we will.

20 *If the adults have been confirmed a service of Eucharist will follow but if they have only been baptized then the following will be done:*

Let us pray

All say the Lord's Prayer. [[CF4a]]

21 O God, our Father, we thank and praise you for the blessing that you have bestowed upon your children today. Be their guardian, and protect them in their coming and going now and forever.

O merciful God in whose church there is one Lord, one faith and one baptism, grant that we may always accept the Lordship of your Son Jesus Christ. May we confess this true faith by our whole lives and may we love all who are baptized in His name. In the name of the same Jesus Christ, who with your Father and the Holy Spirit is worshipped and glorified. **Amen.**

CONFIRMATION SERVICE

⟦1 Rubrics⟧

2 *Bishop:* Our help is in the name of the Lord
who has made the heaven and earth

3 *Bishop:* Let us pray
The congregation kneels and the bishop says
I will set out and go back to my father and say to him: Father, I have sinned against heaven and against you. I am no longer worthy to be called your son.
Let us examine ourselves in silence.
Silence
Bishop: Let us confess our sins in penitence before God Almighty.
O God our father, we have sinned against you in thought, word and deed. We have not loved you with our whole heart, nor have we loved our neighbour as ourselves. We beseech you, have mercy upon us, cleanse us from our sins, and help us to conquer our weaknesses, through Jesus Christ our Lord. Amen.
Bishop: May the almighty and most merciful Lord, grant you the remission of all sins, give you the chance to reform your life, grace of the Holy Spirit and peace.
Amen.

4 *The congregation sits. The local presbyter asks the confirmands to stand.*
Presbyter: Respected spiritual father, on behalf of *so and so congregation* I present these candidates before you to be confirmed and accepted in the Holy Communion.
Bishop: Be mindful of the fact that the persons who are being presented before us have been duly prepared and are worthy of laying on of hands.
Presbyter: I have arranged for their teaching and have tested them. In my opinion they are worthy.

5 *Bishop:* Dearly beloved in Christ! Through God's grace, at the time of your baptism you were accepted in the fellowship of Christ. You received the seal of being a part of the family of God.
Now you have personally come of your own will, to make the covenant that was made at the time of your baptism, to openly confess your faith in the Lord Jesus Christ, to consecrate yourself for him and accept the blessings which he wants to bestow upon you.
You have also come that according to the tradition of the apostles we may lay hands on you and pray that the Holy Spirit may dwell in your hearts and strengthen you in all goodness.
You have also come that this congregation may also accept you in the communion of the Eucharist and that together we may worship and serve God all our lives.
Candidates may be seated.

6 *Bishop:* Hear the word of God regarding the fruit of the Spirit
One or two of the following passages or any other suitable passages may be read by the Bishop
Romans 8.12–17, Ephesians 3.14–21, John 14.15–18 Or Acts 1.8
The Bishop may give a brief sermon/talk. After this he may sit on his chair while the candidates stand at their respective places.

7   *Bishop:* You who are about to be confirmed must confess obedience to Christ and renounce all evil, therefore I ask.

Do you turn to the Lord Jesus Christ?

Yes, I turn to the Lord Jesus Christ.

Bishop: Do you repent of your sins?

Yes, I repent of my sins.

Bishop: Do you renounce Satan, and all kinds of idol worship and superstition?

Yes, I renounce Satan, and all kinds of idol worship and superstition.

8   *Bishop:* You have come in order to be confirmed, you stand before the Lord and his church, therefore, you must confess the faith into which you were baptized.

The candidates recite the Apostle's Creed.

9   *After this any one of the following orders may be followed:*

9a Order 1

Bishop: You have come to be confirmed and to submit yourself to the Lord Jesus so that you may serve his church and share in his table. Therefore I ask:

Do you promise to remain God's faithful servant and witness? Will you attend church regularly? Will you incessantly serve the church? And contribute gladly towards the Lord's work?

Yes, I promise.

Bishop: Now all the candidates will pray along with the Presbyter.

The candidates will kneel and pray the following:

O God, my God, father of our Lord Jesus Christ! I am not mine own but yours. Trusting in your grace, as your child I commit myself to you so that I may faithfully love and serve you all my life.

9b Order 2

Bishop: Now all the candidates must pray along with the Presbyter.

All the candidates kneel.

O God, my God, Father of our Lord Jesus Christ! I am not mine own but yours. Trusting in your grace, as your child I commit myself to you so that I may faithfully love and serve you all my life.

Amen

Bishop: If you wish to commit yourself to the Lord Jesus Christ that you may serve his church and share in his table, you must say "Yes, I promise" when your name is called out.

Do you promise to remain God's faithful servant and witness? Will you attend church regularly? Will you incessantly serve the church? And contribute gladly towards the Lord's work?

The presbyter calls the candidates one by one and each one stands and says

Yes, I promise.

Amen.

10   *Bishop:* Now we will sing hymn number...and ask God for the blessings of His Spirit.

Any suitable hymn may be sung at this time.

11   *Bishop:* Almighty God our heavenly father, who through baptism, has accepted these children in your household, and has granted them his Holy Spirit, we beseech you to strengthen them in their faith through the same Spirit, and that you increase the blessings of your grace in them day by day. Increase in them the spirit of wisdom and understanding, the spirit of expedience and power, the spirit of knowledge and the fear of the Lord and by your mercy preserve them for eternal life, through your Son and our Lord Jesus Christ.

Amen.

12   *Bishop:* May the congregation please stand.

The candidates and congregation stand. One presbyter holds the list of the candidates in his hand and another presbyter stands behind the bishop with the crosier/bishop's staff in his hand. The bishop can either sit or stand.
Bishop: When your name is called out you must come forward and kneel in order to obtain God's blessings.
The presbyter calls the candidates one by one. They come and kneel before the Bishop.
Bishop: (*places both hands on the candidate's head*). O God, in your heavenly grace strengthen your servant (name) so that s/he may always remain yours. And until s/he does not reach your holy kingdom, may continue obtain your Holy Spirit day by day.
Candidate and Congregation: (*After every confirmation*): **Amen.**
Every candidate must then return to their respective seats and pray.

The candidates and congregation stand. One presbyter stands behind the bishop with the crosier/bishop's staff in his hand. The bishop can either sit or stand.
Bishop: Now you must approach one by one, and kneel in order to obtain God's blessings.
The candidates approach one by one and kneel before the Bishop.
Bishop: (*Places both hands on the candidate's head*). O God, in your heavenly grace strengthen your servant (name) so that s/he may always remain yours. And until s/he does not reach your holy kingdom, may continue to obtain your Holy Spirit day by day.
Candidate and Congregation: (*After every confirmation*): **Amen.**
Every candidate must then return to their respective seats and pray.

13   *Bishop:* Let us pray.
Oh Holy God! We give you thanks because we are undeniably living members of the body of your dear son. Grant that with a thankful heart, we may remain steadfast in this Holy Communion. We pray especially for these young people who have been confirmed today. When they approach your holy table and partake of the body and blood of Christ, grant that they may receive the understanding of his love and may receive a share of his grace. You be their guardian and watch over all their comings and goings both now and forevermore. **Amen.**

14   *Bishop:* Now all those who have been confirmed may stand.
Since you have confessed your faith before God and this congregation, and have received God's blessings, I invite you to Holy Communion in the name of Jesus Christ who is the Lord and head of the church.

15   The Lord bless you and keep you; the Lord make his face to shine on you and be gracious to you; the Lord turn His face toward you and give you peace. **Amen.**

16   *The congregation can also join in the priestly blessing. The confirmed candidates may remain standing facing the congregation.*

17   *Presbyter or (Presbyter and congregation):* Dearly beloved, we the members of this congregation welcome you with happiness to the joint life of the church. With you, we also promise to give priority to the church in our prayers, presence, giving and services. We assure you that we will remain your friends and will continue to pray for you, so that you may continue to grow in the knowledge and love of God and his son our Lord Jesus Christ. May it be that on earth we serve him in the unity of the Holy Spirit and in heaven we obtain the full communion of saints.

18 *The local presbyter may welcome the candidates with suitable signs such as, patting on the head, or members of the pastorate committee could garland them, cards and books may also be presented after the service.*

19 *If there is no communion service a hymn may be sung during which the offerings are collected. One of the candidates can collect the special offerings from the others whether in the form of an envelope or garland and bring them to the bishop who will pray for all the offerings.*

20 *After this the congregation may say the Lord's Prayer. In case of Holy Communion, the candidates should be served first.*

21 *Bishop:* Go forth into the world in peace; be of good courage; hold fast to that which is good; render to no one evil for evil, strengthen the fainthearted, support the weak, help the afflicted, revere all people, love and serve the Lord, rejoicing in the power of the Holy Spirit.

22 *The congregation may stand or remain kneeling.*
Bishop: Now may God who is the fountain of peace perfect you in everything, so that you may fulfil His will, and may he create in everything that which is pleasing to Him. And may the blessing of almighty God, Father, Son and the Holy Spirit be upon you and remain with you. **Amen.**

23 *A processional hymn may be sung.*

27. The Church of North India

The Portuguese 'discovery' of India led to the creation of trading stations and conclaves, e.g. Goa, and Christian mission in North India. This was followed by the Dutch and then the British East India Company. The latter had important centres in Calcutta and Bombay with chaplains there to minister to the company. The growth of the army in India also led to many army chaplains. After the change in the Charter in 1813, Anglican missionaries began to work across North India. The missionaries translated the Book of Common Prayer into various Indian languages.[68] The first Anglican diocese was Calcutta in 1813, and bishops from India were at the first Lambeth conference. In 1930 the Church of India, Burma and Ceylon became an independent Province and created its own Book of Common Prayer,[69] which was translated into several languages.[70]

The Church of North India was formed in 1970 with the uniting of six churches. The church began by producing a series of booklets which by its silver jubilee it combined into *The Book of Worship* (1995). The uniting churches included some from a Baptist tradition and thus *The Book of Worship* includes services for a believer's baptism position as well as a service of infant baptism. The baptismal services begin with a catechumenal rite 'a service for receiving a candidate for baptism'. This is followed by a service of 'believers baptism', 'thanksgiving of parents after the birth of a child', 'the baptism of children', 'baptism in an emergency', 'the public reception of person is baptised outside of public worship', 'conditional baptism', 'the blessing of children commonly called the dedication of children' and 'the order of confirmation'.

The rubrics suggest that in some places certain prayers found in an appendix may be supplemented with experimental prayers authorized by the bishop. It is also clear from the rubrics that in some places the presbyter may use extempore prayer rather than the set prayer in the text. The rubrics allow baptism in a font, or a pond, or a tank, or a river, and elements of inculturation may be seen in the use of lyrics, and the use of a Deepak, and of the possibility of the candidate dancing in response to their baptism. While previous patterns within the uniting churches are allowed to continue, it is clear that the growing expectation is that confirmation will be done by the bishop. The Church of North India has an optional use of the baptismal formula in the passive. This may be in light of the full communion agreement with the Mar Thoma Syrian Church.

---

68 G 107: 1–17 Marathi, 52: 1–4 Hindi, G 77: 1 Kashmiri, G 78: 1–2 Khasi, G 13: 1–16 Bengali.
69 J 67–76, 95–102.
70 G 107: 18–19 Marathi, G 78: 3 Khasi, G 13: 17 Bengali.

THE BOOK OF WORSHIP 1995

BELIEVERS' BAPTISM

PRESENTATION OF THE CANDIDATES

1 *The presbyter, the candidates, those presenting them and the congregation stand in appropriate places near the font, or pond, or tank, or river.*

2 Blessed be God who in his generosity and mercy has saved us through the washing of regeneration and renewal in the Holy Spirit.
Blessed be God, who poured forth the Holy Spirit upon us plentifully through Jesus Christ our Saviour, so that being justified by his grace we might share in eternal life.

3 We rejoice that God has created in *these persons* the desire to be baptized. By receiving baptism *they* will publicly demonstrate *their* commitment to Christ and *their* oneness with his Church in worship, witness and service to the world. Let *these candidates* be now presented.

4 *Those presenting the candidates say*
I/We present ... *(Name)* to be baptized.

5 *When all the candidates have been presented, the presbyter asks each candidate in turn,*
(Name) have you been baptized before?

6 *If the reply is 'No' the presbyter says,*
(Name) do you desire to be baptized?
I do.

7 Let us pray.
God our heavenly Father,
you alone are the source
of all good desires and right actions.
we thank you for calling *these persons*
into a closer union with Christ in baptism
Purify *their* intentions;
grant *them* a clear vision of the life in Christ
and courage to yield completely
to the leading of the Holy Spirit;
and unite *them* and us
in the fellowship of your Son,
our Lord and Saviour Jesus Christ.
Amen.

THE MINISTRY OF THE WORD

8 Beloved in Christ from time immemorial water has been regarded by people of many faiths as a symbol of life and spiritual cleansing.

Baptism in water signifies at the same time that we have died in our sinful nature and have risen again to new life in union with Christ. In this sign God gives assurance of his grace to those who are baptized with sincere repentance and faith.

They receive forgiveness of all their past sins; they receive new birth through the Holy Spirit; they are made members of the Church, the body of Christ; and they are given power to grow continually in obedience to the Lord Jesus Christ.

Listen to what the apostle Paul wrote to those who had been baptized, in his letter to the Romans, the 6th chapter, verses 3 to 11:

⟦This passage of Scripture is included in the text.⟧

Alleluia! To God be the glory.
May this word of God be fulfilled in our lives. Amen.

DECLARATION OF FAITH
RENUNCIATION AND PROMISE

You who have come to be baptized have heard that baptism is a sign of sharing in the death and resurrection of Christ and of receiving new life in him.

It is therefore necessary for you to be willing to accept this new life as a gift from God. He alone can transform your life and enable you to continue in the new life as a disciple of Christ.

You must therefore in the presence of this congregation renounce all that is evil and contrary to God's will, and openly declare your faith in him and your desire to follow the Lord Jesus Christ.

Therefore I ask you:

10 Do you believe and trust in Jesus Christ as Lord and saviour of all?
Yes, I do.

11 Do you believe in trust in one God, the father Almighty who created all things?
Yes, I do.

12 Do you believe in the Holy Spirit who sanctifies, strengthens and guides the people of God?
Yes, I do.

13 Do you repent of all your past sins and of all that you know to have been unworthy of God in your life?
Yes, I do.

14 Do you renounce Satan and all the powers of wickedness that rebel against God?
Yes, I do.

15 Do you renounce all sinful desires that draw us away from the love of God and from the love of our fellow human beings?
Yes, I do.

16 Will you obey Christ, boldly bear witness to him in the world, and love and serve others as he did?
Yes, I will, with God's help.

17 You therefore desire to be baptized and to commit yourself to Jesus Christ as your Saviour, Lord and Guide in the fellowship of his church.
Yes, I do.

18 Let us all with joy and boldness profess our faith together.

19 *The Apostles' Creed shall be said or song by all.* ⟦**CF1a**⟧

THE BAPTISM

20 *A psalm, or hymn, or lyric may be sung. The Thanksgiving for the Gift of Water (Appendix, Section 37 [Section 33 in this book]) may be used.*

21 *Then the presbyter prays as follows, or in his/her own words:*

Almighty and everlasting God, your blessed son our Lord Jesus Christ has commanded us to make disciples of all nations, and to baptize them in the name of the Father, and of the Son, and of the Holy Spirit. Send your Holy Spirit, heavenly father, to sanctify this water, and grant that *these persons* now to be baptized in it may die to *their* sinful nature and rise to the new life in union with Christ. May *they* be filled with your power and peace, and grow as *members* of the body of Christ. To him, to you father, and to the Holy Spirit, be all honour and glory to the end of the ages. **Amen.**

22 *The presbyter baptizes each person in one of the following ways..., saying the following words:*
(*Name*), I baptize you in the name of God, the Father, the Son and the Holy Spirit.
or
(*Name*), be baptized in the name of God, the Father, the Son and the Holy Spirit.
Amen.

23 *When all the candidates have been baptized, the Doxology, or a lyric, or a him may be sung.*
We are the body of Christ.
In the one Spirit we were all baptized into one body.

Glory to the Father, and to the Son and to the Holy Spirit;
as it was in the beginning, is now, and ever shall be to the end of ages. Amen.

24 *After the baptism one or more of the optional additional ceremonies... may be added.*

⟦The direction is added that where possible confirmation and reception into communicant membership should follow immediately. There are then directions for the celebration of the Lord's Supper. The service ends with the following material.⟧

WELCOME INTO THE CHURCH

27 *The newly baptized stands facing the congregation, who also stand.*

Three representatives of the congregation come forward and say with the presbyter to the newly baptized:
Beloved in Christ, we welcome and receive you into the Fellowship of Christ's Church. Rejoice and take your part with us in building up the body of Christ for the salvation of all.

28 *The newly baptized may also be garlanded, or any other local customs of welcoming them may be followed.*

29 *The newly baptized take their place in the congregation.*

THANKSGIVING AND PRAYER

30 *The presbyter prays his/her own words, or as follows.*
The following prayer may also be used just before the final Blessing if there is a celebration of the Lord 's Supper.
Almighty God, in your mercy you draw the hearts of believers to yourself through the revelation of your love in Jesus Christ our Lord.
We thank you for this work of grace in *those* who *have* now been baptized, and for planting in them the seed of new life in fellowship with you and with all your people.
We pray that *they* may be continually strengthened by your spirit in a deeper knowledge of view, and in holiness of life.
Grant that they may go forward in faith and obedience to your will, was sure hope in your promise of eternal life; through Jesus Christ our Lord to whom with you and the Holy Spirit your praise and glory for ever. **Amen.**

⟦31 Directions are given for further prayers, the Lord's Prayer, the sermon, hymns or lyrics, and a presbyteral benediction of the Aaronic blessing with the Trinitarian conclusion.⟧

APPENDIX

⟦32 The rubric says that the elements in the appendix are optional. And more similar material may be produced for experiment with the approval of the bishop.⟧

33 *THANKSGIVING FOR THE GIFT OF WATER*
Thanks be to God, who created water and by determining its functions and bounds removed for us its threat of chaos and death.
Blessed be God.

Thanks be to God that, when floods threaten the survival of the human race and brought to people sense of their sins, he pardoned that iniquities and promised that floods should destroy the earth no more. The rainbow in the clouds is the sign of his beauty and favour.
Blessed be God.

Thanks be to God that, when his people fled from their oppressors, he led them through the Red Sea from bondage to freedom.
Blessed be God.

In the fullness of time God sent his servant John whose baptism of repentance prepared the people for the kingdom of God and for the baptism of the Holy Spirit through Jesus Christ our Lord.
Blessed be God.

The Lord Jesus passed through the waters of death, but God raised him from the dead and open to us the gates of eternal life.
Blessed be God.

In ancient times God promised to pour out his spirit upon all people. Led by his holy spirit, we now turn to God and call him father. He gives us new birth and leads us from untruths to truth, from darkness to light, from death to eternal life.
Blessed be God. The grace of our Lord Jesus Christ, the love of God and the Fellowship of the Holy Spirit be with us all. Amen.

OPTIONAL ADDITIONAL CEREMONIES

34 *SIGNING THE FOREHEAD WITH THE SIGN OF THE CROSS*
The presbyter dips his/her finger in water and signs the forehead of the newly baptized with the sign of the cross, saying:
I sign new with the sign of the cross of Jesus Christ. Do not be ashamed to confess Christ who was crucified and to fight always against all forms of evil.

35 *GIVING OF A LIGHTED DEEPAK OR CANDLE*
The presbyter gives a lighted deepak or candle to the newly baptised, saying:
Christ the light of the world leads you from darkness to light, from untruths to truth, from death to eternal life. Walk in his light.

36 *PUTTING ON A WHITE GARMENT*
The presbyter places on the newly baptised a white garment, saying:
Put on this white garment in token of your putting on Christ's purity and his risen life which makes you new.

[[37 Further optional ceremonies include, giving a testimony, and act of thanksgiving prayer, or a song, or a dance. A copy of the New Testament may also be given to the candidate.]]

THE BAPTISM OF CHILDREN

THE MINISTRY OF THE WORD AND CONFESSION OF FAITH

1   The parents, the sponsors with the child to be baptised and the congregation assemble near the font all the vessel containing the water for baptism, or pond, or tank, or River.

2   Hear the gracious words of our Lord Jesus Christ which tell us of God's love and concern for children: [[Mark 10.14]]
    If such as God's love for children then we can with confidence pray, that he will grant them the gift which will enable them to grow up as his own sons and daughters.
    Our Lord Jesus Christ also said [[John 3.3]]. Such a new birth God alone can give and it is promised to us through the working of the Holy Spirit in the sacrament of baptism [[John 3.5]]. God will grant this gift to *this child* in baptism when we ask in faith.
    Throughout the ages the church of God has been built up of those who receive God's gift of new birth and were incorporated into the body of Christ in their baptism either in infancy or as adults.
    As the Lord Jesus Christ had forgiveness of sins and healing to the paralytic in response to the faith of his friends who brought him to the Lord, so God will grant new birth to *this child* by the power of the Holy Spirit when we ask him in faith. Let us therefore place *this child* in God's loving hands, trusting that he will give *him* all that is necessary for *his* salvation and growth in grace.

3   Let us pray.
    Oh God our loving father, you desire that none of your children should perish, and you have raised up your Church so that in its common life your children may receive spiritual nourishment and grow in your likeness. We thank you for promising new life and fellowship with you to those who are born of water and the Holy Spirit. We thank you for the sacrament of baptism which signifies that in union with Christ they died to sin and rise again to new lists of life.

4   **O loving Father, we bring *this child* to you, who alone can renew and save those who come to you in faith. Receive *him* and make *him* yours for ever in the body of Christ; renew and save *him* and make *him* an instrument of your redeeming love in the world. We ask this in the name of Jesus Christ our Lord. Amen.**

5   Now to him who by the power at work within us is able to do far more abundantly than all that we can ask or think, to him be glory in the Church and in Christ Jesus to all generations, for ever and ever. **Amen.**

THE PARENTS' AND SPONSORS' PROMISES

6   *Each parent and sponsor (or godparent) makes the promises as follows:*

7   Do you who have brought this child for baptism promised before God and in the presence of this congregation that you will steadfastly affirm and uphold the faith the church?
    Yes, I do.

8   Do you promise to help this child to believe and trust in God the father Almighty, who created heaven and Earth?
    Yes, I do.

9   Do you promise to help this child to believe and trust in Jesus Christ, the Son of God, who for our salvation died on a cross, was raised from the dead, lives now in glory as the Saviour and Lord of all, and will come again to judge the living and the dead?
Yes, I do.

10 Do you promise to help this child to believe and trust in the Holy Spirit of God who renews, guides and strengthens the people of God?
Yes, I do.

11 Do you promise that by your prayers for this child, by your own manner of life, and your guidance, you will help him as he grows up to pray and worship God, to study the Bible, to follow the example and teaching of the Lord Jesus Christ, to share generously what he has with others and to take an active part in the Church's witness to Christ?
Yes, I do.

12 Do you also promise that you will also help this child to grow in the knowledge and experience of Christ, that when he comes to the age of discretion, he will be led to make his personal and public profession of faith in Christ and be received into the communicant membership of the church?
Yes, I do.

Let us pray in silence that the Holy Spirit may enable you to be faithful to your promises.
Silence

13 Do you now wish this child to be baptised?
I do.

THE BAPTISM

14 *A Psalm, or hymn, or lyric may be sung, or the Thanksgiving for the Gift of Water (Appendix... Or similar devotional material) may be used.*

15 *The presbyter prays as follows, or in his/her own words:*
Let us pray.
O holy and loving Father, your word became flesh so that, in union with him, all people may be enabled to be your children. Accept this child, we pray and make him your own in the body of Christ. Send your Holy Spirit and sanctify this water, that, as water cleanses and refreshes the body, so this child now to be baptised in this water may be born anew, and may have the blessing of eternal life in Jesus Christ our Lord, who with you, O Father, and with the Holy Spirit lives and reigns to the ends of the ages. **Amen.**

16 *The presbyter asks the parents (or the sponsors) to name the child.*

17 *The presbyter baptizes each child in one of the ways prescribed..., saying*
(*Name*), I baptize you in the name of God, the Father, the Son, and the Holy Spirit.
or
(*Name*), be baptized in the name of God, the Father, the Son, and the Holy Spirit.
Amen.

RECEPTION INTO THE CHURCH

18 *When all the children have been baptized, the congregation stands.*
We are the body of Christ.
In the one Spirit we were all baptized into one body.

Glory be to the Father, and to the Son and to the Holy Spirit; as it was in the beginning, is now and ever shall be to the end of the ages. Amen.

19 We receive this child into the fellowship of Christ's church.
We welcome him in the name of Christ.

⟦20 Directions are given to use the optional additional ceremonies.⟧

THANKSGIVING AND PRAYER

21 Almighty God, our heavenly Father, in your mercy you have called all people to enter your kingdom through the redeeming work of Christ our saviour. We thank you for making this child your own this day through baptism by giving him new birth in water and the Holy Spirit and making him a member of the body of Christ. Guide, strengthen and sanctify him all the days of his life. Enable his parents (and sponsors) to fulfil the promises they have made so that under their care this child may grow up in the knowledge of your love and in devotion to you; through Jesus Christ our Lord to whom with you, Father, and the Holy Spirit, one God in wisdom, power, and love we offer thanks and praise, now and always. **Amen.**

Almighty God, we thank you for fellowship in the household of faith with all those who have been baptized into Christ. Keep us faithful to our Christian calling and so make is ready for that day when the whole creation shall be made perfect in your Son, our Lord and saviour Jesus Christ. **Amen.**

⟦22 Directions are given for intercessory prayer, the Lord 's Prayer, and two benedictions. An appendix contains a Thanksgiving for the gift of the water as in 37 above (33 in this book). The optional ceremonies of the sign of the cross and giving of a lighted Deepak are included. The rubrics are exactly the same but the text is completely different.⟧

23 *THE SIGN OF THE CROSS*
We sign this child with the sign of the cross as a sign that *he* now belongs to Christ who was crucified.

24 *GIVING OF A LIGHTED DEEPAK OR CANDLE*
Receive this lighted Deepak/candle. Hold it in the hand of your child. Remember the words our Lord spoke to us all: 'You are the light of the world'.

THE ORDER OF CONFIRMATION WITH THE PUBLIC PROFESSION OF FAITH OF THOSE BAPTIZED AS CHILDREN AND RECEPTION INTO COMMUNICANT MEMBERSHIP OF THE CHURCH

THE PREPARATION

1 *At the beginning of the service the minister may give this or some other Call to Worship*
Thus says the Lord who made you, I will pour my Spirit upon your descendants and my blessing on your offspring. *Isa. 44.2–3*
Come let us praise him!

2 *Before or after the Call a hymn, a canticle or a psalm may be sung.*

3 *The Bishop greets the people, saying*
Grace and peace to you from God our Father and the Lord Jesus Christ.
And also to you.

4 *If the Lord's Supper is to follow the Confirmation, or if the Bishop so desires, the Confession of Sin here follows.*
⟦A confession of sin⟧

5   ⟦An absolution by the bishop.⟧

6   *The Bishop speaks to the congregation, either in his own words, or saying*
Beloved in Christ, we have come together today in God's presence to do three things.
The first is to be present while each of those to be confirmed publicly accepts for
himself or herself God's promise of salvation in Christ. You will be their witnesses
that they have committed themselves to Christ, their Lord and Saviour.
The second is to support these candidates with your prayers. Especially we shall pray
that through the laying on of hands in Confirmation each of them may increasingly
experience the grace and power of God's Holy Spirit; for only so can they grow in the
love of God and be true followers of Jesus Christ.
The third is that you, the members of the particular congregation to which they
belong, may welcome them into the fellowship of those who share in the holy
sacrament of the Lord's Supper.

7   *The Bishop speaks to the candidates, either in his own words, or saying*
Those who brought you as a child for baptism made a solemn pledge that you would
be nurtured in the Christian faith in God, Father, Son and Holy Spirit. You are here
today in order that you may give your own assent to the pledge which was then made
in your name.

You have come to declare your faith in the Lord Jesus Christ, your acceptance of him
as your Saviour, and your commitment to him for ever.

In your baptism each of you was made a member of the body of Christ and was
received into his Church, which is the family and household of God. You have now
come to receive from God the spiritual gift which he has promised to those who
believe in him; for in accordance with the practice of the Apostles I shall lay my hand
on each of you and pray that the Holy Spirit may strengthen you to follow Christ and
to be his faithful witness.

8   *The Bishop and people pray together*
Almighty God, our heavenly Father, you have made us your children in Christ
through your Holy Spirit in baptism. Grant that, strengthened by your Spirit in
Confirmation, we may share in the glorious liberty of your people and live as sons
and daughters of your kingdom; through your Son Jesus Christ our Lord, who with
you, Father, and the Holy Spirit, lives and reigns, one God, world without end. **Amen.**

THE MINISTRY OF THE WORD

⟦9–13 Ezekiel 36.26–28; or Jeremiah 31.31–34; Romans 8.11–17; or 1 Cor 12.12–13; Gal
5.22–25; John 14.15–17; or Mat 16.24–27. A sermon is given.⟧

THE PROFESSION OF PERSONAL DISCIPLESHIP

14   *The Congregation sits. The presbyter(s) reads the names of those whom he is presenting.
Each candidate stands when his or her name is called.*

The Bishop says to the candidates
You who desire to be confirmed must first profess your allegiance to Christ and your
rejection of all that is evil. *You* must have already counted the cost of being a disciple
of Jesus Christ. He says, Anyone who wishes to be a follower of mine must leave self
behind; he must take up his cross, and come with me: But he also promises that in his
company no burden is too hard to bear.

15 *The Bishop says to all the candidates or to each in turn*
Do you accept Jesus Christ as your Lord and Saviour?
Yes, I do.
Do you, therefore, renounce all that is evil?
Yes, I do.
Will you follow Jesus Christ in the fellowship of his Church?
Yes, I will.

THE DECLARATION OF FAITH

16 *The Bishop says to the candidates*
You are determined to be true followers of Christ and to renounce all that is evil. The power to do this is promised to those who hold fast to God in faith and hope.

17 Do you believe and trust in God the Father, who created you and all the world?
Yes, I do.

Do you believe and trust in his Son Jesus Christ, who has redeemed you and all mankind?
Yes, I do.

Do you believe and trust in his Holy Spirit, who renews and transforms you and all the people of God?
Yes, I do.

THE PROMISES

18 *The Bishop says to the candidates*
The sincerity of our faith is proved when it is active in love. I therefore urge you to make your daily life worthy of the Father of all who loves you and has made you his children, worthy of his Son who died for you, and worthy of his Spirit who dwells in you.

Will you strive through regular prayer and reading of the Bible to grow in God's love and to learn his will for your life?
Yes, I will.

Will you strive to respond to this great love of God by a life of joyful obedience to him and of love and care for others?
Yes, I will.

Will you join as far as possible with your fellow Christians in public worship on Sundays, and especially in the Lord's Supper?
Yes, I will.

God calls his Church to share with all people the good news of his love made known in Christ. Will you take your part in doing this?
I shall try with God's help to make Christ known,
by what I am, by what I say, by what I do for others.

19 *The candidates and congregation kneel.*
Let us pray in silence that the Holy Spirit may enable you to be faithful to your promises.
Silence

20 *After the silence those to be confirmed, led by the Bishop, say together*
O God, my Father, I am not my own but yours; I rely on your grace and the power of your Holy Spirit, and give myself to you as your child, to love and serve you all the days of my life.

THE CONFIRMATION

Immediately after this the Bishop administers Confirmation.

21 *The Bishop stands facing the candidates, and says*
The love of God is poured into our hearts,
Through the Holy Spirit he has given us.

22 *The Bishop and the presbyters stretch out their hands towards those to be confirmed, and the Bishop says this prayer, in which the whole congregation joins.*

**Almighty God, our heavenly Father,
in baptism we were made your children
and members of your Church
by the water of rebirth and the renewing
power of your Holy Spirit.
Grant now to these your children the fullness
of the same Spirit,
the Spirit of wisdom and understanding,
the Spirit of counsel and inward strength,
the Spirit of knowledge and true godliness,
and fin them, O Lord, with the Spirit of your holy fear.**

23 *The candidates to be confirmed come forward and kneel either in turn before the Bishop, or in a row, as instructed. The Presbyter, just before the Bishop confirms each candidate, announces clearly to the congregation the name of that candidate.*
The Bishop lays his hand on the head of each candidate in turn, saying

Strengthen, O Lord, your child/servant with your Holy Spirit. **Amen.**

24 *After all the candidates have been confirmed, or after each individual candidate, the Bishop says*
Defend, O Lord, these your children/servants: make them strong with your heavenly grace, that they may continue yours for ever, and daily grow in your Holy Spirit more and more, until they come to your everlasting kingdom. **Amen.**

25 ⟦The Lord's Prayer **CF4a** may be said.⟧

26 *The Bishop says*
Almighty and everliving God, we thank you for the great blessing bestowed on these your children/servants through the laying on of hands. By this sign they are assured of your unfailing goodness towards them. We commit them to your fatherly care. Grant that they may serve you all the days of their life, and finally know the bliss of your eternal presence; through Jesus Christ, our Saviour. To him, to you, Father, and to the Holy Spirit, one God in wisdom, power and love, we offer our thanks and praise, now and for ever. **Amen.**

THE WELCOME

27 *All stand. The Bishop and presbyters welcome, according to local custom, the newly confirmed persons. The Bishop says*

We admit you and welcome you into communicant membership of the Church.

28 *The newly confirmed persons turn and face the congregation. Each presbyter and congregation welcome their own newly confirmed members, saying to them*
We, the members of the congregation, welcome you with joy, as you come to share with us at the Lord's Table. We promise you our friendship and our prayers. God grant that we may together serve him here on earth in the unity of the Spirit and in the bond of love, and come to the perfect fellowship of the saints in light.

29 *The newly confirmed persons say together*
    Thank you.

⟦30 Directions are given for the Lord's Supper and a blessing.⟧

28. The Church of Bangladesh

Bangladesh shares the history of the other churches in the subcontinent with Christianity coming at first through trade. CMS and the Oxford Mission to Calcutta worked in this area. The Book of Common Prayer 1662 was translated into Bengali.[71] The Diocese of Calcutta was set up in 1813, and in 1952 the Diocese of Dhaka was created. At this time the church was a part of the independent Province of India, Pakistan, Burma and Ceylon, and the provincial Prayer Book was translated into Bengali.[72] In 1970 the church became a part of the Church of Pakistan and towards the end of the liberation war in 1971 the church became an independent Province.

The church has used the Bengali edition of the CNI liturgy, but from the 1980s developed its own liturgical tradition. In 1997 the church produced a full prayer book in Bengali. This includes a service of baptism, for adults and children, and service confirmation.

PRAYER BOOK OF THE CHURCH OF BANGLADESH 1997

[Translated by John Webber]

THE ORDER FOR HOLY BAPTISM

[Seven introductory rubrics are given, including the preference for baptism to be on a Sunday.]

[A rubric on how to include a baptism in the eucharistic rite.]

1 Dear brothers and sisters in Christ, through baptism our heavenly Father frees us from sin and death, accepts us as his children and makes us inheritors of eternal life. By it, he joins us to Christ's body, the Church, and gives us his grace and strength that we might follow Christ and lead our lives according to his will. Come, let us pray for those who today will receive baptism.

2 Almighty God, shepherd of your chosen people, as you freed your children from the hand of the enemy through the water of the Red Sea, so free these your sons and daughters from the power of Satan, wash them from their sin and make them sharers in Christ's death, so that they might be worthy to share in his resurrection. May this be done through your chosen and beloved Son Jesus Christ. **Amen.**

THE READING OF SCRIPTURE

[2 Three lessons, and a sermon, but no Creed.]

---

71 G 13:1–16.
72 G 13: 17, J 67–76, 95–102.

THE PROMISES

3   You have brought these children here for baptism. From now on these will be your special responsibilities:
You shall bring them regularly to the Lord's House for worship, that they may join in fellowship with God's family.
You will teach them all that is necessary for Christians to know.
By your prayer and example, you will help them, that as they grow up, to grow into maturity in Christ.
Are you willing to take on these responsibilities?
Yes, we are.

4   *The minister shall ask these questions of those who are to receive baptism. In the case of children, the minister shall question their parents and godparents.*

For those who receive baptism, it is necessary that they promise to forsake Satan and all his works, follow Christ and believe in God. Therefore I ask you:
Do you renounce all that is evil?
Yes, I renounce it.
Will you accept Jesus as your Lord and Saviour, and follow and obey him?
Yes, I will.
Do you believe in God, Father, Son and Holy Spirit?
Yes, I believe.

5   All the members of the church ought to help those who will be baptised to grow in Christ-like love, fellowship and prayer. Are you willing to take on this responsibility?
Yes, we are willing.

6   Come, let us now proclaim our own faith together with those who have just now proclaimed their faith in God.

7   *Then, the congregation will join in the Apostles' Creed.*
[The Apostles' Creed **CF1a**]

BLESSING OF THE WATER

8   Come let us pray for those who will now receive baptism that they may be filled with the blessing of God.

Silence

The Lord is amongst us.
His Spirit is in our midst.

Lift up your hearts to God.
We lift our hearts to the Lord.

Come, let us thank and praise God.
That is right and fitting.

Holy King of heaven and our Father, the everlasting God, through your only Son our Lord Jesus Christ, it is not only fitting to thank and praise you, but it is our joyful responsibility.

Therefore, we now especially give you thanks that through our Lord Jesus Christ you have accepted us as your children, given us the title of subjects of your kingdom, and given us your Holy Spirit. You have given us the command to make the good news of your salvation reach all the people of the earth, and to baptise them in the name of the Father, the Son and the Holy Spirit. Therefore, we now humbly pray that you will protect these your sons and daughters from sin and death.

Lord in your mercy **Hear our prayer.**
Fill them with your holy and life-giving Spirit.
Lord in your mercy **Hear our prayer.**
Keep them in the faith and fellowship of the church.
Lord in your mercy **Hear our prayer.**
Teach them to love, so that they may love you with all their hearts and their neighbours as themselves.
Lord in your mercy **Hear our prayer.**
Lead them from darkness into light, that they may fully receive your eternal peace.
Lord in your mercy **Hear our prayer.**
Almighty God, we humbly pray, that you will bless this water through the power of your Holy Spirit, that those who will be washed from their sins and receive new birth in this water will grow in the resurrection life of our Saviour, the Lord Jesus. With him and the Holy Spirit all honour, glory and power be yours for ever and ever. **Amen.**

BAPTISM

9 *The minister will ask the names of those who will receive baptism and their parents/ witnesses will introduce them one by one by name to the minister. The minister shall immerse them in water or pour water over them and say:*

[Name] I baptise you in the name of the Father and the Son and the Holy Spirit. Amen.

10 *When all have been baptized, the minister will sign the forehead of each with the sign of the cross and say,*

We sign you with the sign of the cross and receive you into the community of those who follow Christ.

Never be ashamed to confess the faith of Christ crucified and serve Him as a faithful disciple throughout your life.

11 *At the giving of white clothing, the minister will say:*

Clothe yourself with holiness and live your life in grace.

At the time of giving the candle, the minister will say:

The light of Christ light up your heart and mind with light and lead you on the way of light.

12 *A hymn of praise may be sung. Then all can go forward from the place of baptism to the altar.*

13 *After each of the prayers below, silence may be kept.*

Let us pray.

For those who have been baptised we now pray with joy and thanksgiving, and at the same time we pray also for ourselves that we all may remain faithful to Jesus Christ.
Lord in your mercy **Hear our prayer.**
We pray also for the families of those who have been baptised that their homes may be unswerving in love for each other, in knowledge and wisdom.
Lord in your mercy **Hear our prayer.**
For all people we pray and especially for the peace of the world.
Lord in your mercy **Hear our prayer.**
We pray for those who are in the midst of any danger, suffering, difficulty and problems.

Lord in your mercy **Hear our prayer.**
We pray that following the example of the saints we may be sharers in the eternal joy of Christ's kingdom.
Lord in your mercy **Hear our prayer.**
Lord, bless us that we who have received baptism into the death of Jesus Christ may walk in the strength of this resurrection and may share eternal joy with him. **Amen**

14 *Then worship shall continue with the Sharing of the Peace in the order of the Lord's Supper. If there is not to be a celebration of the Lord's Supper, worship will conclude with the Lord's Prayer and a blessing.*

SOME ADDITIONAL MATTERS CONCERNING HOLY BAPTISM

15 *At the time of baptism, the ceremony of clothing with a white garment and the lighting of a lamp may proceed as below.*

16 *The priest may take each candidate for baptism by the right hand and say to the godparents.*
Give the name of this child/person.

17 *The minister shall immerse them in water or pour water over them and say:*

[Name] I baptise you in the name of the Father and the Son and the Holy Spirit. Amen

18 *Then the priest shall say:*

We have received this person into the fellowship of Christ's religion and signing him/her with the sign of the cross, we proclaim this that this person shall not be ashamed to confess the faith of Christ crucified but rather as a faithful soldier and child, bearing Christ's banner, shall fight against sin, the world and Satan until death. Amen

19 *Then [or after the baptism] every baptised person may wear a white cloth. When clothing each person, the priest can say these words:*

This white cloth is a sign of holiness. By God's grace, in Holy Baptism, this holiness was given to you, so that from now on, you may exercise vigilance in living a holy life, and that in a short while, at the end of life, you may inherit eternal life.

20 *Then the priest may say to the baptised persons:*

God give you the grace of baptism, that you may obediently follow all his commands, and may walk worthy of your Christian calling. Go forth in the strength of the Spirit, so that you do not fulfil the will of the flesh. The fruit of the Spirit is love, joy, peace, long-suffering, compassion, good behaviour, faithfulness, gentleness and self-restraint. Always keep in remembrance that baptism is for us a sign of faith, by which we mean following our Saviour Christ's example and being like him. To him be all glory offered now and for ever. Amen.

ORDER FOR CONFIRMATION/LAYING ON OF HANDS

[SERVICE OF RECEPTION INTO THE CHURCH'S FULL FELLOWSHIP]

Note: The Plan for Church Union stipulates that a bishop or presbyter may conduct this act of worship.

It will be celebrated in the context of the Lord's Supper.

PREPARATION

1 *A hymn may be sung*

2 *The Bishop/Presbyter will greet the congregation with these words:*
The mercy and peace from God our Father and the Lord Jesus Christ be poured over you.
And over you

I will arise and go to my father and will say to him: Father, I have sinned against heaven and before you. I am no longer worthy to be called your son.
Luke 15.18–19
Lord, do not judge me. For in your sight, nobody is counted as without fault.

CONFESSION AND ABSOLUTION OF SIN

3 Come, in penitence and faith, let us confess our sins.
Almighty God our heavenly Father, we have sinned against you in thought, word and deed. through neglect, weakness and our own free will. We have not done what we ought to have done, rather we have done what we ought not to have done. For all these faults, we are truly sorry and truly repent. Forgive all our sins through our Lord Jesus Christ, who died for us, and, with renewed purpose, give us the strength to live our lives according to your will. Amen

The Bishop or Presbyter will say:
Almighty God have mercy upon you, forgive you, free you from all sin, confirm and strengthen you in all goodness and grant you eternal life, through our Lord Jesus Christ. **Amen.**

4 *Glory to God in the Highest will be sung.*

5 Dear brothers and sisters in Christ, we have come together today to fulfil three tasks: Firstly, you are to be present as those who are to be confirmed confess before the congregation that the promise of God's salvation through Christ has been fulfilled, and you are to be witnesses as they receive Jesus as Lord and Saviour and surrender themselves into his hand.
The second is this: that you may help these candidates with prayer, and especially, today we pray that at the time of confirmation, through the laying of hands on their heads, they may each, day by day, understand in greater measure the mercy and strength of God's Holy Spirit, that their lives may grow in the love of God and that each may be a true follower of Jesus Christ.
The third is this: you may make known to them the invitation extended to them to the fellowship of the sacrament of the Lord's Supper, as members of the world wide church, and within the local church of which they are members.

6 *The Presbyter shall read out the name of all who are present. When the candidates' names are read, they shall stand up one by one.*

7   *The Bishop/Presbyter will address the candidates in these or his own words:*

At the time of Baptism, you became part of God's family, a member of the Church. Those who brought you for Baptism formally made promises on your behalf that you would be brought up in the faith of God, Father, Son and Holy Spirit. Today you are present for this purpose that you, yourselves, may freely and sincerely agree to those promises made in your name. You will confess your faith in the Lord Jesus Christ, accept him as your Saviour and commit yourselves into his hands for ever.

You are present here so that you may receive those spiritual gifts promised to all believers. Therefore, following the example of the apostles, I will lay my hands upon each of you and pray that the Holy Spirit will give you the strength so that, following Christ, you may be his faithful witnesses.

Finally, you have come so that the members of your own pastorate/parishes can extend to you the invitation to the fellowship of those who receive the Lord's Supper, in which fellowship you will praise and serve God.

8   *A prayer for the gift of the Holy Spirit and the Collect for the day shall be said.*

O God, as on the day of Pentecost you taught your disciples by pouring out on their hearts and minds the light of your Holy Spirit, so now, pour out the strength of your Holy Spirit on the lives of your children, these candidates for confirmation, so that their lives may be fit to be strengthened by the manifold gifts of the Holy Spirit, to be guided by your wisdom and in all situations in their life to receive the benefit of your comfort. And may he who lives and reigns for ever with You and that same Spirit, one God, our Lord Jesus Christ through his strength bring this prayer to fulfilment. **Amen.**

THE READING OF SCRIPTURE

⟦9 Three readings of Scripture, a sermon, but no Creed.⟧

THE RENEWAL OF THE BAPTISMAL COVENANT

11 Those who will receive confirmation must confess their obedience to the commandments and renounce all that is evil. You have no doubt reckoned what is the cost of being a disciple of Jesus Christ, who said 'If anyone wants to come after me, let him forget himself and take up his cross and follow me.' But he has also promised that with him no burden is too heavy to bear. Therefore I ask you:

Are you willing to renounce all that is evil?
Yes, I am willing.
Do you accept Jesus Christ as your Lord and Saviour?
Yes, I do.
Are you firmly resolved to journey with Christ as his disciples?
Yes, I am firmly resolved.

You are witness of all these promises. Will you, according to your ability, help these people to fashion their lives according to the example of Christ?
Yes, we will.

CONFESSION OF FAITH

12 You are firmly resolved to truly follow Christ and renounce all that is evil. In the Bible, he promises his spiritual strength to those who believe in God and put their trust in him. Therefore I ask you:

Do you believe and trust in God the Father who created all that is in the world?
I believe and trust in him.

Do you believe in the Lord Jesus Christ who gave you and all the human race freedom?

I believe and trust in him.

Do you believe in the Holy Spirit who renews and transforms you and all God's people?

I believe and trust in him.

Come, let us join with those who have even now confessed their faith in God and confess our own faith in him.

Then the congregation will join in the Apostles Creed [[CF1a]].

PROMISES

13a Our faith will be proved to be true by works of love. Therefore, I earnestly entreat you that, in your daily life, you will be worthy of the Father, who loves you and has made you his children, worthy of God the Son, who died for you, and worthy of His Spirit, who directs you. Therefore, I ask you:

Will you, meet regularly with other Christians and join in various acts of worship, and especially through participating in the Lord's Supper, and through prayer and reading of the Bible, strive to know the will of God and grow in His love?

With the help of God I will.

Will you maintain the unity of the Church of Bangladesh and through accepting a part in its witness and service be a dedicated member of it?

With the help of God I will.

Will you, through your lives, your words and work, your strength, time and money, take your part, with all others, in the gospel of God's love proclaimed in Christ.

With the help of God I will.

Will you ban evil from your life and whenever you fall into any sin will you strive to return to the Lord with repentance?

With the help of God I will.

Or the following short form may be used.

SHORT FORM

13b At the time of your baptism, before God and the church, important vows and promises were made in your name – that you would not walk in the path of evil, that you would accept Jesus as Lord and Saviour, and that you would live in accordance with God's will. Do you today accept all these promises for yourself, as your own responsibility?

Yes, I do.

Will you be witnesses to Christ's salvation through your life, words and work?

I will.

Will you regularly join in worship and remain in the fellowship of the church. Will you faithfully serve your neighbour and be assiduous in giving?

With the help of God, I will.

LAYING ON OF HANDS

14 *The Bishop/Presbyter addresses the candidates:*

You have accepted Christ and confessed your faith and trust in God and have proclaimed your love for Him, and that you will remain obedient to him and will live within the fellowship of the Church. Therefore, kneeling, you will now pray that the Holy Spirit will strengthen you to keep faithful to your promises.

15a *For a short while, all will keep silence and fall to their knees. Those who are to have hands laid on them will say all together with the Bishop/Presbyter:*

Lord, I am not mine, I am yours. I offer myself as your son/daughter. According to your will, make use of me and give me the strength to love and serve you until the last day of my life. Amen

or

15b **Lord, make me an instrument of your peace. Where there is hatred, may I sow love, where there is injury, pardon, where there is division, unity: in the midst of unbelief, may I bring faith, in the midst of despair, hope, in darkness may light shine out, where there is sorrow may I bring your joy, O Lord. And when I am dealing with the faults of others, may I always be compassionate. We ask this in your Holy name. Amen**

16 *The candidate kneeling, the Bishop and those presbyters who are present, will extend their hands over them. The congregation will say the following prayer with the Bishop.*

Heavenly Father, we give you thanks that through the death and resurrection of Jesus Christ you have given us new life. Renew the covenant made with these your children at the time of their baptism, make them strong through the assistance of your Holy Spirit and keep them firm in your mercy for ever. Amen.

17 *The Bishop/Presbyter shall lay hands on the head of each candidate and say the words that follow. If he wills, he may also anoint the forehead with blessed oil. Parents and relatives may be present by the side of the candidates.*

Lord, fill your child _____ with the strength of your Holy Spirit, that he/she may be yours for ever. **Amen.**

18 Almighty and eternal God, of your mercy, like a father protect them for ever, may your Holy Spirit always stay with them, that, understanding your word and being obedient to it, they may serve you in this life and may live with you in the life to come, through the Lord Jesus Christ, **Amen.**

RECEPTION INTO THE FELLOWSHIP OF THOSE WHO RECEIVE THE LORD'S SUPPER

19 *The Bishop/Presbyter will address the candidates:*
I admit and welcome you into the fellowship of those who receive the Lord's Supper.

The bishop and the Presbyter of the pastorate may give some form of greeting to the candidates, such as offering their right hand. Members of the Pastorate Committee may also join in.

20a *The newly confirmed facing the congregation, the congregation shall say together:*

As the congregation, we welcome you with joy, that you may join with us at the Lord's Table for his Supper. We promise you our friendship and our prayers. May God bless you so that maintaining the fellowship of the Holy Spirit, we may serve Him together in this world and gain full fellowship with the saints in the Kingdom of Heaven.

or

20b *A representative of the congregation may give a word of welcome.*

INTERCESSIONS

21   Listen to what the Apostle Paul says:
'As you therefore have received Christ Jesus the Lord, continue to live your lives in him, rooted and built up in him and established in the faith.' He also tells us that we should be clothed with garments appropriate to God's chosen people.

Lord God, our Father, bless us that receiving Christ Jesus as Lord, we may dwell in him, and, responding to the needs of others, may like Jesus Christ, have compassion in our hearts for others.
Lord in your mercy **Hear our prayer.**

May we, forsaking all kinds of selfishness and pride, clothe ourselves with the humility of Jesus Christ.
Lord in your mercy **Hear our prayer.**

May we, freeing ourselves from all kinds of anger, find place in our hearts for the patience and forbearance of Jesus Christ.
Lord in your mercy **Hear our prayer.**

May we, driving far from us all kinds of bitterness and intolerance. May we, like Jesus Christ, clothe ourselves with hearts full of mercy.
Lord in your mercy **Hear our prayer.**

May we, in all that we do, keep in our hearts the likeness of the love of Jesus Christ.
Lord in your mercy **Hear our prayer.**

Here special thanksgiving and intercessions may be added.

To the Father, Son and Holy Spirit may all glory and praise be given:
As it was in the beginning, is now and ever shall be. **Amen.**

22   *The service will continue, beginning with the Sharing of the Peace in the Order of the Lord's Supper.*

FINAL BLESSING

23   Go forth into the world in peace;
be of good courage;
hold fast that which is good;
render to no one evil for evil;
strengthen the fainthearted;
support the weak;
help the afflicted;
honour everyone;
love and serve the Lord,
rejoicing in the power of the Holy Spirit;
And the blessing of God almighty, Father, Son and Holy Spirit, be with you and remain with you always. **Amen.**

A PLEDGE TO LIVE A CHRISTIAN LIFE

1. *I will pray every day, morning and evening.*

2. *I will read the Bible every day with prayer and reflection.*

3. *Every Sunday, I will join with other Christians for an act of worship or for the Lord's Supper.*

4. *After self-examination I will regularly receive the Lord's Supper, at the very least once a month.*

5. *During Lent and Advent, I will practice self-denial and abstinence, especially on Fridays.*

6. *Regularly, and generously, I will give to God's purposes: for the work of the church [at least 3% of income] and to help those in need.*

7. *I will learn, maintain and proclaim to others the faith delivered to the Church.*

8. *I will observe and maintain the teaching of the church concerning marriage and will bring up children that they may love and serve the Lord.*

9. *I will play a full part in the witness of the Church.*

10. *I will love and serve neighbour and the people of my homeland.*

29. The Church of South India

Christianity came to India by St Thomas in AD 63. There has been a continuous church of Thomas Christians in South India. Roman Catholicism came with the Portuguese and Anglicanism with the East India Company, the first factory founded in 1614. Protestant mission began in South India in 1710 with the SPG and then SPCK employing Lutheran missionaries in what is now Tamil Nadu. The Book of Common Prayer was translated into Tamil[73] and later by CMS missionaries into Malayalam.[74] In 1835 the bishopric of Madras was created and then divided as the church grew. In 1927 the Church of India, Burma and Ceylon was created severing ties with the Church of England. Considerations of church union began in 1928.

The Church of South India was formed in 1947 and gradually began to develop its worship in a series of separate booklets and order for holy baptism being published in 1955 and a second edition in 1960. The *Book of Common Worship* (1962) brought together all these services into one volume and was a significant development in the Anglican Communion. Jagger[75] included the 1962 rites of thanksgiving after childbirth, infant baptism and confirmation in his book.

The *Book of Common Worship* (2006) is the current definitive volume incorporating and making various revisions, not least writing the services in modern English. There are great similarities between the 1962 volume and the 2006 rite. The baptismal material in the 2006 book includes directions for conditional baptism and emergency baptism. The person may be baptized in a font, pond, tank or river. There is an admission service for a catechumen prior to adult baptism, a service for adult baptism (also called in the headings believers' baptism), an order for thanksgiving after childbirth (which is expected to be performed before infant baptism), a service of the baptism of infants and a service of confirmation. It is clear from the services that confirmation is optional for a person who is baptized as an adult, depending upon the tradition of the local congregation. Also confirmation may be administered by a bishop or a presbyter. Again this depends on local tradition.

---

73 G 169: 1.
74 G 101: 1.
75 J 301–314.

HOLY BAPTISM OF PERSONS ABLE TO ANSWER FOR THEMSELVES

1   *The minister ascertains beforehand that the candidates have not already been baptized.*

2   *When the people are gathered at, or proceeding to the place of baptism, a hymn may be sung, after which the minister says:*
Our help is in the name of the Lord
Who has made heaven and earth.

PRESENTATION OF THE CANDIDATES

3   *The candidates may be presented to the congregation. Where appropriate; they may be presented by their sponsors.*

4   *The minister asks those candidates for baptism who are able to answer for themselves:*
Do you wish to be baptized?
I do.

5a Let us pray: Almighty God, you Shepherd of Israel, who did deliver your chosen people from the bondage of Egypt, and did establish with them a sure covenant, have mercy on your flock, and grant that N, who is/are by baptism to be received into your heritage, may be delivered from the bondage of sin through the covenant of grace, and attain the promise of eternal life which you have given us in your Son our Lord and Saviour Jesus Christ, who lives and reigns with you and the Holy Spirit, one God, world without end. **Amen.**

or

5b God, our Lord, you alone are the source of all good desires and right actions. We thank you for calling N into a closer union with Christ in baptism. Purify *his/her/their* intentions; grant *him/her/them* a clear vision of the life in Christ and the courage to yield completely to the leading of the Holy Spirit; and unite *him/her/them* and us in the fellowship of your Son, our Lord and Saviour Jesus Christ. **Amen.**

EXHORTATION

6   Dearly beloved, we are gathered together to administer holy baptism to N, that according to Christ's command *he/she/they* may be sealed as a *member/members* of Christ, *child/children* of God, and *heir/heirs* of the kingdom of heaven.

From time immemorial, water has been regarded by people of many faiths as a symbol of life and spiritual cleansing. By the sign of water God cleanses from sin, renews life, and prefigures the reconciliation of all things promised in Christ. Baptism proclaims the faith of the Church. In baptism we are given the Holy Spirit as the pledge of this reconciliation. The same Spirit binds us to each other and to Christ, and inspires us to be the foretaste of the reign of God.
Hear therefore, the words of our Lord and Saviour Jesus Christ:

[The exhortation continues with a series of Bible verses: Matthew 28.18–20; John 3.5; Acts 2.38; Romans 6.3–4; Galatians 3.27–28; 1 Peter 2.9; Ephesians 4.4–6.]

7a *The minister expounds the teaching of Scripture concerning baptism in his/her own words.*

7b *Or the minister says:*
Obeying the word of our Lord Jesus, and confident of his promises, we baptize those whom God has called. In baptism God claims us, and seals us to show that we belong to God. God frees us from sin and death, uniting us with Jesus Christ in his death and

resurrection. By water and the Holy Spirit, we are made members of the Church, the body of Christ, and joined to Christ's ministry of love, peace and justice:

You *N* have come to be baptized, have heard that baptism is a sign of sharing in the death and resurrection of Christ and of receiving new life. It is therefore necessary for you to be willing to accept this new life as a gift from God. God alone can transform your life and enable you to continue in the new life as a disciple of Christ.

THE DECISION

8 You must therefore in the presence of this congregation openly declare your faith in him and your desire to follow the Lord Jesus Christ.

I therefore ask you:

Do you believe and trust in Jesus Christ as Lord and Saviour of all?

Yes, I do.

Do you believe and trust in one God, the Father almighty who created all things?

Yes, I do.

Do you believe in the Holy Spirit who sanctifies, strengthens and guides the people of God?

Yes, I do.

9 Do you repent of all your past sins, and of all that you know to have been unworthy of God in your life?

Yes, I do.

Do you renounce all sinful desires that draw us away from the love of God and from the love of our fellow human beings?

Yes, I do.

Will you obey Christ, boldly bear witness to him in the world, and love and serve others as he did?

Yes, I will, with God's help.

10 Do you therefore desire to be baptized and to commit yourself to Jesus Christ as your Saviour, Lord and Guide in the fellowship of his Church?

Yes, I do.

THE PROFESSION OF FAITH

11 Do you believe in one God, the Father, the Son, and the Holy Spirit?

I believe.

Let us all with joy and boldness profess our faith together:

All stand

〚12 Apostles' Creed **CF1a**〛

THE PROMISES

13 Those who are baptized are called to worship and serve God.

Do you desire to be baptized in this faith?

I do.

Will you continue in the apostles' teaching and fellowship, in the breaking of bread, and in the prayers?

With the help of God, I will.

Will you persevere in resisting evil, and, whenever you fall into sin, repent and return to the Lord?

With the help of God, I will.

Will you proclaim by word and example the good news of God in Christ?

With the help of God, I will.

Will you seek and serve Christ in all people, loving your neighbour as yourself?
With the help of God, I will.

Will you acknowledge Christ's authority over human society, by prayer for the world and its leaders, by defending the weak, and by seeking peace and justice?
With the help of God, I will.

(If the candidates are husband and wife, the minister says to them:

Will you, in obedience to Christ's teaching, continue together in love, and nurture your children in the Christian faith?
By God's grace, we will.

14 May Christ dwell in your heart(s) through faith, that you may be rooted and grounded in love and bring forth the fruit of the Spirit. **Amen.**

15a Let us pray in silence for those about to be baptized, that they may receive the fullness of God's grace.
The people may kneel. Silence is kept for a space.
Then, the minister says:
The Lord be with you:
And also with you.
The minister prays in his/her own words.

15b *Or, the following litany or the prayer that follows is said:*
Blessed are you, O Lord God, heavenly Father, who has created all things and given us the element of water:
Blessed are you, O Lord.
Blessed are you, O Lord Jesus Christ, the only begotten Son of God, who was baptized in the Jordan and did die and rise again:
Blessed are you, O Lord.
Blessed are you, O Lord, the Holy Spirit, who did descend upon Jesus Christ and upon the church:
Blessed are you, O Lord.
Be present, O God, with us who call upon your threefold name, and bless this water, that it may signify the washing away of sin, and that those who are baptized therein may be born again to eternal life:
Gracious God, hear us.
Grant them your Holy Spirit, that they may be baptized into the one body, and ever remain in the number of your faithful and elect people:
Gracious God, hear us.
Grant that, being united with Christ in his death and resurrection, they ,may be dead to sin, and live to righteousness:
Gracious God, hear us.
Grant that they may put off the old person and become a new creation in Christ Jesus:
Gracious God, hear us.
From darkness, lead them to light; from death lead them to everlasting life: **Gracious God, hear us.**

or

15c Almighty and everlasting God, your blessed Son our Lord Jesus Christ has commanded us to make disciples of all nations, and to baptize them in the name of the Father, and of the Son, and of the Holy Spirit. Send your Holy Spirit, heavenly Father, to sanctify this water, and grant that *N* now to be baptized in it may die to *his/her/their* sinful nature and rise to the new life in union with Christ. May *he/she/they* be filled with your power and peace, and grow as a *member/members* of the body of Christ. To him, to you Father, and to the Holy Spirit, be all honour and glory to the end of the ages. **Amen.**

THE BAPTISM

16 *All stand; and the minister, having asked for the name/s, dips each candidate in the water, or pours, or sprinkles water upon him/her saying:*
N, I baptize you in the name of the Father, and of the Son, and of the Holy Spirit. **Amen.**

THE SIGN OF THE CROSS

17 *The minister makes the sign of the cross on the forehead of each candidate, saying:*
Christ claims you for his own. Receive the sign of his cross.

Then minister says for all together:
May you never be ashamed to confess the faith of Christ crucified, but continue as Christ's faithful servant unto your life's end.

18 The Lord bless you and keep you: the Lord make his face to shine upon you, and be gracious to you: the Lord lift up his countenance upon you, and give you peace. **Amen.**

19 *Then the doxology may be sung:*
Praise God, from whom all blessings flow;
Praise him all creatures here below;
Praise him above, ye heavenly host;
Praise Father, Son and Holy Ghost. Amen.

20 *A procession may be made from the place of baptism into the body of the church.*

THE PUTTING ON OF A WHITE GARMENT

21 *The newly baptized may now put on white garments. When they have assembled, the minister says to them:*
We will rejoice greatly in the Lord:
Our souls shall be joyful in our God.
For he has clothed us with the garments of salvation:
He has covered us with the robes of righteousness.
Put off your old nature, and be renewed in the spirit of your minds:
We will put on the new nature, created after the likeness of God.

THE LIGHT

22 *The newly baptized may be given lighted lamps or tapers. When they have received them, the minister says:*
Let your light shine before others, so that they may see your good works; and give glory to your Father in heaven. *Matthew 5.16*
Or some other brief forms of words may be used.

THE THANKSGIVING

23 *The minister says, or the minister and people say together:*
We give you humble thanks, most merciful Father, that it has pleased you to receive *this/these* your *servant/s* for your own *child/children* by adoption and to incorporate *him/her/them* into your holy Church. And we humbly ask you to grant that *he/she/they* may increasingly show forth in *his/her/their life/lives* that which he/she/they now is/are by your calling; so that as *he/she/they is/are* made *a partaker/partakers* of the

death of your Son, *he/she/they* may also be *a partaker/partakers* of his resurrection, and finally, with all your church, inherit your everlasting kingdom; through the same Jesus Christ our Lord. **Amen.**

24   Almighty God, in your mercy you draw the hearts of believers to yourself through the revelation of your love in Jesus Christ our Lord. We thank you for this work of grace in N who *has/have* now been baptized, and for planting in *him/her/them* the seed of new life in fellowship with you and with all your people. We pray that *he/she/they* may be continually strengthened by your Spirit in a deeper knowledge of you, and in holiness of life. Grant that *he/she/they* may go forward in faith and obedience to your will, with sure hope in your promise of eternal life; through Jesus Christ our Lord, to whom with you and the Holy Spirit, be all praise and glory for ever. **Amen.**

WELCOME

25   *The minister may say to the congregation:*
These our brothers and sisters in Christ have, after profession of their repentance and faith, been received into the household of God. I charge you, and especially the elders among you, to befriend them, and to remind them what solemn promises they have made before this congregation. Support them therefore with your prayers, and encourage them to attend diligently to right instruction in God's holy Word, [and so to prepare themselves for confirmation,]* that, being established in faith by the Holy Spirit, they may come with due preparation to receive the Lord's Supper, and may go forth into the world to serve God faithfully in the fellowship of his church. Will you endeavour to do all these things?
We will, God being our helper; and we receive *him/her/them* into our fellowship.
* *This phrase may be omitted if the church traditions do not insist on the rite of confirmation after adult baptism.*

26   *And then speaking to the newly baptized, the minister says*
N, today God has touched you with his love and given you a place among his people. God promises to be with you in joy and in sorrow, to be your guide in life, and to bring you safely to heaven. In baptism God invites you on a life-long journey. Together with all God's people you must explore the way of Jesus and grow in friendship with God, in love for his people, and in serving others. With us you will listen to the Word of God and receive the gifts of God. May God, who has received you by baptism into his Church, pour upon you the riches of his grace, that within the company of Christ's pilgrim people you may daily be renewed by his anointing Spirit, and come to the inheritance of the saints in glory. **Amen.**

27   *The minister introduces the Peace in these or other suitable words:*
We are all one in Christ Jesus. We belong to him through faith, heirs of the promise of the Spirit of peace.
The peace of the Lord be always with you;
And also with you.
The minister may say:
Let us offer one another a sign of peace.

LORD'S PRAYER

28   [[CF4b]]

29   *If the baptism is administered otherwise than at the Lord's Supper or at Morning or Evening Worship, the minister dismisses those that are gathered together with the following:*

May God almighty, the Father of our Lord Jesus Christ, grant that you may be strengthened in your inner being with power through his Spirit, that Christ may dwell in your hearts through faith, as you are being rooted and grounded in love, that you may have the power to comprehend, with all the saints the breadth and length and height and depth of the love of Christ which surpasses all knowledge, so that you may be filled with all the fullness of God. **Amen.**

ORDER FOR HOLY BAPTISM OF INFANTS

1   *The minister ascertains beforehand that the children have not already been baptized.*

2   *When the people are gathered at, or proceeding to, the place of baptism, a hymn may be sung, after which the minister says:*
Our help is in the name of the Lord:
Who has made heaven and earth.

3   Let us pray
Almighty God, you Shepherd of Israel, who did deliver your chosen people from the bondage of Egypt, and did establish with them a sure covenant, have mercy, we ask you, on your flock, and grant that these children, who are by baptism to be received into your heritage, may be delivered from the bondage of sin through the covenant of grace, and attain the promise of eternal life which you have given us in your Son our Saviour Jesus Christ, who lives and reigns with you and the Holy Spirit, one God, world without end. **Amen.**

4   *The people may be seated.*

EXHORTATION

5   Dearly beloved, we are gathered together to administer holy baptism to these children, that according to Christ's command, they may be sealed as members of Christ, children of God, and heirs of the kingdom of heaven.

Hear therefore, the words of our Lord and Saviour Jesus Christ: [The exhortation continues with a series of Bible verses: Matthew 28.18–20; John 3.5; Mark 10.13–16.]

Jesus Christ is the same yesterday, today and forever. He loves children and is ready to receive them to embrace them with the arms of his mercy, and then we can with confidence pray, that he will grant them that gift which will enable them to grow up as his own sons and daughters; and will give them the blessing of eternal life.

Our Lord Jesus also said. Very truly, I tell you, no one can see the kingdom of God without being born from above. *John 3.3*

Such a new birth God alone can give and it is promised to us through the working of the Holy Spirit in the sacrament of baptism. God will grant his gift to this child in baptism when we ask in faith. Throughout the ages the Church of God has been built up of those who received God's gift of new birth and were incorporated into the body of Christ in their baptism either in infancy, or as adults.

As the Lord Jesus granted forgiveness of sins and healing to the paralytic in response to the faith of his friends who brought him to the Lord, so God will grant new birth to this child by the power of the Holy Spirit when we ask him in faith. Let us therefore place this child in God's loving hands, trusting that he will give *him/her* all that is necessary for *his/her* salvation and growth in grace.

6 *The minister expounds the teaching of the Scripture concerning baptism in his/her own words, and then says:*

7 Let us pray.
O God our Lord, you desire that none of your children should perish, and you have raised up your Church so that in its common life your children may receive spiritual nourishment and grow in your likeness. We thank you for promising new life and fellowship with you to those who are born of water and the Holy Spirit. We thank you for the sacrament of baptism; which signifies that in union with Christ, they die to sin and rise again to newness of life.

O loving and merciful God, we bring this *child/children* to you, who alone can renew and save those who come to you in faith. Receive *him/her* and make *him/her* yours forever in the body of Christ; renew and save *him/her* and make *him/her* an instrument of your redeeming love in the world. We ask this in the name of Jesus Christ our Lord.

Now to him who by the power at work within us is able to do far more abundantly than all that we can ask or think, to him be glory in the Church and in Christ Jesus to all generations, for ever and ever. **Amen.**

THE PROFESSION OF FAITH

8 *All stand. The minister says to the parents (and godparents):*
It is the duty of those who present children for baptism to make confession of the faith in which they are baptized and to promise to bring them up in the way of Christ.

Do you believe and trust in God the Father almighty, who created heaven and earth?
We believe.
Do you believe and trust in Jesus Christ, the Son of God, who for our salvation died on a cross, was raised from the dead, lives now in glory as the Saviour and Lord of all, and will come again to judge the living and the dead?
We believe.
Do you believe and trust in the Holy Spirit of God who renews, guides and strengthens the people of God?
We believe.

9 *The minister says to the congregation:* Let us therefore profess our faith.
The Apostles' Creed is said or sung by all: ⟦**CF 1**⟧

10 *The minister says to the parents (and godparents):*
Do you who have brought this child for baptism promise before God and in the presence of this congregation that you will yourself steadfastly affirm and uphold the faith of the Church?
We do, God being our helper.
Do you promise that by your prayers for this child, by your own manner of life, and by your guidance, you will help *him/her* as *he/she* grows up to pray and to worship God, to study the Bible, to follow the example and teaching of the Lord Jesus Christ, to share generously what *he/she* has with others and to take an active part in the Church's witness to Christ?
We do, God being our helper.
Do you promise that you will help this child to grow in the knowledge and experience of Christ, and encourage *him/her* later to be received into the full fellowship of the Church by confirmation; so that, established in faith by the Holy Spirit, *he/she* may partake of the Lord's Supper and go forth into the world to serve God faithfully in his Church?
We do, God being our helper.

The minister says to the congregation:

Dearly beloved, will you be faithful to your calling as members of the church of Christ, so that these and all other children in your midst may grow up in the knowledge and love of him?

We will, God being our helper; and we welcome him/her/them into our fellowship.

THE BAPTISM

11a Let us pray in silence for the *child/children* about to be baptized, that *he/she/they* may receive the fullness of God's grace.

The people may kneel.

Silence is kept for a space. Then the minister says:

The Lord be with you:

And with your spirit.

The minister prays in his/her own words.

11b *Or, the following litany or the prayer that follows is said:*

Blessed are you, O Lord God, heavenly Father, who has created all things and given us the element of water:

Blessed are you, O Lord.

Blessed are you, O Lord Jesus Christ, the only begotten Son of God, who was baptized in the Jordan and did die and rise again:

Blessed are you, O Lord.

Blessed are you, O Lord, the Holy Spirit, who did descend upon Jesus Christ and upon the Church:

Blessed are you, O Lord.

Be present, O God, with us who call upon your threefold name, and bless this water, that it may signify the washing away of sin, and that those who are baptized therein may be born again to eternal life:

Gracious God, hear us.

Grant them your Holy Spirit, that they may be baptized into the one body, and ever remain in the number of your faithful and elect people:

Gracious God, hear us.

Grant that, being united with Christ in his death and resurrection, they may be dead to sin, and live to righteousness

Gracious God, hear us.

Grant that they may put off the old person and become a new creation in Christ Jesus

Gracious God, hear us.

From darkness, lead them to light; from death lead them to everlasting life:

Gracious God, hear us.

or

11c O holy and loving God, your Word became flesh so that, in union with him, all people may be enabled to be your children. Accept this child, we pray, and make *him/her* your own in the body of Christ. Send your Holy Spirit and sanctify this water, that, as water cleanses and refreshes the body, so this child now to be baptized in this water may be born anew, and may have the blessing of eternal life in Jesus Christ our Lord, who with you, O Father, and with the Holy Spirit lives and reigns to the end of the ages. **Amen.**

12 *All stand; and the minister; having asked for the child's name, pours or sprinkles water upon each child, saying:*

N, I baptize you in the name of the Father, and of the Son, and of the Holy Spirit. **Amen.**

THE SIGN OF THE CROSS

13 *The minister says over each child baptized:*
We have received this child into the congregation of Christ's flock and do sign him/her
with the sign of the cross *(here the minister may make a cross upon the child's forehead).*

Then the minister says:
May this child never be ashamed to confess the faith of Christ crucified, but continue
as Christ's faithful servant unto *his/her* life's end.

14 The Lord bless you and keep you: the Lord make his face to shine upon you, and
be gracious to you: the Lord lift up his countenance upon you, and give you peace.
Amen.

15 *Then the doxology may be sung:*
Praise God, from whom all blessing flow;
Praise him all creatures here below;
Praise him above, ye heavenly host;
Praise Father, Son and Holy Ghost. Amen.

16 *A procession may be made from the place of baptism into the body of the church.*

THE LIGHT

17 *The parents of the children baptized may be given lighted lamps or tapers. When they have
received them, the minister says:*
Let your light shine before others, so that they may see your good works; and give
glory to your Father in heaven. *Matthew 5.16*

18 *Or some other brief forms of words may be said.*

THE THANKSGIVING

19a *The minister says, or the minister and people say together:*
We give you heartfelt thanks most merciful Father, that it has pleased you to receive
this child/these children as your own *child/children* by adoption and to incorporate
him/her/them into your holy Church. And we humbly ask you to grant that *he/she/*
they may more and more show forth in *his/her life/their lives* that which *he/she is/they*
are now by your calling; so that, as *he/she is/they are* made partakers of the death of
your Son, *he/she/they* may also be partakers of his resurrection, and finally with all
your Church, inherit your everlasting kingdom; through the same Jesus Christ our
Lord. **Amen.**

or

19b Almighty God, our heavenly Father, in your mercy you have called all people to enter
into your kingdom through the redeeming work of Christ our Saviour. We thank you
for making *this child/these children* your own this day through baptism, by giving
him/her/them new birth in water and the Holy Spirit, and making *him/her a member/*
them members of the body of Christ. Guide, strengthen and sanctify *him/her/them*
all the days of *his/her life/their lives*. Enable *his/her/their* parents (and godparents) to
fulfil the promises they have made, so that under their care *this child/these children*
may grow up in the knowledge of your love and in devotion to you; through Jesus
Christ our Lord, to whom with you, Father, and the Holy Spirit, one God in wisdom,
power and love, we offer thanks and praise, now and always. **Amen.**

The minister says:

20 Faithful and loving God, whose blessed Son shared at Nazareth the life of an earthly
home; bless we ask you, the *home/homes* of *this child/these children*, and grant

wisdom and understanding to all who care for *him/her/them*, that *he/she/they* may grow up in your constant fear and love. Pour upon *him/her/them*, your healing and reconciliation, and protect *his/her home/their homes*. Fill *him/her/them* with your loving kindness and presence, and establish *him/her/them* in the joy of your kingdom, through the same your Son Jesus Christ our Lord. **Amen.**

21   *A hymn may be sung here, and the thank offering is taken.*

22   **Lord's Prayer**
     ⟦**CF4b**⟧

23   *If the baptism is administered otherwise than at the Lord's Supper or at Morning or Evening Worship, the minister dismisses those that are gathered together with this blessing:*
     May God almighty, the Father of our Lord Jesus Christ, grant that you may be strengthened in your inner being with power through his Spirit, that Christ may dwell in your hearts through faith, as you are being rooted and grounded in love, that you may have the power to comprehend, with all the saints the breadth and length and height and depth of the love of Christ which surpasses all knowledge, so that you may be filled with all the fullness of God. **Amen.**

AN ORDER OF SERVICE FOR THE RECEPTION OF BAPTIZED PERSONS INTO THE FULL FELLOWSHIP OF THE CHURCH COMMONLY CALLED CONFIRMATION

INTRODUCTION
     ⟦Introductory rubrics.⟧

1   *The minister says:*
     Our help is in the name of the Lord:
     Who has made heaven and earth.

2   Let us pray:
     The people kneel, and the minister prays in his/her own words:

3   *After the prayer, the minister says:*
     Who shall ascend the hill of the Lord? And who shall stand in his holy place? Those who have clean hands and pure hearts, who do not lift up their souls to what is false, and do not swear deceitfully. They will receive blessing from the Lord, and vindication from the God of their salvation. *Psalm 24.3–5*
     Let us examine ourselves in silence.

4   *All are silent for a space. After this, the minister says:*
     Let us humbly confess our sins to the almighty God:
     O God, our Father, we have sinned against you in thought, word and deed: we have not loved you with all our heart; we have not loved our neighbours as ourselves. Have mercy upon us, we ask you; cleanse us from our sins; and help us to overcome our faults; through Jesus Christ our Lord. Amen.

5   *The minister says:*
     May the almighty and merciful Lord grant to us pardon and remission of all our sins, time for amendment of life, and the grace and comfort of the Holy Spirit. **Amen.**
     Or he/she may say you *and* your *instead of* us *and* our.

6   *The minister reads the names of the candidates, who stand up as their names are called and come forward.*

EXHORTATION

7   *The minister speaks to the congregation and the confirmation candidates in his/her own words explaining the meaning and significance of confirmation or says:*
Beloved in Christ, we have come together today in the presence of God as witnesses to the act of confirmation, wherein these persons standing before us publicly commit themselves to Christ, their Lord and Saviour, and accept for themselves God's promise of salvation in Christ.

As a congregation, we are here to support these candidates with prayers. Especially, we shall pray that through the laying on of hands in confirmation each of them may experience the abundant grace and power of the Holy Spirit, and that they may grow in the knowledge of the love of God, and be true and worthy followers of Jesus Christ.

As a congregation we welcome them into the fellowship of those who share in the holy sacrament of the Lord's Supper; and share the responsibility of mission entrusted to us; to be the instrument and foretaste of God's reign of love, justice and peace.

Dear confirmation candidates, you have come to declare your faith in Lord Jesus Christ, your acceptance of him as Saviour, and your commitment to him, and the mission entrusted to you to be the ministers of the Gospel of Christ.

Those who brought you as a child for baptism made a solemn pledge, that you would be nurtured in the Christian faith, in God the Father, the Son and the Holy Spirit. You are here today, in order that you may give your own assent to the pledge that was then made, in your name.

Through baptism you were made the members of the body of Christ and were received into his Church, which is the family and household of God. In the community of the people of God, you have been learning of God's purpose for you and for all creation. You are being nurtured in the faith and are called to- witness to the Gospel of Jesus. You have now come to consecrate yourselves to God of your own choice, and receive the gifts that God wants to bestow on you. You have now come that in accordance with the practice of the apostles, we may lay our hands on you and pray that the Holy Spirit may strengthen you to follow Christ, and to be God's effective and meaningful witness.

8   *The minister and the people pray together:*
Almighty and loving God, you have made us your children in Christ through your Holy Spirit in baptism. Grant that, strengthened by your Spirit in confirmation, we may share in the glorious liberty of your people and live as sons and daughters of your kingdom; through your Son Jesus Christ our Lord, who with you, Father, and the Holy Spirit, lives and reigns, one God, world without end. Amen.

THE MINISTRY OF THE WORD

⟦9   Ezekiel 36.26–28; or Jeremiah 31.31–34; Romans 8.12–17; or Galatians 5.22–25; John 14.15–17; or Matthew 16.24–27. Sermon.⟧

THE PROFESSION OF FAITH

10   *The candidates stand, and the minister says:*
Do you believe and trust in God the Father, who created you, and all the world?
Yes, I do.
Do you believe and trust in his Son Jesus Christ, who has redeemed you, and all people?
Yes, I do.

Do you believe and trust in his Holy Spirit, who renews and transforms you, and the whole creation?
Yes, I do.

11 Let us therefore together profess our faith:
The Apostles' Creed is said or sung by all: [[CF1a]]

THE PROMISES

12 *The minister continues:*
The sincerity of our faith is proved when it is active in love. I therefore urge you to make your daily life worthy of our Lord God who loves you, and has made you his children; worthy of his Son, who died for you, and worthy of his Spirit, who dwells in you.
Will you strive to respond to this great love of God by a life of joyful obedience to him, and of love and care for others?
Yes, I will, God being my helper.
Will you keep God's holy will and commandments and walk in them all the days of your life?
Yes, I will, God being my helper.
Will you be a faithful member of this congregation, share in its worship and ministry through your prayers and gifts, your study of the Bible and service, and so fulfil your calling to be a disciple of Jesus Christ?
Yes, I will, God being my helper.
Will you devote yourself to the Church's teaching and fellowship, especially to the breaking of bread and the prayers?
Yes, I will, God being my helper.
God calls his Church to share with all people the good news of his love made known in Christ. Will you participate and involve yourself in this mission of the church?
I shall try with God's help to make Christ known, by what I am, by what I say, by what I do for others.

13 *The minister says:*
Beloved, you have affirmed your faith in God through Christ our only Saviour, and expressed your desire to obey him, and live in fellowship with his people. Will you now kneel and pray in silence that the Holy Spirit may enable you to be faithful to your promises?
Silence

14 *Then the candidates led by the minister, say together:*
O God, my Lord, I am not my own, but yours; I rely on your grace and the power of your Holy Spirit, and give myself to you as your child, to love and serve you all the days of my life.

THE CONFIRMATION

15 *The minister calls the congregation to pray in silence for the candidates. Silence is kept for a space.*
A hymn or lyric praying for the Holy Spirit may be sung kneeling.

16 *The minister says the following prayer alone. Or he/she may invite the congregation to say it with him:*
Gracious God, by water and the Spirit you claimed us as your own, cleansing us from sin, and giving us new life. You called us to be your children, and made us members of your body – the Church; and gave us the privilege to be your servants in this world. Renew now, the covenant you have made in the baptism of these your children;

continue the good work you have begun in them; grant them now the power of your Holy Spirit; the spirit of wisdom and understanding; spirit of counsel and inward strength; spirit of knowledge and of the fear of the Lord. Send them forth in the power of your Holy Spirit to love and serve you with joy and to be a foretaste of your reign of justice and peace. In the name of Jesus Christ Our Lord, we pray. **Amen.**

17 *The minister lays his/her hand upon the head of each of the candidates in turn, saying:*
Strengthen O Lord this your child with your heavenly grace, that *he/she* may continue yours forever, and daily increase in your Holy Spirit, until *he/she* comes into your everlasting kingdom. **Amen.**

18 *When all have been confirmed, the minister says:*
The Lord be with you.
And with your spirit.
Let us pray:

[[Lord's Prayer **CF4b**]]

The minister prays:

19a Almighty and ever-living God, who, according to the promise of your Son our Saviour Jesus Christ, have ordained your Church to be the temple of the Holy Spirit: mercifully hear our prayers for these your children, upon whom we have laid our hands. Let your protective hand be over them; let your Holy Spirit ever be with them; and so lead them in the knowledge and obedience of your word, that they may serve you all their days and be with you for ever; through our Lord and Saviour Jesus Christ, who with you and the Holy Spirit, lives and reigns, ever one God, world without end. **Amen.**

or

19b Almighty and ever-living God, we thank you for the great blessing bestowed on these your children through the laying on of hands. By this sign they are assured of your unfailing goodness towards them. We commit them to your protective care. Grant that they may serve you all the days of their life, and finally know the joy of your eternal presence; through Jesus Christ, our Saviour. To him, to you, Father, and to the Holy Spirit, one God in wisdom, power and love, we offer our thanks and praise, now and for ever. **Amen.**

THE RECEPTION

[[Directions for the service.]]

20 *The newly confirmed persons stand and face the congregation, while the minister and the congregation stand and together say to them:*
We, the members of the congregation, welcome you with joy, as you come to share with us at the Lord's Table, and as partners in the common life of the Church. We promise you our friendship and our prayers that you may grow in the knowledge and love of God, and of his Son Jesus Christ our Lord. We do not live to ourselves, and we do not die to ourselves. If we live, we live to the Lord, and if we die, we die to the Lord; so then, whether we live or whether we die, we are the Lord's. May God grant us all strength and commitment to work together for his reign of justice and wholeness here on earth, and give us grace to experience life in all its fullness, with all the saints now, and in the world to come. Amen.

21 *The newly confirmed persons turn again to the minister.*
Each is given a membership card. The Bible or New Testament, or the Book of Common Worship of the Church of South India may also be given.

22 *The minister says to them:*
In token of our love in Christ, we give you the greeting of peace.
The peace is given and a hymn is sung, during which the offerings of the newly confirmed,
and of the congregation are received.

23 *If there is no celebration of the Lord's Supper, the minister gives this blessing:*
Go into the world in peace and the blessings of God almighty, the Father, the Son,
and the Holy Spirit, be upon you and remain with you forever. **Amen.**

30. The Church of Ceylon (Sri Lanka)

Christianity was present in Sri Lanka from the sixth century with the mission work of the Church of the East. Western Christianity arrived with the Portuguese in the sixteenth century, followed by the Dutch and later the British. In 1799 the first colonial chaplain arrived to support the colonial bureaucracy. Missionary societies came after the change in the East India Company Charter opening up mission work in South India and Sri Lanka. The Prayer Book was translated into Sinhala[76] and later included 1928 variations,[77] and portions of the CIPBC Prayer Book.[78] In 1930 Sri Lanka became a part of the Church of India, Burma and Ceylon. The formation of united churches, particularly that of North India in 1970, led to the end of the Province.

The two dioceses of the Anglican Church of Ceylon are extra-provincial to Canterbury. The see of Colombo was created in 1845 and the Diocese of Kurunegala was formed in 1950. The two dioceses inherited the *Book of Common Prayer* 1960 of CIPBC and any local rites that had been produced.[79] The church has been gradually revising its liturgy and has produced new texts for baptism, confirmation (and the Eucharist). The new rites of baptism and confirmation went through a three-year period of experimentation approved by the Episcopal Synod (which includes the Archbishop of Canterbury) followed by final authorization by the General Assembly in 2013. They are published in English, Tamil and Sinhala. There has been considerable discussion about inculturation in Sri Lanka. The catechumenal rites have not been revised, and thanksgiving for the birth of a child is a time for spontaneous prayer rather than a written liturgy. Reception and reaffirmation are included in the baptismal service, being presbyteral rites. It is expected in the Church of Ceylon that people will be confirmed before they receive communion.

ENTRY INTO THE CHURCH 2013

NOTES

1   Baptism marks the entry into the One Holy Catholic and Apostolic Church of which the Church of Ceylon is a part. Holy Baptism is full initiation by water and the Holy Spirit into Christ's Body, the Church, in the name of the Father, and of the Son and of the Holy Spirit. It is complete sacramental initiation, into the Christian community commanded by Christ, given once-for-life, and being a calling and gift of God is unrepeatable and irrevocable *(Rom. 11.29)*. Being the one covenant *(Eph. 4.4–6)* applicable to persons of

76 G 157: 1.
77 G 157: 11.
78 G 157: 12.
79 J 95. G 459/3.

any age on God's own initiative and action, the theology and ritual of Holy Baptism is common both to infants and adults and expressed by a common liturgical order.

2   Parents, spiritual parents and the local congregation have a special responsibility to bring those who are baptised on reaching an age of discernment before the Bishop after sufficient instruction to renew their baptismal promises, to publicly repent their sins, and to make a personal commitment of faith, and then by the laying on of hands by the Bishop to be strengthened and confirmed with grace by the stirring of the indwelling Holy Spirit already begun in Baptism. At such a confirmation and at other times the congregation too renews their baptismal commitment which is also done when a baptised person of another Christian communion is received into the Church of Ceylon. These are all related to the One Covenant made in Baptism.

3   Baptism, Confirmation and Reception should be administered during the main public service on a Sunday to involve the majority of the congregation. The Constitution suggests that it is specially suitable for candidates to be collected and for baptisms to be done on the Easter Vigil, Pentecost, Church of Ceylon Sunday (closest to July 08), All Saints Sunday, and the Sunday after the Epiphany (Jan 06) – Rule 1 Chapter 24.

4   The Liturgy of Baptism is used for both infants and believers baptism after the sermon at a Holy Eucharist, in the full view of the congregation. Much extempore prayer and spontaneity is encouraged but the sequence should not be changed: Hallowing of water, exhortation, renunciation, declaration of faith, baptism and welcome.

5   The number of spiritual parents, their qualifications and the instruction to be given are stated in the Constitution Chapter 24 Canon 9.

6   A threefold administration of water (whether by immersion or dipping or pouring) is a very ancient practice of the Church and is commended as testifying to the faith of the Trinity in which the candidates are Baptised. The circumambulation round the Font three times has a similar symbolism and in addition has the cultural symbolism of the death of the old self being born again into the new life of God the Trinity – the same ceremony at Sri Lankan funerals.

7   The anointing with sacred chrism and laying hands, the giving lighted tapers or clay lamps (preferably from the Easter Candle), the vesting with a white garment, and the epheta are optional symbolic ceremonies signifying respectively the salvation in the anointed Christ through the Spirit, enlightenment through Christ (Eph. 5.14), putting on the purity of a Christian life clothed with power from on high (Gal. 3.27; Acts 1.8), and hearing and proclaiming the faith; which should not obscure the symbolism of Baptism with water and the Holy Spirit but should enrich the Liturgy. The thilaka (forehead mark) with sandalwood and salt paste symbolic of God's protection and the spreading fragrance of a Christian example, the use of oil and an ekel for protection and health (exorcism), the water cutting for cleansing and rain, and the cutting of a lock of hair at a first visit to a holy place, are cultural ceremonies in Sri Lanka which too are optional. If such ceremonies are used the congregation needs to be edified as to their Christian meaning.

8   It would be appropriate for the kiss of peace at the welcome after the Baptism to be demonstrably exchanged between the President, newly initiated, Spiritual parents, and the congregation. It is also appropriate for the lessons to be read by the candidates or sponsors, a testimony and public repentance to be given by an adult candidate, and the bread and wine and/or milk-rice or honey and curd (for later consumption by the congregation) be presented by the newly initiated or their parents and sponsors.

THE LITURGY OF HOLY BAPTISM FOR SRI LANKA

⟦The notes direct that the service begins after the Liturgy of the Word. Testimony may be given by adult candidates.⟧

THE REQUEST AND DECLARATION PRAYER

1   *We as parents, guardians, sponsors and adult candidates, having had instructions in the Faith according to the Constitution, seek Baptism and or dedication present these candidates for Baptism and also requests this congregation to nurture them in the Lord.*

Do you recognize that baptism embodies God's own initiative in Christ and expresses a response of faith made within the believing community and requiring a responsible attitude towards Christian nurture?

We accept the free gift of God's grace, love and call given unconditionally and for the growth of these persons within the Christian community (and promise to bring them to repentance of evil and affirmation of Faith at an age of reason before a Bishop).

Our Lord Jesus Christ said: 'Go and make disciples of all nations baptizing them in the name of the Father, and of the Son and of the Holy Spirit, and teaching them to obey all that I have commanded.' (Our Lord also said: 'Let the little children come to me, for it is to such as these that the kingdom of God belongs.')

On the day of Pentecost Peter declared:
'Repent and be baptized every one of you in the name of Jesus Christ so that your sins may be forgiven; and you will receive the gift of the Holy Spirit. For the promise is for you and your children, every person whom the Lord our God calls.'

Let us therefore pray for those to be reborn and for those of us who will nurture these persons in their life in the Christian Church.

2a *Extempore prayer.*
Local new birth customs may then be done, e.g. oiling of the body, (cleansing) striking with an ekel (protection), marking a sandalwood cross on the forehead, (claiming for Christ).

or

2b God the Ultimate Reality, you sent your Child, our Lord Jesus Christ to renew in forgiveness humanity's covenant of grace with you, through its sign and seal, the Sacrament of Holy Baptism of water and the Spirit, in which we die to sin, and are buried and raised with Christ our Liberator out of the water, to be born again to a newness of life.

It incorporates us to Christ and unites us to one another in a common discipleship in the Church in every time and place, by the cleansing power of the Holy Spirit *(body and head may be oiled with gingerly oil)* that nurture the life of faith and anticipates your reign when those who have been claimed for your own would be fully redeemed.

Protect *this/these* your *child/children (may strike gently with an ekel)* about to be baptized, from Satan and all evil, and bring *her/him/them* from darkness to light to be well and happy in your loving-kindness and grace throughout life *(may mark across of sandalwood paste on the forehead)*.

Grant also wisdom and love to these parents and spiritual parents that they and this congregation may fulfil their responsibilities to *this/these child/children/candidate/s* to bring them up in a lifelong growth of grace in Christ; through Jesus Christ our Lord. **Amen.**

THE THANKSGIVING

(offered near the water of baptism)

3　Homage to the One God, the Ultimate Reality
That You Are – The Father, the Son and the Holy Spirit. Amen.
Homage to the One God, the Ultimate Reality –
That You Are – The Father, the Son and the Holy Spirit. Amen

Lift up your hearts
We lift them to the Lord
Let us give thanks to the Lord our God
It is right to give God thanks and praise

4　Gracious God, we thank you for your gift of water and the Holy Spirit, which
sustains life, cleanses, satisfies and provides life giving power.
From the beginning your grace has been made known through water and the Spirit.
(The Light of Christ. **Hallelu Yah**).
Your Spirit moved over the waters at the creation of light and life, and by the water
of the flood you made a sign of the waters of Baptism that makes an end of sin and
the birth of a new life. *(Salt may be added to the water symbolic of the salt of the earth).*
(The Light of Christ. **Hallelu Yah**).
You led your people by light and spirit to freedom through the waters of the Red Sea.
(The Light of Christ. **Hallelu Yah**).
In the fullness of time you sent the Lord Jesus, who was baptized in the waters of the
Jordon and anointed by the Holy Spirit. *(Olive oil may be hallowed symbolic of the seal
of the Holy Spirit).* (The Light of Christ. **Hallelu Yah**).
The Lord Jesus Christ was immersed in the baptism of the deep waters of suffering
and death and was raised to life, and then sent your Spirit to set hearts aflame and
enlighten all people in Christ. (The Light of Christ. **Hallelu Yah**).

*The Presbyter stretches hands over the water and the candidates (making the sign of the
cross)*
Pour out your Holy Spirit that those baptized in (this) water may with thanksgiving
die to sin, be raised with Christ and be born to new life in the family of your Church;
(The Light of Christ. **Hallelu Yah**).
and please may this Baptism today be a sign to all of us of the reign of God and of the
life of the world to come. Amen, (The Light of Christ. **Hallelu Yah**).

THE EXHORTATION

5a　Dear parents and spiritual parents, You have brought *this/these child/children* to be
baptized with water and the Holy Spirit to become full members of the Church of
Christ. You must now agree to bring *her/him/them* up as Christians that they may
grow stronger in the practice and faith of Christ.

5b　N.N. You are now to be baptized. You will be born again of water and the Holy
Spirit and thus be admitted as a full members of the Church of Christ. See that you
grow in the faith of Christ day by day, keeping yourself safe from the poison of sin
and evil.

I am willing, with God's help.

As a sign that you accept this responsibility I urge you and others here present
to renew now the vows of your own baptism (and you the candidates who can
understand to reject sin) repent your past lapses, and profess your faith in the Lord
Jesus Christ, the faith of the Universal Church into which every Christian is baptized,
and in which you and this parish will help these children/persons to grow. This gift

and calling of God are irrevocable *(Rom 11.29)* – Holy Baptism must never again be repeated in a lifetime.

THE RENUNCIATION

6a Do you turn to Christ.
I turn to Christ.
Do you renounce Satan and all evil.
I do.
Do you repent of all your sins and all that denies God.
I do.

Silence for repentance
Holy God, Holy and Mighty, Holy and Immortal, Have mercy on us.
Holy God, Holy and Mighty, Holy and Immortal, Have mercy on us
Holy God, Holy and Mighty, Holy and Immortal, Have mercy on us

or

6b *Any other form of Confession from the Eucharistic Liturgy. The Presbyter will then pronounce the Absolution in this or any other manner:*
God is faithful and just and forgives our sins and cleanse you/*us* from all unrighteousness. (May God lead you from darkness into the light of Christ through the guidance of the All Holy Spirit.) **Amen.**

DECLARATION OF FAITH

7a Let us make profession of our common Christian belief

⟦The Apostles' Creed **CF1a** said by all⟧

or

7b Do you believe and trust in God the Father, who made the World?
I believe and trust in God.

Do you believe and trust in God the Son, Jesus Christ, who redeemed humankind?
I believe and trust in our Lord Jesus Christ.

Do you believe and trust in God the Holy Spirit, who gives life to the people of God?
I believe and trust in the Holy Spirit.

This is the faith of the Church
This is our faith.
We believe and trust in one God:
Father, Son, and Holy Spirit.

Will you obediently keep God's holy will and commandments and walk in the same all the days of your life?
I will, by God's help.

or

7c *The Thisaranaya*

I take refuge in you Parent God,
I take refuge in you Christ Lord,
I take refuge in you blest Spirit,
I take refuge in you Three as One God.

I look for refuge in your Holy Church,
I look for refuge in your own precepts laws,

I look for refuge in your noble word,
I look for refuge in your community.

CALL FOR COMMITMENT

8 This Sacrament lays solemn obligations upon you, the people of God. Be faithful
   to your calling as members of the Church of Christ, so that this child/person *(these
   children of God)* and others present may grow up in the knowledge and love of
   Christ. In acceptance of this responsibility let us all stand.

THE HOLY BAPTISM

⟦The notes add that a threefold circumambulation of the font may happen; either before or
after the baptism.⟧

9 *The President immerses or pours water on each candidate three times saying:*
   N. is baptized in the Name of the Father, and of the Son, and the Holy Spirit. **Amen.**

   (These Eastern words indicate that Baptism is by God and not by a human)
   *(A lock of hair may then be sheared from the crown of the candidate's head, which is a
   national custom at a first visit to a religious place and a traditional baptismal custom in the
   Christian East.)*

   *The President may then anoint each candidate in the forehead making the sign of the cross,
   and lay hands on the head.*
   N. receive the Seal of the gift of the Holy Spirit: may it make you a faithful witness to
   Christ of God. **Amen.**

10 *Reception from another Christian communion or conditional Baptism or symbolic
   reaffirmation of Baptism of those who so insist in adult life may then take place with a
   blessing. Pots of water from font and/or lighted candles may be passed from hand to hand
   through the congregation as an offering of thanksgiving for renewal of baptismal promises.
   The newly baptized are taken to face the congregation.*

WELCOME

11 *The newly baptized are clothed in a white garment (Gal. 3.27, Titus 3.5) and on their
   behalf the parents and spiritual parents given a lighted lamp or candle (Eph 5.14) a
   Warden or senior member of the congregation saying:*

   N.N. For you there is a new creation, liberated to a new humanity and clothed in
   Christ, and renewed by the Spirit of light to be a full member of the body of Christ,
   the Church, being called out of darkness into Christ's marvellous light. **Hallelu Yah!**

   We welcome you into the Fellowship of Christ's Church. Hallelu Yah! Hallelu Yah!
   All applaud.

THE PEACE

REAFFIRMATION AND RECEPTION

11a *As the congregation too has reaffirmed their Baptismal Promises or anyone else who
   specifically wishes to do so, the Presbyter turns to them, raises hands in blessing and says:*

   May the Holy Spirit, who has begun a good work in you direct and uphold you in the
   service of Christ and the reign of God. **Amen.**

11b *There may be some who insist on the use of water in adult life in re-affirming their
   Baptismal promises. Though this must be discouraged so as not to appear as a re-baptism,
   they may be washed ONCE with a minimal quantity of the baptismal water without any
   loud splashing, and following or similar text used by the Presbyter:*

N, as you have already been baptized in the name of the Father, and of the Son, and of the Holy Spirit, so now in commemoration of THAT ONE BAPTISM ONCE, and in renewal of its meaning to you, you are symbolically washed in this water in the name of the One God – Creator, Liberator and Sanctifer. **Amen**

11c *If there is reasonable doubt as to a person being baptized with water in the name of the Holy Trinity, that person is baptized in the usual manner, using the following words by the Presbyter:*

If you have not been Baptized, *N* is baptized in the name of the Father, and of the Son and of the Holy Spirit, wherein to be sealed with the Holy Spirit to make you a faithful witness to Christ of God. **Amen.**

11d *When a person of good standing in another Christian Communion wishes to be received into the Church of Ceylon, or after recovery of a person who received an emergency baptism privately, the reception is done at the baptismal font, the Presbyter saying a blessing using the following or similar words:*

N, we recognize you as a member of the one holy catholic and apostolic Church, and we receive you into the fellowship of this Communion/*parish*. God: the Father, Son, and Holy Spirit, bless, preserve, and keep you. **Amen.**

11e *Pots of water from the font and/or lighted candles may be passed from hand to hand throughout the congregation in symbolism of thanksgiving for the renewal of baptismal promises/covenant. Either at the font or after being taken to face the congregation the newly baptized may be clothed in a white garment (Gal. 3.27, Titus 3.5) and adult candidates, parents and spiritual parents given a lighted candle or lamp (Eph 5.14). All those around the font then process to face the congregation.)*

WELCOME

Presbyter or a Lay Officer: N.N. for you there is a new creation, liberated to a new humanity and clothed in Christ, and renewed by the Spirit of light to be a full member of the body of Christ, the Church, being called out of darkness into Christ's marvellous light. Hallelu Yah! Hallelu Yah!

We welcome you into the fellowship of Christ's Church. Hallelu Yah! Hallelu Yah!

CONFIRMATION

1 *The Confirmation candidates, clergy and Bishop arrive at the main entrance. All stand. The Presbyter and the confirmation candidates move to the font.*
Bishop 'In Samaria, the Spirit had not come upon them; they had only been baptized in the name of the Lord Jesus. Then Peter and John laid their hands on them and they received the Holy Spirit'. *(Acts 8.16–17)*

2 Blessed be God.
Blessed be God's reign forever. Amen.

3 *Having had instructions in the faith we who have been baptized as full members of the Church of God, and now having come to an age of reason, seek Holy Confirmation and reception into responsible membership of the Church.*

4 Sisters and brothers, by God's own initiative and grace in Christ, through the sign of baptism and in the power of the Holy Spirit we become God's people, the Church. Today, of your own free will, you will publicly renounce evil and profess your faith in Christ and the Holy Trinity and by the sign of the laying on of hands and anointing in

Holy Confirmation; the Holy Spirit is stirred within us to strengthen us to a new life to be witnesses of Christ's Good News.

We accept the offer of God's grace and for our own growth within the Christian Community.

4   *During the singing of the hymn, the candidates dip their hands in the water in the Font and mark their fore heads symbolically as a sign of their baptism(full admission to the Church) to be strengthened today by Confirmation and receiving Holy Communion with their sisters and brothers in Christ.*

⟦Hymn, lighting of the oil lamp, invitation to confession, confession, absolution (1 John 1.9), Gloria.⟧

5   *Collect for the day*
    or
    God of grace by the power of the Holy Spirit you have given us new life in the waters of baptism; strengthen us to live in righteousness and true holiness, that we may grow into the likeness of your Son Jesus Christ. Amen.

MINISTRY OF THE WORD

⟦Lessons, psalm/hymn, Gospel and sermon.⟧

CONFIRMATION

6   *The candidates and Clergy stand; the congregation takes their seats*
    Bishop of… we present theses candidates for the laying on of hands.

You are now to be confirmed: in love God will clothe you in a new life; As a sign that you are ready to commit yourself in Faith to the service of Christ and the Church after having attained an age of reason. I urge you and others here present to declare your Faith in the Lord Jesus Christ, the Faith in which every Christian is initiated into the Universal Church, to love you God with your very being, to fight against the power of evil, and to repent of all your past lapses.

7   Do you turn to Christ?
    I turn to Christ.
    Do you repent of your sins?
    I repent of my sins.
    Do you renounce evil?
    I renounce evil.

8   Will you obediently keep God's holy will and commandments and walk in the same all the days of your life?
    I will, by God's help.

THE AFFIRMATION OF FAITH

9   Do you believe and trust in God the Father, who made the world?
    I believe and trust in God.
    Do you believe and trust in God the Son, Jesus Christ, who redeemed humankind?
    I believe and trust in the Lord Jesus Christ.
    Do you believe and trust in God the Holy Spirit, who gives life to the people of God?
    I believe and trust in the Holy Spirit.

This is the faith of the Church.
This is our faith.

**We believe and trust in one God:
Father, Son and Holy Spirit.**

or

9b [[Apostles Creed **CF1a**]]

10 Let us pray in silence, for those who have declared their commitment to Christ and
God's Church
*All pray in silence for the descent of the Holy Spirit on the Candidates and a Hymn to the
Holy Spirit is sung solemnly.*

11 *Hymn* [[Hymn of invocation on candidates.]]

The Bishop and Clergy then stretch out their hands and pray for those to be confirmed.

12a [[Confirmation prayer **CF5** 'your children' instead of 'your servants'.]]

or

12b **Almighty and ever living God, by the water of rebirth and the renewing power of
your Holy Spirit you freed your sons and daughters from sin and gave them new life.
Renew and increase in these your servants, the Covenant you made with them in
baptism, and stir up the fullness of the same Spirit within them the Spirit of wisdom
and insight the Spirit of counsel and power, the Spirit of knowledge and of reverence
for the Lord, so that they may continue to be yours forever in the royal priesthood of
all believers and witness in their lives the fruits of Love, Joy, Peace, Patience, Kindness,
Trustfulness, Gentleness and Self-Control, through Jesus Christ our Saviour Amen.**

13 *The Bishop sits and then lay the right hand on each candidate's head and (may anoint with
Chrism/olive oil) saying the following or similar words*

Servant of God, (Name) be sealed and strengthened daily with the gift of the Holy
Spirit. Amen.

14 *The newly confirmed will now face the congregation*
We present to you the newly confirmed members of the Body of Christ. (Hallelu Yah)
**We welcome you into the Fellowship of Christ's Church, as a fellow inheritor with us
of God's reign and of the royal priesthood of all believers. Put on Christ, hear God's
word, and live and preach Christ. (Hallelu Yah! Hallelu Yah!)**

15 *The Lay Officers or the previous year's confirmation candidates will welcome the newly
confirmed with a lighted lamp lamp or beetel leaves. Bells are rung and all applaud.*

[[16 Intercessions, greeting of peace, hymn, ministry of the sacrament.]]

31. The Church of the Province of Myanmar (Burma)

The first mission work in Myanmar was Roman Catholic from 1602. The East India Company sent chaplains after 1826, but it was not till 1854 that mission work was begun by the SPG. In 1877 the Diocese of Rangoon was formed out of the Diocese of Calcutta. The present Province was formed in 1970 when the Church of India, Pakistan, Burma and Ceylon divided into separate churches. The Province thus inherited the 1960 BCP of CIPBC. This book was republished in 1984 without change as *The Book of Common Prayer of Christ's Church of Burma*.[80] It had previously been translated into Burmese (translations of BCP 1662 from 1884 onwards)[81] and other tribal languages. While there is a new eucharistic rite, the church has yet to publish new baptismal rites.

The 1960 CIPBC rites for baptism of infants and confirmation are found in Jagger.[82] There is in fact further baptismal provision which is worth mentioning briefly. There is a form for the admitting a catechumen. Also compared to the BCP 1662 the order of services is reversed and thus starts with the baptism of adults, and the baptism of infants follows. The supplement also contained an order for reception of people from other churches and permissive ceremonies at baptism and an alternate form of confirmation. Included here is the baptism of adults, not found in Jagger.

THE BOOK OF COMMON PRAYER OF CHRIST'S CHURCH OF BURMA

THE BAPTISM OF ADULTS OR CHILDREN
ABLE TO ANSWER FOR THEMSELVES

〚1 Rubrics〛

2 *The Priest shall ask the godparents and parents,*
   Has this person (child) been already baptized, or no?

3 *If they shall answer No, then shall the Priest shall speak to them of the meaning and purpose of baptism, saying,*
   Dearly beloved, seeing that God wills all men to be saved from the fault and corruption of the nature which they inherit, as well as from the actual sins which they commit, and that our Saviour Christ says, None can enter into the kingdom of God, except he be regenerate and born anew of Water and of the Holy Spirit; I beseech you to call upon God the Father, through our Lord Jesus Christ, that of his bounteousness he will grant to this person (child) that thing which by nature he cannot have; that

---

80 G 16:7.
81 G 16:1.
82 J 95–102.

he may be baptized with Water and the Holy spirit, and received into Christ's holy Church, and be made a lively member of the same.

4 *Then shall the Priest say, all standing*
Let us pray.
Almighty and everlasting God, who of thy great mercy didst save Noah and his family in the ark from perishing by water; and also didst safely lead the children of Israel thy people through the Red Sea, figuring thereby thy Holy Baptism; and by the Baptism of thy well-beloved Son Jesus Christ, in the river Jordan, didst sanctify of water to the mystical washing away of sin; We beseech thee, for thine infinite mercies, that thou wilt mercifully look upon this person (child); wash him and sanctify him with the Holy spirit, that he, being delivered from thy wrath, may be received into the ark of Christ's Church; and being steadfast in faith, joyful through hope, and rooted in charity, may so pass the waves of this troublesome world, that finally he may come to the land of everlasting life, there to reign with thee world without end ; through Jesus Christ our Lord. **Amen.**

5 *After which he may also say this prayer.*
Almighty and immortal God, the aid of all that need, the helper of all that flee to thee for succour, the life of them that believe, and the resurrection of the dead ; We call upon thee for this person (child), that he, coming to thy Holy Baptism, may receive remission of their sins by spiritual regeneration. Grant that's the may enjoy the everlasting benediction of thy heavenly washing, and may come to the eternal kingdom which thou hast promised by Christ our Lord. **Amen.**

⟦6 Reading John 3.1–8 or Matt. 28.18–20.⟧

7 Beloved, being persuaded of the good will of our heavenly Father towards this person (Name), declared by his Son Jesus Christ; let us faithfully and devoutly give thanks to him, and say together.
Almighty and everlasting God, heavenly Father, we give thee humble thanks, for that thou hast vouchsafed to call us to the knowledge of thy grace, and to faith in thee: Increase this knowledge, and confirm this faith in us evermore. Give thy Holy Spirit to this person (child), that he may be born again, and be made and heir of everlasting salvation; through our Lord Jesus Christ, who lives and reigns with thee and the Holy Spirit now and for ever. Amen.

THE PROMISES

8 Well-beloved, who are come hither desiring to receive Holy Baptism, you have heard how the congregation has prayed, that our Lord Jesus Christ would vouchsafe to receive you and bless you, to release you of your sins, to give you the kingdom of heaven, and everlasting life. Our Lord Jesus Christ has promised to grant all these; which promise he, for his part, will most surely keep and perform.

9 I ask you therefore in the presence of these your witnesses, and this whole congregation,

Do you renounce the devil and all his works?
I renounce them all.
Do you renounce the vain pomp and glory of the world, with all covetous desires of the same?
I renounce them all.
Do you renounce the sinful desires of the flesh, so that thou wilt not follow, nor be led by them?
I renounce them all.

10 Do you believe in God the Father Almighty, Maker of heaven and earth?
I believe.
Do you believe in Jesus Christ his only Son our Lord, who was conceived by the Holy Spirit, born of the Virgin Mary, suffered under Pontius Pilate, was crucified, dead, and buried, He descended into hell; the third day he rose again from the dead, He ascended into heaven, and sits at the right hand of God the Father Almighty; and from thence he shall come to judge the quick and the dead?
I believe.
Do you believe in the Holy spirit; the holy Catholic Church; the Communion of Saints; the Remission of sins; the Resurrection of the body; and everlasting life after death?
I believe.

11 Will you be baptized in this faith?
That is my desire.

Will you bear faithful witness to the Lord Jesus Christ, even unto death?
I will.

Will you then obediently keep God's holy will and commandments, and walk in the same all the days of thy life?
I will.

THE BLESSING OF THE WATER

12 The Lord be with you.
And with thy spirit.
Lift up your hearts.
We lift them up unto the Lord.
Let us give thanks unto our Lord God.
It is meet and right so to do.
It is very meet, right, and our bounden duty that we should give thanks unto thee, O Lord Holy Father Almighty, Everlasting God, for that thy most dearly beloved Son Jesus Christ, for the forgiveness of our sins, did shed out of his most previous side both water and blood, and gave commandment to his disciples, that they should go teach all nations, and baptize them in the name of the Father, the Son, and the Holy Spirit. Hear, we beseech thee, the prayer of lay people; sanctify this water to the mystical washing away of sin; and grant that this persons (child), now to be baptized therein, may receive the fullness of thy grace, and ever remain in the number of thy faithful and elect children: through Jesus Christ our Lord, to whom, with thee, in the unity of the Holy Spirit, be all honour and glory, now and evermore. **Amen.**

13 *Then shall the Priest say,*
Merciful God, grant that the old Adam in him who shall be baptized in this water may be so buried, that the new man may be raised up in them. **Amen.**
Grant that all evil desires of the flesh may die in him, and that all things belonging to the Spirit may live and grow in him. **Amen.**
Grant that he may have power and strength to have victory, and to triumph, against the devil, the world, and the flesh. **Amen.**
Grant that they, being here dedicated to thee by our office and ministry, may also be endued with heavenly virtues, and everlastingly rewarded, through thy mercy, O blessed Lord God, who dost live, and govern all things, world without end. **Amen.**

⟦14 Rubric saying the blessing of the water may occur at the beginning.⟧

THE BAPTISM

15 *Then shall the Priest take each person to be baptized by the right hand, and shall say to the godparents,*
Name this person (child).

N. I baptize thee in the name of the Father, and of the Son, and of the Holy Spirit. **Amen.**

16 We receive this person (child) into the congregation of Christ's flock, + and do sign him with the sign of the Cross, in token that hereafter he shall not be ashamed to confess the faith of Christ crucified, and manfully to fight under his banner, against sin, the world, and the devil; and to continue Christ's faithful soldier and servant unto his life's end. **Amen.**

+ Here the priest shall make a cross upon the persons (child's) forehead.

17 God preserve you in the grace of your baptism without reproach, that you may obediently keep his commandments and walk worthy of your Christian calling. Walk by the Spirit and you shall not fulfil the last of the flesh; for the fruit of the spirit is love, joy, peace, long-suffering, kindness, goodness, faithfulness, meekness, self-control. Remember always that baptism represents unto us our profession, which is, to follow the example of our Saviour Christ, and to be made like under him, to whom be all glory, now and in eternity. **Amen.**

THE THANKSGIVING

18 Seeing now, dearly beloved brethren, that this person (child) is regenerate, and grafted into the body of Christ's Church let us give thanks unto Almighty God for these benefits. Let us remember that it is our duty to encourage him in our fellowship, and to support him in our prayers, and to strengthen him by our example, that he made daily advance in all virtue and godliness of living. And therefore let us now with one accord make our prayers unto God, that this person (child) may lead the rest of their life according to this beginning.

19 *Then shall be said by Priest and people together*
[[Lord's Prayer **CF4c**]]

20 We yield thee hearty thanks, most merciful Father, that it hath pleased thee to regenerate this person (child) with thy Holy Spirit, to receive him for thine own children by adoption, and to incorporate him into thy holy Church. And humbly we beseech thee to grant that as he is made partaker of the death of thy Son, he may née be partaker of his resurrection; so that serving the here in newness of life, he may finally, with all thy holy Church, inherit thine everlasting kingdom; through Christ our Lord. **Amen.**

21 *Here, when a child is baptized, may follow this prayer for the home:*
Almighty God, our heavenly Father, whose blessed Son did share at Nazareth the life of an earthly home: bless, we beseech the, the home of this child and grant wisdom and understanding to all that have the care of him; that he may grow up in thy constant fear and love; through the same thy Son Jesus Christ our Lord. **Amen.**

22 *If any husband and wife are baptized together, this prayer may be said:*
O God, who hast taught us that it should never be lawful to put asunder those whom thou by matrimony hast made one, and hast consecrated the state of matrimony to such an excellent mystery, that in it is signified and represented the spiritual marriage and unity betwixt Christ and his church; look mercifully upon these thy servants that both this man may love his wife according to thy Word, (as Christ did love his spouse the church, who gave himself for it, loving and cherishing it even as his own flesh,)

and also that this woman may be loving and amiable and faithful to her husband, and in all quietness, sobriety, and peace, be a follower of holy and godly matrons. O Lord, bless them (both), and grant them to inherit thine everlasting kingdom; through the same Jesus Christ our Lord. **Amen.**

23 *Then, if the Baptism be administered otherwise than at Morning or Evening Prayer, the priest shall dismiss those that are gathered together, saying:*
May God Almighty, the Father of our Lord Jesus Christ, from whom every family in heaven and on earth is named, grant you should be strengthened with might by his Spirit in the inner man; that Christ may dwell in your hearts through faith, and ye be filled unto the fullness of God. **Amen.**

24 The blessing of God Almighty, the Father, the Son, and the Holy Spirit, be amongst you and remain with you always. **Amen.**

〖25 Rubrics that direct the candidate should be confirmed as soon as possible, and directions if the service includes the baptism of children unable to answer for themselves. Finally a rubric on the unrepeatability of baptism.〗

32. The Church of the Province of South East Asia

Christianity in the Malayan archipelago may go back to Arab traders and Christians from the Church of the East in the seventh century. The Portuguese conquered in 1511 bringing Roman Catholicism. The British East India Company began a settlement in 1786 with the first full chaplain appointed in 1805. Mission work in Borneo began in 1841 with the Rajah Sir James Brooke recruiting a clergyman for Sarawak. In 1855 the Bishop of Labuan was consecrated for Sarawak, an independent kingdom outside of British influence, and the Book of Common Prayer was translated into local languages.[83] In 1909 the Diocese of Singapore was formed.

The Province of the Anglican Church in South East Asia was inaugurated in 1996, but constituent dioceses are much older with one bishop going to the first Lambeth Conference. It was created out of four dioceses that were extra-Provincial with different Anglican backgrounds. The church operates in a number of languages: English, Chinese, Tamil and Malay. It also has extensive mission work with tribal peoples and in some neighbouring countries. The church inherited a number of different diocesan services. The Diocese of Singapore had a *Service Book 1986* which contained services of baptism and confirmation in English and Chinese. *A Prayer Book for Thailand 1989* is in English and Thai with slightly different texts. These illustrate the diocesan diversity before the Province was formed. The *Service Book 1999* is the first official Provincial rite, and includes services of baptism and confirmation. While it uses material from the ASB there are also considerable divergences, with its own local material. It contains services for baptism, of adults and children, and confirmation. The services are carefully simplified no doubt to facilitate ease of translation. There are a set of rites for the catechumenate, for both urban and tribal mission. Issues of children and communion have not been discussed.

SERVICE BOOK 1999

BAPTISM

THE PREPARATION

⟦1–2 Directions, rubrics, sentence, hymn.⟧

3   The Lord be with you
     and also with you.

     Heavenly Father, by the power of your Holy Spirit you give to your faithful people new life in the water of baptism.

---

83 G 28: 1 Dayak, G 18: 35, 37 Chinese, G 100: 1 Malay.

Guide and strengthen us by that same Spirit, that we who are born again may serve you in faith and love, and grow into the full stature of your Son Jesus Christ, who is alive and reigns with you and the Holy Spirit, one God now and forever. **Amen.**

THE MINISTRY OF THE WORD

⟦4–6 Rubrics, reading, sermon, hymn.⟧

THE DECISION

7 *Those who are to be baptised, the parents and godparents of children to be baptised stand before the Minister. He says*
Our Lord Jesus Christ suffered death on the cross and rose again from the dead for the salvation of mankind. Baptism is the outward sign by which we receive for ourselves what he has done for us; we are united with him in his death; we are granted the forgiveness of sins; we are raised with Christ to new life in the Spirit.

Those of you who have come for baptism must affirm your allegiance to Christ and your rejection of all that is evil.

When no children are to be baptised, the following words in brackets are omitted.
(Those parents and godparents who present children for baptism must bring them up to follow Christ and to fight against evil. These children about to be baptised depend greatly on you for help and encouragement to grow up in the Christian faith.)

8 Therefore I ask these questions:
(Parents and godparents must answer both for themselves and for these children.)

Do you turn to Christ?
I turn to Christ.
Do you repent of your sins?
I repent of my sins.
Do you renounce the devil and all his works; the empty show and glory of the world, with all the covetous desires of it; and the carnal desires of the flesh, so that you will not follow nor be led by them?
I renounce them all.

9 May almighty God deliver you from the powers of darkness, and lead you in the light and obedience of Christ. **Amen.**

THE BAPTISM

10 *The Minister stands before the water of baptism and says*
Praise God who made heaven and earth,
who keeps his promise forever.

Almighty God, whose Son Jesus Christ was baptised in the river Jordan:
we thank you for the gift of water to cleanse us and revive us;
we thank you that through the waters of the Red Sea, you led your people out of slavery to freedom in the promised land;
we thank you that through the deep waters of death you brought your Son, and raised him to life in triumph.
Bless this water, that your *servants* who *are* washed in it may be made one with Christ in his death and in his resurrection, to be cleansed and delivered from all sin.
Send your Holy Spirit upon them to bring *them* to new birth in the family of your Church, and raise *them* with Christ to full and eternal life.
For air might, majesty, authority, and power are yours, now and forever. **Amen.**

11 *The Minister says to adults who are to be baptised*
You must now declare before God and his Church the Christian faith into which you are to be baptised and in which you will live and grow.

To parents and godparents of children who are to be baptised he says
You must now declare before God and his Church the Christian faith into *which these children* are to be baptised, and in which you will help *them* live and grow. You must answer for yourselves and for *these children*.

Then he says
Do you believe and trust in God the Father, who made the world?
I believe and trust in him.
Do you believe and trust in God the Son, Jesus Christ, as your Saviour and Lord?
I believe and trust in him.
Do you believe and trust in God the Holy Spirit, the giver of life?
I believe and trust in him.

This is the faith of the Church.
This is our faith.
We believe and trust in one God
Father, Son, and Holy Spirit.

The Minister then baptises the candidates. He dips each one in the water or pours water on the candidate and says

N, I baptise you in the name of the Father and of the Son, and of the Holy Spirit.
Amen.

12 *The Minister makes THE SIGN OF THE CROSS on the forehead of each one and says*

I sign you with the cross, the sign of Christ.

Do not be ashamed to confess the faith of Christ crucified.
Fight valiantly under the banner of Christ
against sin, the world, and the devil and continue
his faithful *soldiers* and *servants to* the end of your *lives*.

13 *The Minister or other person may give A LIGHTED CANDLE to each adult who has been baptised, and to a parent or godparent for each child saying to each*
Receive this light.
This is to show that you have passed from darkness to light.
Shine as a light in the world to the glory of God the Father.

14 *The Minister and the congregation, representing the whole Church, welcome the candidates.*

God has received you by baptism into his Church.
We welcome you into the Lord's Family.
We are members together of the body of Christ;
we are children of the same heavenly Father;
we are inheritors together of the kingdom of God.
We welcome you.

Almighty God, we thank you for our fellowship in the household of faith with all those who have been baptised in your name. Keep us faithful to Christ and the promises we made at our Baptism, persevering to the end so that we may share with all your people the joy and perfection of your new creation; through Jesus Christ your Son, our Saviour and Lord. **Amen.**

[[15 Final rubrics.]]

CONFIRMATION

THE PREPARATION

⟦1–2 Sentence, hymn, greeting.⟧

THE PRAYERS OF PENITENCE

⟦3–6 Summary of law, introduction to confession, confession, absolution; as ASB.⟧

6 Heavenly Father, by the power of your Holy Spirit you give to your faithful people new life in the water of baptism. Guide and strengthen us by that same Spirit, that we who are born again may serve you in faith and love, and grow into the full stature of your son Jesus Christ, who is alive and reigns with you and the Holy Spirit, one God now and for ever. **Amen.**

THE MINISTRY OF THE WORD

⟦8–13 Readings, hymns and sermon.⟧

THE RENEWAL OF BAPTISMAL VOWS

14 Dearly beloved in the Lord, in ministering Confirmation the Church follows the example of the Apostles of Christ. For in the 8th Chapter of the Acts of the Apostles we read:
⟦Acts 8.4–5; 12; 14–17⟧
The Scripture here teaches us that a special gift of the Holy Spirit is bestowed through laying on of hands with prayer. And because this gift comes from God alone, let us who are here present pray to Almighty God, that he will strengthen with his Holy Spirit in Confirmation those who had been baptised as his children.

You, then, who are to be confirmed must now declare before this congregation that you are steadfastly purposed with the help of the gift of the Holy Spirit, to lead your life in the faith of Christ and in obedience to God's will and commandments; and must acknowledge yourselves bound to fulfil the Christian duties to which your Baptism has pledged you.

15 *The candidates stand before the Bishop; he says*
You have come here to be confirmed. You stand in the presence of God and his Church. With your own mouth and from your own heart you must declare your allegiance to Christ and your rejection of all that is evil. Therefore, I ask these questions:

Do you turn to Christ?
I turn to Christ.
Do you repent of your sins?
I repent of my sins.
Do you renounce the devil and all his works; the empty show and glory of the world, with all the covetous desires of it; and the carnal desires of the flesh, so that you will not follow nor be led by them?
I renounce them all.

Then the Bishop says
You must now declare before God and his Church that you accept the Christian faith into which you were baptised, and in which you will live and grow.

Do you believe and trust in God the Father, who made the world?
I believe and trust in him.

Do you believe and trust in God the Son, Jesus Christ as your Saviour and Lord?
I believe and trust in him.
Do you believe and trust in God the Holy Spirit, the giver of life?
I believe and trust in him.

The Bishop turns to the congregation and says
This is the faith of the Church.
This is our faith.
We believe and trust in one God,
Father, Son, and Holy Spirit.

THE CONFIRMATION

16 *The Bishop stands before those to be confirmed and says*

Our help is in the name of the Lord
who has made heaven and earth.
Blessed be the name of the Lord
now and forever. Amen.

17 *The Bishop stretches out his hand towards them and says*
Almighty and everliving God,
you have given your servants new birth
in baptism by water and the Spirit,
and have forgiven them all their sins.
Let your Holy Spirit rest upon them:
the Spirit of wisdom and understanding;
the Spirit of counsel and inward strength;
the Spirit of knowledge and true godliness;
and let their delight be in the fear of the Lord.
Amen.

18a *The Bishop lays his hand on the head of each candidate, saying*
Confirm, O Lord, your servant N with your Holy Spirit.

and each one answers **Amen.**

or

18b [Confirmation Prayer **CF5**]

19 *The Welcome*
God has received you by Baptism and Confirmation into His church

The whole Congregation says, loudly and clearly
We welcome you into the Lord's Family.
We are members together of the body of Christ;
We are children of the same heavenly Father;
We are inheritors together of the kingdom of God.
We welcome you.

THE COMMUNION

[20 Directions are given to continue with Holy Communion.]

CONFIRMATION WITHOUT HOLY COMMUNION

[21 Various prayers are given in this context.]

33. Hong Kong Sheng Kung Hui

Christianity came to China in 635 with Alopen from the Church of the East in the Tang Dynasty. The church flourished for a while but then suffered persecution. In 1246 a Franciscan delivered letters from the Pope to the Great Khan, where Christians lived as part of his court. In 1294 John of Monte Corvino arrived in Beijing for mission work. He found the Church of the East to be present there and began a Catholic church. This remained until 1369 when Western Christians were expelled. In 1557 the Portuguese settled in Macau and this enabled the Jesuit Matthew Ricci to begin his mission in China. This too suffered by the Chinese suspicion of foreigners and the country closed to mission work. The Treaty of Nanking in 1842 at the end of the shameful Opium War led to five treaty ports and Hong Kong as a British colony. Various Protestant missionaries now began work in China with Anglicans from Britain, America and Canada. Bishop Boone arrived from America in 1844, and in 1849 an English diocese was formed in Hong Kong. Each diocese tended to produce its own Chinese translation of prayer books.[84] The Holy Catholic Church of China came into being in 1912 and was recognized by the 1930 Lambeth Conference as an independent Province. With the rise of Communist rule, the Province detached Hong Kong from the rest of the Chinese church. In 1998 Hong Kong and Macau became an autonomous Province in the Anglican Communion.

Hong Kong is presently undergoing liturgical revision. The current Book of Common Prayer dates from 1998. In 2015 new rites for the Easter Vigil were developed which included baptism and confirmation. The service of Baptism and Confirmation was produced in 2016. The following is the official English translation, the service being written first in Chinese.

INITIATION RITE 2016

HOLY BAPTISM AND CONFIRMATION/RECEPTION

WITHIN A CELEBRATION OF HOLY COMMUNION

⟦Translated by Chunwai Lam⟧

⟦1 Rubrics saying this come after being a catechumen and is presided over by the bishop. Five days are given as particular baptismal days, and the service is public.⟧

THE GATHERING

Sentence

2 *All stand. The Presider or a deacon or an assisting priest says the Sentence.*

---

84 G 18: 1ff.

Processional Hymn

3 *While singing, the choir and the altar party proceed to the church.*
Greeting

4a *The Presider greets the community.*
The grace of our Lord Jesus Christ, and the love of God, and the fellowship of the
Holy Spirit, be with you all.
And also with you.

4b *The following greetings may be used.*
Proper Sundays
Blessed be God: Father, Son, and Holy Spirit;
Blessed be his kingdom, now and for ever. Amen.
or
In the name of the Father, and of the Son and of the Holy Spirit;
Amen.

4c *From Easter to Day of Pentecost*
Alleluia! Christ is risen.
The Lord is risen indeed. Alleluia!

⟦5 The Gloria⟧

COLLECT

6 Let us pray.
All keep a moment of silence.
The Presider says the Collect of the Day, after which all respond, **Amen.**
The following Collect may be used instead.
Almighty God, by your grace all baptized in water and in Spirit are joyfully reborn
and be able to turn away from their evil ways and to seek only good deeds; grant us
we ask your guidance and faith in you that we, being baptized into Christ's death and
be raised with him, can walk in newness of life and live like him, through our Lord
Jesus Christ, to whom with you and the Holy Spirit be honour and glory, now and for
ever.
Amen.

THE MINISTRY OF THE WORD

⟦7 Two readings, gospel and homily.⟧

HOLY BAPTISM

8 *A deacon or an assisting priest holding the Paschal Candle leads the candidates for baptism
and their Godparents to proceed to the baptismal font, which is normally located at the
church entrance.*
The Presider, the candidates and their parents and godparents stand beside the font.
The whole congregation is welcome to accompany the candidates at the font.

During Epiphany
At river Jordan Jesus was baptized by John so as to fulfill the righteousness of God
who promises to redeem his people. May we who by baptism be also made righteous
and be given such grace.
Easter Vigil and Easter Day
Our Saviour Lord Jesus Christ conquered death has unfolded the paschal mystery,
that by being baptized with him into death we can be raised with him to eternal life.

Day of Pentecost
We are all blessed by the Holy Spirit who shines to us and inspires us. May we who by baptism be made children of God and be given strength to be God's witnesses.
Saints Days and other Holy Days
It is through baptism that we are called to enter into the fellowship of faith. May we who by baptism be born anew and be united into the body of Christ who makes us one in him.
Proper Sundays
Jesus said, 'Unless one is born of water and the Spirit, one cannot enter into the kingdom of God.' So may we who by baptism be given hope and assurance that we are called into the household of God.

PRESENTATION

9 *The candidates may be presented to the congregation by their godparents. Infant candidates may be presented by their parents and godparents.*

Presenters **I present to be baptized and be received into the house of God.**

If Confirmation or Reception is to be taken place, the candidates are also to be presented.

Presenters **I present to be confirmed and ask for your prayers.**
or I present to be received and ask for your prayers.

10 Holy Baptism is the first Sacrament of the Church. Jesus commissioned his disciples saying, 'Go therefore and make disciples of all the nations, baptizing them in the name of the Father and the Son and the Holy Spirit.'
Inspired by the Holy Spirit Peter the apostle talked about baptism in these words: 'Repent, and let each of you be baptized in the name of Jesus Christ for the forgiveness of your sins; and you shall receive the gift of the Holy Spirit. For the promise is for you and your children, and for all who are far off, as many as the Lord our God shall call to Himself.'

If there are infants to be baptized, the following may be added:
While preaching the gospel, Jesus saw people bringing their children to him who then said to his disciples: 'Permit the children to come to me; do not hinder them; for the kingdom of God belongs to such as these.' In like manner the Church takes this as the teaching of Christ to welcome children and believes that it is by God's grace that they be admitted to the Sacrament of Baptism. The Church has been upholding these teachings that we all live in sins and our souls have always been weak and fragile, and we can live anew only through the merits of God's saving grace. So with prayers of support from the congregation and the grace of God bestowed upon you, do stand firm and have faith in Christ, that you are able to enter into the fellowship of Christ and walk side by side with those in the ongoing journey of faith.

11 *The presider asks the adult candidates for baptism.*
God chooses you and gives you grace by calling you to be God's children who are born of water and the Spirit.
Dearly beloved, do you desire to be baptized?
I do.

12 *The presider asks the parents and godparents of the infant candidates.*
Dearly beloved, you bring the *child* for baptism, will you be responsible to take the role of parents and godparents: through prayers and examples of love and care to bring up the *child* in Christian faith and life?
I will.

13 *The presider asks the candidates for Confirmation.*
Dearly beloved, we welcome you to receive the laying on of hands in order that your faith be fortified. Are you willing by the help of the Holy Spirit to stand firm on the knowledge of God which you have inherited from the Church and to live like Christ?
I am.

14 *The presider asks the candidates for Reception.*
Dearly beloved, there is one body and one Spirit and we are called to one Lord, one faith, one baptism. Are you willing by the help of the Holy Spirit to be united into one holy catholic Church in communion with all the faithful?
I am.

15 *The presider asks the congregation.*
Through baptism God calls us to the knowledge of his grace and faith in him. Will you as members of this congregation accept and support *them* to enter into Christian faith and living?
We will, with God's help.

PROMISE

16 *The presider asks the following questions to the candidates who can speak for themselves, and to the parents and godparents who speak on behalf of the infants.*
In baptism God calls us to follow Christ, to turn away from darkness and enter into light so that we might die to sin and live to righteousness. Therefore I ask,
Do you reject the devil and all rebellion against God?
I reject them.
Do you renounce all sins and all sinful desires and corruption of evil?
I renounce them.
Do you repent of the sins that separate us from God and neighbour?
I renounce them.
Do you turn to Christ as Saviour?
I turn to Christ.
Do you submit to Christ as Lord?
I submit to Christ.
Do you come to Christ, the way, the truth and the life?
I come to Christ.

PRAYERS FOR THE CANDIDATES

17 Dearly brothers and sisters, let us pray as we are to celebrate our death and resurrection.
Deliver *them*, O Lord, from the way of sin and death.
Lord, hear our prayer.
Open *their* hearts to your grace and truth.
Lord, hear our prayer.
Fill *them* with your holy and life-giving Spirit.
Lord, hear our prayer.
Teach *them* to love others in the power of the Spirit.
Lord, hear our prayer.
Send *them* into the world in witness to your love.
Lord, hear our prayer.
Bring *them* to the fullness of your peace and glory.
Lord, hear our prayer.

Grant, O Lord, that all who are baptized into the death of Jesus Christ your Son may live in the power of his resurrection and look for him to come again in glory; who lives and reigns with you and the Holy Spirit, now and for ever. **Amen.**

THANKSGIVING OVER THE WATER

18 *Before the blessing prayers the Presider or one of the candidates or godparents pours water into the font.*

19 Blessed be God who created all things in heaven and earth,
who keeps his promise for ever.
We give thanks to the Lord our God.
It is right to give God thanks and praise.

We give you thanks, Almighty God, for sending your Son Jesus Christ who was baptized in the river Jordan and was anointed as Christ by your Holy Spirit to bring us salvation and new life.
Lord, our Saviour,
give us life.
We give you thanks that through waters of the Red Sea, you led your people out of slavery to freedom in the Promised Land.
Lord, our Saviour,
give us life.
We give you thanks for the water of baptism. In it we are buried with Christ in his death. By it we share in his triumphant resurrection. Through it we are born anew by the Holy Spirit.
Lord, our Saviour,
give us life.
Now sanctify this water, we pray you, by the power of your Holy Spirit, that those who here are cleansed from sin and born again may continue for ever in the risen life of Jesus Christ our Saviour.
Lord, our Saviour,
give us life.
Sanctify us also that we who believe in you may be renewed and share with Christ in his wholeness and eternity through power of the Holy Spirit. To him, to you, and to the Holy Spirit, be all honour and glory, now and for ever. **Amen.**

RENEWAL OF BAPTISMAL VOW

20 *The Presider addresses the congregation.*
Dear brothers and sisters, we have been saved and renewed through the baptism of water and Holy Spirit. I, therefore, ask you to profess together with *these candidates* the faith of the Church.
All face to the baptismal font.

[Apostles' Creed **CF2b**]

Will you persevere in resisting evil and, whenever you fall into sin, repent and return to God?
I will, with God's help.
Will you proclaim by word and example the good news of God in Christ?
I will, with God's help.
Will you seek and serve Christ in all persons, loving your neighbour as yourself?
I will, with God's help.

Will you strive for justice and peace among all people, and respect the dignity of every human being?
I will, with God's help.

BAPTISM

21 *Each candidate is presented by name to the Presider, or to an assisting priest, who then immerses, or pours water upon the candidate, saying,*

22 I baptize you in the name of the Father, and of the Son, and of the Holy Spirit. **Amen.**

23 *A sign of cross (anointing by the bishop or the priest appointed) is made on the forehead of each candidate.*
We receive into the congregation of Christ's flock; and do sign *him* with the sign of the cross, in token that hereafter *he* shall not be ashamed to confess the faith of Christ crucified, and bravely to fight under his banner, against sin, the world, and the devil; and to continue Christ's faithful soldier and servant unto *his* life's end. **Amen.**

WELCOME

24 There is one body and one Spirit and we are called to one Lord, one faith, one baptism.
We are happy to receive you into this fellowship of faith and welcome you to be with us as the people of God.

25 *This follows a round of applause.*
Asperges may be used here to signify that we are all baptized in water and the Spirit. After which all return to their seats.
Confirmation and Reception follows.

CONFIRMATION

26 *At the centre of the sanctuary, the Bishop leads the congregation to pray for the candidates for Confirmation or Reception.*

27a *The Bishop lays hands upon each candidate.*
⟦*Confirmation prayer* **CF5** *in singular.*⟧

27b Stir up your power, O Lord, in your servant; by your Holy Spirit, fortify *him*, strengthen *him*, empower *him* to do your will all the days of *his* life. **Amen.**

RECEPTION

28 We recognize you as a member of the one holy catholic and apostolic Church, and we receive you into the fellowship of this Communion (of Hong Kong Sheng Kung Hui/ The Anglican/Episcopal Church of Hong Kong). **Amen.**

30 *The Bishop shakes hand with each candidate.*

PRAYERS OF THE PEOPLE

31 *One of alternative prayers provided in the Eucharist Prayer (Rite II) may be used.*
All stand.
Dear brothers and sisters, it is the grace of God that we walk as children of light and enter into the fellowship of faith through baptism. Therefore, let us stand before God without fear and without reproach, and offer God our prayers.
For those who are baptized today: May God continually guide them who have now been born again of water and the Holy Spirit, and have become the *children* of God, and *members* of the Church. May the Spirit abide in them that they may have the determination to imitate Christ and to live a pious life.

Silence

Lord, in your mercy,

Hear our prayer.

For the tests and trials we encounter each day: May God strengthen us, especially when we are alone and helpless, that we may overcome the temptations of the devil which would only lead us to rebel against God and to estrange ourselves from God.
Silence

Lord, in your mercy,

Hear our prayer.

For the worries we undertake: May God grant us that we may grow in faith in which we can have trust in God and will no longer worry about what to eat and what to drink, believing that by what the Son Jesus have taught us our body and mind are always at peace.
Silence

Lord, in your mercy,

Hear our prayer.

For family and its members: May God bless our home and each member of our family; establish among us that peace which is the fruit of righteousness, take away from us lust and vanity, arrogance and pride, grant us knowledge and discipline, patience and piety, charity and kindness, and in love we found our family.
Silence

Lord, in your mercy,

Hear our prayer.

For the fellowship of faith: May God unite us as one through the guidance of the Holy Spirit, that we are able to bear willingly one another's burden and humbly serve one another in the Church.
Silence

Lord, in your mercy,

Hear our prayer.

For all those who suffer in body, mind, or spirit, (especially for): May God comfort and heal them; give them courage and hope in their troubles.
Silence

Lord, in your mercy,

Hear our prayer.

For all who have died in the communion of all the saints, (especially for): May God have mercy upon them, that they may have a place in God's eternal kingdom.
Silence

Lord, in your mercy,

Hear our prayer.

O Lord, we are your possessions for you seek us and enable us to have sought you and make us to be your faithful servants; for the sake of your love accept the prayers of your people, and strengthen us to do your will; through Jesus Christ our Lord.
Amen.

THE MINISTRY OF THE SACRAMENT

[32 The service continues with the peace and the Eucharist.]

DISMISSAL

BLESSING

[33 A blessing is given.]

GIVING OF A LIGHTED CANDLE

34　*The newly baptized, accompanied by their parents and godparents, come forward to the sanctuary.*

35　*The Presider or godparents give each newly baptized a lighted candle.*
God has delivered us from the dominion of darkness and has given us a place with the saints in light.
You have received the light of Christ; walk in this light all the days of your life.
Shine as a light in the world to the glory of God the Father.

36　*Here may be sung a Recessional hymn.*
The Choir and those belong to the altar party may recede.

SENDING OUT

37　*At church door, a deacon or the Presider dismisses the congregation.*
Let us go forth into the world, rejoicing in the power of the Spirit. (Alleluia! Alleluia!)
Thanks be to God. (Alleluia! Alleluia!)

34. The Episcopal Church in the Philippines

The first missionaries in the Philippines were Roman Catholic Augustinians in 1565, with the development of Spanish rule. In 1898 the Americans invaded, and a service was held by an Episcopal chaplain for the soldiers. The invasion opened the land to Protestant missions. There had been discontent in the Roman Catholic population due to the lack of the appointment of indigenous priests and bishops. This led to the development of the Philippine Independent Church in 1902, a church in full communion with the Anglican Communion.[85] In 1901 the General Convention of the Episcopal Church made the Philippines a missionary district. 1902 the Episcopal mission began when Bishop Brent arrived, particularly focusing on American soldiers and administration, Chinese immigrants, Muslims in the south and unevangelized tribes in the mountains. Portions of the 1892 Episcopal prayer book were translated into Igorot. In 1946 the Philippines was given independence from America. Parts of the Episcopal Church's 1979 Book of Common Prayer were translated into Tagalog. In 1990 the Episcopal Church in the Philippines became an autonomous Province.

The current rites of the Episcopal Church in the Philippines are from the *Book of Common Prayer* (1999). This closely follows the Book of Common Prayer 79 of the Episcopal Church. A distinctive contribution from the ECP is a Vigil on the Eve of Baptism. There is also a renewal of baptismal vows during the Easter vigil. The text in this chapter notes the similarities with the Episcopal Church, but does not repeat that text.

BOOK OF COMMON PRAYER 1999
HOLY BAPTISM

⟦1 Introduction called Concerning the Service.⟧

⟦Sections 2 to 4, the introductory material, are exactly the same as BCP 79.⟧

⟦ECP adds here the Gloria, or the Te Deum, or the Kyrie, or the Triagion.⟧

⟦5 The collect is as in BCP 79.⟧

⟦6 The Lessons and sermon as in the Eucharist.⟧

PRESENTATION AND EXAMINATION OF THE CANDIDATES

7   The Candidate(s) for Holy Baptism will now be presented.

The parents, godparents and sponsors present the candidates individually saying,
I present N for baptism.

---

85 J 291–300. G 1961/4,5.

The officiant asks the following questions to the parents, godparents, and sponsors
Will you be responsible for seeing that this person is brought up in the Christian faith and life?
I will, with God's help.

Will you by your prayers and witness help this person to grow into the full stature of Christ?
I will, with God's help.

10   *The candidates who can speak for themselves answer the following questions. Parents and godparents speak for the younger candidates.*

Do you desire to be baptized?
I do.

⟦The renunciations and profession follow exactly the BCP 79.⟧

THE PRESENTATION FOR CONFIRMATION, OR RECEPTION OR REAFFIRMATION

11   *The candidates are presented by their priest or another person designated.*
I present *this person* for Confirmation.
or I present *this person* for reception.
or I present *this person* who desires to reaffirm their baptismal vows.

12   *The following questions are answered by the candidates*
Bishop: Do you reaffirm your renunciation of evil?
I reaffirm the renunciation of Satan and all the spiritual forces of wickedness that rebel against God, the evil powers of this world which corrupt and destroy the creatures of God, and all sinful desires which draw me from the love of God.

Do you renew your commitment to Jesus Christ?
I do, and with God's grace I will put my whole trust in his love and service, follow and obey him as my Lord and Saviour.

⟦13   With a slight change in the rubric the people affirmed their support in the BCP 79 words.⟧

⟦14   With a change to these persons the call to renew the baptismal covenant is as the BCP 79.⟧

THE BAPTISMAL COVENANT

⟦15   Question and answer Apostles' Creed **CF2b**⟧

⟦16   The questions of commitment are the same as the BCP 79 except that after the first an additional question is asked: will you be diligent in the study of Holy Scriptures?⟧

⟦Sections of Psalm 42 or anthem are added for a procession to the font.⟧
Prayers for the Candidates

⟦17   The words for the prayers are exactly as the BCP 79.⟧

THE THANKSGIVING OVER THE WATER

⟦18   The Thanksgiving over the water is as the BCP 79.⟧

⟦An anthem is added here.⟧

CONSECRATION OF THE CHRISM

⟦19   The bishop consecrates chrism with the same words as the BCP 79.⟧

THE BAPTISM

20   *The Officiant immerses, or pours water on the candidate for Baptism, saying,*

N., I baptize you in the Name of the Father, and of the Son, and of the Holy Spirit.
Amen.

If desired the newly-baptized may now put on white garments, while the officiant says,
Through the water of baptism, you have been clothed with the shining garments of
Christ's righteousness. See in these the outward signs of your Christian dignity, and
bring that dignity and stained for life. **Amen.**

A lighted candle may also be given, the officiant saying,
Receive the light of Christ. Let your light so shine before all people that they may see
your good works and glorify your Father who is in heaven. **Amen.**

The following and some anthem may be sung,
You have put on Christ. Alleluia.
In him you have been baptized. Alleluia, alleluia.

Holy church of God, stretch out your hand, and welcome your new-born children,
born anew of water and the Spirit. They have died to sin and our risen with Christ.
Amen.

or

You are now God's children, a new creation in Jesus Christ. Alleluia. **Amen.**
Rejoice, you newly baptized, chosen members of Christ's kingdom; buried with Christ
in his death, you live with him in his resurrection, reborn in him by faith. Enter into
the inheritance of heaven. Alleluia.

21   Let us pray.
[The post-baptismal prayer as the BCP 79.]

22   *Then the Bishop or Priest places a hand on the person's head, marking on the forehead the
sign of the cross using Chrism if desired and saying to each one*

N., you are sealed by the Holy Spirit in Baptism and marked as Christ's own for ever.
Amen.

23   *When all have been baptized, the Celebrant says*
Let us welcome the newly baptized.

24   *Officiant and People*
We receive you into the household of God.
Confess the faith of Christ crucified, proclaim his resurrection,
and share with us in his eternal priesthood.

[25 Rubrics for the Eucharist are given.]

CONFIRMATION, RECEPTION, OR REAFFIRMATION

26   *Bishop*
Let us now pray for *these persons* who have renewed *their* commitment to Christ.

[27 The prayer before confirmation is as in the BCP 79.]

CONFIRMATION

28   *The Bishop lays hands upon each candidate and says*

29a Stir up your power, O Lord, your servant N. By your Holy Spirit give *him* grace to
grow daily in the knowledge and love of you. Empower *him* for your service; and
sustain *him* all the days of *his* life. **Amen.**

29b Direct, sanctify, and govern O Lord, your servant N, that obedient in your love and goodness *he* may daily increase in your Holy Spirit more, until *he* comes to the glory of your heavenly Father; through Jesus Christ our Lord. **Amen.**

RECEPTION

30 N, we recognize you as a member of the one holy catholic and apostolic Church. We receive you into the fellowship of this Communion with all the responsibilities and privileges of a member. God, the Father, Son, and Holy Spirit, bless, preserve, and keep you. **Amen.**

REAFFIRMATION

31a N, may the Holy Spirit, who has begun a good work in you, direct, strengthen, and uphold you in the service of Christ and his kingdom. **Amen.**

or

31b N, may the Holy Spirit, the giver of life and light, strengthen your faith and hope, in which you with all grace, direct you into all truth, and fresh and new after the perfect image of our Lord and Savior Jesus Christ. **Amen.**

32 *The Bishop continues,*
Almighty God, who in the Paschal mystery established the new covenant of reconciliation, grant that all who have been reborn into the Fellowship of Christ's Body, may be empowered by your spirit to show forth in their lives what they profess by their faith, through Jesus Christ our Lord. **Amen.**

⟦33 The peace is then exchanged.⟧

35. The Anglican Church of Korea

The origins of Christianity in Korea are remarkable. In 1777 group of Korean scholars studied the works of Matthew Ricci and were so impressed that they sent one person to Beijing who became a Christian. He then returned and developed a Catholic Church. However, they then suffered a major persecution and the kingdom was closed. An 1882 treaty with the United States changed the situation opening the country to Protestant missionaries. Anglican missionaries arrived in 1890, and as elsewhere the liturgy was translated into Korean[86] although from the beginning the high church nature of the mission meant that the books were never a simple translation of the English Book of Common Prayer. In 1992 the church was recognized as an independent Province.

The Korean texts for baptism and confirmation were heavily based on the Korean translation of The Episcopal Church *Book of Common Prayer* (1979) published in 1986 by the Episcopal Asian Ministry. Because the 1986 translation differs in some respects from the original, this translation has been freshly made from the 2004 Korean text.

In the 2004 Korean *Anglican Prayer Book* baptism immediately follows the Eucharist, both as major sections. Baptism is then followed by a major section of 'Sacramental Rites', beginning with confirmation and including the other non-dominical sacraments. The rite for the Reception of Believers from Other Denominations is included in an 'Appendix' of assorted rites. A point to note in this rite is the direction that all newcomers welcomed into the Anglican Church will be presented for confirmation, regardless of whether they have been episcopally confirmed in their original church or not.

ANGLICAN PRAYER BOOK 2004

[Translated by Christopher John and Nak-Hyon Joseph Joo]

BAPTISM, CONFIRMATION AND
RECEPTION OF BELIEVERS FROM OTHER DENOMINATIONS

[1 Various rubrics about baptism including that it should be in the main Sunday Eucharist.]

BAPTISM

2 *If baptism is administered during the Eucharist, it follows immediately after the sermon.*

---

86 G 81: 1.

RECOMMENDATION OF CANDIDATE(S) FOR BAPTISM

ADULT BAPTISM RECOMMENDATION

3   *Officiant:* Please recommend the candidate(s) to be baptised.
     Sponsor: **I ask you to baptise this person, (N).**
     The officiant questions, one by one, each recommended candidate.
     Officiant: Do you wish to be baptised to become a person of God?
     Candidate: **Yes. I wish to be baptised.**

INFANT BAPTISM RECOMMENDATION

4   *Godparent(s):* I ask you to baptise this baby, (N).
     The officiant questions the parents and godparents.
     Will you be responsible for nurturing this child in Christian belief and life?
     With God's help I will take this responsibility.
     Will you promise, on behalf of this child, to bring (him/her) up by prayer and the
     example of life to grow into the full stature of Christ?
     With God's help I will bring (him/her) up.

BAPTISMAL COVENANT

5   *The officiant asks the candidate(s), and, for infant baptism, the godparents and parents.*
     Now, in front of the Lord and the church, I invite you to promise to keep the Lord's
     commands and fully confess the Christian faith.
     Do you reject all the works of Satan which rebel against God, or disturb the integrity
     of creation?
     Yes, I reject them.
     Will you renounce the evil powers of this world which destroy and corrupt what God
     has made?
     Yes, I renounce them.
     Will you abandon the sinful desires that separate us from God's love?
     Yes, I abandon them.

6   Do you believe in God the creator?
     I believe in God the Father Almighty, maker of heaven and earth.
     Do you believe in Jesus Christ the Saviour?
     **I believe in God's only son, our Lord Jesus Christ, who was conceived by the Holy
     Spirit and born of the Virgin Mary, who suffered under Pontius Pilate, was crucified,
     died and was buried, descended to the world of the dead, who rose on the third day
     from among the dead, ascended to heaven, is seated at the right hand of God the
     Almighty, will judge the living and the dead and who will come again.**
     Do you believe in the Holy Spirit?
     **I believe in the Holy Spirit, the Holy Catholic Church, the communion of Saints, the
     forgiveness of sins, the resurrection of the body and life everlasting.**

7   Will you follow Jesus Christ as Lord and keep his teaching?
     Yes. With God's help I will.
     Will you fully serve Christ's body the Church, through the Eucharist, sharing the
     grace of word and sacrament?
     Yes. With God's help I will.
     Will you constantly renounce evil and whenever you fall to sin, repent and return to
     the Lord?
     Yes. With God's help I will.
     Will you, in Christ, by word and life proclaim the good news of God?
     Yes. With God's help I will.

Will you love your neighbour as yourself, serving them as Christ?
Yes. *With God's help I will.*
Will you strive for justice and peace in order to protect human dignity?
Yes. *With God's help I will.*

8   *The officiant, facing the congregation, addresses them:*
Will you, who have witnessed this confession and vows, work together to strengthen
(those) now to be baptised and help (them) in faithful Christian belief and life?
Yes. We will help (them).

9   *If this is rite is occurring during the Easter vigil the congregation is now sprinkled with
holy water.*

PRAYER FOR THE BAPTISMAL CANDIDATE(S)

10   Now, let us pray together for those to be newly born through the sacrament of
baptism.
Lord God, draw them out of sin and death.
Lord hear our prayer.
Open their hearts with your grace, and awaken them to your truth.
Lord hear our prayer.
God of life, fill their hearts with your Holy Spirit.
Lord hear our prayer.
Keep them in the belief and fellowship of the holy church.
Lord hear our prayer.
Send them to the world making them witnesses to your love.
Lord hear our prayer.
Lead them in your grace and peace.
Lord hear our prayer.
Lord, with the grace of Jesus' crucifixion, help those being baptised that they may be
reborn in the strength of Christ's resurrection, await the Lord's return in glory, and
live in a right faith. We pray this in the name of our Lord Jesus Christ. **Amen.**

PRAYER FOR THE BLESSING OF THE WATER

11   *If necessary this prayer can take place in advance, before worship.*
The Lord be with you.
And also with you.
Let us give thanks to the Lord.
It is right and proper.
Almighty God, at the beginning of creation out of the darkness you were together
with the Holy Spirit over the waters. You led the people of Israel from slavery in
Egypt through the waters of the Red Sea to the promised land. Also, your son, Jesus
Christ, was baptised by water, and after suffering on the cross, broke the ties of death
and rose again, leading us to everlasting life. Therefore, we give you thanks for giving
us this water of salvation and pray that you will give the grace of your Holy Spirit to
those being baptised in this water that they will receive new life and become one with
the body of Christ.
*The officiant touches the water to bless it. If the Easter candle is being used, the blessing
may be given by it.*
Now, by the power of the Holy Spirit + bless this water and make it holy, that those
baptised by this water and the Holy Spirit may be cleansed from sin, born again, and
enjoy new life in the risen saviour, Jesus Christ, for now, and to eternity, the Lord
who rules over all things. **Amen.**

RITE OF BAPTISM

12   *The sponsor(s) lead the candidate(s) to the font and introduce (them) to the officiant.*

13   *The officiant pours water three times over the head of each candidate, saying the following.*
I baptise you in the name of the Father, the Son and the Holy Spirit. **Amen.**

14   *The officiant anoints each of the newly baptised, one by one, with episcopally consecrated oil, saying:*
You have received the seal of the Holy Spirit through baptism and become a child of Christ for ever. **Amen.**

15   *A baptismal candle is lit from the Easter candle and given to each person, saying:*
Receive the light of Christ. You have come from darkness into light and live with Christ. **Amen.**

16   *If the Rite of Baptism finishes:*
Let us pray.
God of salvation, we thank you that by water and the Holy Spirit you have cleansed these persons from sin, and given them rebirth through your grace. We pray that you will keep them in the power of the Holy Spirit and fill their hearts with truth, that they may live in this world with the great joy of serving and loving you. We pray this in the name of our Lord Jesus Christ. **Amen.**

17   *The newly baptised turn to the congregation, and the following is said.*
The whole congregation welcomes the newly baptised.
Let us welcome those who have been baptised and who have received new life with us as members of the body of Christ and to inherit the reign of God.
We welcome you into God's family. From now, living in the grace of God, let us proclaim the good news of Christ.

18   *The Eucharist continues with the Greeting of Peace.*

COLLECT FOR BAPTISM

Almighty God, through baptism we leave the old life of sin and participate in the death and resurrection of your Son Jesus Christ. We pray that we, now reborn to new life in Christ, may live in holiness and righteousness.

〚19   There are directions about readings, propers for baptism in the service book, and directions on conditional and emergency baptism.〛

RITE OF CONFIRMATION

〚1   Rubrics including *Confirmation is the rite by which, through the laying on of hands, a baptised believer receives the strength of the Holy Spirit in order to fulfil the commitment of the responsibility and faith of baptism.*
Those baptised as infants, when they reach a mature age, through suitable instruction, may receive permission to receive Holy Communion, and when of an age to accept the commitment and responsibility of baptism shall receive confirmation from the bishop. Further rubrics to order the service.〛

RECOMMENDATION OF THE CANDIDATE(S) FOR CONFIRMATION

2   *The candidate(s) for confirmation, with their sponsors, come out.*
The priest recommends the candidate(s) for confirmation.
Bishop: Please recommend the candidate(s) for confirmation.
Recommending priest: **I wish you to confirm these candidate(s), NN.**

3   *The officiant questions the candidate(s) for confirmation.*
    Now, before the Lord and the Church, I call on you to repeat the vows which were made at your baptism.
    Do you reject all the works of Satan which rebel against God, or disturb the integrity of creation?
    Yes, I reject them.
    Will you renounce the evil powers of this world which destroy and corrupt what God has made?
    Yes, I renounce them.
    Will you abandon the sinful desires that separate us from God's love?
    Yes, I abandon them.

4   Do you believe in God the creator?
    I believe in God the Father Almighty, maker of heaven and earth.
    Do you believe in Jesus Christ the Saviour?
    I believe in God's only son, our Lord Jesus Christ, who was conceived by the Holy Spirit and born of the Virgin Mary, who suffered under Pontius Pilate, was crucified, died and was buried, descended to the world of the dead, who rose on the third day from among the dead, ascended to heaven, is seated at the right hand of God the Almighty, will judge the living and the dead and who will come again.
    Do you believe in the Holy Spirit?
    I believe in the Holy Spirit, the Holy Catholic Church, the communion of Saints, the forgiveness of sins, the resurrection of the body and life everlasting.

5   Will you follow Jesus Christ as Lord and keep his teaching?
    Yes. With God's help I will.
    Will you fully serve Christ's body the Church, through the Eucharist, sharing the grace of word and sacrament?
    Yes. With God's help I will.
    Will you constantly renounce evil and whenever you fall to sin, repent and return to the Lord?
    Yes. With God's help I will.
    Will you, in Christ, by word and life proclaim the good news of God?
    Yes. With God's help I will.
    Will you love your neighbour as yourself, serving them as Christ?
    Yes. With God's help I will.
    Will you strive for justice and peace in order to protect human dignity?
    Yes. With God's help I will.

6   *The bishop, facing the congregation, asks the following.*
    You have witnessed this confession and profession of vows. Will you strengthen each other, and with those now to be confirmed, work for the reign of God to be fulfilled on this earth?
    Yes. We will do so.

PRAYER FOR THE CANDIDATES

7   Let us pray for those who promise to commit themselves more to Christ through this rite of confirmation.

8   *A short time of silence or a hymn for the invocation of the Holy Spirit.*

9   Almighty God, through his death and resurrection your Son delivers us from the power of sin, and by the Holy Spirit you have bound us to your service. We pray

that you will strengthen the grace given by baptism to your servants here, and now increase the gifts of the Holy Spirit that they carry out properly the task of proclaiming the good news and serving others. We pray this in the name of Jesus Christ, who with the Father and Holy Spirit, is one God. **Amen.**

LAYING ON OF HANDS

8 *The candidates kneel in front of the bishop, who anoints the forehead of each candidate with oil, and lays his/her hands on the candidate's head.*
Lord, send your Holy Spirit to this servant (N). Strengthen his/her faith, and grant that he/she may serve you throughout his/her whole life. **Amen.**

9 *After the laying on of hands, the bishop says:*
Let us pray.
Almighty and Eternal God, we thank you that by your great grace you give us the gifts of the Holy Spirit. We humbly pray that you keep these people in your loving hands and engrave your words in their hearts, that, by what they will and do they may serve the church and live with you for ever. We pray this in the name of Jesus Christ our Lord. **Amen.**

⟦10 Rubrics for the rest of the service and suggested readings.⟧

36. Nippon Sei Ko Kai
(The Anglican Communion in Japan)

Spanish missionaries from the Philippines entered Japan in the sixteenth century. This was followed later by the missionary work of the Jesuits, subsequently closed by persecution of Christians. Japan began to open again in 1858 and soon the Episcopal Church sent Channing Williams as missionary and then Bishop. This was to be followed with missionaries from Britain and Canada. The first prayer book of the Anglican Church in Japanese was published in 1878 including American and English alternatives.[87] In 1887 the different Anglican groups united to form the Holy Catholic Church of Japan. This was recognized as an independent Province in 1930.

The present Book of Common Prayer was authorised in 1990. It includes a service for the admission of a catechumen and the main baptismal provision is of a unified rite of baptism and confirmation.

BOOK OF COMMON PRAYER 1990

⟦Translated by Lydia Morey and Shintaro Ichihara⟧

BAPTISM AND CONFIRMATION SERVICE

⟦Rubrics re service including prayer and fasting.⟧

1 *The font is filled with clear water.*

2 *The presider stands at the place from which morning or evening service is presided.*

3 *The congregation uses one of the following Psalms or a hymn. Psalm 34 (1–7) Psalm 107 (1–7)*

THE EXHORTATION

4 Dearly beloved, the Lord Jesus Christ taught that no-one can enter the kingdom of God unless they are born anew by water and the spirit. Let us pray together for our brothers and sisters who have now come here by the Lord's guidance to receive baptism.

5 **Almighty God, savior of all those who call upon you, life of all those who believe in you, through baptism cleanse the sins of these person(s) here, cause them to be born anew, bring them into Christ's flock, and let them become with us heirs of your kingdom. We pray this through the grace of our Savior, Jesus Christ our Lord. Amen.**

---

87 G 67: 1.

THE WORD

⟦6 Three readings, psalm and sermon.⟧

7 *The presider, assistant, baptismal candidates, baptism and confirmation candidates,*
confirmands and godparents stand around the font. A hymn may be used.
The congregation stands facing the font.

THE VOWS

8 *Each candidate takes the following vows. Where the candidate is an infant, each all*
godparents take them instead.
Is it your will to be baptized (confirmed)?
It is my will.
To godparents of infants, the following is added:
Will you bring this child up whom you have brought in a Christian belief and life?
With the help of God we will.
By prayer and testimony, will you bring this child up to follow the Christ's perfect
example?
With the help of God we will.

Then they take the following vows.

9 Do you renounce Satan that rebel against God, and fight with every evil powers which
corrupt and destroy this world created by God?
By the help of God I do.
Do you renounce all sinful desires, words and actions that draw you from the love of
God?
By the help of God I do.
Do you turn to the Lord Jesus Christ, and accept him as your Savior?
By the help of God I do.
Do you put your whole trust in the Lord Jesus Christ?
By the help of God I do.
Do you believe and obey Christ as your Lord, and promise to follow his example all
your life?
By the help of God I do.

10 Brothers and sisters who have become witnesses of these vows, will you pray for and
support this person (these persons) so that they will keep these promises all their lives?
We will pray and help with all our strength.

BAPTISM

11 *THE CONSECRATION OF THE WATER*

The Lord be with you
And also with you.
Let us praise God the creator.
The Lord keeps his promises for ever.
Let us pray.
Creator of heaven and earth, almighty God the Father, we thank you for your
creation of water, and that you made as a symbol of purification and giving of new
life to all things. Your Son, who was sent by you, was baptized in the river Jordan,
died on the cross, and was raised to new life and completed his work of salvation.
Sanctify this water, and send your Holy Spirit on those who are washed in it: forgive
all their sins, cleanse them and bring them into new life, share in Christ's death and

resurrection, welcomed into your family the Church, and give them eternal life filled abundantly in Christ; Through Jesus Christ our Lord. **Amen.**

12 *CONFESSION OF FAITH*

Baptismal candidates, baptism and confirmation candidates and godparents of infants confess their faith. Those already baptized but now coming for confirmation also confess and declare their faith. Adult candidates confess individually. Godparents confess on behalf of infants.
Do you believe in God, the Father almighty, maker of heaven and earth?
I believe in God, the Father almighty, maker of heaven and earth.
Do you believe in Jesus Christ, the Son, the redeemer of the world?
I believe in Jesus Christ the Son, the savior of the world.
Do you believe in the Holy Spirit, the Lord, the giver of life?
I believe in the Holy Spirit, the Lord, the giver of life.

13 *BAPTISM*

The presider brings each baptismal candidate to the font, and says to the *godparents.*
(Surname and given name of candidate), what is this person's (infant's) Christian name?
The godparents give the Christian name. The presider says that Christian name and then immerse the candidate or pours water upon their head, each time they say the name of the Father, the Son and the Holy Spirit.

(Christian name), I baptize you in the name of the Father, and of the Son, and of the Holy Spirit. **Amen**

14 *Following this, the sign of the cross is marked on the forehead.*
I mark you with the sign of the cross. This is Christ's sign, expressing that you have been added to God's people, you have become Christ's eternally, and that you will fight with sin and the evil powers of this world as a faithful servant of the Lord. **Amen**

15 *THE WELCOME*

Brothers and sisters who have received the blessing of baptism, we are grateful that you have been received into the family of Christ, and have become one with us in Christ.
Let us confess our faith in Christ crucified, proclaim his resurrection, and together share in Christ's priesthood.

16 *Then all say the Apostle's creed.* [[CF1a]]

CONFIRMATION

[[Translated by Lydia Morey]]

[[Rubrics concerning the service including age, need to learn catechism, and directions to fit with service type and date.]]

1 *Bishop:* We have been buried with Christ through participation in his death through baptism.
This is so that we too may live for new life, as through the glory of the Father Christ was raised from the dead. *(Rom 6.4)*
Beloved brethren, let us pray for the person(s) here, already baptized, now requesting confirmation through the Lord's leading.

Almighty God, saviour of those who call on you, life of those who trust in you, we thank you that you have guided and caused the good desire to be confirmed in these person(s). Please bless these person(s) and grant their desires. We pray this through Jesus Christ our Lord. Amen.

THE WORD

2 ⟦Three readings, psalm and sermon.⟧

3 *A hymn may be used here.*
   Each confirmand stands with their godparents or witnesses in front of the Bishop.

RE-AFFIRMATION OF BAPTISMAL VOWS.

4 *Bishop:* Brothers and sisters who have come to receive the laying on of hands. Based on their baptismal vows, those who request the laying on of hands must renew their promises to be faithful to Christ and resist the power of evil for themselves in front of God and this congregation.
   Do you believe in omnipotent Father, the creator of heaven and earth?
   I believe in the omnipotent Father, creator of heaven and earth.
   Do you believe in Jesus Christ his Son, the saviour of the world?
   I believe in the Son Jesus Christ, the saviour of the world.
   Do you believe in the Holy Spirit, the giver of life?
   I believe in the Holy Spirit, the giver of life.

   Will you resist Satan who disobeys God, and fight with every power of evil which degrades and destroys this word created by God?
   By the help of God we will (fight).
   Throughout your life, will you learn from the example of the life of Christ, and love God and your neighbour?
   With the help of God, we will.

CONFIRMATION (LAYING ON OF HANDS)

5 *Bishop:* Our help is in the name of the Lord
   Who has made heaven and earth.
   Bishop: Let us praise the name of the Lord.
   We will pray him until eternity.
   Bishop: The Lord be with you.
   And also with you.
   Bishop: Let us pray.

6 *The Bishop stands, extends his has to the confirmands, and says:*
   Heavenly father, through the water and the Spirit you have already forgiven the sins of these your servant(s) and brought them into the new life in the Lord. Please fill them with the Holy Spirit, give them wisdom and understanding, foresight and courage, the blessing of knowing God, and a heart to love and respect God. **Amen.**

THE LAYING ON OF HANDS

7 *The godparents lead the confirmands to kneel in front of the Bishop. The Bishop lays his hands on each of their heads and says*
   Bishop: (Baptismal name, given name -) I lay my hands on you in the name of the Father, the Son, and the Holy Spirit. Lord, strengthen your disciple(s) through your Holy Spirit, and cause him/her to become one who serves the Lord more and more. **Amen.**

8 *Bishop:* Let us pray for our brothers and sisters who have received the laying on of hands.

Lord, protect these your servants with your heavenly blessing. Make them eternally the Lord's; may they daily be filled with the Holy Spirit until they (we) reach your kingdom, and cause them to become those (with us) who do the Lord's works. We pray this in the name of the Lord Jesus Christ. Amen.

9 *Bishop:* Let us pray.

Heavenly father, following the example of your apostles, we have now laid hands on these your servants and asked for a special blessing of the Holy Spirit. Please stretch your hand and fill them more and more with your blessing, constantly nourish and strengthen them through the body and blood of your Son, make them those who respect your word and obey it in their hearts, and at last bring them to life eternal. We pray this through the name of Jesus Christ. **Amen.**

⟦10 Rubrics concerning ending the service and receiving Communion.⟧

G. Australasia

37. The Anglican Church of Australia

Christianity arrived in Australia with the fleet of prisoners, departing England in 1787, bound for Botany Bay, which included a chaplain. Free settlers began to arrive in 1793. In 1814 Australia became a part of the Diocese of Calcutta, but by 1824 an Archdeacon of New South Wales was appointed. In 1836 the first Bishop of Australia was consecrated. 1850 saw a conference of Australian bishops and in 1872 a constitution was formed for the Australian church. Constitutional questions continued to trouble the history of the church; in 1962 Australia was recognized as a separate Province.

The report *Prayer Book Revision in Australia* (1966) began a process of liturgical revision. The 1967 baptismal rites were included in Jagger.[88] In 1978 *An Australian Prayer Book* included a full set of rites. This was then replaced by *A Prayer Book for Australia* (1995). This latest book includes services for: holy baptism, confirmation, Holy Communion with reaffirmation of vows and reception; holy baptism in morning and evening prayer; confirmation with reaffirmation and reception; reception into communicant membership. Separate from baptism there is a service for 'thanksgiving for a child'. In 2009 the services for baptism in Communion, and baptism with morning prayer were modified and made available for trial use.

Sydney Diocese did not approve *A Prayer Book for Australia* and has been developing its own liturgical resources. The Archbishop of Sydney's liturgical panel produced *Common Prayer: Resources for Gospel shaped gatherings* in 2012. These include services for baptism, confirmation, naming and reception. These services are not included in this book as they are rites for Sydney Diocese rather than provincially approved rites. Sydney Diocese in 2005 endorsed the possibility of the administration of confirmation by presbyters and in 2006 passed an ordinance not requiring confirmation before communion for those baptized as adults.

Children are admitted to Holy Communion before confirmation by Canon 6 which was passed by General Synod in 1985, provided it is adopted by a diocese and with episcopal guidelines. An example of this can be found online with Sydney's 'Regulations for admission' 2010. The national church has a Catechumenate Network which provides resources for the catechumenate as a way of Christian formation.

---

88 J 125–133.

A PRAYER BOOK FOR AUSTRALIA 1995

HOLY BAPTISM CONFIRMATION IN HOLY COMMUNION TOGETHER WITH PROVISION FOR REAFFIRMATION OF BAPTISMAL VOWS AND RECEPTION

GATHERING AND PREPARATION

⟦1–2 Hymn and liturgical greeting.⟧

3   *A Sentence of Scripture appropriate to the day or the occasion may be read, or the following dialogue used.*
There is one Body and one Spirit;
there is one hope in God's call to us.
One Lord, one Faith, one Baptism,
one God and Father of all.

4   *The minister may continue with these or similar words*
Baptism is the gift of our Lord Jesus Christ.
When he had risen from the dead, he commanded his followers to go and make disciples of all nations, baptising them in the name of the Father, and of the Son and of the Holy Spirit.
We have come together today to obey that command.
Baptism with water signifies the cleansing from sin that Jesus' death makes possible, and the new life that God gives us through the Holy Spirit.
In baptism, the promises of God are visibly signed and sealed for us. We are joined to Christ, and made members of his body, the Church universal.

When children are to be baptised, the minister says
Children are baptised in response to Gods all-embracing love. Parents and godparents who have responded to that love come now to bring their children for baptism. Before this congregation they must express their own trust and commitment to the promises of God, and their intention to bring up their children in the faith and practice of the Church. In due time these children should make their own response to God, and be prepared for confirmation.

When there are candidates for confirmation, the Bishop says
In confirmation those who have been previously baptised come to confirm that baptismal promises and join with the other candidates to receive the laying on of the Bishop's hand with prayer. We pray that those who are baptised and confirmed will be empowered by the Holy Spirit for the ministry and service to which God shall call them.

So we welcome you, *name*(s), with your sponsors [and families].
We give thanks for you, and pray that you may know God's love and faithfulness for ever.

⟦5–7 Kyrie, confession and absolution, Gloria, and collect for the day.⟧

THE MINISTRY OF THE WORD

⟦8–10 Reading(s), gospel and sermon.⟧

THE PRESENTATION

11   *The priest invites all candidates and their sponsors to stand in view of the congregation.*

12   *The priest invites the sponsors of baptismal candidates present the candidates.*
We welcome *those* who come(s) to be baptised I invite their sponsors to present *them* now.
We present name(s) to be baptised.

13   *The priest says to the sponsors of those unable to answer for themselves*
Will you accept the responsibilities placed upon you in bringing *name/this child* for baptism?
I will.
Are you willing to answer on behalf of *name/this child*?
I am.
By your own prayers and example, by your friendship and love, will you encourage *name/this child* in the life and faith of the Christian community?
I will, with God's help.

14   *The bishop invites the sponsors of confirmation candidates to present the candidates.*
We welcome *those who have come* to be confirmed. I invite their sponsors to present them now.
We present name(s) who come(s) to be confirmed.

15   *The bishop invites the sponsors of reaffirmation candidates to present the candidates.*
We welcome *those who have been* baptised and confirmed, and now come to seek God's blessing as *they* reaffirm their faith. I invite their sponsors to present *them* now.
We present name(s) who come(s) to reaffirm their faith.

THE DECISION

16   *The priest says to the candidates who are able to answer for themselves, and to the sponsors of other candidates.*

Before God and this congregation, you must affirm that you turn to Christ and reject all that is evil:

Do you turn to Christ?
I turn to Christ.
Do you repent of your sins?
I repent of my sins.
Do you reject selfish living, and all that is false and unjust?
I reject them all.
Do you renounce Satan and all evil?
I renounce all that is evil.

Almighty God deliver you from the powers of darkness, and lead you in the light of Christ to his everlasting kingdom. **Amen.**

17   *The priest says to the candidates and sponsors*
Will you each, by God's grace, strive to live as a disciple of Christ, loving God with your whole heart, and your neighbour as yourself, until your life's end?
I will, with God's help.

18   *The priest says to the congregation*
You have heard these are brothers and sisters respond to Christ. Will you support them in this calling?
We will.

19   Let us pray.

Grant, merciful God, that *these persons* may be so buried with Christ in baptism that the new nature may be raised up in them. May the fruit of your spirit grow and flourish in *them*. **Amen.**

Give to *their* sponsors (and their families) the desire to share with *them* what you have revealed in your holy Gospel. **Amen.**

(Give to those who come to affirm their baptism, strength and grace that they may faithfully serve you all their lives. **Amen.**)

May *they* know Christ's forgiving love and continue in the fellowship and service of his church. May *they* proclaim, by word and example the good news of God in Christ. **Amen.**

We thank you for the ministry we have in your world and to each other in the household of faith. Hasten the day when the whole creation shall be make perfect in Christ. **Amen.**

20   *Hymn*

THE BAPTISM

21   *At the place where the water for baptism is, the priest begins the thanksgiving.*

(The Lord be with you.

And also with you.)

Let us give thanks to the Lord our God.

It is right to give our thanks and praise.

We give you thanks that at the beginning of creation your Holy Spirit moved upon the waters to bring forth light and life. With water you cleanse and replenish the earth; you nourish and sustain all living things.

Thanks be to God.

We give you thanks that through the waters of the Red Sea you led your people out of slavery into freedom, and brought them through the river Jordan to new life in the land of promise.

Thanks be to God.

We give you thanks for your Son Jesus Christ: for his baptism by John, for his anointing with the Holy Spirit.

Thanks be to God.

We give you thanks that through the deep waters of death Jesus delivered us from our sins and was raised to new life in triumph.

Thanks be to God.

We give you thanks for the grace of the Holy Spirit who forms us in the likeness of Christ and leads us to proclaim your kingdom.

Thanks be to God.

And now we give you thanks that you have called *name/these your servants* to new birth in your Church through the waters of baptism.

Pour out your Holy Spirit in blessing and sanctify this water so that those who are baptised in it may be made one with Christ in his death and resurrection. May they die to sin, rise to newness of life, and continue forever in Jesus Christ our Lord, through whom we give you praise and honour in the unity of the Spirit, now and for ever. **Amen.**

22   *The priest says to the candidates able to answer for themselves, and to the sponsors of the other candidates*

I now ask you to affirm as yours the faith of the Church.

[Apostles' Creed **CF2b**]

This is the faith of the church.
This is our faith:
We believe in one God:
Father, Son and Holy Spirit.

23 *Each candidate is brought to the water.*
The minister baptises by dipping the candidates in the water, or pouring water over them,
saying

Name, I baptise you in the name of the Father, and of the Son, and of the Holy Spirit.

And each one of them answers with their sponsors and the congregation
Amen.

AFTER BAPTISM

24 *When all have been baptised, the priest makes a cross on the forehead of each person,*
saying
Name, I sign you with the sign of the cross to show that you are marked as Christ's
own for ever.

Live as a disciple of Christ: fight the good fight, finish the race, keep the faith.
Confess Christ crucified, proclaim his resurrection, look for his coming in glory.

25 God has brought you out of darkness into his marvellous light.
Shine as a light in the world to the glory of God the Father.

26 God has called you into his Church.
We therefore receive and welcome you as a member with us of the body of Christ, as a
child of the one heavenly Father, and as an inheritor of the kingdom of God.

⟦Further directions. 27 A hymn.⟧

CONFIRMATION

28 *The Bishop says*
Our help is in the name of the Lord
who made heaven and earth.
Blessed be the name of the Lord
now, and for ever. Amen.

Almighty and ever living God, you have given your servants new birth by water and
the spirit, and have given them their sins.
Strengthen them, we pray, with the Holy Spirit that they may grow in grace.
Increase in them the spirit of wisdom and understanding, the spirit of discernment and
inner strength, the spirit of knowledge and true godliness, and fill them with wonder
and awe at your presence, through Jesus Christ our Lord. **Amen.**

29 *Those who are to be confirmed kneel before the Bishop, who lays a hand upon each of*
them saying
Strengthen, Lord, your servant, name with your Holy Spirit. (Empower and sustain
him/her for your service.) **Amen.**

The congregation joins with the Bishop in saying this prior after all the candidates have
received the laying on of hands, but the Bishop may use this prayer instead of the prayer
'strengthen, Lord…' when laying hands on each candidate.

⟦Confirmation prayer **CF5**⟧

REAFFIRMATION

30 *Those receiving the laying on of hands for reaffirmation kneel before the bishop, who lays hands on each saying*
    Name, may the Holy Spirit who has begun a good work in you direct and uphold you in the service of Christ and his kingdom. God, the Father, the Son and the Holy Spirit, bless, preserve and keep you. **Amen.**

RECEPTION

〖31 Those wishing to be received by now presented according to a rite later in the book.〗

〖33–38 The text now includes a service of the Eucharist.〗

THE SENDING OUT OF GOD'S PEOPLE

39 Let us pray.
    Gracious God, in baptism you make us one family in Christ your Son, one in the sharing of his body and his blood, one in the communion of his Spirit. Help us to grow in love for one another and come to the full maturity of the body of Christ.

〖40–41 A congregational post-Communion prayer and a hymn.〗

42 *If there has been no confirmation the bishop may say to the congregation*
    All who have been baptised and confirmed are called to study the Bible, to take part in the life of the Church, to share in the Holy Communion, and to pray faithfully and regularly. We are called to share with others, by word an example, the love of Christ and his gospel of reconciliation and hope. We are called to love our neighbours as ourselves, to honour all people and to pray and work for peace and justice. I invite all of you to commit yourselves anew to this calling.
    We will gladly do so, in the strength of the Holy Spirit.

〖43–44 A blessing by the priest or bishop, the dismissal by the deacon.〗

38. The Anglican Church of Papua New Guinea

Christianity came to Papua New Guinea with the division of the island between the Netherlands, Germany and Britain, the British annexing the south in 1888 and turning the territory over to Australia in 1902. Protestant missionaries arrived in 1870 and Anglicans in 1891. The first bishop was appointed in 1897 for the New Guinea mission. The church grew as a part of the Province of Queensland Australia. It became a Province in 1976, dividing from the Australian church.

The Province has hundreds of different languages, the official languages of the country being English, Tok Pisin and Motu. There was a period of development of the liturgy, *Occasional Offices* 1976 being a trial of the present services. The *Anglican Prayer Book* 1991 includes services of thanksgiving for the gift of the child, admission of catechumens, adult baptism and confirmation, infant baptism and confirmation.

ANGLICAN PRAYER BOOK 1991

THE BAPTISM AND CONFIRMATION OF THOSE WHO ARE OLD ENOUGH TO ANSWER FOR THEMSELVES

NOTES

1   *Candidates for baptism should be given thorough instruction. In new areas it is normal for a person to be a hearer for one year and then to be a catechumen for two years.*

2   *The consent of the diocesan or regional bishop must be obtained before an adult is baptised.*

3   *A person wanting baptism must show that he really desires to put away things that are not Christian, that he is going to accept Christ as his Lord and Saviour and really wants to live the Christian life, and that he is truly sorry for all that he has done wrong.*

4   *Candidates should confess their sin in the presence of a priest before baptism. (The absolution is not given.)*

5   *Candidates should be prepared for confirmation at the same time, so that they can receive Holy Communion and be strengthened in the faith into which they have been baptized.*

THE FIRST PART OF THE SERVICE

1   *A hymn or Psalm 34.1–8 may be said.*

2   The Lord be with you.
    And with you.
    Let us pray.

Almighty God, when Jesus Christ was baptized in the River Jordan, you told the world that he was your only Son; so now grant that in baptism these servants of yours may be made members of Christ through your Holy Spirit; and that they may become your children in the family of your Church. We ask this for the sake of Jesus Christ, our Lord. **Amen.**

[3 Ministry of the Word: *Ezekiel 36.25a, 26–28. Then a hymn or psalm 107.1–9. 1 Corinthians 12 vvs 12–13. TEV. A hymn or Psalm 97.9–12 may be sung or said. Mark 1.1–11. Sermon.*]

4 *Then the Ministers, candidates and people go to the place of baptism. A hymn or Psalm 42.1–7 may be sung or said.*

THE DECISION AND THE THREE PROMISES.

5 *Bishop (or Priest):* You have come here to be baptized. God and His Church are here with you. You must promise to love and obey Christ and to turn away from all that belongs to Satan. You must tell us in what you believe, so I ask you:

Do you turn to Christ?
I turn to Christ.
Do you repent of your sins?
I repent of my sins.
Do you reject Satan and all his works?
I reject Satan and all his works.

6 Do you believe in God?
[The Apostles Creed **CF1a**]

7 Do you promise to obey God's holy will and commandments?
I do.

THE BLESSING OF THE WATER

8 *Bishop (or priest):* The Lord be with you.
And with you.
Let us pray.
We thank you, almighty Father, through your Son Jesus Christ, because by his death and resurrection you have broken the power of evil; and by sending the Holy Spirit you have made us new men, in the family of your Church.
We ask you to bless this water, so that those who are baptized in it may be born again in Christ; so that, as they are baptized into his death, and receive forgiveness for all their sins, they may know the power of his resurrection, and may walk in newness of life, through Jesus Christ our Lord.

THE BAPTISM

9 *Each candidate shall come to the water and give his Christian name(s) to the Minister. The Minister baptizes him saying:*

N ... I baptize you in the name of the Father, and of the Son, and of the Holy Spirit. Amen

THE SIGNING OF THE CROSS

10 *The Minister shall make a cross on the forehead of each candidate saying:*
I sign you with the sign of the cross.

When all have been baptized the Bishop and people say together:

This is to show that you must confess Jesus as your Lord. You must tell his Good News to others. You must fight for him against sin, the world, the devil. You must love him and serve him faithfully all your life.

11　*Then the Minister may give a lighted candle to each candidate, saying*:
Receive this light.
When all have received a candle and taken their places among the Christians the Ministers and people say together:
This light is a sign that you have passed from darkness into light, that you may shine as a light in the world, to the glory of God.

THE WELCOME

12　*Ministers and people say together*:
By this baptism, God has received you into his Church. Therefore we also welcome you into the family of our Lord, as fellow-members of the Body of Christ, as children of the same heavenly Father, as inheritors with us of the kingdom of God.

13　*Then a hymn may be sung*:
The bishop and other ministers take their places in the church for the Confirmation and the Eucharist.

THE CONFIRMATION

14　*All the candidates shall kneel. Then the Bishop shall say*:
Our help is in the Name of the Lord.
Who has made heaven and earth.
Blessed be the Name of the Lord.
Now and for ever.

15　*Stretching out his hands towards those to be confirmed the Bishop shall say*:
Almighty and everliving God, you have freely given a new birth to these your servants by water and the Spirit, you have given them forgiveness of all their sins, pour on them your Holy Spirit, the Spirit of wisdom and understanding; the Spirit of guidance and inward strength; the Spirit of knowledge and true godliness; and fill them Lord with the Spirit of your holy fear. **Amen.**

16　*The Bishop shall then lay his hand on the head of each, and may anoint him, saying*:
Lord, confirm your servant (N ...) with your Holy Spirit (and seal him with the oil of salvation to eternal life.) ***Amen.***

17　*When all have been confirmed the Bishop shall say*:
Lord, defend these your servants with your heavenly grace, that they may daily increase in your Holy Spirit more and more and continue yours for ever. Amen.

18　*There may be a hymn.*

⟦19　Directions are given if there is no Eucharist and final prayers.⟧

BAPTISM OF BABIES AND YOUNG CHILDREN

NOTES

1　*In Baptism water shall be poured on the head of the candidate three times, or he may be dipped in the water three times.*

2　*Care should be taken to see that the parents and Godparents are worshipping Christians.*

3   *The Priest shall see that the parents and Godparents are instructed in good time before the baptism.*

4   *The parents should be told that they must teach their child to know and love the Lord Jesus within the family of his church; by bringing him to public worship in the church, by praying with him, by giving him a good example of Christian life.*

5   *The Godparents shall help the parents to do all this, and should pray regularly for the child.*

6   *Parents and Godparents should encourage the child to be confirmed (when old enough) and to become a regular communicant.*

7   *The Priest should make sure at the time of giving instruction that the child has not been baptized already.*

THE SERVICE

(1   *This shall normally take place at the Eucharist after the Gospel, or at Evensong after the second lesson.)*

2   *The Priest, standing at the font, will say:*
The Lord be with you.
And with you.
There is one body and one spirit.
There is one hope in God's call to us.
One Lord, one faith, one baptism.
One God and Father of us all.

3   Our Lord Jesus Christ took the children in his arms, placed his hands on each of them, and blessed them, saying, 'Let the children come to me! Do not stop them because the kingdom of God belongs to such as these. Remember this! Whoever does not receive the kingdom of God like a child will never enter it.' *(Mark 10.16, 14b, 15 T.E.V.)*

Again He said, 'I tell you the truth: no one can see the Kingdom of God unless he is born again. No one can enter the Kingdom of God unless he is born of water and the Spirit'. *(John 3.3, 5b T.E.V.)*

He also said to His disciples after His resurrection, 'I have been given authority in heaven and on earth. Go, then, to all peoples everywhere and make them My disciples: baptize them in the name of the Father and of the Son and of the Holy Spirit, and teach them to obey everything I have commanded you. And remember! I will be with you always to the end of the age'. *(Matthew 28.18–20 T.E.V.)*

Let us pray for these children whom we bring to baptism in the Name of the Lord and say together:

Heavenly Father, grant that by your Holy Spirit these children may be born again, and brought to know you in the family of your Church; that in newness of life they may overcome evil and grow in grace all their lives: through Jesus Christ our Lord.

THE PRESENTATION

4   *The Priest shall say to the parents and Godparents who present the children for baptism:*
Will you bring up these children to take part in the worship of the church, and help them to pray by your example and teaching? *I will.*
Will you encourage them to come to confirmation and communion when they are old enough? **We will.**

THE THREE PROMISES

5 *The Priest shall say to parents and Godparents:*
You have brought these children to be baptized. You must promise to try to love and obey Christ, and to turn away from all that belongs to Satan.

In the name of these children I ask you:
Do you reject Satan and all his works?
I reject Satan and all his works.

6 Do you believe in God?
⟦The Apostles Creed **CF1a**⟧

7 Do you promise to obey God's holy will and commandments?
I do.

THE BLESSING OF THE WATER

8 The Lord be with you.
And with you.
Let us pray.
We thank you, almighty Father, through your Son Jesus Christ, because by his death and resurrection you have broken the power of evil; and by sending the Holy Spirit you have made us new men, in the family of your Church.
We ask you to bless this water, so that those who are baptized in it may be born again in Christ; so that as they are baptized into his death, and receive forgiveness for all their sins, they may know the power of his resurrection, and may walk in newness of life, through Jesus Christ Our Lord.

THE BAPTISM

9 *The Priest takes the child and says*:
Name this child.

10 *The Priest baptizes the child saying*:
N ..., I baptize you in the Name of the Father, and of the Son, and of the Holy Spirit. Amen.

THE SIGNING OF THE CROSS.

11 *The Priest shall make a cross on the forehead of the child saying*:
I sign you with the sign of the Cross.
Then the Priest gives the child back.

When all the children have been baptized the Priest and people say together:
This is to show that you must confess Jesus as your Lord. You must tell his Good News to others. You must fight for him against sin, the world, and the devil. You must love him and serve him faithfully all your life.

12 *Then the Priest may give a lighted candle to the parent or Godparent of each child, saying*:
Receive this light.
When all have received a candle and taken their places among the Christians the Priest and People say together:
This light is a sign that you have passed from darkness into light, that you may shine as a light in the world, to the glory of God.

THE WELCOME

13 *Priest and people say together:*

By this baptism, God has received you into his Church. Therefore we also welcome you into the family of our Lord,
as fellow-members of the Body of Christ,
as children of the same heavenly Father,
as inheritors with us of the kingdom of God.

THE PRAYERS

14 *Priest:* Let us pray:
   ⟦The Lord's Prayer **CF4b**⟧

15 Father, we thank you that by your Holy Spirit these children have been born again, to become your own children, and members of your Church; grant that they may grow in the faith in which they have been baptized; grant that they themselves may come for confirmation in that faith; and grant that all things belonging to the Spirit may live and grow in them, through Jesus Christ our Lord. **Amen.**

16 We pray that you will bless the parents of these children; give them the spirit of wisdom and love, so that their home may be like your kingdom, through Jesus Christ our Lord. **Amen.**

⟦17 Further directions.⟧

THE CONFIRMATION OF THOSE ALREADY BAPTISED SOME TIME AGO

NOTES

1 *Care should be taken to see that the candidates know the Creed, the Lord's Prayer, the Ten Commandments, in their own language, and are instructed in the Christian Faith as summarised in the Church catechism.*

2 *Candidates should have proved that they are regular worshippers who desire to serve Christ day by day.*

3 *It is desirable that candidates should prepare for their confirmation and first communion by using the Sacrament of Penance.*
   (Normally the Confirmation takes place at the Eucharist and the first part of the service follows the Gloria, replacing the Collect, Epistle and Gospel of the day, except on major feasts when the Collect, Epistle and Gospel of the feast are used).

THE FIRST PART OF THE SERVICE

1 *Bishop:* The Lord be with you.
   And with you.
   Let us pray:
   Almighty God, our heavenly Father, through your Holy Spirit you have called these servants of yours, and made them your children in baptism. We pray that you will fill them with the Holy Spirit, and strengthen them by the Body and Blood of your Son, so that they may continue to be your servants and receive your promises, through Jesus Christ, your Son, our Lord. **Amen.**

⟦2 Ministry of the Word. 1 Corinthians 12.12, 13; John 14.15–17; Sermon.⟧

THE DECISION

3 *Bishop*: Those who are to be confirmed must promise to be faithful to Christ and to reject all that is evil. Therefore I ask:

Do you turn to Christ?
I turn to Christ.
Do you repent of your sins?
I repent of my sins.
Do you reject Satan and all his works?
I reject Satan and all his works.

THE PROFESSION OF FAITH

4 *Bishop*: You have come here to be confirmed. You stand here in the presence of God and His Church. You must now proclaim the Christian Faith in which you were baptised. I therefore ask you to say the Apostles' Creed.

[The Apostles Creed **CF1a**]

5 Do you promise to obey God's will and commandment?
I do.

THE CONFIRMATION

6 *The Bishop will now call upon the whole congregation to kneel in silence, and to pray for the candidates that they may be filled with the Holy Spirit through the laying on of hands.*

7 *After a period of silence a hymn to the Holy Spirit may be sung. Then the Bishop shall say*: Our help is in the name of the Lord.
Who has made heaven and earth.
Blessed be the name of the Lord.
Now and for ever.

8 *Stretching out his hands towards those to be confirmed the Bishop shall say*: Almighty and everliving God, you have freely given a new birth to these your servants by water and the Spirit, you have given them forgiveness of all their sins. Pour on them your Holy Spirit;
the Spirit of wisdom and understanding;
the Spirit of guidance and inward strength;
the Spirit of knowledge and true godliness;
and fill them Lord with the spirit of your holy fear. Amen.

9 *The Bishop shall then lay his hand on the head of each, and may anoint him, saying*: Lord, confirm your servant (N ...) with your Holy Spirit (and seal him with the oil of salvation to eternal life.). **Amen.**

10 *When all have been confirmed the Bishop and people shall say*:
Lord defend these your servants with your heavenly grace, that they may daily increase in your Holy Spirit more and more and continue yours for ever. Amen.

[11 Further directions are given for ending the service in different contexts.]

39. The Anglican Church in Aotearoa, New Zealand and Polynesia

Christianity began in New Zealand with the preaching of Samuel Marsden on Christmas Day 1814. The early church was a Maori church, the missionaries relying on the Maori for protection. The English prayer book was translated into Maori.[89] In 1840 the Treaty of Waitangi was signed, which was to form the basis of relationships between Maoris and settlers. Selwyn was appointed as the first bishop in 1841 and in 1844 had gathered the first synod of the church; in 1857 the church became a separate Province. The constitution was revised in 1992 to better follow the terms of the Treaty of Waitangi.

Prayer book revision began in New Zealand in 1964. It started with a series of booklets of services for trial use including *Christian Initiation* (1976) and *Holy Baptism & Confirmation* (1984). This led to the publication of *A New Zealand Prayer Book He Karakia Mihinare o Aotearoa* in 1989. There was considerable debate on baptism and confirmation in the Province. In 1980 the process began of admitting to Communion before confirmation, canon G7 simply saying 'All the baptised may receive the Holy Communion'. This led to a view of confirmation as a pastoral rite, and not a completion of baptism. The rite is unusual with the recitation of the creed after the baptism, reflecting Christian formation as a process of growing into the faith in which you were baptized. In 2002 a resolution passed General Synod to allow variation in the order of the baptism service and was included in the 2005 edition of the Prayer Book. In 2016 new services were brought to General Synod including the proposal for the abolition of confirmation. These were not accepted and will be discussed again at the next synod in 2018. Unauthorized rites for the catechumenate also exist.

A NEW ZEALAND PRAYER BOOK HE KARAKIA MIHINARE O AOTEAROA
1989

THE LITURGY OF BAPTISM AND THE LAYING ON OF HANDS FOR CONFIRMATION AND RENEWAL

⟦A pastoral introduction is provided with information on emergency and conditional baptism. Rubrics direct that oil set apart for this purpose may be used at the signing with the cross.⟧

⟦1 The rubrics suggest this should take place in the Eucharist after the ministry of the word.⟧

---

89 G 106: 1.

GOD'S CALL

2   E te whanau a te Karaiti / Dear friends in Christ,
God is love, God gives us life. We love because God first loves us. In baptism God
declares that love; in Christ God calls us to respond.

3   *If there are no candidates for baptism, the service continues at The Presentation for the
Laying on of Hands for Confirmation and Renewal.*

THE PRESENTATION FOR BAPTISM

4   *Each candidate for baptism is presented individually by a sponsor or, in the case of a child,
by a parent or godparent, who says*

I present N *(my child)* to be baptised and made a member of the Body of Christ, the
Church.

5   *The bishop or priest says*
From the beginning the Church has received believers by baptism. Believers' children
have also been baptised so that with help and encouragement they should grow up
in Christ and by the grace of God serve Christ all the days of their life. On the day
when the apostles first preached the Gospel of Christ's resurrection, Peter urged his
hearers 'Repent and be baptised, every one of you, in the name of Jesus the Christ for
the forgiveness of your sins, and you will receive the gift of the Holy Spirit. For the
promise is to you and to your children, and to all who are far away, everyone whom
the Lord our God may call.'

(Names) How do you respond to this promise?

Each candidate for baptism replies   *The parents and godparents of each child reply*
I hear God's call and come for baptism.   We hear God's call and ask for baptism.

6   *The bishop or priest says to the candidates, and (for children), to the parents and
godparents*
Do you renounce all evil influences and powers that rebel against God?
I renounce all evil.

Do you trust in Christ's victory which brings forgiveness, freedom and life?

The candidates reply   *The parents and godparents reply*
**In faith I turn to Christ my way,   In faith I turn to Christ, my way,
my truth, my life.   my truth, my life, as I care for this child.**

People: **May God keep you in the way you have chosen.**

THE BAPTISM

7   Praise God who made heaven and earth
whose promise endures for ever.

We thank you God for your love in all creation, especially for your gift of water to
sustain, refresh and cleanse all life.
We thank you for your covenant with your people Israel, through the Red Sea waters
you led them to freedom in the promised land. In the waters of the Jordan your Son
was baptised by John and anointed with the Holy Spirit.
Through the deep waters of death Jesus fulfilled his baptism. He died to set us free
and was raised to be exalted Lord of all. It is Christ who baptises with the Holy Spirit
and with fire.
Amen. Come Holy Spirit.

We thank you that through the waters of baptism you cleanse us, renew us by your Spirit and raise us to new life.

In the new covenant we are made members of your Church and share in your eternal kingdom.

Through your Holy Spirit fulfill once more your promises in this water of rebirth, set apart in the name of our Lord Jesus Christ.

Amen! Praise and glory and wisdom, thanksgiving and honour, power and might, be to our God for ever and ever.

Amen!

8 *The bishop or priest baptises each candidate for baptism, either by immersion in the water, or by pouring water on the candidate, saying*

[Name], I baptise you in the name of the Father, and of the Son, and of the Holy Spirit.	*[Ingoa]*, he iri-iri tenei naku i a koe, i runga i te ingoa o te Matua, te Tama, me te Wairua Tapu.
Amen. God receives you by baptism into the Church. Child of God, blessed in the Spirit, welcome to the family of Christ. a te Ariki.	**Amine. Kua tohia koe e te Atua, ki roto i tana kahui he tamaiti mana, i roto i te Wairua. Nau mai, haere mai, ki te whenua**

9 *The bishop or priest makes the sign of the cross on each of the baptised, saying*

We sign you with the cross, the sign of Christ.　　　Ka tohia koe ki te ripeka a te Karaiti.

10 *A lighted candle may be given by a representative of the congregation, who says,*

Walk in the faith of Christ crucified and risen. Shine with the light of Christ.　　　Takahia te ara, i roto i te whakapono o te Karaiti i ripekatia nei, i ara ake i te mate. Tiaho i roto i te maramatanga o te Karaiti.

11 *If there are no candidates for the laying on of hands, the Liturgy of Baptism continues at The Affirmation.*

THE PRESENTATION FOR THE LAYING ON OF HANDS FOR CONFIRMATION AND RENEWAL

12 *The bishop stands before the congregation.*
The baptised who come to profess (or to re-affirm) their faith and receive the laying on of hands by the bishop are brought forward and presented to the bishop with these words
Bishop N, I present N to profess their faith
(Bishop N, I present N to re-affirm their faith).

13 *The bishop shall then say*
N, we welcome you as you come to profess [and/or reaffirm] your faith. At your baptism you were made a disciple of Christ, and we signed you with the cross. Come now to receive the laying on of hands with prayer, to strengthen you for the work of God's kingdom.

THE AFFIRMATION

14 *The congregation, the newly baptised, and any candidates for laying on of hands, stand to respond in these affirmations.*

Praise to God who has given us life.
Whakamoemititia te Atua, te Kai-homai i te ora.
Blessed be God for the gift of love.
Kia whakapaingia te Atua, mo tana oha o te aroha.
Praise to God who forgives our sin.

Whakamoemititia te Atua, e muru nei i o tatou hara.
Blessed be God who sets us free.
Kia whakapaingia te Atua, e whakawatea nei i a tatou.
Praise to God who kindles our faith.
Whakamoemititia te Atua, te ahi ka o te whakapono.
Blessed be God, our strength, our hope.
Kia whakapaingia te Atua, to matou kaha, to matou tumanako.

15 *The bishop or priest says to all those present who are baptised Christians*

Let us, the baptised, affirm that we renounce evil and commit our lives to Christ.	Tatou kua tohia nei, me whakarere te kino tahuri pumau ki a te Karaiti.

Blessed be God. JESUS IS LORD! | **Whakapaingia te Atua, KO IHU TE ARIKI!**

16 *The bishop or priest then says to the candidates for laying on of hands and the newly baptised, and/or in the case of children, their parents and godparents*

What is your faith?	He aha to whakapono?

They respond

I believe and trust in God the Father, maker and sustainer of all things, and in God the Son, my Saviour Jesus Christ, and in God the Holy Spirit, giver of life and truth. This is my faith.	*E whakapono ana ahau ki te Atua, te Matua, te Kai-hanga o nga mea katou, ki te Atua, te Tama, taku Kai-hoko, a Ihu Karaiti, ke te Atua, te Wairua Tapu, te Kai-homia i te ora me te tika. Ko tenei taku whakapono.*

17 *If children have been baptised, the bishop speaks to the parent(s) and godparents*
How then will you care for this child?
The parent(s) and godparents reply together
I will love this child and share my faith with her/him.

18 *The bishop or priest says to the congregation*
As the community of faith, we rejoice at this baptism and will share with *N* what we ourselves have received: a delight in prayer, a love for the word of God, a desire to follow the way of Christ, and food for the journey.
The bishop or priest then says to the child
N, you are now a pilgrim with us. As a member of Christ's body, the Church, you will be challenged to affirm your faith in God and receive the laying on of hands in confirmation. May you grow in the Holy Spirit, fulfil your ministry and follow Christ your whole life long.
The bishop or priest then blesses the family
God bless you with wisdom and love, may this child find in you, your homes and families, Christ's love and understanding. **Amen.**

19 *The bishop or priest, with the people, prays*
God of love we thank you for our calling to be disciples of Christ. Help us to nurture *this child* in the faith we share. May *s/he* grow to love, worship and serve you, and bring life to the world. Amen.

20 *If there is not to be a laying on of hands, the service shall continue at The Celebration of Faith.*

COMMITMENT TO CHRISTIAN SERVICE

21 *The people being seated, all the candidates for the laying on of hands stand before the bishop, who says*

Either

21a Those who are baptised are called to worship and serve God. From the beginning, believers have continued in the apostles teaching and fellowship, in the breaking of bread, and in the prayers.
Will you commit yourself to this life?
I will, with God's help.
Will you forgive others, as you are forgiven?
I will, with God's help.
Will you seek to love your neighbour as yourself, and strive for peace and justice?
I will, with God's help.
Will you accept the cost of following Jesus Christ in your daily life and work?
I will, with God's help.
With the whole Church will you proclaim by word and action the Good News of God in Christ?

or,

21b Those who are baptised are called to worship and serve God. From the beginning, believers have continued in the apostles teaching and fellowship, in the breaking of bread, and in the prayers.
Will you commit yourself to this life?
I will, with God's help. Through God's grace, I will forgive others as I am forgiven, I will seek to love my neighbour as myself, and strive for peace and justice; I will accept the cost of following Jesus Christ in my daily life and work; with the whole Church I will proclaim by word and action the Good News of God in Christ.

THE LAYING ON OF HANDS

22 *The candidates being conveniently placed, the bishop continues*
Let us pray for these who have declared their commitment to Christ's service.
Silence

Our help is in the name of the eternal God
Ko te Ingoa o te Atua ora tonu, to tatou oranga,
who is making the heavens and the earth.
Te Kai-hanga i te rangi, i te whenua.
Come Holy Spirit
Haere mai, e te Wairua Tapu
bearing your gifts of grace
uhia mai tou aroha noa.

God of mercy and love, new birth by water and the Spirit is your gift, a gift that none can take away; grant that your servants may grow into the fullness of the stature of Christ. Fill them with the joy of your presence. Increase in them the fruit of your Spirit: the spirit of wisdom and understanding, the spirit of love, patience and gentleness, the spirit of wonder and true holiness.

E te Atua o te aroha noa, nau i whakarite te wai hei tohu whanau hou, e kore nei e taea te wewete. Tukua kia tipu au pononga ki te tino kaumatuatanga e tutuki ai i to te Karaiti, kia hari tonu ai ki roto i a koe. Kia hira ake ai ki roto i a ratou nga hua o te Wairua: ara te wairua matau, marama hoki, te wairua aroha, humarie, ngawari, he wairua hari me te tapu pono.

23 *The bishop lays hand(s) on each candidate in silence and then prays.*

FOR CONFIRMATION

24 Creator Spirit, strengthen N with your gifts of grace, to love and serve as a disciple of Christ. Guide, protect, uphold *her/him* that *s/he* may continue yours forever. **Amen.**

E te Wairua Kai-hanga, whakakahangi a *Ingoa* ki nga manaakitanga o tau aroha noa, kia pumau ai te mahi, te aroha, i nga ara a te Karaiti. Arahina, tautokona, tiakina ia kia u tonu ai ki a koe, ake tonu atu. **Kororia ki te Atua.**

FOR RENEWAL

25 Creator Spirit, rekindle in N your gifts of grace, renew *her/his* life in Christ and bring to completion all that your calling has begun. **Amen.**

26 *At the conclusion of the laying on of hands for all the candidates, the bishop prays*
Living God, empower your disciples to bring life to the world.
The people respond
Amen! May we and they together be found in Christ and Christ in us.

Te Atua ora tonu, tukua mai tou mana ki au pononga hei mau i to ora ki te ao.

Amine! Ko tatou katou ka kitea i roto i te Karaiti me ia hoki i roto i a tatou.

THE CELEBRATION OF FAITH

27 *All standing, the bishop or priest says to the congregation*
Let us rejoice with those who have committed themselves to Christ, and celebrate the faith of our baptism.
Do you believe in God the Father?
I believe in God the Father almighty, creator of heaven and earth.

Do you believe in Jesus Christ, the Son of God?
I believe in Jesus Christ, God's only Son, our Lord, who was conceived by the Holy Spirit, born of the Virgin Mary, suffered under Pontius Pilate, was crucified, died and was buried; he descended to the dead. On the third day he rose again; he ascended into heaven, is seated at the right hand of the Father, and will come again to judge the living and the dead.

Do you believe in God the Holy Spirit?
I believe in the Holy Spirit, the holy catholic Church, the communion of saints, the forgiveness of sins, the resurrection of the body, and the life everlasting. Amen.

⟦28 The service continues with the peace. Directions are given for derived services e.g. baptism only, lessons are provided for different services.⟧

AN ALTERNATIVE ORDER FOR THE LITURGY OF BAPTISM ONLY
(2005 EDITION)

These sections are used following the New Testament lesson or gospel or sermon

God's Call
The Affirmation (but not including the post-baptismal questions and exhortation to parents, godparents, child and congregation)
The Celebration of Faith
Commitment to Christian Service
The Baptism
The continuation of the Liturgy of the Eucharist, or Prayers

40. The Church of Melanesia

The voyages of Captain Cook aroused interest in the South Sea Islands. The first missionaries of the LMS were sent out in 1796. Bishop Selwyn inaugurated mission work in 1848. In 1861 John Coleridge Patteson became the first bishop and was martyred 10 years later. A Mota Prayer Book was published in 1879; Mota being the language of the mission at that time.[90] In 1938 the first English Prayer Book was published; the mission switched to English. A new service book *Melanesian English Prayer* was produced in 1965 and much reprinted with services of infant baptism and confirmation. In 1975 the Church of Melanesia became an independent Province. There was a revision of confirmation in 1996 in *Occasional Offices*. A new baptismal service *Revised Order of Service for Holy Baptism* 2001 was produced particularly to take into account adult baptisms.

The preface to the 2001 service says that it has drawn on the previous forms and contemporary Anglican prayer books, particularly the *Book of Alternative of Services* of the Anglican Church of Canada. One of the main aims was to produce a single service for people of all ages, the existence of different rites for different ages being seen as theologically confusing. It wanted to express the theological fullness of baptism. It also wanted to include the congregation in the renewal of baptismal promises, showing baptism is an ongoing reality. The commission was aware that confirmation is viewed as unnecessary by many liturgical scholars in the case of adult baptism. However the canons of the Church of Melanesia require confirmation before receiving Communion. Therefore they included a short service of confirmation in the service. They wish to be clear that baptism is fundamental.

The confirmation section is very short, simply two prayers (17, 18). It is not given any subheading and does not include chrism, which is administered as a part of baptism. It is expected when a bishop is present that they should preside at the baptism.

THE REVISED ORDER OF SERVICE FOR HOLY BAPTISM 2001

CONCERNING THE RITE

[Opening rubrics direct baptism to be at a main service, preferably a Eucharist or on baptismal feast days.]

THE GATHERING OF THE COMMUNITY

1a The grace of our Lord Jesus Christ, and the love of God,
   and the fellowship of the Holy Spirit, be with you all.
   And also with you.

---

90 G 113: 1.

1b *For daily use:*
Arise, shine out, for your light has come.
The glory of the Lord is shining upon you.

1c *For all Sundays in the year:*
This is the day that the Lord has made.
Let us rejoice and be glad in it.

1d From Easter to Pentecost:
Alleluia! Christ is risen.
The Lord is risen indeed. Alleluia!

2 There is one body and one Spirit,
There is one hope in God's call to us;
One Lord, one faith, one baptism,
One God and Father of us all.

3 THE COLLECT OF THE DAY

4 THE PROCLAMATION OF THE WORD

THE READINGS
⟦Three reading with a psalm or hymn.⟧

5 *SERMON*

6 *The celebrant and candidates for baptism proceed to the font.*

PRESENTATION AND EXAMINATION OF THE CANDIDATES

7 The candidate(s) for baptism will now be presented and examined.

7A *ADULTS AND OLDER CHILDREN*
Candidates able to answer for themselves are presented by the parish priest or catechist as follows:
I present this person to receive the sacrament of baptism.

The celebrant asks each candidate by name
N Do you desire to be baptized?
Yes, I do.

7B *INFANTS AND YOUNGER CHILDREN*
Candidates unable to answer for themselves are presented individually by their parents and sponsors as follows:
I present this child to receive the sacrament of baptism.

8 *When all have been presented the celebrant asks the parents and sponsors:*
Will you be responsible for seeing that the child you present is nurtured in the faith and life of the Christian community?
I will, with God's help.
Will you by your prayers and example help this child to grow into the full stature of Christ?
I will, with God's help.

9 *Then the celebrant asks the following questions of the candidates who can speak for themselves, and of the parents and sponsors who speak on behalf of the infants and younger children*

Do you renounce Satan and all the spiritual forces of wickedness that rebel against God?
I renounce them.
Do you renounce the evil powers of this world which corrupt and destroy the creatures of God?
I renounce them.
Do you renounce all sinful desires that separate you from the love of God?
I renounce them.

Do you turn to Christ and accept him as your Saviour?
Yes, I do.
Do you put your whole trust in his grace and love?
Yes, I do.
Do you promise to obey him as your Lord?
Yes, I do.

After all have been presented, the celebrant addresses the congregation saying:
Will you who witness these vows do all in your power to support these persons in their life in Christ?
We will.

PRAYERS FOR THE CANDIDATES

10 *Celebrant:* Let us now pray for these persons who are about to receive the sacrament of new birth.
Leader: Deliver them, O Lord, from the way of sin and death,
Lord, hear our prayer.
Open their hearts to your grace and truth,
Lord, hear our prayer.
Fill them with your holy and life-giving Spirit,
Lord, hear our prayer.
Teach them to love others in the power of your Spirit,
Lord, hear our prayer.
Send them into the world in witness to your love,
Lord, hear our prayer.
Bring them to the fullness of your peace and glory,
Lord, hear our prayer.

Grant, we pray you, O Lord,
that all who are baptized
into the death of Jesus Christ your Son
may live in the power of his resurrection
and look for Him to come in glory,
who lives and reigns now and for ever. **Amen.**

THE CELEBRATION OF BAPTISM

THANKSGIVING OVER THE WATER

If baptism takes place in church, water is now poured into the font. The celebrant blesses the water, using one of the following forms:

11a The Lord be with you,
And also with you.
Let us give thanks to the Lord our God,
It is right to give our thanks and praise.
We give you thanks, almighty God and Father, for by the gift of water you nourish and sustain all living things.
Blessed be God forever.
We give you thanks that through the waters of the Red Sea, you led your people out of slavery to freedom in the promise land.
Blessed be God forever.
We give you thanks for sending your Son Jesus. For us he was baptized by John in the river Jordan. For us he was anointed as Christ by your Holy Spirit. For us he suffered the baptism of his own death and resurrection, setting us free from the bondage of sin and death, and opening to us the joy and freedom of everlasting life.
Blessed be God forever.
We give you thanks for your Holy Spirit who teaches us and leads us into all truth, filling us with his gifts that we might proclaim the gospel to all nations and serve you as a royal priesthood.
Blessed be God forever.
We give you thanks for you have called N to new life through the waters of baptism. Now sanctify this water, + that your servants who are washed in it may be made one with Christ in his death and resurrection, to be cleansed and delivered from all sin. Anoint them with your Holy Spirit and bring them to new birth in the family of your Church, that they may become inheritors of your glorious kingdom.

We give you praise and honor and worship through your Son Jssus Christ our Lord, in the unity of the Holy Spirit, now and forever.
Blessed are you, our strength and song, and our salvation.

Or the following:

11b The Lord be with you.
And also with you.
Let us give thanks to the Lord our God.
It is good and right to do so.

We thank you, Almighty God, for creating water to give life and to revive and cleanse all creatures.
Over the waters the Holy Spirit moved in the beginning of creation. Through waters you led the children of Israel out of their bondage in Egypt into the land of promise. In water your Son Jesus received the baptism of John and was anointed by the Holy Spirit as the Messiah, the Christ, to lead us, through his death and resurrection, from the bondage of sin into everlasting life.

We thank you, Father, for the water of baptism. In it we are buried with Christ in his death. By it we share in his resurrection. Through it we are reborn by the Holy Spirit. Therefore in joyful obedience to your Son, we bring into his fellowship those who come to him in faith, baptizing them in the name of the Father, and of the Son, and of the Holy Spirit.

Now sanctify this water, + by the power of your Holy Spirit, that those who are here cleansed from sin and born again, may continue forever in the risen life of Jesus Christ our Savior.

To him, to you, and the Holy Spirit, be all honor and glory, now and for ever. **Amen.**

Let us join with those who are committing themselves to Christ
and renew our own baptismal covenant.

THE BAPTISMAL COVENANT

⟦11 Question and Answer Apostles' Creed **CF2b**⟧

Will you continue in the apostles' teaching and fellowship, in the breaking of the bread, and in the prayers?
I will, with God's help.
Will you persevere in resisting evil and, whenever you fall into sin, repent and return to the Lord?
I will, with God's help.
Will you proclaim by word and example the good news of God in Jesus Christ?
I will, with God's help.
Will you seek and serve Christ in all persons, loving your neighbor as yourself?
I will, with God's help.

THE BAPTISM

Each candidate is presented by name to the celebrant, or to an assisting priest or deacon, who then immerses, or pours water upon the candidate saying:

12 N, I baptize you in the name of the Father, and of the Son, and of the Holy Spirit. **Amen.**

The celebrant then makes the sign of the cross on the forehead of each one (using chrism) saying:

13 N, I sign you with the cross,
and mark you as Christ's own forever. **Amen.**

After all have been baptized, the celebrant then prays over the newly baptized, saying:

14 Heavenly Father,
we thank you that by water and the Holy Spirit you have bestowed upon your servants the forgiveness of sin,
and have raised them to the new life of grace.
Sustain them, O Lord, in your Holy Spirit. Give them an inquiring and discerning heart, the courage to will and to persevere,
a spirit to know and to love you,
and the gifts of joy and wonder
in all your works. **Amen.**

THE GIVING OF THE LIGHT

The celebrant, or an assisting priest or deacon, then gives to each of the newly baptized a lighted candle, saying:

15 Receive the light of Christ,
to show that you have passed from darkness to light.
May the flame of faith be kept alive in your heart.

Let your light shine before others that they may see your good works and glorify your Father in heaven.

16   Let us welcome the newly baptized.

We welcome and receive you
into the household of God.
Confess the faith of Christ crucified, proclaim his resurrection,
And share with us in his eternal priesthood.

17a *If any of the newly baptized are to be confirmed, the bishop lays hands on their heads and*
says:
Strengthen, O Lord, your servant N with your Holy Spirit; empower him/her for your
service; and sustain him/her all the days of his/her life. **Amen.**

    Or this:

17b Keep, O Lord, your servant N with your heavenly grace, that *he/she* may continue
yours forever, and dally increase in your Holy Spirit more and more, until *he/she*
comes to your everlasting kingdom. **Amen.**

18   *Then the bishop prays:*
Almighty and everliving God, let your fatherly hand
ever be over these your servants;
let your Holy Spirit ever be with them;
and so lead them in the knowledge and obedience of your Word,
that they may serve you in this life, and dwell with you in the life to come;
through Jesus Christ our Lord. **Amen.**

⟦19 There are directions on conditional baptism.⟧

EMERGENCY BAPTISM

20   *In cases of emergency, any baptized person may administer Baptism according to the*
following form. Pour water three times on the person to be baptized saying:

If you are living, N I baptize you in the name of the Father, and of the Son, and of the
Holy Spirit. **Amen.**

The person is signed with the saying:
N I sign you with the cross,
and mark you as Christ's own forever. Amen.

Other prayers such as the following may be said
Heavenly Father,
We thank you that by water and the Holy Spirit
you have given your servant the forgiveness of sin
and raised him/her to the new life of grace.
Strengthen him/her with your presence,
and uphold him/her in your mercy and safekeeping,
now and forever. **Amen.**

⟦21 Directions on emergency baptism.⟧

⟦22 The service finishes with the peace and the Eucharist.⟧

Appendix A: Common Forms

Ecumenical Common Forms used in baptism come from the English Language Liturgical Consultation (ELLC) published in *Praying Together* (Canterbury Press, 1990) and available online. Other Common Forms are from Anglican Liturgy.

COMMON FORM 1 (CF1) APOSTLES' CREED

ELLC 2 the Apostles' Creed CF1a

I believe in God, the Father almighty,
creator of heaven and earth.
I believe in Jesus Christ, God's only Son, our Lord,
who was conceived by the Holy Spirit,
born of the Virgin Mary,
suffered under Pontius Pilate,
was crucified, died, and was buried;
he descended to the dead.
On the third day he rose again;
he ascended into heaven,
he is seated at the right hand of the Father,
and he will come to judge the living and the dead.
I believe in the Holy Spirit,
the holy catholic Church,
the communion of saints,
the forgiveness of sins,
the resurrection of the body,
and the life everlasting. Amen.

Traditional Apostles' Creed CF1b

I believe in God the Father almighty,
maker of heaven and earth:
And in Jesus Christ his only Son our Lord,
who was conceived by the Holy Ghost,
born of the Virgin Mary,
suffered under Pontius Pilate,
was crucified, dead and buried.
He descended into hell;
the third day he rose again from the dead;
he ascended into heaven,

and sitteth on the right hand of God the Father almighty;
from thence he shall come to judge the quick and the dead.
I believe in the Holy Ghost;
the holy catholic Church;
the communion of saints;
the forgiveness of sins;
the resurrection of the body,
and the life everlasting.
Amen.

COMMON FORM 2 (CF2), QUESTION AND ANSWER APOSTLES' CREED

CF2a with (and trust), CF2b without (and trust)

Do you believe (and trust) in God the Father?
I believe in God, the Father almighty,
creator of heaven and earth.
Do you believe (and trust) in his Son Jesus Christ?
I believe in Jesus Christ, his only Son, our Lord,
who was conceived by the Holy Spirit,
born of the Virgin Mary,
suffered under Pontius Pilate,
was crucified, died, and was buried;
he descended to the dead.
On the third day he rose again;
he ascended into heaven,
he is seated at the right hand of the Father,
and he will come to judge the living and the dead.
Do you believe (and trust) in the Holy Spirit?
I believe in the Holy Spirit,
the holy catholic Church,
the communion of saints,
the forgiveness of sins,
the resurrection of the body,
and the life everlasting.
Amen.

COMMON FORM 3 (CF3) MODERN QUESTION FORM FROM ASB

Do you believe and trust in God the Father, who made the world?
I believe and trust in him.

Do you believe and trust in his son Jesus Christ, who redeemed mankind?
I believe and trust in him.

Do you believe and trust in his Holy Spirit, who gives life to the people of God?
I believe and trust in him.

COMMON FORM 4 (CF4), THE LORD'S PRAYER

ELLC 1 the Lord's Prayer CF4a 'time of trial'; CF4b 'lead us not into temptation'.

Our Father in heaven,
hallowed be your name,
your kingdom come,
your will be done,
on earth as in heaven.
Give us today our daily bread.
Forgive us our sins
as we forgive those who sin against us.
Save us from the time of trial (or lead us not into temptation)
and deliver us from evil.
For the kingdom, the power, and the glory are yours
now and for ever. Amen.

Note where translations are made the original may not be an ecumenically agreed text.

Traditional Lord's Prayer CF4c

Our Father, who art in heaven,
hallowed be thy name;
thy kingdom come;
thy will be done;
on earth as it is in heaven.
Give us this day our daily bread.
And forgive us our trespasses,
as we forgive those who trespass against us.
And lead us not into temptation;
but deliver us from evil.
For thine is the kingdom,
the power and the glory,
for ever and ever.
Amen.

CONFIRMATION PRAYER CF5

Defend, O Lord, these your servants with your heavenly grace,
that they may continue yours for ever,
and daily increase in your Holy Spirit more and more
until they come to your everlasting kingdom. Amen.

Appendix B: The Mar Thoma Syrian Church

The Mar Thoma Syrian Church is a reformed Oriental Church in full communion with the Anglican Communion. Christianity began in South India with the apostle Thomas. The Syrian Christians, who are strong in Kerala, see themselves in continuity with that tradition. In the early nineteenth century CMS brought a Mission of Help to the Syrian community. In 1836 an indigenous Reformation began, and CMS turned to work with the local people, creating an Anglican church, which became part of the Church of South India. The reforming Syrians eventually establish themselves as the Mar Thoma Syrian Church, which is now a worldwide church, through the Indian diaspora. The text of the service is from the official English translation *Order of Services* 1988. There is no service of confirmation as candidates for baptism are chrismated, but there is a service of admission to First Communion. The text assumes a deacon, marked D, otherwise the conventions of this book are followed.

ORDER OF SERVICES 1988

HOLY BAPTISM AND CHRISMATION

INTRODUCTION

1   *The Child or the adult who receives Holy Baptism joins the Christian Church as its member. Identifying himself/herself with the death and the resurrection of Jesus Christ who is the head of the Church, he/she receives divine graces through Him.*

2   *There are some who doubt the efficacy of baptizing Children. To think that Jesus who welcomed Children and blessed them during his ministry will not receive them today is fallacious. When four persons brought a paralytic to Jesus it was because of their faith that he healed the patient. So also, on account of the Centurion's faith Jesus healed his servant. The daughter of the Canaanite women was healed because of the mother's faith. So we can surely hold that the faith of the parents or other members of the Christian faith can provide an occasion for bestowing divine blessings on children. It must be definitely emphasized that both the parents and the god-parents of children receiving baptism have great responsibility to bring them up in devotion to God and in the Christian faith.*

3   Glory to the Father and to the Son, and to the Holy Spirit.
    Shower upon us, weak and sinful as we are, O Lord, your blessings and mercies in this world and in the world to come, now and for ever. Amen.
    Make us worthy, O Lord, for this ministration of Holy Baptism which you have commanded through your holy Apostles. Grant salvation to this child who has come now for Baptism, through the mediation of us your sinful servants, and may we all obtain blessings and mercy, now and for ever. Amen.

KUKLYON

⟦4   Ps 23 read responsorially.⟧

EKBA

5   O Lord, may the seal of your grace guard us your faithful people. Help us, who trust in the life-giving and divine grace of Holy Baptism to obtain salvation, as the Hebrews were saved from the Destroyer by the blood smeared on the door – posts and the lintel: and by the unfading light of that the salvation may we see the Holy Trinity. **Amen.**

O Lord God of the heavenly hosts, bless this your servant who now joins your holy Church. Enlighten his mind that he may see the vanity of this world and renounce all the works of death, and so offer to you, Father, Son and Holy Spirit, Praise and glory now and for ever. **Amen.**

6 D Stomen kalos   *or*   Let us stand and attend
     Kurie eleison   *or*   **Lord have mercy**

PROMION

7   Let us pray to the Lord for his grace and mercy.
     Merciful Lord, have mercy and help us.

Help us, O Lord, continually to offer to you praise, adoration, worship, thanksgiving and glory.

To our Lord Christ, who is the true and indescribable Light, and who in his divine wisdom has instituted this holy Baptism for his spiritual flock, be honour, praise and adoration, now at the Baptism of this your servant and all the days of our life. **Amen.**

SEDRA

8   O Lord Jesus Christ you have gathered us from straying in sin. You have invited us to observe your holy commandment and admitted us to your spiritual fold. You have called us to the streams of salvation and the fountain of eternal life, and with your life- giving voice have offered to cleanse us from our heart's defilement. Lord, bless this your servant who has come to receive the seal of life. Accept him/her into your fold. Number him/her among your sheep. May your countenance shine upon him. Make him/her worthy of regeneration to become a child of your Father. Enable him/her to put off the old man and to put on the imperishable new man. Help him/her to grow to the full stature of Christian perfection and after a peaceful and holy life bring him/her to eternal glory.
     We praise you, with the Father and the Holy Spirit, now and for ever. **Amen.**

     Chant

⟦9a   In Malayalam⟧ *or*

9b   O Lord, protect with your Cross this person who has come for Baptism. Zechariah's son said that he baptized with water, but the One who was to come after him would baptize with the Holy Spirit.

John the Baptist came to the river Jordan. The Mighty One hidden to the angels drew near to be baptized by him. Our Lord came for baptism, and John witnessed to him. The voice of the Heavenly Father from above said, 'This is my beloved Son'.

O Lord, abundant in blessings, we pray for this your servant who has come prepared for holy baptism. May he/she be sealed for eternal life, may he/she become an heir in your household, may he/she bound by your holy commandments and offer praise and thanksgiving to you, Father Son and Holy Spirit. **Amen.**

10 D As the deer longs for the running brooks: so longs my soul for you, O God. Halleluiah. *(Psalm 42.1)*

11 D From the Epistle of St. Paul to the Romans.
Praise to you, O Lord of the Apostles. O Lord, grant us grace to discern your word.
⟦Romans 5.20–6.8⟧

12 D Purge me with hyssop and I shall be clean: wash me and I shall be whiter than snow. Make me hear of joy and gladness: let the bones which have broken rejoice.

13 D Brethren, let us stand in silence and reverence and listen to the proclamation of the living word of God from the Gospel of our Lord Jesus Christ.

Peace be with you all.+
May the Lord make us all worthy to listen to his word.
The Holy Gospel of our Lord Jesus Christ, which proclaims life and salvation to the world as recorded by the Evangelists Luke and John.
Blessed is he that has come and will come again. Praise to the Father who sent him for our salvation. May his blessings be ever upon us.
In the days of Jesus the Christ, our Lord and Saviour, the word of Life, God incarnate of the Blessed Virgin Mary, it happened in this way …
So we believe and affirm.

⟦14 Luke 3.15–16 and John 3.5–6⟧

15 Peace be with you all.+
And also with you.

EXORCISM AND RENUNCIATION

16 *The priest makes the sign of the cross with his thumb on the forehead of those to be baptized, saying:*
(Name) is sealed in the Name of the Father +
and of the Son +
and of the Holy Spirit +
Amen.

17 O Lord God, cast out all the wicked dealings of the Evil One from this your creation and handiwork, who has been sealed in your holy name. + Rebuke the rebellious Traitor. + Cleanse him from the spirit of deceit. +.May he not be the dwelling place of Satan, but the sanctuary of God. **Amen.**

18 *Then one of the Godparents (the Godfather in the case of a boy, the Godmother in the case of a girl) holding the left hand of the child with his/her left hand, repeats thrice the words of renunciation after the priest.*
I who am being baptized – renounce Satan-all his angels – all his hosts – all his worship – and all his deceits.

Then, holding the right hand of the child with his/her right hand, the Godparent repeats thrice:
I who am being baptized – believe and accept Jesus Christ – and all the divine teachings – entrusted to our holy Fathers – through the apostles and prophets.

Then the Godparent places his/her right hand on the child's head and repeats:
I renounce Satan.
I believe in Christ.
I renounce Satan.
I believe in Christ.
Renouncing Satan,
I fully believe in Christ.

PROFESSION OF FAITH

19 Let us affirm our faith:

⟦Nicene Creed slight variations and no filioque.⟧

20 D Stomen kalos *or* Let us stand and attend
Kurie eleison *or* **Lord have mercy**

Lord, by sending your Holy Spirit, out of nothing you have created this *child* as a living being, and by your love you have made *him* worthy of Holy Baptism. O Lord, build *him* upon the foundation of your holy apostles. Plant *him* to grow and flourish in your Church. Make *him* open to the mystery of the anointing of the Holy Spirit. Perfect *him* with your divine gifts. May the hearts of these your worshippers be kindled with your light that they may be free from the bondage of sin. **Amen.**

PREPARATION OF CANDIDATE AND WATER

21 *The priest anoints the forehead of the candidate with Syth and says:*
As a token of being born anew as a child of God, *(Name)* is sealed with holy oil, in the name of the Father + and of the Son + and of the Holy Spirit + . **Amen.**

22 *Then the priest, mixing hot and cold water in the font, blesses the water:*
O Lord, accept our humble prayers by the mercies, grace and love for mankind of our Lord Jesus the Messiah, and sanctify this water. O Lord, you have given us the fountain that truly cleanses us from all the defilements of sin. As you are the one who saves us, washes us clean and grants all good gifts, we offer praise and thanksgiving to you and to your only Son and to the Holy Spirit. **Amen.**

KUKAYA

⟦23a Chant in Malayalam.⟧
or

23b Hear this, all you nations. John stood in the river Jordan. The Messiah entered the water, sanctified it and was baptised in it. When he came up out of the water heaven and earth honoured him; sun, moon, stars and clouds praised him who sanctified all rivers and streams.

Barek Mor.
Glory to the Father and to the Son and to the Holy Spirit:
As it was in the beginning, is now and shall be for ever.
Amen.

24 Baptism is given to us as a sign of the fountain of life. God the Father, Son and Holy Spirit sanctified it: The Father says, 'This is my beloved Son'. The Son bowed his head and received baptism. The Holy Spirit descended upon him like a dove. We believe in the Holy Trinity through whom the world came to life.

O Lord, bless us and help us.

We beseech you, O Lord, sanctify this water by your mercy and abundant grace.

Grant that those who are baptized in this water may put off the defiling lusts of the old man and put on the new man that recreates them into the image of the Creator. We offer praise and thanksgiving to you, to your only Son and to your Holy Spirit. **Amen.**

The priest beats his hands upon his chest thrice and says:
Answer unto us, O Lord, answer unto us O Lord, answer unto us, O Lord, and by your grace have mercy upon us.
Kurie eleison, Kurie eleison, Kurie eleison.
or
Lord have mercy, Lord have mercy, Lord have mercy.

The priest makes the sign of the cross three times on the water and says:
Almighty God, grant those who are baptised in this water cleansing from defilement, freedom from bondage, remission of sins, forgiveness of trespasses, + a holy inheritance, imperishable garments, newness of the Holy Spirit + and identification with the death and resurrection of your only begotten Son. **Amen.**

25   *The priest holds up the container of Muron and says:*
Glory to the Father and to the Son and to the Holy Spirit:
As it was in the beginning, is now and shall be for ever. Amen.

26   We pour the holy oil upon this water: In the name of the Father + and the Son + and of the Holy Spirit +. **Amen.**

BAPTISM

27   O Lord, perfect *him* who is now being baptized. Cleanse this your servant by your saving baptism and make *him* a fellow-heir with your Messiah. Let *him* be renewed and dignified through the fullness of your grace. May *he* use the gifts that you bestow upon *him*. We will offer praise and thanksgiving to you, and to your Son and to the Holy Spirit, now and for ever. **Amen.**

28   *The candidate is placed in the water facing east and water is poured thrice over his head by the priest.*
(Name) is baptized in the hope of the remission of sins and eternal life. In the Name of the Father + the Son +and the Holy Spirit +. **Amen.**

The following may be chanted in Malayalam or English as the candidate is dried.

⟦29a Chant in Malayalam.⟧ *or*

29b   Lord, bless us and accept our worship. Lord stretch forth your right hand and bless this your servant. Give him grace from above to glorify your majesty. Grant him your Holy Spirit that he may do your will and praise your holy name. O Lord, who hear our prayer and answer our supplications, hear our prayer now, forgive us and grant us your blessings.

CHRISMATION

EXHORTATION

30   You who by baptism are the light of the world, be strong by the Holy Spirit with power from on high. Renounce the transient and deceitful lusts of fallen humanity and turn your face away from them. May you be strengthened by the Holy Spirit to hold forth the word of God in the midst of unbelievers, always conscious that you are striving towards the eternal life promised to the faithful. May you be made worthy to reign with the Messiah for ever, according to the riches of his grace. **Amen.**

31   *Then the priest anoints the baptised person with Myron, saying:*
(Name) is anointed with holy oil as a sign of the gift of the Holy Spirit given to true believers. In the name of the Father + and of the Son + and of the Holy Spirit.

Basmo dabo, udabero, wede ruho hayo quadish leolam, olmeen. Amen. **Amen.**

CROWNING

32   Lord God, adorn your servant with the crown of the radiance and glory of your holy name. May his life be subject to your sovereignty and reflect the glory of your majesty. May he show forth the grace of sonship, be adorned with the crown of glory, and be worthy to offer praise and thanksgiving to you, to your Father and the Holy Spirit, now and for ever. **Amen.**

    Chant

⟦33a Chant in Malayalam⟧ *or*

33b Brethren, sing praises to the son of Almighty God who adorns you with the crowns desired by kings. In Paradise Adam earned a curse. But you have received glory by water. In your chambers the angels rejoice and the spiritual ones are happy. Brethren, you have received heavenly treasure. Take care that you are not robbed by the evil one. He has made you sheep of his heavenly pastures: sing praises to the heavenly king. Unfading crowns have been placed on your heads: Let your lips sing his praises. Children through baptism depart in peace and worship the crucified Christ.

⟦34   Exhortation to the parents and godparents.⟧

BLESSING

35   My beloved, depart in peace as I commend you to the grace and blessings of the Holy Trinity.+
Amen.
May God the Father be with you: the Holy Son keep you: and the Holy Spirit make you perfect.+
Amen.
May this Holy Trinity guard you from the damnation of sin and save you from all evil, now and for ever.+
Amen.

Appendix C: Joint Liturgical Group 1992

The Joint Liturgical Group, established in 1965, has been a significant ecumenical contribution to liturgy in the United Kingdom. In 1992 they produced *Confirmation and Re-affirmation of Baptismal Faith*, or what is more commonly known as joint confirmation. Local ecumenism has been developing within the Church of England and that there are numbers of places where there are shared buildings, joint congregations and, with relevant permission, exchange of ministry. The ecumenical canons of the Church of England, Canon B43 and B44, order these arrangements. Canon B44 specifically allows joint services of baptism and confirmation. The ecumenical bodies asked JLG to produce a suitable rite.

There are two key features in this rite with respect to confirmation. At the confirmation itself a number of hands may be laid on the candidate. Thus in an Anglican, Methodist and Reformed shared congregation three ministers simultaneously lay on hands and say the prayer together. The candidates are later welcomed into each of the constituent churches, which also allows participating churches who do not have confirmation, e.g. Brethren, to share the right hand of fellowship. The people are then declared to have full membership in all constituent churches.

CONFIRMATION AND RE-AFFIRMATION OF BAPTISMAL FAITH 1992

ORDER OF SERVICE

1   Hymn

PROCLAIMING BAPTISM

2   We invite those who have been baptized to join with us in celebrating our baptism in which we are united with Christ and with each other.

Grace and peace to you from God our Father and the Lord Jesus Christ.
God is faithful, who calls us to share in the life of his Son.

Grace to those who are set apart in Jesus Christ.
Peace to all who in every place call upon his name.

By one Spirit we were all baptized into one body and all given one Spirit to drink.
All who have been baptized into Christ Jesus have been baptized into his death.

We were buried with him by baptism into death.
So that, as Christ was raised from the dead by the glorious power of the Father, we also may set out on a new life.

If you confess with your lips that Jesus is Lord and believe in your heart that God raised him from the dead you will find salvation.
Everyone who calls upon the name of the Lord will be saved.

Welcome one another as Christ has welcomed you for the glory of God.
The kingdom of God is justice, peace and joy in the Holy Spirit.

3a   *A minister takes a bowl of water and says to the people:*
This water reminds you of your baptism into Jesus Christ.
The officiating ministers then move among the people, sprinkling them with water and repeating the words:
Remember your baptism into Jesus Christ. Share the joy of all who have been baptized.

or

3b   *A minister, where appropriate, standing at the baptistry or font, says to the people:*
Remember your baptism into Jesus Christ. Share the joy of all who have been baptized.

4   *When the officiating ministers have returned to their places, a minister says:*

Blessed be God the Father;
Creator of all things.

Blessed be God the Son;
**Baptized in Jordan,
crucified at Calvary,
risen and glorified.**

Blessed be God the Spirit;
Lord and giver of life.

5   Let us pray.
Loving Father, we praise you
for our confidence and hope in Jesus Christ.
We thank you for our shared life in one Church,
our baptism into Jesus Christ,
and our experience of your Spirit
in fellowship and service.
Anoint your church with your Holy Spirit.
Draw together your divided people
Bless [those who are to be baptized today, and]
those who now respond to your call
and take a further step in the Christian way;
through Jesus Christ our Lord. **Amen.**

ENTRY OF BAPTISMAL CANDIDATES

6   *If there are candidates for baptism, they should be brought in (or brought forward) and presented to the assembly at this point.*

MINISTRY OF THE WORD

⟦7–12 Readings, hymns and sermon.⟧

(BAPTISM AND) RESPONDING TO BAPTISM

⟦13 Directions for a baptism.⟧

14 *Those (to be baptized and those) responding to baptism in confirmation, reaffirmation of faith, or recognition by all participating churches stand.*

Sisters and brothers in Christ in baptism God assures us of his gracious favour, brings us into his family, makes us accepted in the Beloved, and brings us through death to life in Christ Jesus.

Therefore I ask you to declare your allegiance to Christ and your rejection of all that is evil.
Do you repent of your sins, renounce all evil, and turn to Christ?
I do.

Do you trust in Jesus Christ as your Saviour and Lord?
I do.

Will you obey Christ and serve him in the Church and in the world?
With his help, I will.

15 You are now asked to affirm the Christian faith into which we are baptized, and in which we grow.

⟦Question and answer Apostles' Creed **CF1a**⟧

16 Baptism into Jesus Christ calls us to a life of service. From the beginning, believers have continued in the apostles' teaching and fellowship, in the breaking of bread, and in the prayers.
Will you commit yourself to this way of life?
I will, with God's help.

Will you forgive others as you are forgiven?
I will, with God's help.

Will you seek to love your neighbour as yourself, pray for the world and its leaders, and strive for justice and peace?
I will, with God's help.

Will you accept the cost of following Jesus Christ in your daily life and work?
I will, with God's help.

With the whole Church will you proclaim by word and action the Good News of God in Christ?
I will, with God's help.

⟦17 Rubrics for a baptism.⟧

18 *The officiating ministers say*:
Our help is in the name of the Lord
who has made heaven and earth.
Blessed be the name of the Lord
now and for ever. Amen.

19 **FOR THOSE BEING CONFIRMED:**

The ministers stretch out their hands and say:

Either A
God of mercy and love,
by water and the Holy Spirit
you have freed these your servants from sin
and have given them new life.
Grant that they may grow
into the fullness of the stature of Christ.

May your Holy Spirit rest upon them:
the Spirit of wisdom and understanding;
the Spirit of right judgement and power;
the Spirit of knowledge and true godliness;
the Spirit of our Lord Jesus Christ. **Amen.**

or B
Almighty and everliving God,
you have given your servants new birth
in baptism by water and the Spirit,
and have forgiven them all their sins.
Let your Holy Spirit rest upon them:
the Spirit of wisdom and understanding;
the Spirit of counsel and inward strength;
the Spirit of knowledge and true godliness;
and let their delight be in the fear of the Lord. **Amen.**

The ministers each lay a hand on the head of each person and say together:
Confirm, o Lord, your servant N with your Holy Spirit; (empower him/her for your
service and sustain him/her all the days of his/her life). **Amen.**

20 **FOR THOSE RE-AFFIRMING FAITH**
The ministers stretch out their hands and say:
God of mercy and love,
in baptism you welcome the sinner
and restore the dead to life.
You create a clean heart in those who repent,
and give your Holy Spirit to those who ask.
Grant that these your servants may grow
into the fullness of the stature of Christ.
May your Holy Spirit fill them
with faith in Jesus Christ,
with love for all your people,
and with strength, joy and hope
in the service of your kingdom. **Amen.**

The ministers each lay a hand on the head of each person, and say together:
Renew, O Lord, your servant N with your Holy Spirit; (uphold him/her in his/her
commitment to Christ, and direct him/her in the service of your kingdom.) **Amen.**

21 **FOR THOSE BEING RECOGNISED BY THE PARTICIPATING CHURCHES**
The ministers stretch out their hands and say:
God of mercy and love,
by one Spirit
we all have been baptized into one body
and made to drink of the one Spirit.
Grant to these your servants
the strength and joy of your Holy Spirit
within the fellowship and service of your kingdom.
Pour out upon your whole church
overflowing love towards all,
knowledge and discernment of your will,
steadfastness in your service,
and joy in our Lord Jesus Christ. **Amen**

The ministers each lay a hand on the head of each person, and say together:

Continue, O Lord, to bless with your Holy Spirit your servant N as a member of your Church; (enlarge his/her vision and make him/her faithful within the fellowship and service of this Christian community). **Amen.**

22   *When the prayers are concluded, the people stand and say:*
⟦Confirmation prayer **CF5**⟧

WELCOME AND PEACE

23   *The ministers say together to those who have received the laying on of hands:*
You have been baptized into Jesus Christ and made to drink of the one Spirit; enjoy with us the love of God within the one holy catholic and apostolic church.

Each officiating minister says in turn:
I welcome you within the life of ... [denomination]

A member or members of the congregation(s) of the LEP say(s):
In the name of ... Local Ecumenical Project we welcome you.

Greetings from individual congregations may follow.
May God bind us together in a fellowship of love.
We promise you our friendship and our prayer.
We pray that God will use us together
to make his love and goodness known.

⟦24–29 Directions for the peace, intercessions, the Eucharist and the blessing.⟧